official
Guide®

T0163819

The
Disneyland
Story

The Unofficial Guide to the Evolution
of Walt Disney's Dream

From 1962 to 1966, McDonnell Douglas sponsored
the Rocket to the Moon ride, as indicated by the
word *Douglas* on the rocket in the background.

Sam Gennawey
Foreword by Jeff Kurtti

OPPOSITE PAGE, CLOCKWISE FROM TOP LEFT: Plenty of benches line the sidewalks near Sleeping Beauty Castle in 1955; Jungle Cruise in Adventureland; Frontier Trading Post in 1955; Space Mountain in 1977; streetcar on Main Street, U.S.A.; Big Chief Thunder at Rivers of America in 1955; *Mark Twain* riverboat; horse-pulled buggy on Main Street, U.S.A. THIS PAGE, CLOCKWISE FROM TOP LEFT: Maxwell's Intimate Apparel, also known as the Wizard of Bras, in 1955; Tomorrowland as seen in 1955; Schweitzer Falls, named after the famous African missionary, along the Jungle Cruise in Adventureland; a mechanical elephant along the Jungle Cruise; a shady spot in Frontierland to enjoy some Fritos, circa 1955.

ABOVE LEFT: Overview of Frontierland. ABOVE RIGHT: The *Mark Twain* riverboat, raf
to Tom Sawyer Island, and Mike Fink Keel Boat float by in the Rivers of America,
circa 1956. BELOW: Jungle Cruise in 1955.

ABOVE, LEFT TO RIGHT: Annette Funicello as Peter Pan at the Chicken of the Sea restaurant, circa 1961; Skull Rock; Sleeping Beauty Castle. LEFT: Motor Boat Cruise. BELOW, LEFT TO RIGHT: Sleeping Beauty Castle draws guests in to the park; Clock of the World provided the time for anywhere in the world; *Moonliner* rocket in 1956.

The Circarama theater was eventually renamed Circle-Vision 360°.

ABOVE: Swift Market House on Main Street. LEFT: House of the Future. RIGHT: Flying Saucers inspired Luigi's Flying Tires at Cars Land. BELOW: The *C. K. Holliday* train at the Frontierland station.

A marching band and horse-pulled streetcar head down Main Street, U.S.A.

The Disneyland Story

THE *unofficial* GUIDE®
TO The Evolution of Walt Disney's Dream

SAM GENNAWEY

DEDICATION

LIKE WALT DISNEY, I have always been surrounded by great women. To my mom, Jeanette, who encouraged me to read; Susan Foster de Quintana, who encouraged me to write; and Marsha Rood, who encouraged me to teach.

Every effort has been made to ensure the accuracy of information throughout this book, and the contents of this publication are believed to be correct at the time of printing. Nevertheless, the publishers cannot accept responsibility for errors or omissions, for changes in details given in this guide, or for the consequences of any reliance on the information provided by the same. Assessments of attractions and so forth are based upon the author's own experience; therefore, descriptions given in this guide necessarily contain an element of subjective opinion, which may not reflect the publisher's opinion or dictate a reader's own experience on another occasion.

Published by:
AdventureKEEN
2204 First Avenue South, Suite 102
Birmingham, AL 35233

Copyright © 2014 by Sam Gennawey. All rights reserved. No part of this publication may be reproduced, stored in a retrieval system, or transmitted in any form or by any means, electronic, mechanical, photocopying, recording, scanning, or otherwise, except as permitted under Section 107 or 108 of the 1976 United States Copyright Act, without either the prior written permission of the Publisher or authorization through payment of the appropriate per-copy fee to the Copyright Clearance Center, 222 Rosewood Dr., Danvers, MA 01923; 978-750-8400; fax 978-646-8600; or on the web at copyright.com. Requests to the publisher for permission should be addressed to Keen Communications, LLC, 2204 First Avenue South, Suite 102, Birmingham, AL 35233, 205-322-0439, fax 205-326-1012.

Unofficial Guide is a registered trademark of Keen Communications in the United States and other countries and may not be used without written permission. Used under license. All other trademarks are the property of their respective owners. Keen Communications is not associated with any product or vendor mentioned in this book.

Cover and photo insert design by Scott McGrew

Text design by Vertigo Design and Annie Long

Photo credits for insert: *page 1:* Jeff Kurtti; Disneyland (top left); Mary Barry (center); *page 2:* Disneyland (top left); Jeff Kurtti (top right and bottom); *page 3:* Jeff Kurtti; *page 4:* Joseph and Lois Osburn; Jeff Kurtti (Space Mountain); *page 5:* Joseph and Lois Osburn; *page 6:* Jeff Kurtti; *page 7:* Jeff Kurtti; Mary Barry (Flying Saucers); *page 8:* Disneyland

For information on our other products and services or to obtain technical support, please contact us from within the United States at 888-604-4537 or by fax at 205-326-1012.

Keen Communications, LLC, also publishes its books in a variety of electronic formats. Some content that appears in print may not be available in electronic formats.

ISBN 978-1-62809-095-6 (hardcover); eISBN 978-1-62809-013-0

5 4 3 2 1

CONTENTS

ACKNOWLEDGEMENTS

IN FEBRUARY 2012, I had the privilege of interviewing Jack Lindquist, Disneyland's first president. In a room filled with hard-core Disney enthusiasts, he recalled a time when Walt Disney said that he was not as interested in all of the promotional stuff, the parades, and the shows. Walt figured that he hired good people who would do a great job and meet his standards. He was concerned about creating a great place with great rides, and creating a place that was beautiful.

This book is not a survey of the wonderful entertainment programs at Disneyland, such as the parades and fireworks, nor a warts-and-all backstage peek at what it was like to work as a cast member, nor a testimonial to the amazing things people do at theme parks. This is a biography of a place called Disneyland. Like all biographies, the story starts with the birth of the park, winds its way through the trials of its adolescence, and ends as Disneyland works its way to middle age.

Early on, Walt Disney instituted a protocol for his artists and his employees that everybody would be called by their first names. Throughout the book, I refer to Mr. Disney as Walt. This is not meant to indicate intimacy or informality. I will not be extending the same convention to the other personalities who are part of this story. When I refer to Disney, I am speaking of either Walt Disney Productions or what is known today as The Walt Disney Company.

Finally, this book would not be possible without Leon and Jack Janzen. They were the publishers, writers, graphic layout artists, and distributors of *The "E" Ticket,* a magazine dedicated to Disneyland, along with glimpses at other historic Southern California amusement areas. From 1986 to 2009, I would rejoice when I found a new edition in my mailbox. Their brilliant work, which remains available today through The Walt Disney Family Museum, is the inspiration behind my obsession in trying to understand why Disneyland has become something greater than the sum of its parts.

I would like to acknowledge the following people for their help in making this book possible: Jack Janzen, Leon Janzen, Jeff Kurtti, Diane Disney Miller, Ron Miller, David Price, Harrison "Buzz" Price, Heidi Floren, Jason Schultz, Len Testa, Werner Weiss, David Zanolla, Jim Korkis, Laila Miletic-Vejzovic, Suphi Burka Ogreten, Rebecca Hammond, and Jane Newell.

FOREWORD

SAM GENNAWEY IS A SMART MAN and a good friend. That's why, when he told me that he was writing a new book about Disneyland, I screwed a smile on my face and wished him well. Oh, lord, another book about Disneyland. As if the world needs another book about Disneyland, right?

But, as I said, Sam is smart. His passion for history, combined with his professional training as an urban planner and a not-unhealthy obsession with theme parks, gives him an informed and unique viewpoint. I was lucky enough to help him produce a remarkable and erudite presentation for The Walt Disney Family Museum about one of Walt Disney's final projects, a never-realized ski resort development at Mineral King, and his authoritative book *Walt and the Promise of Progress City* is a remarkable achievement.

Sam recognized that a comprehensive history of Walt Disney's park had, surprisingly, never been written. There are certainly excellent books about Disneyland. Randy Bright's 1987 *Disneyland: Inside Story* is one example, but it tells the story (as indicated) from the point of view of its designers and builders. Bruce Gordon and David Mumford's revered *The Nickel Tour* is a rich and enjoyable resource, but it is visual and anecdotal in its approach—it does not pretend any academic or journalistic objective. Even my own *The Art of Disneyland* is (obviously) a work focused on inspirational and developmental art and artists; my *Disneyland Through the Decades* is intentionally more of a scrapbook of reflection and reaction than a history.

What sets Sam's book apart is the alchemy of his experience and viewpoint. In *The Disneyland Story: The Unofficial Guide to the Evolution of Walt Disney's Dream*, he has created not only a scrupulously accurate chronology of the activities and events involved in the creation and operation of Disneyland, but he has also layered it with important context, including key personalities, contemporary historical and cultural issues, and a view of the nuanced mechanics of the park from the standpoint of an urban design expert.

While the combination of these elements might make *The Disneyland Story: The Unofficial Guide to the Evolution of Walt Disney's Dream* seem about as appealing as eating a bowl of dust, the addition of Sam's deep passion for the subject and his enthusiasm in sharing his research and perspective make this volume not only a must-have history for the aficionado but a damn good read as well.

Whether you know everything about Disneyland, or have a desire to know everything about Disneyland, *The Disneyland Story: The Unofficial Guide to the Evolution of Walt Disney's Dream* is a thorough, unique, entertaining, and ultimately indispensable account of the myriad elements that compose the Happiest Place on Earth.

Jeff Kurtti is one of the leading authorities on The Walt Disney Company and its history. The author of more than 25 books, Kurtti served as a production coordinator on the 1984 Los Angeles Olympic Arts Festival. For several years, he worked for Walt Disney Imagineering, the theme park design division of The Walt Disney Company, and then for the Corporate Special Projects department of Disney. Most recently, he was creative director, content consultant, and media producer for the cornerstone exhibit at The Walt Disney Family Museum in San Francisco, California.

CAST *of* CHARACTERS

KEN ANDERSON Disney Legend, animator, Imagineer, art director, worked at Disney 1934–1982

XAVIER ATENCIO Disney Legend, animator, Imagineer, worked at Disney 1938–1984

TONY BAXTER Disney Legend, Imagineer, worked at Disney 1965–2013

AL BERTINO animator, Imagineer, worked at Disney 1935–1977

MARY BLAIR Disney Legend, conceptual artist, Imagineer, worked at Disney 1940–1953, consultant thereafter

WALLY BOAG Disney Legend, entertainer, writer, worked at Disney 1955–1983

BARRY BRAVERMAN Imagineer, worked at Disney 1977–2006

RANDY BRIGHT Disney Legend, Imagineer, writer, historian, worked at Disney 1965–1990

ROGER E. BROGGIE Disney Legend, Imagineer, mechanical wizard, worked at Disney 1939–1975

HARRIET BURNS Disney Legend, first female Imagineer, model maker, worked at Disney 1955–1986

COLLIN CAMPBELL Disney Legend, animator, Imagineer

CLAUDE COATS Disney Legend, animator, background painter, Imagineer, worked at Disney 1935–1989

BILL COTTRELL Disney Legend, first president of WED Enterprises, president of Retlaw, writer, worked at Disney 1929–1982

ROLAND "ROLLY" CRUMP Disney Legend, animator, Imagineer, worked at Disney 1952–1970, 1976–1981, and 1992–1996

ALICE DAVIS Disney Legend, Imagineer, costume design, worked at Disney 1960–1978

MARC DAVIS Disney Legend, animator, Imagineer, worked at Disney 1935–1978

MARVIN DAVIS Disney Legend, senior vice president of WED Enterprises, filmmaker and Imagineer, worked at Disney 1953–1975

ROY O. DISNEY cofounder, Walt Disney Productions, worked at Disney 1923–1972

WALTER E. DISNEY cofounder, Walt Disney Productions, Father to Disneyland, worked at Disney 1923–1966

RON DOMINGUEZ Disney Legend, executive vice president of Walt Disney Attractions West Coast, worked at Disney 1955–1994

MICHAEL EISNER The Walt Disney Company CEO, 1984–2005

MORGAN "BILL" EVANS Disney Legend, Imagineer, landscape design, worked at Disney 1954–1975

JOE FOWLER Disney Legend, retired rear admiral of the U.S. Navy, Disneyland's second general manager, worked at Disney 1954–1978

VAN ARSDALE FRANCE Disney Legend, founder of The University of Disneyland, worked at Disney 1955–1978

BLAINE GIBSON Disney Legend, Imagineer, sculptor, animator, worked at Disney 1939–1983

HARPER GOFF Disney Legend, Imagineer, musician, railfan, worked at Disney 1951–1975

BRUCE GORDON Imagineer, Disney historian, worked at Disney 1980–2007

YALE GRACEY Disney Legend, Imagineer, mechanical wizard, worked at Disney 1939–1975

ROBERT "BOB" GURR Disney Legend, Imagineer, vehicle designer, mechanical engineer, started at Disney in 1954

JOHN HENCH Disney Legend, animator, Imagineer, worked at Disney 1939–2004

ROBERT IGER The Walt Disney Company CEO, 2005–present

RICHARD "DICK" IRVINE Disney Legend, executive vice president of WED Enterprises (later WDI Imagineering), worked at Disney 1952–1976

JACK JANZEN cofounder, publisher, *The E Ticket*

LEON JANZEN cofounder, publisher, *The E Ticket*

FRED JOERGER Disney Legend, Imagineer, model maker, worked at Disney 1953–1979, returned in 1982

WARD KIMBALL Disney Legend, animator, railfan, musician, Renaissance man, worked at Disney 1934–1972

JACK LINDQUIST Disney Legend, Disneyland's first advertising manager, Disneyland's first president, worked at Disney 1955–1993

BILL MARTIN Disney Legend, Imagineer, worked at Disney 1953–1977

SAM MCKIM Disney Legend, child actor, animator, Imagineer, worked at Disney 1954–1987

DIANE DISNEY MILLER Walt Disney's oldest daughter

RICHARD "DICK" NUNIS Disney Legend, chairman of Walt Disney Attractions, worked at Disney 1955–1999

HARRISON "BUZZ" PRICE Disney Legend, consultant, Stanford Research Institute, Economics Research Associates, Harrison Price Company

WATHEL ROGERS Disney Legend, Imagineer, model maker, Audio-Animatronics, worked at Disney 1939–1987

HEBERT RYMAN Disney Legend, artist, worked at Disney 1938–1989

MARTY SKLAR Disney Legend, Imagineer, vice president of concepts and planning for WDI Imagineering, worked at Disney 1955–2009

DAVE SMITH Disney Legend, founder and former chief archivist of The Walt Disney Archives, worked at Disney 1970–2010

ESMOND CARDON "CARD" WALKER Disney Legend, president and chairman of the board of The Walt Disney Company, worked at Disney 1938–1983

CORNELIUS VANDERBILT WOOD Disneyland's first general manager, 1955–1956

INTRODUCTION

ONCE UPON A TIME, Walt Disney raised three wonderful children: Diane, Sharon, and Disneyland. He nurtured all three and taught them values that would serve them well for all of their lives. He was lucky to watch his daughters grow into adulthood, but he would only live long enough to see Disneyland through its first 11 formative years.

Walt knew that happiness came most frequently when he was with his family, where he could be true to himself and to his inner forces. After World War II, his doctors recommended that he take up a hobby to alleviate the pressures of the movie studio. "A man needs a new set of problems to pull his mind away from the old ones," Walt said."[1] So he looked for a hobby that he could share with his family. Circumstances rekindled his lifelong passion for trains and miniatures.

According to Ray Bradbury, science fiction author and Walt's good friend, "Disney knew from the start that there were two kinds of people in the world: people who enjoy happiness and people who hate it."[2] Walt set out to build a place that would satisfy both kinds of people.

As Walt's passion for his hobbies grew, he wanted to share it with others. This was typical, according to his daughter Diane: "When he bought things, they were to give to somebody, or to do something with, but he wanted to build an amusement park that people could come to and really be happy."[3] Just like him.

Building the park would be a new type of challenge for Walt. Disney historian Michael Broggie said, "During one of his visits to a local train store, he was asked about the size of his layout, since he was frequently ordering additional equipment. Walt told the clerk it would never be finished."[4] He was becoming frustrated with the filmmaking process. "A picture is a thing that once you wrap it up and turn it over to Technicolor, you're through," Walt said. "The last picture I just finished . . . it's gone. I can't touch it. I wanted something I could keep 'plussing' with ideas. The Park is that."[5]

Disneyland was a very personal project that reflected the experiences and values of one man. Walt said the park "would be a world of Americans, past and present, seen through the eyes of my imagination—a place of warmth and nostalgia, of illusion and color and delight."[6]

"I always believed the reason Walt built Disneyland was that he wanted one," said Imagineer Bruce Gordon. "He wanted the biggest train layout; he wanted a place for all his toys. In the park he had an apartment above the fire station. Walt would get up early in the morning, before the park opened, and he'd drive his fire truck around Disneyland. People would think he was crazy, but he was only playing with his toy."[7]

But this adventure was not some lark. Building the largest model train set and meeting the public need would become Walt's next pursuit after animation. He said, "When I say, 'play with it,' I don't mean that. Everything I do I keep a practical eye toward its appeal to the public."[8] This was very important to him. He noted about Disneyland, "When they come here, they're coming because of an integrity that we've established over the years. And they drive hundreds of miles. I feel a responsibility to the public."[8] Just like raising his girls, this was just the never-ending challenge he was seeking.

Walt did not have a roadmap or instruction manual to raise his two daughters, and it was no different for creating his park. Through persuasion and collaboration, Walt and his team carefully and deliberately stumbled along their way, creating a new system to organize the built environment, one that preys on our most basic instincts. They invented the theme park.

The result was that Disneyland would become "a place for people from all over the world to come and bring their private demons, those demons that are not afraid of happiness, to allow them freedom and give them air," wrote Ray Bradbury.[9]

When Walt died, he left a clear mission to serve the public need, a legacy of ideas, and a group of ardent disciples to carry on. Despite their battles with the "sharp pencil boys"[10] who did not get it, the whims of history, and their own doubts and egos, Walt's people were able to maintain momentum, thrive, and teach future generations how to do it the Walt way.

How did this happen? Why did it happen?

1. Bruce Gordon and David Mumford, *Disneyland: The Nickel Tour* (Santa Clarita, CA: Camphor Tree, 2000).
2. Ray Bradbury, "Disneyland, or Disney's Demon for Happiness," *Modern Maturity*, March/April 2002.
3. Diane Disney Miller, interview by Reza Lackey, *Slashfilm*, 7 Feb. 2012.
4. Michael Broggie, *Disney's Railroad Story* (Pasadena, CA: Pentrex, 1998).
5. Wendy Lefkin, ed., *Disney Insider Yearbook: 2005 Year in Review* (New York: Disney Editions, Inc., 2006).
6. Dave Smith, *Walt Disney Famous Quotes* (Lake Buena Vista, FL: Walt Disney Theme Parks and Resorts, 1994).
7. *Walt: The Man Behind the Myth*, dir. by Jean-Pierre Isbouts (2004; Walt Disney Home Entertainment).
8. Walt Disney, interview with Peter Martin, 1961.
9. Bradbury, "Disney's Demon."
10. Jack Kinney, *Walt Disney and Assorted Other Characters* (New York: Harmony Books, 1988).

CHAPTER 1

MOTIVATION

ONE *of* THESE DAYS

IN 1963, Canadian Broadcasting Company broadcaster Fletcher Markel interviewed Walt Disney and asked him where he got the inspiration for Disneyland. Walt said the idea "came about when my daughters were very young and Saturday was always Daddy's day with the two daughters. So we'd start out and try to go someplace, you know, different things." Frequently, Walt and the girls would visit nearby Griffith Park. "I'd take them to the merry-go-round, sit on a bench, you know, eating peanuts." He said it was on that bench that the idea came to him. "I felt there should be something built where the parents and the children could have fun together."[1] His older daughter, Diane, speculated, "It probably went back farther than that, to a big amusement park in Kansas City that I've read he talked about. He and his sister would stand outside the gates and look in. I think he always had it in his mind." She added, "When I was growing up, he was always talking about doing an amusement park someday."[2]

Diane's words ring true. Walt's father, Elias Disney, had moved the family from rural Marceline, Missouri, to urban Kansas City in 1911. Walt was accustomed to the freedom that came with the farm and found comfort and enjoyment going to Electric Park in Kansas City. The amusement park was only 15 blocks from the Disney home, and the 9-year-old boy and his younger sister, Ruth, would frequently visit. Electric Park was modeled after the 1893 World's Columbian Exposition in Chicago. What the young boy saw was a magical place with distinctive architecture outlined by popcorn lights. The landscaping was carefully designed, and the grounds were well maintained. A train ran around the perimeter, and the park rides were integrated into the landscape. Every evening, there was a fireworks show at closing time. Walt continued to visit as a young man while running the Laugh-O-Gram animation studio. On one trip, he turned to one of his employees, Rudy Ising, and said, "One of these days I'm going to build an amusement park." He added prophetically, "And it's going to be clean!"[3]

Fans of the Mickey Mouse and Silly Symphony cartoons further nurtured Walt's nascent ideas for a place to play when they persistently wrote to Walt asking to "meet" the characters. He considered a studio tour, but the facility on Hyperion Avenue was already cramped, and he felt that watching the animation process would not be very entertaining. He said, "You know, it's a shame people come to Hollywood and find there's nothing to see. Even the people who come to the [Disney] Studio. What do they see? A bunch of guys bending over drawings. Wouldn't it be nice if people could come to Hollywood and see something?"[4] Walt was touched by the demand, and he let their requests germinate in the back of his mind.

At the 1937 world premiere of *Snow White and the Seven Dwarfs,* a display with the dwarfs' cottage was placed in front of the Carthay Circle Theater. At one point, Walt turned to animator Wilford Jackson and mentioned that he wanted to build an amusement park scaled to children just like the display. *Snow White* was a huge hit, and the Disney brothers took $3 million from the profits to build a state-of-the-art animation factory on 51 acres in Burbank. While working on the studio master plan, Walt noticed he had a triangular piece of property south of the main facilities between Riverside Drive and the Los Angeles River. He believed this would be a good place to build a park where people could actually come and visit.

In 1939, Walt asked Bob and Bill Jones from the animation studio's Character Model Department to come to his office. The department was responsible for the models and three-dimensional effects for *Pinocchio,* He told the men that he wanted them to work on a project that he had been thinking about and he wanted it to remain confidential because it had nothing to do with the studio.

Walt told the men about his visits to Griffith Park and his belief that things could be done better. He was considering setting aside a few acres on the southeast corner of his new studio for an amusement park. Walt wanted safe rides, including a merry-go-round. He suggested the park should be a beautiful, well-maintained environment like his new studio. He wanted a park designed for the entire family.

The men took six weeks and went around to every kiddie land and amusement park they could find, including the 1939 World's Fair on Treasure Island in San Francisco. They began to form some rough ideas to present to Walt. The Jones brothers suggested visitors enter the town square of a Bavarian village. They were thinking of something like the architecture used in *Pinocchio*. From there, streets would lead to the various attractions, including the merry-go-round. At the front entrance would be a railroad station, where visitors could board a train to ride around the park's perimeter. Walt wanted to control views by placing a high fence and shrubbery around the park's borders.

To interest adults, the brothers suggested a dark ride through the mine from *Snow White and the Seven Dwarfs*. Walt liked what he heard, but he was unsure it could be done. Bob Jones reminded Walt of the mechanical whale model made for *Pinocchio*. That model was animated from below by a series of internal cables. Jones told Walt that the figures in the mine could be operated in a similar manner. As the trains approached the figures, they would be animated by a series of cams that were synced to a film soundtrack loop.[5]

The park idea was looking promising, but the priorities at the Studio had changed. The project was temporarily shelved due to the urgency of *Pinocchio* and *Fantasia*. Then came World War II, and all of that was forgotten.

That is where the story might have ended if it were not for Disney Legend Ward Kimball. Kimball joined the studio as an animator in 1934. He was the first prospective hire to bring along his portfolio, and this greatly impressed Walt. In a May 1959 interview with Burris Jenkins of the *Baltimore News-Post*, Walt said of his directors, "All of them are good, some of them great. Only one genius—that's Ward Kimball there. He can really do anything without effort, too—caricaturist, musician, fine arts painter." He was also the owner of the Grizzly Flats Railroad.

The Grizzly Flats Railroad was in Kimball's backyard in San Gabriel, a suburb of Los Angeles, where he had 900 feet of narrow-gauge track and a restored 1881 coal-burning Baldwin "Mogul" (2-6-0) live steam locomotive. It came from the Southern Pacific's Owens Valley, and Kimball named it the *Emma Nevada*. He also owned a smaller wood-burning 1907 Baldwin 0-4-2 live steam locomotive named the *Chloe*.[6]

Kimball and his wife, Betty, would frequently host "steam-up" parties to give friends and neighbors an opportunity to ride on the railroad. Realizing that he had neglected to include the boss in any of his parties, Kimball invited Walt on October 20, 1945. Walt was shocked and amazed at what he saw. Here was a fully functional steam locomotive hissing and breathing right before his eyes. Kimball appointed Walt chief engineer and gave him the honor to run the *Emma Nevada* on its rollout. Walt refused at first, until Kimball told him, "It's simple, Walt. You take the Johnson bar and you shove it forward, that means it's going forward; you pull it back, it's going to back up.' I talked him into it. And he ran it and I can remember how his mouth dropped open."[7] At that moment, Walt was not thinking about the studio and its problems. What he was thinking about was the awesome and fickle power at his fingertips. According to Kimball, what came over Walt was "a railroader's 'high iron' in his blood" that "he just hadn't discovered . . . yet."[8]

The experience at Kimball's house touched something deep within Walt. Ever since he was a little boy, he had loved trains. He would marvel at the stories from his Uncle Mike Martin, who was an engineer for the Santa Fe Railroad. At 15, Walt took a job as a news butcher on the Missouri Pacific selling sodas, apples, and newspapers. To get the job, Walt had to borrow $30 from his older brother, Roy, so he could post the required bond. Walt returned home, having lost all of his profits to poor money management and forfeiting the bond money, but he did not lose the passion for trains. Many years later, Walt's wife, Lillian, said, "We'd stand and watch the trains come in and after they'd go by, he'd watch the vibrations on the track. I wondered why he did that. [To Walt,] that was recreation."[9] Walt found something that excited him and it could not come at a better time.

A **BIRTHDAY CHRISTMAS PRESENT**

TIMES WERE TOUGH at Walt Disney Productions after World War II. In 1937 Walt had been the toast of Hollywood, the mogul of an animation empire, the critics' darling, and a man who seemed to have the golden touch. By 1947 he was not even sure he could remain in business.

During those 10 years, Walt and the studio released such timeless animated classics as *Pinocchio, Fantasia, Dumbo,* and *Bambi.* Walt and his animators were at the height of their creative powers. World War II changed everything: the lucrative overseas markets dried up, and the revenues generated in Great Britain were frozen. The studio was over-taken by the United States military so that it could protect the nearby Lockheed aircraft manufacturing plant. Walt was left with nothing to do but create training films for the United States government.

The struggle continued after the war. Walt Disney Productions was no longer king of the cartoon shorts. Fred Quimby at Metro-Goldwyn-Mayer was winning all of the awards, and Warner Bros. was winning the box office. Worse yet, Warner spent half as much to produce their cartoons. Walt had *Cinderella* in production, but he knew that animated feature films took a long time, cost a lot of money, and were risky. The future looked more like films such as *Song of the South* and *So Dear to My Heart*, which combined animation with live action elements. These films were faster and less expensive to produce.

It seemed that Walt had been working harder than ever but not getting the same results. By the end of 1946, things got so tough that Walt Disney Productions was forced to take a $1 million loan from RKO to stave off insolvency. He felt the weight. In early 1947 he confided to members of his staff, "I've got to stay up all night think-ing about things for you guys to do." [10] Animator Wolfgang "Woolie" Reitherman said, "There was quite a lot of down feeling at the Stu-dio." Walt knew he needed to find a way to diversify the business as a way to survive. Disney biographer Neal Gabler said, "[Walt] was a man of enormous self-confidence, but at any given point in his life he wasn't sure that he was going to be successful. He was hoping, but he didn't know." [11]

Circumstances at the studio may have provided the necessary dis-content to force Walt to revisit the idea that had been simmering for a long time. Maybe Walt's dream to build an amusement park could save the business. After all, look what happened when he risked it all for Mickey Mouse and Snow White. Maybe the magic could strike a third time. Plus, it might be fun.

The timing for Walt's awakening could not have been better. Imagi-neer John Hench said, "A big impetus was when the doctors told him that he had to have a hobby, and he started making miniatures, and built his live steam model train . . . and that continued until he had his full-size trains at Disneyland." [12] Trains would turn out to be the perfect hobby. It was the start of a new chapter in his life.

In late fall of 1947, Walt contacted his sister, Ruth, and asked her if he could send her son a Lionel electric train set for Christmas. He also called a few other relatives with the same offer for their children. More important, he decided to buy a train set for himself. When it arrived, Walt wrote to his sister, "I bought myself a birthday Christmas present. Something I've wanted all my life—an electric train. Being a girl, you probably can't understand how much I wanted one when I was a kid, but I've got one now and what fun I'm having. I have set up in one of the outer rooms adjoining my office so I can play with it in my spare moments." [13]

As Walt got more serious in 1948, he started purchasing HO-gauge scale model train equipment, and he decided to build the layout himself. He went to the Studio Machine Shop and met Roger Broggie (Disney historian Michael Broggie's father), who was considered the ultimate mechanic. One studio employee said of Roger Broggie, "He could build anything just from scratch." [14] Walt and Broggie built a layout in the office big enough to "fill half a two-car garage," according to Disney biographer Neal Gabler. [15]

When Ward Kimball saw what was happening, he rushed over to animator Ollie Johnston and said, "There's something up in Walt's office you've got to see." [16] The model railroad became an invitation for all of the rail fans at the studio to come out of the woodwork. The business of making movies was slowly becoming less important to Walt; he preferred to play with his trains. This was the break from the studio that Walt was looking for. At one point, he turned to Broggie and asked, "Okay, this is a toy electric train. Now what's for real?" [17] Imagineer Randy Bright said, "Disney's wife, Lillian, believed that it was Walt's longtime fascination with trains that really provided a focus for Disneyland." [18]

When John Hench was working at the Animation Department, he would peer out of his office, which overlooked the area between the Disney Studio and the river. Hench recalled, "I'd often work over the weekends and one Sunday I looked up and saw Walt out there pacing an area, with his long, 3-foot strides. I knew he was measuring space for something . . . he'd walk a certain direction, then walk another way." So one day, Hench asked Walt, "What in the hell are you doing across the street, tramping around in those weeds?" Walt began to tell Hench about his plans for a park. He wanted to build something "near the commissary, as a place for employees' kids to come visit. His plans at that time included a 'singing waterfall' and he was out there pacing out where to put the waterfall." [19]

Walt began to spend time researching other facilities. He believed in doing the homework. He would later tell his team, "When we consider a new project, we really study it—not just the surface idea, but everything about it. And when we go into that new project, we believe in it all the way. We have confidence in our ability to do it right. And we work hard to do the best possible job."[20]

Walt visited Coney Island, Knott's Berry Farm, Travel Town in Griffith Park, the Los Angeles County Fair, and Oakland's Fairyland. Throughout Los Angeles there were small amusement parks, and Walt would visit them all. He became friends with Dave and Bernice Bradley, who ran Beverly Park at the corner of Beverly and La Cienega Boulevards. Walt would talk with Dave for hours, trying to pick his brain. Beverly Park was near the film studios and convenient for celebrities.

The park was very small, only three-quarters of an acre. The Bradleys had leased the property in 1945 and opened the park in 1946 with partner Don Kaye. There was a carousel, a little train ride, and another little boat ride for children. In 1947 they built the first children's roller coaster, the Little Dipper. Bradley made his living building amusement rides, and the park acted as a display for prospective customers.

Walt would visit the small park almost every day. He would find a bench, watch the children play, and then ask them questions about what they had just experienced. He wanted to know how the rides worked and what people ate. He watched how people lined up in the queues and how long it would take before they became impatient. He even took measurements of the queue length. Dave Bradley would end up doing research for Walt, traveling to Europe to photograph rides.

Wendell "Bud" Hurlbut was another supplier of amusement park equipment used throughout the Los Angeles region. He was the creator of the *Calico Mine Train and Timber Mountain Log Ride* at Knott's Berry Farm. In 1948, Walt stopped by his facility a few times. Hurlbut was used to dreamers checking things out and thought that he might have a new customer. Hurlbut approached Walt and asked if he could answer any questions. Walt would bend Hurlbut's ear for hours. It did not take long for Hurlbut to realize that Walt had been studying things and knew a great deal already. Walt invited Hurlbut to take a look at the property adjacent to the studio, and the two men continued to talk.

Hazel George, the Disney Studio nurse and Walt's confidant, noticed that her boss seemed "anxious and aimless," according to Disney biographer Neal Gabler.[21] Walt mentioned to George that Ward Kimball always seemed relaxed. He felt that Kimball's railroading hobby was a big factor. Inspired, George suggested to Walt that he should take a break and visit the 1948 Chicago Railroad Fair in August. As Kimball recalls, "[Walt] calls me out of bed early on a Sunday morning and he says, 'Hey Kimball, this is Walt.' And I always said: 'Walt who?' You know, I knew a lot of other guys named Walt. 'Kimball, this is Walt. There's a swell train show they're opening in Chicago down by the lake. It's supposed to be the biggest event in railroad history and I want to go.' Kimball said, 'Wow, I want to see that.' "[22]

The Chicago Railroad Fair was held at the 1933 Chicago Century of Progress World's Fair. More than 100,000 rail fans attended. The fairgrounds were divided up into themed "villages" representing different tourist destinations and hosted by different rail lines. There was a replica of the French Quarter in New Orleans, a dude ranch, a slice of a national park, and American Indian pueblo. Costumed attendants and appropriate food added to the illusion.

After exploring the fair, Walt and Kimball left Chicago and visited the Henry Ford Museum near Dearborn, Michigan. The museum featured displays of just about anything that a consumer would want. There were complete collections of kitchen appliances, furniture, knives, and guns. The men were especially intrigued by the museum's exhibit depicting the history of transportation, complete with bicycles, tractors, planes, trains, and automobiles.

Adjacent to the museum was a park called Greenfield Village, which featured historical buildings that had been moved to the location, restored, and put on display. Some of the historical structures included Orville and Wilbur Wright's bicycle shop, the original Ford assembly shop, Thomas Edison's Menlo Park Laboratory, a 1913 Dentzel merry-go-round, and a stern-wheeler riverboat. An operating steam train ferried guests around the property.

On August 31, 1948, within days of Walt's returning from his trip, he sent a memo to Dick Kelsey, one of his production designers, outlining his early ideas for Mickey Mouse Park. Walt's vision was a park where guests would enter a main village with an old-fashioned town square that "will be a place for people to sit and rest . . . mothers and grandmothers can watch over small children at play." Surrounding the square would be a railroad station, a town hall, a fire station, a drug store, and other shops. He even proposed "a little jail where the kids could look in. We might even have some characters in it" just like Knott's Berry Farm. The village would have an opera house and a movie theater. Visitors would be able to ride on historic vehicles such as a horse trolley, horse-drawn buckboards, and a steam train. He also proposed other themed areas, such as a Western village and a carnival section.

IDEAS EXCITE ME

WHY WOULD WALT want to build something so unlikely as an amusement park? Industrial trainer Van Arsdale France wrote of the park's early history for the training programs he created, and he speculated that Walt built Disneyland for three primary reasons: taxes, tourism, and the opportunity to reinvent something familiar—the amusement park—into something he, his family, and his friends would enjoy.[23]

Walt was politically conservative, and he was not fond of taxes. Anytime he produced a hit film he had to give some money to the government, and he knew that if he could reinvest his profits, he would pay less in taxes. But Walt did not want to pay fewer taxes to accumulate wealth; he wanted the money available to fund his dreams. "Money is something I understand only vaguely, and think about it only when I don't have enough to finance my current enthusiasm, whatever it may be," he said. "Money—or, rather the lack of it to carry out my ideas—may worry me, but it does not excite me. Ideas excite me."[24]

Prior to the opening of Disneyland, studies had determined that tourism was California's third-largest industry. Typically, most tourists to Southern California would go to the beach, pick an orange, or try to visit a movie studio. Walt felt that a movie-related destination would be a natural attraction.

The post–World War II timing was perfect. The middle class was growing, and they began to purchase automobiles and have more leisure time. They were also restless. Former Disneyland marketing director Edwin Ettinger said, "They felt awkward about all that leisure time thrust onto them and they weren't sure what to really do with it."[25] Walt's amusement park idea could offer something that seemed familiar, predictable, and reassuring.

"Walt had that instinct, that gut feeling of what people wanted, when they wanted it and how much," said Tommy Walker, Disneyland's first entertainment director. "He was tremendously creative, yet he was a practical and common-sense guy."[26] His desire to exceed his guests' expectations was central to the park's success. "I think the reason that Disneyland worked was because Walt Disney liked people in the first place," said John Hench. "He was always trying for better communication, of linking with the audience, of touching them. He said that the only thing wrong with people, if they were acting badly, was because of poor communication. They simply didn't have the right information. Walt blamed all the trouble in the world on wrong information."[27]

Disneyland emerged at a very special moment. After World War II, people were looking for an escape, and the mild weather of Southern California beckoned. The Los Angeles region was ripe for a movie-based tourist attraction. The fact that the metropolitan region was going through a population boom did not go unnoticed. Disneyland would become a pedestrian-friendly urban center surrounded by auto-centric suburban sprawl.

Walt also wanted to create an amusement park that his wife could enjoy. When Lillian asked him, "Why would you want to get involved with an amusement park? They're so dirty and not fun at all for grown-ups. Why would you want to get involved in a business like that?" Walt said, "That's exactly my point. Mine isn't going to be that way. Mine's going to be a place that's clean, where the whole family can do things together." He figured that if she enjoyed herself at his amusement park, he would be doing OK.

IT DOES ME GOOD

WALT'S INTEREST IN MODELS added other dimensions to his amusement park dream. He had visited the 1939 San Francisco Golden Gate International Exposition, and he was taken by a collection of miniature dioramas called the Thorne Collection. It included 32 elaborately detailed scale-model interiors that represented various architectural styles and time periods. The models, built at a scale of 1 inch to 1 foot, combined painstakingly accurate details, materials, and theatrical lighting to create the illusion that somebody could walk into the room at any time.

Walt always loved miniatures; in 1947 he began to collect them in earnest. Over the years, he amassed an impressive collection. On a trip to New Orleans in 1949, Walt purchased a small mechanical bird. When a switch was moved, the bird would demonstrate amazingly lifelike movements and sounds. Walt was fascinated by the little toy. He gave the bird to Roger Broggie and asked him to take it apart and discover how it worked. Broggie said, "It was like taking apart a piece of jewelry. When I finally got it all apart and laid everything out I found a little bellows made of canvas, and some little cams and other parts."[28] Walt was encouraged, and the Disneylandia project was started. He began to consider a traveling display of scale-model interiors with animated figures. This was also the beginning of Walt's interest in animating realistic, three-dimensional figures to a level where the audience could suspend their disbelief.

Many knew Walt to be a workaholic who frequently spent nights at the studio. He had a small apartment adjacent to his office, and it was his refuge. As work pressures mounted and with his interests shifting, Walt wanted to get away and find a new haven. He convinced Lillian that they needed a new home and that the property should be large enough for her gardens and his scale-model live steam locomotive. Lillian agreed, figuring he would be home more often. On June 1, 1949, the Disneys bought 5 acres in Holmby Hills, a neighborhood in Westwood in Los Angeles.

Working with Roger Broggie, Walt built a ⅛-scale live steam locomotive named the *Lilly Belle,* in honor of his wife. Walt insisted on building as much as he could himself. It was very important to him to get his hands dirty. Broggie said, "It was hard to tell Walt anything because he was impatient. But one day he said, 'You know, it does me good sometimes to come down here and find out I don't know all about everything.' "[29] Broggie was impressed and said, "You only had to show him once and then he got the picture." For Walt, working on the *Lilly Belle* and the rolling stock was therapy. He said, "If I had a headache and I went down to that shop, it would clear up and I'd feel fine."[30] The little locomotive would make her inaugural run on a temporary track layout set up at the Burbank studio on December 24, 1950. On May 7, 1951, it would have its maiden run at Walt's home.

The little steamer train may not have been as big as Ward Kimball's *Emma Nevada,* but Walt would have room to create a much more interesting layout: the Carolwood Pacific Railroad ran on 2,615 feet of 7-inch gauge track. A train could travel almost a full mile without running on the same track in the same direction. There was a 90-foot, S-shaped tunnel and a 46-foot-long wooden trestle bridge.

Just like Electric Park railway in Kansas City, the train was integrated into the landscape. To create this fantasy world, Walt had hired Morgan "Bill" and Jack Evans to do the landscaping design. The Evans brothers graded the property, brought in a number of large trees, and embellished the landscape with smaller trees and shrubs. Later, they added an irrigation system and brought in turf.

In 1951 Walt and his good friend, television personality Art Linkletter, visited the world-famous Tivoli Gardens in Copenhagen, Denmark. The park was built in 1843. The buildings were lined with popcorn lights, there was outdoor entertainment, it was priced within reach of everyone, and it was a place for both adults and children. Walt said, "You're dead if you aim only for the kids. Adults are only kids grown up, anyway."[31] As the families walked through the park, Linkletter was fascinated by Walt's childlike delight. Linkletter also noticed that during the visit, Walt would constantly be taking notes. Linkletter asked Walt why, and for the first time Walt revealed his interest in building an amusement park. After Linkletter probed further, Walt told him that he was impressed with how clean the park was, how orderly the layout was, and how there were plenty of places to sit and relax. Tivoli Gardens did not sell alcohol and there was no raucous entertainment. At night everything was well. It was just a nice place to be. Walt learned, "Anything that I build will be kept clean, and the employees should feel that they are part of the show."[32] When he saw the Tivoli Gardens, he turned to Lillian and said, "Now, this is what an amusement park should be."[33]

Tivoli Gardens was the proof Walt needed that he was on the right track. Diane Disney Miller suggested, "It was in his mind that this is what he wanted, and then he saw a place where it was working. He combined everything like the visuals from a movie set. The beautiful landscaping, live music and entertainment . . . everything was integrated."[34]

 EVER BEEN TO KNOTT'S?

ON ANOTHER TRIP IN THE WINTER OF 1951, Walt's passion for trains would lead to a chance meeting with Harper Goff, one of the most important figures in the early development of Disneyland. Goff was an art director, and he was visiting Basset-Lowke, a London store that sold miniature steam trains. He was shopping around for a new locomotive and found exactly what he was looking for. The shop owner told him that it was not available for sale because another customer was interested. However, if the other customer did not come back later in the day, Goff could have it. Goff patiently waited; much to his surprise, the other buyer was Walt Disney.

As the two men talked, Walt asked Goff what he did for a living, and Goff told him. Walt was not aware that Goff was also a member of the

Firehouse Five plus Two, a Dixieland band made up of Disney animators. Goff was stumped when Walt invited him to come to the Burbank studio. He told Walt he was not an animator, but that did not matter.

Walt explained that he was planning to go into live-action filming, plus he was thinking about another project; a "kiddieland" to be called Walt Disney's America. Walt asked Goff if he had ever visited Knott's Berry Farm in Buena Park. He mentioned how much he enjoyed the park and that he was thinking of building something similar. He explained, "I don't want to just entertain kids with pony rides and slides and swings. I want them to learn something about their heritage."[35]

Soon after the chance encounter, Goff visited the studio and was assigned a private room that was off-limits to other studio employees. Goff worked on pencil sketches of a rural, small town for his Main Street. Most of the buildings along the commercial street were one-story structures with tall facades. Walt decided that he needed a two-story street to allow for storage and space for attractions.

Goff had designed a little park with pony rides, statues of the cartoon characters, picnic areas, and a steam train, as well as a roller coaster–type ride that would go over a broken bridge. A museum could be built to house miniature dioramas. The proposal also included a Gulliver's Travels gravity-flow canalboat through Lilliputian Land, complete with animated figures. Also among Goff's earliest sketches is a creepy, dilapidated haunted house situated on a hill over Main Street.

WALT DISNEY'S AMERICA

IN 1951 ARTIST KEN ANDERSON was pulled from the studio and put on Walt's personal payroll. Always looking for a different angle, Walt started working with Ken Anderson to hand-build a ⅛-scale miniature of Granny Kincaid's cabin from the 1949 film *So Dear to My Heart*. He thought he could put the model in the park or maybe even have a traveling show of little dioramas similar to the Thorne Collection, but enhanced with tiny animated figures.

The two men were the only ones with keys to Anderson's private office. Walt wanted 24 Norman Rockwell–type miniature stage sets. Walt's vision was a custom train filled with the displays traveling all around the country. He was going to call it Walt Disney's America. The train would arrive and pull up to a siding. The show would become a special event with a limited run. Visitors would board the rear of the train and walk past the displays. Walt told the men, "It will be like a little labyrinth, and when you break an electric eye the models will come to life."[36] Walt was so confident in the concept that he wrote to a patent attorney trying to secure the rights for dimensional animation that could be synchronized with audio tracks of words and music.

Along with Granny's cabin, Walt had another small team work on Project Little Man, based on a rendering of a miniature stage drawn by Anderson. The illusion was a figure dancing on a stage. In February 1951, Walt hired actor Buddy Ebsen to dance in front of a screen marked with a grid to document the movement. The movements were recorded by punching holes in a mechanical piano roll. A small Buddy Ebsen doll was hooked up via wires to a huge console-type machine, and the piano rolls were fed into the console like a continuous IBM card. The little Buddy Ebsen doll magically repeated the dance steps. To turn the hand-cut cams that moved the figure, the men modified a Bell and Howell movie projector.

Walt hand-built much of the set himself. To get just the right look, Anderson and Walt searched hobby shops for wooden ornaments and other parts. Walt tried carving the dancing figure himself but decided that he needed help, so he commissioned the sculptor Charles Cristodoro to carve the 9-inch figure.

Then they tried a third display. Goff suggested another typically American scene, a barbershop quartet. He envisioned the group singing "Down by the Old Mill Stream," and he built a small nonworking model. Walt liked what he saw and took the model to Disney Legends Fred Joerger, Ken Anderson, and Roger Broggie to see if they could actually get the model to work.

Now Walt was ready to take a big step forward with his park next to the studio. The March 27, 1952, headline of the *Burbank Daily Review* proclaimed, "Walt Disney Make-Believe Land Project Planned Here." This would be the first time that the general public would learn of Walt's interest in owning an amusement park. The article suggested that the park would have "various scenes of Americana, rides in a 'Space Ship' and submarine, a zoo of miniature animals and exhibit halls." The park was budgeted at $1.5 million. The first entitlement step came easily when Burbank's Board of Parks and Recreation approved the plan as long as it was linked to a recreational area on city property. The next step in the process was the approval from the city council. This would not be so easy.

Walt was further inspired by a July 1952 visit to Madurodam, an interactive miniatures park in Scheveningen, The Hague, in The Netherlands. The park was a 1:25 scale model of an ideal Dutch city, and Walt was one of the first visitors. He was able to study how the miniatures had been integrated within the landscape, and he was so impressed that he sent Anderson to study the park.

In September 1952, the Burbank city council rejected Walt's amusement park project. One lawmaker proclaimed, "We don't want the carny atmosphere in Burbank! We don't want people falling in the river, or merry-go-rounds squawking all day long."[37] Walt knew better. He assured them, "A word may be said in regard to the concept and conduct of Disneyland's operational tone. Although various sections will have the fun and flavor of carnival or amusement park, there will be none of the 'pitches,' games, wheels, sharp practices, and devices designed to milk the visitor's pocketbook."[38] At this point, Burbank's approval didn't matter to Walt. His ideas were getting bigger, and he started to consider other properties. He would not be deterred.

To test the Disneylandia concept, Walt entered the Granny Kincaid's cabin miniature in the "Festival of Living" show at the Pan Pacific Auditorium in November 1952. Visitors saw the display light up and heard actress Beulah Bondi, the original Granny Kincaid from the film, recite some lines. He stood back to watch the visitors' reactions, and he was pleased with what he saw. He went back to the studio and told Roger Broggie, "We're going to do this thing for real!"[39]

Walt had Broggie calculate the costs of moving the show from city to city and maintaining the show. Sadly, what Broggie discovered was not good news. It would be impossible to get from point A to point B without having to switch to another carrier. This would be very expensive. Walt was not deterred. He purchased three old Pullman railroad cars from the Southern Pacific and placed them on a siding. When he tried to purchase more cars, he found the price substantially higher. Goff said working with the railroads is what doomed the Disneylandia project. "They had just enough track sidings to do their normal business and this idea called for a 21-car train on a siding with public access," he said. "The railroad companies said they would put in a 'Disney line' with a rental of $13,000 a month or something like that. And the word got around. I think that Walt, who was used to success on his terms, may have expected all these cities to say, 'Oh yes, Mr. Disney, please come to our town.' But then everybody began planning to make a lot of money, just to let Disney in."[40]

CANNIBAL ISLAND

ROY O. DISNEY was not at all thrilled with his brother's obsession about an amusement park. Walt said, "I couldn't get anybody to go with me because we were going through this financial depression, and whenever I'd talk to my brother about it, why he always started to get busy with some figures, so I mean, I couldn't bring it up."[41] Animator Frank Thomas knew Walt was alone and said, "When he started Disneyland, he didn't have a friend in the world."[42]

Roy suggested that Walt start a separate design company apart from the studio to help with these projects. He considered the park to be just another one of "Walt's screwy ideas" and refused to invest more than $10,000 of the studio's money.[43] He figured that Walt could use his own money and do whatever he wanted. Walt said, "I believe the worst thing you can do is sit still. Roy used to try and hold me back but I think I finally convinced him that it takes money to make money."[44]

Walt wanted to call the new company The Walt Disney Company, but the lawyers quickly nixed that idea because it was too similar to the name of the film studio. Walt changed the name to WED Enterprises after his full name, Walter Elias Disney. The business was incorporated on December 16, 1952. WED would allow Walt the freedom to develop his amusement park without the constraints found at the studio. WED would become, as he described it, his sandbox and "you might call it my backyard laboratory, my workshop away from work."[45]

Walt arranged for a name use agreement with the studio, and this generated the revenues that he needed to finance the development of the attractions for Disneyland. He raised additional money by borrowing $100,000 on his life insurance policy. "Even had to sell my home in Palm Springs to use that money to get this thing to a point where I could show people what it would be," he said.[46]

Richard "Dick" Irvine joined WED and acted as the liaison between Walt and the architects. Irvine came from 20th Century Fox. The architectural firm of Pereira & Luckman was hired to design Disneyland, but it was not working out. Architect Welton Becket, a friend of both Irvine and Walt, suggested that Walt hire his own staff. They both figured that no architect was going to understand what Walt was trying to achieve. It was not the nature of their training.

WED Enterprises set up shop on the back lot in Burbank. Walt placed his core group, including Dick Irvine's office, in a ramshackle shed called the Zorro Building. It was a temporary structure that was cold in the winter and hot in the summer. The model shop was located in an old boxcar. The rest of the team was scattered all over the studio lot. Irvine was in charge of a small group, but they were prepared to do things really fast.

Many of the early Imagineers came over from 20th Century Fox. Irvine worked there, and he knew these artists brought with them the knowledge gained from one of the largest back lots in Hollywood. Twentieth Century Fox's back lot was four times the size of Disneyland and had a river town, a main street, a frontier town, a replica of a stern-wheeler steamboat, and so much more.

WED was also having an impact on the animation studio. In *Inside the Dream,* Rolly Crump remembered the company being called Cannibal Island because it "was gobbling up all the people that were in animation."[47] This poaching did not sit well with animator Frank Thomas, who pointed out, "Walt was taking away a lot of our top guys for his pet projects. We'd say, 'Hey, we need him. We can't let him go!' Walt would say, 'Oh no . . . you've got these other guys and they can do the work.' "[48]

Walt liked having movie people around him. He felt that their professional experience taught them how to create continuity between scenes, which would be applied to the way guests moved from land to land and to the attractions. The use of filmmaking techniques in the design of Disneyland would become one of the park's signature elements. Because something like the park had never been done before, Walt knew he needed to find people who were eager, energetic, friendly, and willing to learn. He knew they would make mistakes but they would be learning every step of the way.

The process at WED was very much like the process of making a movie. Every ride idea started with a written synopsis. Then, if the idea gained momentum, designers created artwork of key scenes. Walt just had one demand. He said, "All I want you to think about is when people walk through or have access to anything you design, I want them, when they leave, to have smiles on their faces. Just remember that. It's all I ask of you as a designer."[49]

Disney Legend Harrison "Buzz" Price came up with a special name for the development process. He called it Imagineering.[50] Walt explained that it was "the blending of creative imagination and technical know-how." Animator Claude Coats suggested that Imagineering "means that some imagination all by itself doesn't get anywhere, and engineering all by itself isn't very entertaining. But if you do the two things together, and put them together in an interesting way . . . and publicize it, and market it, etc., . . . that's what makes us the entertainment leaders that we really are."[51] WED employees would become known as Imagineers.

The design process was fluid and personal. Walt avoided big meetings. He did not gather teams of artists, but instead worked with artists who could supply him with ideas. He generally walked into his artists' offices unannounced to see what they were up to. If he did not like what he saw, he would not be negative. Instead, he would say something like, "There must be something else we can do," or "What do you think we could do differently?" and push his talent to go farther than they might have gone on their own. Once decisions started to be made, he would bring in the technical people. His personal touch was a major motivation toward innovation.

When Walt did attend meetings, he would usually take on the role of project cheerleader. He was famous for his passion and enthusiasm, and he assumed that the others would follow. The process would start with an idea, usually from Walt, and then, in typical Disney fashion, the group would start to develop a storyboard, with everybody jumping in to make improvements in the timing, the layout, and other details.

The next step would be to create a small conceptual model, which did not necessarily represent what the public was going to see at all. The model-making process would begin with a small model, perhaps at a scale of $\frac{1}{16}$ of an inch to the foot, or even $\frac{1}{32}$ of an inch. Then a larger model would be made with greater detail at a scale of $\frac{1}{8}$ or $\frac{1}{4}$ of an inch. Sometimes a model of 1 inch to 1 foot would be necessary to achieve the level of reality Walt was seeking. To give the designers a preview of the actual attraction, Roger Broggie and Don Iwerks built a little scope that could be put into the model and give the viewer a realistic look from the guests' point of view. Even a film camera could be hooked up to the scope to record the view. The benefit of this process was the ability to make adjustments early on before fabrication. Walt and the Imagineers could get a true sense of what they were building. Walt could also clearly articulate any changes he wanted to make.

Walt insisted on the use of models because, he said, "renderings lie, but a scale model does not." Walt did not trust his artists because he knew they were so talented they could exaggerate anything and he would not know. Another benefit was the ability to see the finished structure. Sam McKim called the process "visualizations" and explained, "Words are elusive, and even correct elevations and plans don't give a realistic look in perspective."[52]

Walt relied on another trick. Frequently when he came up with an idea, he would ask five or six people to work on it and tell them not to tell the others what they were up to. He would have everybody secretly working on it. Then he would hand over the results to somebody else, who would work the problem. Sometimes he would give out assignments that did not seem to make any sense. His expectation was the Imagineer would spend the time pondering the opportunity because Walt was too busy to think about it at that moment. This gave the Imagineers an opportunity to really research the concept and to generate multiple ideas for Walt to consider. If he liked what he saw, the development process would continue.

Disney artist Rolly Crump said that "the secret to Disneyland is that there were so many different designers that it became this wonderful melting pot of different styles. It's like a gorgeous salad. If it's one designer, you can get something plain. This [approach] lines up with the way Walt used to change his guys around and assign them work they hadn't done before."[53]

Walt also liked options. He would not tolerate people bringing him problems if they had not already thought through potential solutions. Lots of them. Then he could choose which one he thought was best. From these options, it might simply be a matter of him saying yes. However, if an artist presented only one option, that would not be good. Animator Marc Davis recalled a time when somebody went up to Walt and asked, "Hey Walt, what do you think about this?" Walt looked at it and said, "Well, it's awfully hard to choose between one."[54]

Walt was known as a quick study, which garnered him much respect. Also, everyone who knew him claimed he had an amazing memory. His team soon learned his memory could make for tough times if they were not prepared. He would walk from office to office to check on things. He asked lots of questions, and the Imagineers soon learned he would remember all of the answers. He was not shy on calling out people who were not consistent. Walt was known as a tough boss, but he tried to create a fun, creative atmosphere and gave those who tried a lot of room to experiment.

There was an interesting tension within WED. Many Imagineers would not make decisions unless they got input from Walt. This sometimes would backfire. Bill Martin recalled "a time when this one guy was working on some ideas for Fantasyland and I was in the meeting when he was showing these marvelous drawings to Walt. When this guy got all through explaining his stuff he said to Walt, 'You know, if you can't do it this way, I don't know how you're going to do it!' Walt didn't say a word. The next day the guy was gone."[55]

Walt did not like the hard sell, but he appreciated some outside thinking. He taught his Imagineers that they should not be too dogmatic about their suggestions and to retain an open mind. If he did not like it, he would let them know, and the smart Imagineers supplied the boss with multiple options and let Walt decide. He appreciated flexibility and usually had a pretty good idea of what he wanted.

The artists were not working in a vacuum. Walt provided direction and suggestions on how to achieve what he was looking for. He enjoyed the collaboration and took great pride when his artists exceeded even their own expectations. He encouraged his artists with the hope that eventually the answers would evolve and they would come up with stuff in the direction that he wanted. His team knew that he was always a couple of steps ahead of them and he would not give up if he thought he had something. Walt was always curious, and he suggested, "All you've got to do is own up to your ignorance honestly, and you'll find people who are eager to fill your head with information."

Over time, the Imagineers at WED began to think like Walt. They began to figure out what he would like and what would not work. Although he was not known for showering his team with compliments, they knew that they were working on something special, and that was plenty of motivation. Walt was always coming up with new ideas, and the artists had more work than they could possibly imagine. "There was a saying around there that there were a lot of good horses hired by the Disney organization," said McKim. "But they had to pull the wagon in the same direction."[56]

Everybody knew who was in control. His initials were on the door.

TELL *a* STORY VISUALLY

WHEN HE WAS READY to turn his amusement park dream into a reality, Walt began by having his team go out and learn everything that they could about the attractions business. They visited the big amusement parks back East. Bill Martin, Bill Cottrell, Bruce Bushman, and George Whitney visited places like Fairmont Park in Philadelphia, Palisades Park in New Jersey, and other parks in New Orleans, Cincinnati, and so forth. They also visited Knott's Berry Farm and Coney Island, as well as small museums and replica historic towns.

Walt wanted to understand the operations and types of displays, plus crowd and traffic patterns. On the financial side, he wanted to know how much they charged for rides and food, how many guests walked through the turnstiles, and how much money they made. He was interested in all aspects of operating a park, including theft by the guests and the operators.

unofficial **TIP**
George Whitney was the only member of the Disneyland design group with amusement park experience.

Once the team was making good progress with the research, it was time to figure out what Disneyland might look like. Walt assigned that challenge to Marvin Davis when he joined WED in May 1953. Davis would be the land planner in charge of outside areas and responsible for drafting the park master plan. He had worked with Sam McKim, Bill Martin, and Dick Irvine as an art director at 20th Century Fox and had a degree in architecture. He was the perfect guy for the job.

In an early description of Disneyland, Walt said that it would be a "fabulous playground, something of a fair, a city from the *Arabian Nights*, metropolis of the future, a showplace of magic and living facts, but above all a place for people to find happiness and knowledge." He was not afraid to share his thoughts to test the water. When he told his ideas to veterans of the amusement park business, they all suggested he was crazy. Instead of Walt being discouraged, this only reinforced in his mind that he was on the right track.

Marvin Davis began his work building on Goff's early drawings. Goff's earliest efforts resembled a kiddie land because that was what the idea was at the time. There was a train around the perimeter. Goff used Walt's Carolwood Pacific Railroad as inspiration, forever linking Walt's backyard railroad and Disneyland.

Walt was constantly looking over Marvin Davis's shoulder, tweaking the plans. Walt would come in one day with suggestions, Davis would make the changes, and then Walt would tweak it some more. Often, they found themselves right back where they started. Davis recalled doing "133 different drawings and designs, because we had no idea where the Park was going to be or anything to begin with."[57] Davis added, "I really didn't think it would ever come to fruition, but the closer we got with it, and the harder we worked—God, I never worked so hard in my life!—the more real it became. . . . It's proved to me that if you've got enough guts and intelligence and drive, you can accomplish anything."[58]

Walt wanted the park laid out so that he could push guests to visit every corner of the park without them knowing that they were being manipulated to do so. His innovation was the use of a single entrance. Up to this time, all other amusement parks and World's Fairs had multiple entrances. With only one way to get in and out of the park, they knew exactly how many people were in the park at any one time. The assumption was that people would walk up Main Street and then travel counterclockwise, visiting each of the lands. Then they would walk back through Main Street at the end of their day. Marvin Davis knew Walt wanted Fantasyland at the end of Main Street just beyond the castle. A castle was always meant to be the park's centerpiece, and Fantasyland represented the animations studio's heritage. The other lands just fell into place.

Once they settled on the basic organizing principle of a single entrance and various lands distributed around a central plaza, they called it the radial or hub-and-spoke plan. Each of the spokes became main streets within their lands. This legible environment would quickly put guests at ease, avoiding the confusion that comes with entering an unfamiliar place. Frontierland had a main street of an old Western town, and Tomorrowland had a main street of the future. Adventureland had civilization on one side and the jungle on the other, while Fantasyland had a medieval courtyard that acted as its main street. The original plan allowed for more spokes than were actually used.

IT'S *about the* PARK

WHEN THE DISNEY BROTHERS bought the Burbank property in 1939, Walt thought there might be room for an amusement park. However, by 1953, Walt's wish list of ideas had grown. That combined with Burbank's permit rejection the previous year inspired Walt to look for a larger site somewhere else. He first looked at properties nearby, including Descanso Gardens in La Cañada Flintridge, one of California's most beautiful botanical displays. He also considered the police pistol range in Chatsworth—a site that had many positive qualities, including a small brook, rolling hills, and plenty of trees. Walt and Roy found another property farther north in Calabasas in a beautiful valley.

However, many Walt Disney Productions stockholders were not enamored with the project, believing that owning an amusement park was not part of the corporation's charter. They filed and won a lawsuit that prevented the deal from closing. Walt angrily replied, "We are not in the amusement park business. We are in the entertainment business." He tried to explain, "There's nothing like it in the entire world. I know because I've looked. That's why it will be great . . . because it will be unique—a totally new concept in entertainment."[59] To make sure Disney Company was never again an obstacle to his plans, Walt formed Retlaw.

Retlaw—Walter spelled backward—was incorporated on April 6, 1953. The company would provide Walt a way to fund the development of Disneyland. He owned one-third of the company, and his daughters owned the other two-thirds. He negotiated a deal: in return for licensing his name to Walt Disney Productions, he would receive either a 5% royalty from every merchandising transaction, or he would take a share of up to 15% in every Disney project. Considering that the Disney name appeared on virtually everything, the agreement was especially lucrative to Walt and his family.[60]

Walt felt that he had ample justification for the agreement. "I borrowed on the insurance I'd been paying on for 30 years, and sold my house in Palm Springs to get Disneyland to a point where I could show people what it would be," he said. "My wife complained that if anything happened to me, I would have spent all the family money."[61] He did find one early investor, the Bank of America. One day Roy Disney was in his office when he got a call from a banker friend who said, "Walt was in my office today." "Oh?" replied Roy. "It's about the Park. We went over the plans he showed me. You know, Roy, that Park is a wonderful idea," the banker said. Roy asked, "Did Walt try to borrow from you?" and the banker replied, "Yes, he did. And you know what? I loaned it to him." Walt even had Hazel George, the studio nurse and Walt's confidante, to canvas the studio for additional investors. He asked her, "If I were to go outside to finance Disneyland, would you contribute?" She replied, "You bet I would!" She began to canvas the staff, and they formed a group of early believers called the Disneyland Backers and Boosters. Roy was impressed.[62]

Retlaw would own the old-fashioned scale-model steam railroad that would circle Disneyland and, in time, the futuristic monorail that would circle Tomorrowland. "I started designing that—it was a pet of mine," Walt said.[63] The railroad paid 20% of its gross revenues to Walt Disney Productions for the right-of-way. Employees of Retlaw did not work for the studio or Disneyland. They worked directly for Walt. Retlaw was also there to protect the Walt Disney family financially in case things did not go as well as planned.

Walt's new firm was a major sore spot between the Disney brothers. Walt wanted more control over his activities that were not directly related to the studio. He suggested that the arrangement was in the best interest of Walt Disney Productions as well as himself because the studio could now count on the use of his name after he died. Roy felt betrayed. The fact that Roy's family did not benefit was the cause of the friction. Walt Disney Productions was a partnership between the brothers, and Roy did not appreciate the fact that only Walt's daughters and wife would benefit from the deal. He would still work with his genius younger brother, but it was not the same.[64] (Walt Disney Productions ultimately purchased Retlaw on July 8, 1981, for $46.2 million worth of stock.)

With all the legal issues out of the way, it was decided that the hit-or-miss search process was not getting results. One of Walt's movie friends, Nat Winecoff, had a neighbor who was a City of Los Angeles civil engineer. Nat asked the man about new freeways and where they were going. The man replied that "the biggest freeway was going to be the Santa Ana Freeway." The neighbor "insisted everything was going to move in that direction."[65]

Winecoff felt Walt needed professional help to find the perfect property, and he knew that Roy had hired SRI in 1953 to find a location for the studio fantasy props. Winecoff suggested to Walt that he might want to hire them as well. SRI was formed in 1946 to study the expandability of aircraft industries, and they had done multiple location studies for large corporations. Walt put SRI under contract in June to conduct a comprehensive feasibility study of the Los Angeles–Orange County basin.

The SRI project manager was C. V. Wood Jr., but it was theme park legend Harrison "Buzz" Price who ran the numbers. Walt paid the firm $25,000 for the location study. The only constraints were a minimum of 100 undeveloped acres at a price of no more than $4,500 per acre, preferably flat and with one owner. The ideal location would be somewhere between Chatsworth and Pomona on the north and Tustin and Balboa on the south. It should not be near the beach because Walt did not "want to attract the barefoot beach crowd."[66]

Price divided the region into 10 geographically homogenous districts. Then he eliminated the districts that were already fully developed, were producing oil, suffered from a bad topographic feature, or were under governmental control. By doing this, he immediately eliminated 8 out of the 10 districts. One of the remaining districts was located in the Santa Ana Freeway corridor called the Whittier-Norwalk area, and the other was farther south in Orange County. SRI did a complete search of land records and looked at a variety of factors, including utility conditions, accessibility, topography, and environmental characteristics, such as temperature, rainfall, and smog. All in all, 43 possible sites were identified; upon closer inspection, that list was narrowed down to four.

There were two candidate locations in Los Angeles County. The first was a 170-acre undeveloped site located on the Orange County boundary, lying along the Southern Pacific Railroad and the Santa Ana Freeway rights-of-way. It was accessible from the Valley View Avenue off-ramp, and it was for sale. The other site, in La Mirada, was also served by the Valley View off-ramp. Known as the McNally Ranch, the site consisted of five parcels totaling 750 acres owned by the Shaw Construction Company.[67]

The only site in Orange County was the Willowick Country Club just outside of Santa Ana. The lack of direct access to arterial highways was deemed a major fault. After the primary search had been completed, the SRI team learned of another property in a more accessible part of Orange County, but it did not rise to their attention initially because it was made up of 17 parcels.

A man named Fred Wallich told SRI about a 145.35-acre property in unincorporated Orange County near Anaheim. That property was bounded by Ball Road (on the north) to Cerritos Avenue (on the south) and Harbor Boulevard (on the east) to West Street. Wallich was not a property owner, and no one knows if he had any financial interest at all. He told SRI, "I know many of the owners are considering selling to a housing subdivision." It would be like buying from one owner. Earne Moeller, head of the Anaheim Chamber of Commerce, described the site as ideal. He said, "There was the freeway and two major highways. The land was level and the utilities were in. It could be annexed to Anaheim and for all purposes [Disney] regarded this as the number one site." The site became known as the Ball Road subdivision.[68]

An Analysis of Location Factors for Disneyland was delivered on August 28, 1953. The study provided Walt with a list of potential sites ranked by desirability. Price and Wood made a presentation, and Walt selected the Ball Road subdivision, far south of the existing population centers, for further consideration. Winecoff liked the Anaheim location. It seemed so far away from city. "We found out you should never have a park in the city," he said. "It was just a 30-minute drive from Los Angeles, and people would enjoy such a ride."[69]

When Walt visited the area to check things out for himself, the real estate team first showed him a different property that was available a couple blocks north of Ball Road and about a mile and a half west of West Street, at Euclid Street. On the west side of Euclid was an unkempt Catholic cemetery owned by the Los Angeles Diocese. When Walt was told they planned to clean it up, he said, "I wouldn't bring my guests past this for love nor money. Do you have another site?"[70]

When they went to the Ball Road subdivision, Walt got very excited about the site and immediately authorized SRI to contact the property owners. A key piece of property was known as the Bauer property at the intersection of Ball Road, Harbor Boulevard, and Manchester Avenue. It was leased to the Viking Trailer Manufacturing Company. Retlaw put up a $10,000 deposit for a purchase option and agreed to expedite things to buy Viking's fixed assets for $100,000.

With that done, the Disney team stopped to have lunch at Knott's Berry Farm. "Don't you know that some s.o.b. overheard us and picked up some property at the same location," Nat Winecoff said. "Somebody came along and raised the price of the property and we got annoyed."[71] Walt walked away from his $10,000 deposit "when we could not put up with the sellers," Winecoff said.[72] They were back to looking at the other sites.

"It looked like the City might lose out," said Anaheim City Manager Keith Murdoch.[73] Murdoch talked with Moeller to see if he had any ideas. Moeller suggested that they stick to the same area but slide the northern boundary down from Ball Road to Winston Road and the southern boundary down to the Edison right-of-way near Katella Road. Murdoch liked the suggestion. "I sat in my office one Sunday afternoon, looking at maps. I spotted this area outside the city adjacent to another site that had been turned down," Murdoch recalled.[74] He knew Walt needed a site north of the Edison transmission lines due to the nature of television technology at the time. It was critical that they had the ability to transmit uninterrupted line of sight to the antennas atop Mount Wilson, in the San Gabriel Mountains northeast of Los Angeles.

Moeller recommended to Walt that he use local real estate people to work with the property owners in the revised site. Most of the property owners knew that it was Walt Disney who was interested in the properties by this time. To make the deal happen, all Murdoch had to do was to figure out a way to deal with Cerritos Avenue, which would have cut through the property. After some research he learned, "It's no small matter to close a road in the County."[75] However, state code did allow for abandonment if adjacent property owners agreed.

Just one property owner not in agreement would have killed the deal. When they updated Walt, he said, "If you can abandon that street, you got a deal."[76] Moeller was successful and the deal was closed. Moeller said that the orange-growing business wasn't good, and this was a chance to find a way out. Most properties sold for approximately $4,000 an acre, with one owner holding out for $5,000.[77]

Walt's team liked Anaheim. It had a cooperative city manager and police chief, plus an interested chamber of commerce. "Anaheim was sort of a growing area and the freeway project was such that eventually freeways would hit Anaheim as a sort of hub," Walt said.[78] Anaheim was eager to collaborate with Walt Disney; in the summer of 1953, Disney artist Roy Williams was hired to design one whole division of floats with Disney characters for the Anaheim annual Halloween Festival parade. Burr Williams of Anaheim (not related) said that if the city had not "made such a good impression on that first visit with the officials at Disney Studios in Burbank, Disneyland probably would not have moved down here at all."[79]

One of the couples who sold their property to Walt Disney was Paul and Laura Dominguez. Mrs. Dominguez was born in the house at the corner of West Street (then known as Sugar Avenue) and Cerritos Avenue. When her parents were married in 1896, Tim Carroll, Anaheim's first horticulturist, gave the newlyweds a pair of rare Canary palms. One of those trees still stands in Adventureland.[80]

Their son, Ronald Dominguez, was 18 at the time his family sold their 10-acre farm to Walt. He remembered, "My mother didn't want to sell. We sold for about $30,000, as I recall. I was excited when I learned [Walt] Disney was buying it, but I had to keep my mouth shut until all of the site was acquired."[81] Dominguez said that his mother "tried to buy seven acres across the street for $22,000, but my dad couldn't see it." Paul Dominguez would have been wise to listen to his wife; Ronald said that three years later the property sold for $100,000 per acre.

unofficial **TIP**
Ronald Dominguez would later become a Disneyland employee and rise to the position of vice president.

BANKERS DON'T HAVE IMAGINATION

WALT WAS SO PROUD of his new property in Anaheim that he wanted to show it off to Art Linkletter, who agreed to a road trip to see the site. A driver picked Linkletter up, and they drove south toward

Anaheim. Anaheim was 22 miles southeast of metropolitan Los Angeles. The new freeway ended at Rosecrans Avenue. From there, it was 8 miles of stoplight traffic to Harbor Boulevard. Surrounding them was nothing but vacant land. Linkletter was becoming concerned.

Since some of the real estate transactions were not completed, Walt reminded Linkletter that everything he was about to see was confidential. When they finally arrived, Linkletter thought Walt was crazy. Walt told Linkletter that the SRI people had said that a city would develop at the location, and that Orange County was going to be a very rich source of audience. At that point, Linkletter realized that Walt was serious.

With the property in hand, Walt was ready to move forward. He got his brother to go to New York to raise money for the Disneyland project in late September 1953. All Roy needed from Walt was a prospectus and some sort of illustration, so he could sell his brother's idea. Walt prepared a prospectus that took the reader step-by-step through the park as he first envisioned it. Many of the core elements would remain as planning continued. "The idea of Disneyland is a simple one. It will be a place for people to find happiness and knowledge," he wrote. "Disneyland will be something of a fair, an exhibition, a playground, a community center, a museum of living facts, and a showplace of beauty and magic." He promised a unique experience. "Like Alice stepping through the Looking Glass, to step through the portals of Disneyland will be like entering another world. Within a few steps the visitor will find himself in the Civic Center, a small mid-Western Town at the turn of the century." Visitors would board a steam train at Main Street and take a grand circle tour, visiting True-Life Adventureland, the World of Tomorrow, Lilliputian Land, Fantasy Land, Recreation Park, Frontier Country, Treasure Island, the home of the Mickey Mouse Club, Holidayland, and back to Main Street.

The prospectus described a three-block-long commercial street with "the nostalgic quality that makes it everybody's hometown." It is a shopping and dining district and the location for "the broadcasting theatre for the Walt Disney Television Show." Down the side streets would be the mayor's house, a boarding house for guests, and The Little Church Around the Corner. Main Street would lead to the hub: "The cross roads of the world of Disneyland."

At the entrance to True-Life Adventureland would be "a beautiful botanical garden of tropical flora and fauna." The main attraction would be the "Explorer's Boat with a native guide for a cruise down

the River of Romance." Along the banks are "birds and animals living in their natural habitat . . . alligators lurking along the banks, and
otters and turtles play[ing] in the water about you."

Walt's prospectus continued, "The theme for the World of Tomorrow is the factual and scientific exposition of Things to Come." Visitors would enter using the moving sidewalk and see "fascinating
exhibits of the miracles of science and industry." This would also
be "the home of the exciting World of Tomorrow Television Show."
Rides would include a monorail train and "The Little Parkway system
where children drive scale-model motor cars over a modern freeway."
There would be "the Magic House of Tomorrow, with mechanical
features that obey the command of your voice like a Genie. You say
'Please' and the door opens, a polite 'Thank you' will close it." Even
dining would be a futuristic experience with "conveyor-belts [that]
carry your food through the electronic cooking device of tomorrow
where you will see it cooked instantly to your liking." The big attraction would be the rocket spaceship to the moon.

Over in Lilliputian Land, an Erie Canal barge would take visitors
"through the famous canals of the world, where you visit the scenic
wonders of the world in miniature." Along with the boats, visitors
could take "a little diamond-stacked locomotive engine 17 inches high
[that] steams into the tiny railroad station. You sit on top of the Pullman coaches like Gulliver, and the little 9-inch engineer pulls back
the throttle taking you on the biggest little-ride in the land." Even
the food would be themed with "miniature ice-cream cones, or the
world's smallest hot-dog on a tiny bun."

Fantasy Land would be "within the walls and grounds of a great
medieval castle whose towers loom 70 feet into the air." Along with a
carousel would be a Snow White ride-through, a walk-through Alice
in Wonderland, and a fly-through with Peter Pan.

Certainly borrowing from the nearby Knott's Berry Farm, Frontier
Country is "where the Stagecoach meets the Train and the Riverboat
for its trip down the river to New Orleans." A Western main street
with a harness shop, a blacksmith shop, a livery stable, and a sheriff's
office would be open to the public. Another attraction would be "a
practical working farm operated with real live miniature horses, cows,
oxen, and donkeys." A Pony Express ride and a pack mule ride would
round out the offerings.

Visitors who came to meet Mickey Mouse would find him on Treasure Island in the middle of a river. A multistory hollowed-out tree

with a tree house on top would be the headquarters for the Mickey Mouse Club. The island would also serve as the location for the *Mickey Mouse Club* television show.

Holidayland would continuously change to reflect the seasons. In the summer it is "the Fourth of July . . . and Circus Time . . . with a Circus Parade down Main Street." In the fall it is time for "the Harvest Festival . . . Halloween . . . Girl Scout week . . . Thanksgiving." Winter brings an "ice skating rink, sleigh rides, and Bob-Sled Hill with real snow." Over in Recreation Land is a "shady park set aside for reservations by clubs, schools or other groups for picnics and special outings."

Walt was not content merely to write a prospectus to prepare for Roy's fund-raising trip to New York. On the morning of September 26, 1953, Walt called Herb Ryman, one of his favorite artists, and said, "Hi, Herbie. I'm over here at the Studio. I wonder if you could come over here. Just come the way that you are, I'll be out front waiting for you." Ryman said, "I was curious, and flattered that he picked up the phone and called me. I had no idea what he wanted." Walt met Ryman at the front gate and took him to the Zorro building. What transpired there has become known in Disney history circles as the Lost Weekend.[83]

Ryman asked Walt what he was doing, and he replied, "Well, we're going to do an amusement park." Ryman said, "That's good and exciting. So what do you want to see me about?" Walt confided, "My brother Roy has to go to New York on Monday morning. He's got to talk to some bankers there. You know bankers don't have imagination, none at all. You have to show them what you're going to do. Roy has to show them what this place is going to look like." Ryman got excited and asked, "Well, I'd like to see what this place is going to look like, too. Where have you got all this stuff?" Walt said, "You're going to do it."[84]

"No, I'm not," Ryman immediately replied. He later recalled, "Walt paced back and forth—we were alone in the room. He went over to the corner and he turned his head around with his back to me and said, 'Will you do it if I stay here with you?' 'Yes, I'll do it if you stay here.'" For the next two days, Walt described his dream, and Ryman put it to paper. When the two men were done, Ryman went home and told his mother what had just happened and she recorded the episode in her diary.[85]

"Every time I'd get to thinking of television I would think of this Park," Walt said, "and I knew that if I did anything like the Park that

I would have some kind of a medium like television to let the people know about it."[86] Roy went to New York and made a deal with Leonard Goldenson of the American Broadcasting Company (ABC). Disney would supply the network a 1-hour weekly television series and ABC would invest in Disneyland. Disneyland would be jointly owned by Walt Disney Productions and the American Broadcasting Company/Paramount Theaters, each with a 34.8% interest, Western Printing and Lithographing with a 13.79% interest. Walt Disney retained 17.25% for himself.

Planning for the park continued; in October Marvin Davis had developed a concept for Tomorrowland that showed a moving sidewalk, the Drive Yourself Freeway System, and the Rocket to the Moon. Some of the earliest ideas were starting to drop out. Davis also had plans for a Circus Land, but that was abandoned because of the live animals.

WE MIGHT NEED RACING BOATS

ACCORDING TO DISNEY HISTORIAN David Mumford, one of Walt's early ride concepts was the River of Romance, "a tribute to Americana and the original had guests gliding through the Everglades and down the Suwannee. By 1953, the boat ride design had become a jungle excursion."[87] The initial site plan had a big lake with an island in the middle filled with tropical trees and foliage. Motorboats would leave a dock and circumnavigate the island. Harper Goff decided that the concept would not work. He told Walt, "What you've got is everybody on that boat, if you go counterclockwise around the island, having to look to the left. The boat isn't going to go sideways, so half the people will have to look over the shoulders of people beside them."[88]

Goff's next suggestion was to have the boats enter a river on the island, with sights for people to look at from both sides. Walt agreed. As the plan continued to evolve, Goff also learned that Walt wanted the attraction to last a certain length of time. So Goff drafted a plan with a lake with an island at the center. The boats would cross the lake and then could enter the river on the island. Walt looked at the plan and asked how long it would take to get across the lake and how fast the boats would get back to pick up another load. Goff had no idea. He did not know how fast the boats could go. Walt was becoming increasingly frustrated and kept asking about the time estimates. Goff then suggested that they could build a smaller ride, but Walt would have none of that. This was going to be a marquee attraction. When Goff suggested they purchase racing boats so the boats could speed back to the dock, Walt said no. He wanted them out there a certain length of time, and he did not want them to go fast. Goff brought in architects to help, but they could not get it to work either. They made cutouts of the boats and then began to argue with one another. Finally, Goff decided the lake and island concept did not work. Stymied, Goff took out a fresh piece of paper and started over. Goff proposed a compromise. He began with a river ride where the boats would return to the same place they started. The ride would evolve into the Tropical Rivers of the World; by the time Disneyland opened in 1955, it had become the Jungle Cruise.

 ## CAN DO!

BY THE BEGINNING OF 1954, it seemed like it was all finally starting to come together. Walt had done the research, had bought the land, and had generated lots of ideas. Plus, he put together a team that he thought could make those ideas a reality. Now he just needed to get it done.

Like any of his film productions, Walt needed a director to manage the project and carry out his vision on a day-to-day basis. He needed somebody who was experienced with large and complex projects. He had been very impressed with the real estate study project manager from SRI, C. V. Wood Jr. In January Walt appointed Wood vice president and general manager of Disneyland.

Industrial labor relations expert Van France said that Wood had "a brilliant, computerized mind. He was warm and loyal to his friends, cold as steel when necessary. He can turn on a hidden charm button and sell anybody almost anything."[89] Walt liked that. What Walt likely did not know was that Wood was setting up his own team inside the Disneyland organization. He hired friends and former colleagues from the aircraft construction industry, such as France and human resources manager Fred Schumacher.

Wood came from Amarillo, Texas, where most people knew him as "Woody" when he was the director of industrial engineering at the company that would later become General Dynamics. France worked with him and said, "Up against Woody, P. T. Barnum might lose in the persuasion category." According to France, "Walt was very impressed with Wood and felt he could be instrumental in getting the Disneyland project off the ground."[90] Walt appreciated Wood's skill at getting outside companies to invest as licensees, and he treated him like a son.

France had worked with Wood before, and he reconnected with his old boss in 1954. Wood and France would bring a new discipline to the show business people at the studio, WED, and Retlaw. As men who had to train hundreds to build aircraft, they were used to policies, procedures, and organizational charts. Walt was able to blend the aircraft manufacturing culture with the film culture, and he called this "show thinking."[91] That way of thinking would soon become the standard for the Disneyland project, and those who could not adapt did not last long.

Walt hired his son-in-law Ron Miller to be the liaison between the artists at WED and the construction people. "I think at first [Ron] didn't like it," said Diane Disney Miller. "He worked under C. V. Wood and definitely felt he was there as the son-in-law of Walt. He was nothing but an errand boy. He had nothing to do, didn't know what was happening. Woody at the time had Ron thinking Dad's some kind of crackpot, that he can't do all these wild things he wanted to do at Disneyland."[92] The arrangement was short-lived; Miller was drafted into the United States Army a few months later.

Fortunately, Walt had also hired Rear Admiral Joseph W. Fowler U.S.N. (Ret.), who had served in the Navy during World War II. He was building large housing tracts in Northern California when he met with Walt and Wood. Walt was looking for an expert on ships for the *Mark Twain* project and became instantly enamored with Fowler. In late winter 1954, the two men convinced Fowler to come to Southern California and become the construction manager for the park.

Fowler was known for replying to the most impossible requests with a "Can do!" Walt really liked that. After reviewing the drawings for Disneyland, Fowler was heard to say that everything was just a lot of "blue sky plans." Fowler's assessment was bleak: of the 20 first-day attractions, only 6 were likely to open, 11 were doubtful, and 3 were definitely not going to open on time.[93] This was not the news Walt was looking for, but he had no choice but to press on because on April 2, 1954, Walt put his reputation on the line by publicly announcing the deal with ABC to broadcast the Disneyland television series and the opening of his park in July 1955.

On May 1, 1954, the hometown paper broke the story about the location of Walt's park. The *Anaheim Bulletin* headline screamed "Disneyland Comes Here."[94] The newspaper reported that the Disney brothers purchased 160 acres for an "entertainment and educational project" near the intersection of Manchester Boulevard (Highway 101) and Harbor Boulevard.

The *Orange County Register* interviewed Walt on May 11, and he said, "The land cost $1,000,000 and getting that was the toughest job. The Stanford Research Institute surveyed the area and selected Anaheim as best." He told the reporter, "We found one tract there but when people found out what it was for, the price went up. So we found another section. We had to contact 15 owners, as far away as Ohio, to buy the land."[95]

As an example of the pace of development, consider Peter Pan's Flight. In late spring 1954, Herb Ryman started working on the concepts for the Peter Pan ride with a huge rainbow as the climax. By late September, the project was in the hands of Marvin Davis, who had to figure out how to make Ryman's drawings work as a ride. Davis came up with the guests flying through three large rooms and suggested that the galleon's flight path go clockwise. He added two new scenes, Crocodile Creek and Hangman's Tree, and cut Ryman's huge rainbow at the end. Then the project moved over to Bill Martin in November; he kept the three rooms but changed the direction of the galleons to counterclockwise and eliminated Crocodile Creek and Hangman's Tree. By May 1955, less than a year after Ryman started work, the plan was finalized, and Ken Anderson was designing interiors and fabricating the attraction.

The same thing was happening in Tomorrowland. Work had begun on the Autopia miniature car attraction. Hartmann Engineering was hired to design and build the cars, but the project was not going well. Dick Irvine thought it might be best to bring the project in-house. Roger Broggie had already started to develop a bumper system when WED hired auto stylist Bob Gurr, who had heard about the job through his friend Don Iwerks, son of Disney Legend Ub Iwerks. Although Gurr was trained as a car stylist, he had no direct experience with mechanical engineering. That would all change, and he very quickly taught himself the necessary skills. Gurr was also recruited to test the Peter Pan and Mr. Toad vehicles.

Walt finally broke ground on July 12, 1954. As part of the land acquisition process, Walt had promised to let the Claussens family keep their home at the northwest corner of Cerritos Avenue and Harbor Boulevard for their daughters. With that promise, they were the first family to sell. While clearing the site, the construction crew piled up a stack of orange trees and lit it on fire. Earne Moeller said, "The wind changed and the house burnt to the ground to the extreme embarrassment of the Disney group."[96]

On July 21, 1954, C. V. Wood made a presentation to city officials and the Anaheim Chamber of Commerce. Wood described the site evaluation process that led to the "best location money can buy." The response from the business community was positive and overwhelming. The *Anaheim Bulletin* editorial by Howard Loudon proclaimed, "Opportunity is knocking at your door, and it is knocking hard, through the medium of a fantastic one-man development called Disneyland." They recognized, "It is natural to be concerned over a development so large, so fabulous, so new. No one can possibly know the repercussions that will develop when this new concept in entertainment opens." However, they did know that "any business established to bring happiness cannot develop into a detriment to the community in which it is situated."[97]

20 FEET *of* EARTH

EARLIER IN THE YEAR, landscaper Bill Evans and his brother, Jack, had received a call from Fred Schumacher, who was the personnel director, to talk about the park. Schumacher set up a meeting between Walt and the brothers, and Walt immediately offered them the job to supply the landscape for Disneyland. Of course, the brothers said yes.

The Evans brothers started by taking Walt to their home to give him an idea of what could be done. The brothers had created various environments within the canyon near their home. One area looked like a tropical jungle, while another was an example of an old English garden. They had an area that looked wild, yet was actually built from scratch. They used the gardens as a way to educate Walt on the type of plant materials necessary to create the mood he was seeking.

Later that week, Walt took the Evans brothers for a walk in Anaheim, and what they saw was wall-to-wall orange trees, with a few avocados, and maybe a couple of dozen walnut trees. Bill Evans noticed that they were knocking down trees in the parking lot, and he immediately put a stop to that. He figured replacing the mature trees would cost at least $500 each.

Evans took a transparency of the master plan and placed it over an aerial photograph of the property at the same scale. He marked all the trees that were not in the middle of the street or in the Rivers of America and tried to work around them. Evans tagged trees that were to be saved with green ribbons, and he tagged trees to be removed with red ribbons. His efforts were futile. As it turned out, the bulldozer operator was color-blind and they lost dozens of trees that were 50–100 years old. More than 12,000 orange trees were removed.

One goal for the landscape design was screening out the real world. If Walt wanted to take his guests to the American Wilderness or an African jungle, he needed to make sure people were not seeing a freeway exchange, high-rise buildings, or transmission lines from inside the park. Evans had to figure out a way to eliminate any visual intrusions. The solution was to build a berm to shut out the sound outside. "Trees alone won't do that. It takes about a 100 feet of dense trees to block sound, but you can do that with about 20 feet of earth," said Evans. "Then we garnish the berm with all the landscaping we can afford, and in this way we exclude the twentieth century."[98]

McNeil Construction was awarded the contract to build the park on August 26, 1954. The first challenge was to prepare the site by moving hundreds of tons of soil around to create rivers, mountains, and the earthen berm that would surround the park and protect it from the outside world.

An official groundbreaking ceremony had been scheduled for August 25, but it was canceled two weeks beforehand due to a threatened protest demonstration. Even though the Disneyland project was welcomed by much of the local community, there were some who were not so pleased. Two Garden Grove businessmen sued Anaheim on September 17, 1954, due to the boundaries of the 608-acre annexation area that included Disneyland. The initiative was put on the ballot in November. Annexation was important to Disneyland because of sewer connections and the benefit of working with responsive local municipal leaders instead of countywide supervisors.

Earne Moeller recalled later that to ensure victory, the borders of the annexation effort were gerrymandered so that there would be reasonable assurance of victory. The annexation election was carried out and Anaheim prevailed—56 property owners in favor to 2 opposed.[99] Landowners and the cities of Orange and Santa Ana appealed the election in district court, and Anaheim prevailed once again. On January 5, 1955, Disneyland became part of Anaheim, and the city grew from 6.98 square miles to 11.17 square miles.

SNEEZE TWICE

THE ABC BROADCAST DEBUT of Disneyland on October 27, 1954, was a landmark moment for television and the amusement park industry. The first episode was called "The Disneyland Story," and it would be the first time that most of the public would learn about Walt's plans. Never before had a major motion picture studio placed such a large bet on the medium. Most movie moguls felt the electronic box would kill their businesses, and they shied away. Walt was not afraid. Just as he had done with sound, color, stereo, and so many other breakthroughs, he embraced technology.

The show was set in the Disneyland Plans Room. Walt personally hosted the show and gave the audience a preview of the show and the park. He began with artist Peter Ellenshaw's bird's-eye illustrative drawing of the park as seen from 2,000 feet.[100] Then he showed off the models for Main Street, Sleeping Beauty Castle, and the Jungle Cruise. Walt was especially proud of the model of the *Mark Twain,* built by Yale Gracey, which he kept in his office for many years.

Ward Kimball introduced the Tomorrowland segment with a preview of the Man in Space episode, director Norman Foster talked about Davy Crockett and Frontierland, and director Ben Sharpsteen reviewed the plans for Adventureland. The television broadcast was a huge hit, with a 28.4 rating and capturing 52% of the viewing audience. This was unheard of for a new show.

At the same time, Walt was accustomed to the building process for movie sets and became frustrated at what he thought was a lack of progress at the site in Anaheim. Goff speculated that Walt "thought he could just 'sneeze twice' and there would be work completed each time he went down there."[101] Walt was beginning to wonder if anything was going to happen other than pushing dirt around, so he decided to take matters into his own hands and would constantly visit the construction site, hoping that his presence would speed things up. Goff spent a lot of time with Walt explaining to him what was going on. It still did not help.

There were a lot of challenges with the planning that had to be corrected in the field. An old riverbed that had a slight fall from the north to the southwest ran through part of the site. Quite a bit of grading was necessary to create a new river, an island, and a jungle river.

The original plan had the guests walking north along Main Street to the Plaza Hub in front of the castle and then going in a counterclockwise direction visiting each of the lands. Tomorrowland was to be located on the west side of the park so that it would be the final stop. Instead, Frontierland and Adventureland had to be placed together because of the way they share the water system. Another benefit was the opportunity to use an existing row of eucalyptus trees used as windbreak behind City Hall that provided a way to screen the back side of Main Street from the Jungle Cruise.

Walt did not want another Coney Island or Long Beach Pike. He wanted something radically different. He looked for the qualities that were missing at the typical amusement park, and these included courtesy, cleanliness, imagination, and landscaping. Old-time amusement parks were mostly wood and pavement. Walt wanted a park filled with shows and attractions. Existing amusement parks were not very attractive or a pleasant place to be. Disneyland was meant to be different. Walt wanted to use trees and gardens to create a relaxing environment. He wanted his guests to feel comfortable just sitting and enjoying the views, watching a riverboat pass by, or listening to music in a shady spot. Providing shade would be a very important asset in the hot days of summer. At night, the park would come alive with twinkle lights mounted in the trees.

Disneyland would become one of the most diverse botanical gardens in the United States. Approximately 90% of the plant material was nonindigenous to California. There were more than 800 species of plants and trees, including specimens from Australia, Mexico, Europe, and Asia.

Evans was given a very tight budget, very little time, and a mandate to achieve the illusion of full growth landscapes. At the park's grand opening, Evans was able to create a reasonably believable jungle, appropriate formal plantings in the Plaza Hub and Town Square, and nothing but tiny 5-gallon trees in Frontierland. Tomorrowland was even more barren.

Bill Evans began a tradition of using familiar plant materials in unfamiliar ways. For example, in a traditional setting such as Main Street, his team selected less conventional plantings to separate it from community parks and to give it a Disney flair. Evans depleted nurseries from Santa Barbara to San Diego. They spent $400,000 on 1,200 full-size trees and 9,000 shrubs and used 32,000 sacks of cement and 3.5 million board feet of lumber. They moved 5 million square feet of pavement and 300,000 cubic yards of earth.

"In the year before Disneyland opened, you just couldn't escape Walt," Evans said. "He toured the place daily."[102] Evans recalled a time when he had planted a pepper tree beside the Plaza Pavilion Restaurant. Walt, Fowler, and Evans were walking by the restaurant when Walt turned to Fowler and asked, "Joe, that tree looks a little close to the walkway doesn't it?" Fowler then turned to Evans and asked, "How about moving that tree, Bill?" Evans did as he was told and "moved all 10 tons of it a little ways back" about 10 feet overnight. The next day, as the men walked past the same spot, Evans said, Walt "didn't say a word. He just smiled."[103]

One of the things Walt was not smiling about was the progress of Tomorrowland. On September 10, 1954, he suspended work and had his team concentrate on more achievable goals. However, there was good news as well. Walt's team had found a Dentzel carousel built in 1875 that had been at Toronto's Sunnyside Park since the 1920s. It was delivered to Disneyland in October. A lot of work needed to be done to get the carousel into shape, but the centerpiece of Fantasyland, one of the inspirations for the park, had finally arrived.

Van France was a master at organizational design, and he described the team building Disneyland as a hybridized organization. Everybody knew the boss was Walt, even those loyal to C. V. Wood. However, there were many other stakeholder groups, each with its own special interest.[104]

France called the first group "the entrenched studio employees." They were the brilliant people that Walt had worked with for years. Some of them thought that the amusement park was an odd thing for Walt to be doing and were not too excited about the potential effects on the studio. Even so, all of them wanted to help out because Walt had asked them.

The next group was "the WED Enterprises people." These were the true believers. They were all handpicked by Walt to build and design Disneyland. Some of the WED people came from the Disney Studio, while others came from other parts of Hollywood. Admiral Joe Fowler and Dick Irvine made sure that the team stayed on track. Bob Gurr said, "Walt trusted Dick Irvine to direct his set designers for the overall Disneyland architecture. Art director Emile Kuri made sure the interiors were going to be beautiful. Roger Broggie was entrusted with all the unique mechanical rides. Admiral Joe Fowler made sure all the construction was happening fast.

Then there were "Woody's Texans." C. V. Wood worked hard at building a team loyal to him. Most were personal friends. Another group somewhat related were "Woody's aircraft and Stanford people." This was the original group of professionals who worked on the location study or worked with Wood in the aircraft industry. They were critical in getting the park actually built.

Finally, there were the "lessees." Walt relied on other companies for money and services to complete the project. The lessees included representatives from the companies that had invested in Disneyland, such as Eastman Kodak or Swift and Company. There were also a bunch of smaller companies that would operate the venues inside the park.

As 1955 began, Walt was beginning to regret his decision in September to put Tomorrowland on hold until after the grand opening. In November 1954, Walt and John Hench had given a tour to Ralph Damon of TWA, who had decided to sponsor the Rocket to the Moon. With TWA sponsorship in place, Walt wanted his guests to see the complete show. Now that he had TWA interested in funding the Rocket to the Moon ride, he told Joe Fowler on January 15 to get started on Tomorrowland. To expedite the process and save some money, they eliminated the proposed dancing fountains and the moving sidewalks at the entrance. At the same time, they pulled the plug on the Frontierland Miniature Museum. This is where Walt thought he could place some of the work done for Disneylandia, including Granny Kincaid's cabin, Project Little Man, and the barbershop quartet.

In the final weeks before the park opening and the television broadcast, the construction site was in overdrive. This was welcome news to the union workers who were working seven days a week. Overtime pay in most cases was into double time, and some tradesmen were grossing more than $1,000 a week.

One of the things they built was a beautiful bandstand set in the middle of the town square in Main Street USA. It was large enough for a 16-piece band, painted white, and perfect for a Victorian-era civic center. France described it as "a one-of-a-kind, a Picasso, a Van Gogh, a Walt Disney original."[105] On one Sunday, Walt was looking at the bandstand and said, "There's something damned wrong with where that bandstand now is."[106] Walt did not like how the bandstand blocked the view of the train station from Sleeping Beauty Castle.

The bandstand was moved to the other end of Main Street, just west of the castle. In the spring of 1956, Walt had the bandstand moved once again to make room for the Carnations Plaza Gardens. The bandstand became the centerpiece of Magnolia Park in Frontierland when it opened on May 31, 1956. When that area was demolished to make way for New Orleans Square, the bandstand was put backstage and then finally sold to Roger's Gardens nursery in Corona del Mar.

A 65-foot flagpole was installed in place of the bandstand at the center of the town square. Walt had paid $5 for the base of a flagpole found at the scene of an auto accident on Wilshire Boulevard, where a car had run into a lamppost. At the base of the flagpole was the dedication plaque, which read, "To all who come to this happy place; Welcome. Disneyland is your land. Here age relives fond memories of the past, and here youth may savor the challenge and promise of the future. Disneyland is dedicated to the hard facts that have created America—with the hope that it will be a source of joy and inspiration to all the world." That plaque was protected by cannons by Hutchkiss in Paris, France.

Opening day was quickly approaching, and Walt decided that it was time to show off the park to some of the studio employees. He had hoped that he could alleviate some of their concerns and reassure them that the boss was not going crazy. The private dining room at the Walt Disney Studio in Burbank was called the Penthouse Club and was located on the top floor of the Animation Building. Membership was limited to senior members of the studio staff. Members and their families were invited to a holiday picnic at Disneyland on July 4, 1955.

The party was going to feature a ride on the *Mark Twain* and the Santa Fe & Disneyland Railroad. The two steam trains were fired up, with Walt as engineer for the *C. K. Holliday* and Ward Kimball in charge of the *E. P. Ripley*. Roger Broggie reported that the trains performed well. Kimball said, "This was a big day for Walt, on that 4th of July. To the 80 or 90 people that were there that day, the Park was basically a big empty place, with a lot of work going on. They rode the trains and the *Mark Twain*, looked at how the construction was going, ate a picnic lunch and that was about it. People began leaving, when the sun went down. But to Walt, the locomotives were under steam!" Kimball remembered, "We were like kids, playing trains."[107]

On July 13, with just a few days to go before the park's grand opening, 300 special guests were invited to attend the Tempus Fugit Celebration at the Golden Horseshoe Saloon. The Golden Horseshoe had the authentic flavor of an 1840 saloon and was a direct lift from the dance hall featured in the film *Calamity Jane*. Harper Goff was the set designer for both projects. The saloon was named after the

OVER TIME, Walt would adopt the stage left box at the Golden Horseshoe Saloon as his own. Comedian Wally Boag said, "If Walt was in the Park they would notify us and that box (the one under the steer horns) would be kept empty . . . and he showed up a lot. He would always stay after the show and talk to us." Roy was also a fan. "Roy and his party didn't want the box," said Boag. "They would sit at a front table, right in the middle. They would talk to the musicians and wait until we came out and they'd say, 'Hey . . . it was great again!' Walt would stay too, but Roy was a little more down to earth."[112]

In 1985 the *Golden Horseshoe Revue* set a Guinness World Record with 42,921 performances, the greatest number of any theatrical presentation. Boag would repeat the role of Pecos Bill in nearly 40,000 of those performances. More than 16 million guests would see the show during its run.

authentic Golden Horseshoe in New York. Paintings from Charles M. Russell and Frederick Remington adorned the walls, which also featured 15 sets of Texas longhorns.[108]

The party celebrated Walt and Lillian's 30th wedding anniversary, and they promised "cruising down the Mississippi on the *Mark Twain*'s maiden voyage, followed by dinner at Slue-foot Sue's Golden Horseshoe!"

On the day of the party, Joe Fowler was on the project site as usual and went to the *Mark Twain* for a final inspection. On board was a woman sweeping the deck. She handed him a broom and said, "This ship is just filthy . . . let's get busy and sweep it up." After getting over the shock, Fowler realized that the woman was Lillian Disney.[109]

Walt walked with Jack Sayers toward the front gate at 6 p.m. to meet his guests. When they got there, Walt exclaimed, "Where is everybody?" Sayers had no idea and he told Van France later, "He's blaming me because the guests are probably hung up in traffic." Inevitably, the guests began to arrive to this remote site in motor coaches and cars.

The entertainment was the debut performance of the *Golden Horseshoe Revue*, "an Old-West stage show with comedy and singing in a 30-minute production starring comedian Wally Boag, songstress Betty Taylor, tenor Fulton Burley, and the Golden Horseshoe Girls," according to the press release. "There were quite a few important people in the audience . . . Hedda Hopper and Irene Dunn were there," comedian Wally Boag remembered. "It was mostly a dress rehearsal, but it was our first show as far as I'm concerned."[110]

Walt's daughter Diane has claimed that this party may have been one of the happiest days in her father's life. As the evening came to a close, she recalled asking her father if she could drive him home. He said, "Well, sure, honey." As he climbed into the backseat of the car, she said, "He had a map of Disneyland, and he rolled it up, and tooted in my ear as with a toy trumpet." As she drove, the car grew silent. Diane looked at the backseat and he was sound asleep, with "his arms folded around the map like a boy with a toy trumpet." She claims, "The next morning he . . . bounded out of the house at 7:30 and headed for Disneyland again."[111]

1. Walt Disney, interview by Fletcher Markel, *Telescope* (CBC), 25 Sept. 1963.
2. Diane Disney Miller, interview by Peter Sciretta, *Slashfilm,* 7 Feb. 2012.
3. Ibid.
4. *The Spirit of Disneyland* (Anaheim, CA: Walt Disney Productions, 1984).
5. Ibid.
6. Michael Broggie, *Walt Disney's Railroad Story* (Pasadena, CA: Pentrex, 1998).
7. Katherine Greene and Richard Greene, *Inside the Dream* (New York: Disney Editions, Inc., 2001).
8. "Walt Disney and Ward Kimball on the Track to Disneyland," *The "E" Ticket,* Number 12, Winter 1991–92, 20–31.
9. Greene and Greene, *Inside the Dream.*
10. Neal Gabler, *Walt Disney: The Triumph of the American Imagination* (New York: Knopf, 2006).
11. Ibid.
12. "Another Kind of Reality," *The "E" Ticket,* Number 17, Winter 1993–94, 16–25.
13. Gabler, *Triumph.*
14. Jeff Kurtti, *Walt Disney's Imagineering Legends and the Genesis of the Disney Theme Park* (New York: Disney Editions, Inc., 2008).
15. Gabler, *Triumph.*
16. Broggie, *Railroad Story.*
17. Ibid.
18. Randy Bright, *Disneyland: Inside Story* (New York: Abrams, 1987).
19. *Disneyland: The First Quarter Century* (Burbank, CA: Walt Disney Productions, 1979).
20. Dave Smith, *Walt Disney Famous Quotes* (Lake Buena Vista, FL: Walt Disney Theme Parks and Resorts, 1994).
21. Gabler, *Triumph.*
22. Steve DeGaetano, *Welcome Aboard the Disneyland Railroad!* (Winter, CA: Steam Passages Publications, 2004).
23. Van Arsdale France, "Backstage Disneyland: A Personal History" (unpublished manuscript, 1980).
24. Smith, *Famous Quotes.*
25. Orrin Klapp, *Overload and Boredom* (Westport, CT: Greenwood Press, 1986), 148.
26. Herman Wong, "Disneyland: Can It Top 15 Years of Success?," *Los Angeles Times,* 17 July 1970.
27. John Hench with Peggy Van Pelt, *Designing Disney: Imagineering and the Art of the Show* (New York: Disney Editions, Inc., 2008).
28. Wendy Lefkin, ed., *Walt Disney Imagineering: A Behind the Dreams Look at Making the Magic Real* (New York: Hyperion, 1996).
29. Bruce Gordon and David Mumford, *Disneyland: The Nickel Tour* (Santa Clarita, CA: Camphor Tree, 2000).
30. Ibid.
31. Smith, *Famous Quotes.*
32. Ibid.
33. *The Spirit of Disneyland.*
34. Bright, *Inside Story.*
35. Jeff Kurtti, interview with author, 12 Jan. 2011.
36. Wendy Lefkin, ed., *Disney Insider Yearbook: 2005 Year in Review* (New York: Disney Editions, 2006).

37. "Walt Disney Make-Believe Land Project Planned Here," *Burbank Daily Review*, 27 March 1952, A1.
38. Smith, *Famous Quotes*.
39. Lefkin, ed., *Insider Yearbook*.
40. Ibid.
41. Walt Disney, interview with Peter Martin, *Saturday Evening Post*, summer 1956.
42. Gerald Peary, "Walt's World," *The Boston Globe*, 19 April 1992.
43. John Taylor, *Storming the Kingdom* (New York: Ballantine Books, 1988).
44. Ibid.
45. Gordon and Mumford, *Nickel Tour*.
46. *First Quarter Century*.
47. Greene and Greene, *Inside the Dream*.
48. Ibid.
49. Disneyland University, "The Dream is a Reality" (Anaheim, CA: Disneyland, July 1975).
50. Tim O'Brien, *Ripley's Legends: Pioneers of the Amusement Park Industry*, Vol. 1 (Nashville, TN: Ripley's Entertainment, 2006).
51. Lefkin, ed., *Behind the Dreams*.
52. "Visualizing Disneyland with Sam McKim," *The "E" Ticket*, Number 18, Spring 1994, 8–21.
53. Rolly Crump with Jeff Heimbuch, *It's Kind of a Cute Story* (Clearwater, FL: Bamboo Forest, 2012).
54. "Designing Disneyland with Marc Davis," *The "E" Ticket*, Number 7, Summer 1989, 4–17.
55. "Disneyland Art Director Bill Martin," *The "E" Ticket*, Number 20, Winter 1994–95, 10–19.
56. "Visualizing Disneyland with Sam McKim," *The "E" Ticket*, Number 18, Spring 1994, 8–21.
57. "Planning the First Disney Parks," *The "E" Ticket*, Number 28, Winter 1997, 8–19.
58. Ibid.
59. *First Quarter Century*.
60. John McDonald, "Now the Bankers Come to Disney," *Fortune*, May 1966.
61. *Spirit of Disneyland*.
62. Ibid.
63. McDonald, "Bankers Come to Disney."
64. Taylor, *Storming the Kingdom*.
65. Alan Trudell, "Disney—It Almost Got Away," *Anaheim Bulletin*, 5 Jan. 1978.
66. *Spirit of Disneyland*.
67. *An Analysis of Location Factors for Disneyland* (Menlo Park, CA: Stanford Research Institute, 28 Aug. 1953).
68. Mike Kilroy, "How Disney Chose OC for His New Land," *Orange County Register*, 5 Dec. 1996.
69. Trudell, "It Almost Got Away."
70. Earnest W. Moeller, "An Historical Sketch for the Archives of Mother Colony Room" (presentation, Anaheim Main Public Library, Anaheim, CA, July 14, 1980).
71. Trudell, "It Almost Got Away."
72. Ibid.
73. Moeller, "Historical Sketch."
74. Ibid.
75. Ibid.
76. Ibid.
77. "Landscaping Keeps Kingdom Enchanting," *Anaheim Bulletin*, 15 July 1980.

78. *First Quarter Century.*
79. Moeller, "Historical Sketch."
80. Mildred Yorba MacArthur, letter, May 1957, Mildred Yorba MacArthur Papers, Anaheim Heritage Center, Anaheim Public Library, Anaheim, California.
81. Jack Boettner, "Disney's Magical Little Park after Two Decades," *Los Angeles Times,* 6 July 1975.
82. France, "Backstage Disneyland."
83. John Stanley Donaldson, *Warp and Weft: Life Canvas of Herbert Ryman* (Las Vegas: Incanio Press, 2010).
84. Ibid.
85. Ibid.
86. Gabler, *Triumph.*
87. Gordon and Mumford, *Nickel Tour.*
88. Ibid.
89. France, "Backstage Disneyland."
90. Ibid.
91. *Spirit of Disneyland.*
92. Taylor, *Storming the Kingdom.*
93. Gordon and Mumford, *Nickel Tour.*
94. "Disneyland Comes Here," *Anaheim Bulletin,* 1 May 1954.
95. Aline Mosby, "Cartoonist Has Fabulous Future Planned for Anaheim Disneyland," *Orange County Register,* 11 May 1954.
96. Moeller, "Historical Sketch."
97. Howard Loudon, "Disneyland . . . Friend or Foe," *Anaheim Bulletin,* 8 July 1955.
98. Karal Ann Marling, *Designing Disney's Theme Parks: The Architecture of Reassurance* (New York: Flammarion, 1997).
99. Moeller, "Historical Sketch."
100. Jeff Kurtti and Bruce Gordon, *The Art of Disneyland* (New York: Disney Editions, Inc., 2005).
101. "An Interview with Harper Goff," *The E Ticket,* Number 14, Winter 1992, 4–11.
102. Lefkin, ed., *Behind the Dreams.*
103. Ibid.
104. France, "Backstage Disneyland."
105. Christy Gustitis-Ritner, "Then and Now," *Disneyland Line,* 8 May 1992.
106. Ibid.
107. "On the Track to Disneyland," *The "E" Ticket,* Number 12, Winter 1991–92, 20–31.
108. Disneyland Operations Department Group II, *Background Information: Adventureland, Frontierland, New Orleans* (Anaheim, CA: Disneyland, 26 Jan. 1970).
109. Kurtti, *Imagineering Legends.*
110. Wally Boag and Gene Sands, *Wally Boag: Clown Prince of Disneyland* (New York: Disney Editions, Inc., 2009).
111. Ibid.
112. Jim Korkis, The *Revised Vault of Walt: Unofficial, Unauthorized, Uncensored Disney Stories Never Told* (Orlando, FL: Theme Park Press, 2012).

CHAPTER 2

STUMBLING FORWARD: 1955

▌ *An* **ESTABLISHING SHOT**

DISNEYLAND WAS MORE than the attractions and pathways on the map that Walt clutched in his arms the night of the Tempus Fugit celebration. It was, according to Disneyland University, the "road map of Walt Disney's life." And just as a parent's life events influence the child's developing character, Walt's experiences shaped his "child," Disneyland. "From his boyhood days through his interest in space travel," Walt's inspirations accompanied the guests every step of the way.

It is no surprise, then, that what set Disneyland apart from other amusement parks or World's Fairs was its reliance on storytelling and the application of optical tricks commonly used in filmmaking as an integrated part of the environmental design. This approach was a reflection of Walt's experience as a filmmaker and his desire to surround himself with people who shared the same professional background.

"A film makes sense to the audience because the director takes them from scene one to scene two and so on, in a logical flow of events and relationships," John Hench said. "If the director were to leapfrog from scene one to scene 52, it would be like sending the audience out for dinner in the middle of the film."[1] Disneyland would be the first public environment explicitly based on a cinematic point of view. That was the difference between a theme park and an amusement park.

Walt wanted to capture the experience of visiting a movie palace and enjoying the magic of the show but with a twist. The guests had to step through the screen and become part of the show. Walt described the property as a 70-acre stage where each visitor becomes an actor reliving memories and turning his dreams into reality. What Marvin Davis found fascinating about the project was that "no one before

Walt had used moviemaking experience and techniques to tell a story visually in a three-dimensional park setting."[2]

According to John Hench, Walt wanted a place "where each scene relates to another in logical sequence." He explained, "Walt was one of the first people to understand this type of visual literacy—really of using form in a literate way. Reality is inside the park and fantasy is outside of it."[3]

"Walt had a keen sense of how images fit together and how they took their meaning from each other and he knew how to eliminate contradictions," Hench said. "Ideas can be approached through a sequence, just like a book with chapters. Each succeeding chapter takes its meaning from the ones that precede it, and Walt used this for, of all things, an amusement park. Main Street was the most obvious example . . . it had a kind of an optimistic message."[4]

"Ours are not typical amusement parks, and they never will be," Hench said. "Walt was a very intuitive guy . . . and he knew how to communicate ideas using traditional theatrical techniques that were appropriate. He used these methods for an amusement park and the others not only didn't discover this, they wouldn't 'see' it if they discovered it, and wouldn't have seen any use for it."[5] He suggested, "Some of the newest parks tried, but they didn't learn the lessons very well and the results are quite chaotic. The use of the step-by-step process of evolving a sequence (like in films), and to try to make a visual system out of all the elements is hard to do."[6]

Hench explained, "Most urban environments are basically chaotic places, as architectural and graphics information scream at the citizen for attention. This competition results in disharmonies and contradictions that serve to cancel each other. A journey down almost any urban street will quickly place the visitor into visual overload as all of the competing messages merge into a kind of information gridlock."[7] Disneyland is different. It "is symbolic that all is right with the world. There, the guest walks through an atmosphere of order and cleanliness and comes away feeling that things must be all right, after all," Hench said. "Unlike in society's modern cities, they can drop their defenses in Disneyland and look other people in the eye. Actually, what we're selling throughout the Park is reassurance. We offer adventures in which you survive a kind of personal challenge—a charging hippo, a runaway mine train, a wicked witch, an out-of-control bobsled. But in every case, we let you win. We let your survival instincts triumph over adversity. A trip to Disneyland is an exercise in reassurance about oneself and one's ability to maybe even handle the real challenges in life."[8] He suggested, "All you have to do is come through the gates and you have a temporary respite from the next week's problems and last week's hurt. And the message is, we made this place just for you, our guests. You are who we were thinking about when we built Disneyland."[9]

Disney archivist Dave Smith said, "Disneyland's true appeal, we admit now, is to adults. Children don't need it. Their imaginations are enough. For them, Disneyland is only another kind of reality, somewhat less marvelous than their own fantasies."[10]

Harrison "Buzz" Price said, "Walt taught the post-war world that there was a positive way to look at the imperfect society. Political life could be screwed up, wars and pestilence could occur, economics could get out of balance and we could be up to our ass in debt. But, there was a positive way to look at all of this and that was the message that Walt set out to put into his attractions."[11]

However, Hench claimed, "For all its success, the Disney theme show is quite a fragile thing. It just takes one contradiction, one out of place stimulus to negate a particular moment's experience."[12] For example, he suggested if you took a "streetcar conductor's costume away and put him in double-knit slacks and a golf shirt, replace that old gay nineties melody with a rock number, replace the themed merchandise with digital clock radios and electric hair dryers, tack up a felt-tip drawn paper sign that says, 'Keep Out,' place a touch of Astroturf here, add a surly employee there, it really doesn't take much to upset it all." Guests came with such high expectations. "We realized that people come to Disneyland with an extraordinary mind set. They don't just hope they'll be entertained . . . they take it for granted, there's a conviction that they'll have a good time." The formula for success was "attention to infinite detail, the little things, the minor picky points that other companies just don't want to take the time, the money, the effort, to do right."[13]

An OPENING DAY GUIDED TOUR of the DISNEYLAND "MOVIE SHOW"

IN THE 1950S THE LOVE AFFAIR with the automobile was reaching new heights in Southern California. Drive-in movie theaters, drive-in restaurants, and drive-in churches were all the rage. It was assumed by park officials that most guests would arrive by car, typically exiting at

Harbor Boulevard once the Santa Ana Freeway was open. Dominating the street was a large sign that could easily have been a theater marquee. The entrance to the parking lot was easily visible to the driver who would be tired of the traffic and the excitable kids.

Walt knew that first impressions mattered, and one of the greatest sensitivity points in the entire Disneyland experience was the parking lot. The parking lot was the outer lobby. As guests drove into the parking lot, they would be guided to one of the 12,175 empty parking stalls by uniformed parking attendants acting more like ushers.

A short walk from their car, the guests would board one of several tractor-drawn rubber-tired trams with convenient side seating. The tram would deliver the guests to one of the many ticket booths. The abundance of ticket booths meant that guests did not have to wait long to purchase their general admission tickets.

Marking the entrance was the Santa Fe & Disneyland Railroad's Main Street Depot, perched high on an earthen berm. Like a motion picture, the Disneyland story started with an establishing shot. The depot was visible from the entire parking lot, so it had to be impressive. To add to the experience, guests might also get a peek at the *C. K. Holliday,* an authentic steam-powered locomotive, stopping at the station to pick up passengers. Or guests might see the *E. P. Ripley,* another steam locomotive, pass by on its way to Frontierland.

Past the turnstiles was the "inner lobby." The redbrick pavers symbolized the red carpet for the VIPs at any important movie event. The space provided families room to gather, collect themselves, and not feel rushed.

At the movies, just as the main attraction begins, the studio that was responsible for the production displays its logo. In the 1950s, this opening statement raised audience expectations as to the type of picture they were about to see. For example, Universal's spinning globe with a plane flying around the equator meant that they were likely to see a low-budget thriller or horror film. The MGM lion promised a lavish musical production or a film featuring the biggest stars. Disneyland was no different. At the center of the "lobby" was a large floral display of Mickey Mouse. The Mickey Mouse emblem meant fun, and fun is what the audience could expect once they passed through the portal and stepped onstage.

Another way Walt defied conventional wisdom was the use of a single entrance. Since movie theater operators only have one entrance and exit, they always know how many people they are serving. Walt wanted the same level of control at Disneyland. An additional benefit of the single entrance was that it reduced the level of stress for a guest visiting an unfamiliar place. The site plan provided for one entrance that moved people through a narrow corridor toward an open space. This layout could accommodate large crowds, and it provided immediate orientation.

What Disneyland called the "stage curtains" were the two tunnels that passed under the railroad tracks to the left and right of the station. Above each tunnel, Walt wanted to place a plaque that would sum up his expectations for the park. He got a memo on June 22, 1955, with the first draft, which read, "Disneyland, where you leave today . . . and visit the world of fantasy, yesterday, and tomorrow." Walt took a look and made a few changes, and today the plaque reads, "Here you leave today and visit the world of Yesterday, Tomorrow, and Fantasy." Walt was so focused on the details that he even indicated the size, proportions, and location of the plaque in the memo's margins.[14] However, the plaque was not ready in time for the grand opening.

As the show began, the opening scene was just on the other side of the railroad tracks. Borrowing from filmmakers, the tunnels acted as a cross dissolve between one realm to another, from the outside world into "the world of Yesterday, Tomorrow, and Fantasy." In the movies, when the director needed to take the viewer from one scene to another seamlessly, he or she superimposed the tail end of the first clip onto the beginning of the second clip and faded the clips in and out.

The tunnels created the same sensation; once through to the other side, the guests would find themselves in Main Street U.S.A., "center stage" for the first scene of the Disneyland experience. Gone were the asphalt sea of a parking lot, the overhead electrical transmission lines, and the hustle and bustle of the freeway. The train station on the berm effectively blocked the view of the outside world, and guests were immersed in a plaza surrounded by grand civic buildings of a bygone era.

SCENE ONE: MAIN STREET U.S.A.

MAIN STREET U.S.A. was made up of three primary features: the town square plaza; a narrow retail corridor called Main Street, which was two blocks long with Center Street at the halfway point; and the plaza hub at the end of Main Street. Every detail had been subject to Walt's scrutiny. "[Walt] went over my plans with a fine-tooth comb," Imagineer Bill Martin said. "I'd drawn some sidewalks on the blueprints with square corners and Walt said, 'Bill, people aren't soldiers! They don't turn in sharp angles! Curve the sidewalks! Make the corners round!' "[15] Some of the cresting and railings came from old plantations in Nashville and Memphis, Tennessee, as well as San Francisco and Sacramento, California.

Town Square

Surrounding the flagpole at the center of Town Square were civic buildings, such as the opera house, city hall, and the police department. Defining the south end of Town Square was the ornate Victorian Main Street train station. The architecture combined elements from several 1890s stations found in a book from Ward Kimball's collection called *Buildings and Structures of American Railroads*. The structure featured a gabled roof, cupolas, and the town clock. Inside was a small exhibit with the history of the American West and a snack bar. Guests could watch the progress of the trains circling the park with a display map of Disneyland with lights that duplicated the block light system. On the siding was the handcar given to Walt Disney by the Kalamazoo Mfg. Co.

On the east side of town square was the Disneyland branch of the Bank of America, the only bank in America opened Saturdays, Sundays, and holidays and where guests could purchase specially printed money orders without charge.[16] Next door was the opera house, which was not accessible to the public until the "Babes in Toyland" exhibit in 1961. The fire station was "complete with horse-drawn hose and chemical wagon" with an alarm system purchased from the City of Los Angeles.

Hidden above the fire station was Walt's private apartment. As described earlier, Anaheim was not very close to Burbank. With only a couple of motels in the area, Walt thought it was important that he have a place to stay and work. So he had a 500-square-foot apartment built for him above the fire station. He lived in the apartment full-time for weeks prior to the park's opening. Archivist Dave Smith said, "He probably felt that his constant presence would help get his pride-and-joy opened."[17]

Walt had set designer Emile Kuri work with his wife, Lillian, to come up with a place that reflected her taste. She chose to work in the Victorian style, as appropriate for Main Street, with the room dressed in rose and green. Many of the details throughout the apartment reflected Lillian's love of roses. Roses were carved into the high-backed chairs and used in the patterns for throw pillows, chair coverings, and china. Walt and Lillian owned most of the decorative items, including the two antique music boxes. There was a tiny bathroom with a shower and a small dressing area. Hidden behind louvered accordion doors was a kitchenette. The couches could be folded out to make additional beds.

Walt's daughter Diane Disney Miller said, "That little apartment was a big part of the experience. It was above the Fire House, right near Adventureland, and you could hear the soundtrack of the natives singing all night long. They didn't turn it off!"[18] She noted, "Mother and Dad spent the night there all the time, often with my children." Walt was known to suffer from insomnia and came up with ideas in the middle of the night. John Hench said, "He used to come in every morning with more ideas than anybody could ever use."[19]

Miller described to Disney historian Michael Broggie of a time when one of the fans got a little too close. Her father was in the apartment "reading a magazine, just relaxing, when the next thing he knows this red-haired kid pops his head up through the opening where the brass pole came up from the Fire House below." The intruder climbed up the fire pole and moved the desk that was covering the hole. Walt's reaction was, "Man, we've gotta nail that thing down! People are trying to get in this place everywhere!"[20] Later on they added a terrace so that the family could enjoy meals outdoors.

Main Street Corridor

Main Street's condensed retail corridor was lined with 1850s gaslight lampposts from Baltimore, Boston, and Philadelphia. A few came from the Hollywood Auditorium at a cost of $25 apiece. Walt remembered when he was a boy delivering newspapers at 3:30 a.m. in Kansas City seeing the lamp-lighters turn the gas off every morning and turn them back on every night on the way home from school. Disneyland also had a lamp lighter. Authentic to the period were hitching posts of all sorts.

The shops along Main Street were clustered into four blocks. The first cluster was the 100-odd block on the west, and across the street was the 100-even block. Past Center Street were the 200-odd and -even blocks. In 1955 many of the shops were operated by outside vendors. Walt did not have the time, the knowledge, or the money to open these stores.

Even though Walt was forced to use outside vendors for many of the restaurants and stores, he was not happy about it. Because they were independent from the park, he struggled to have them open every day or to keep consistent hours. Plus, many of the vendors did not believe the park was going to last the first year, so they figured they had a limited time to extract as much money as they could before packing up. So Walt instructed his team to learn everything they could about the retail and food business with the intention of bringing it in house as soon as they could.

The biggest store on Main Street was the Emporium of Orange County, prominently at the corner of the 100-odd block and town square. The Emporium was an old-fashioned dry goods store and offered items that could be found throughout the park. Emile Kuri's interior captured an understated elegance. The display windows were set low enough for a small child to see, and the artwork was elaborate.

On one side of the Emporium was the Bekins Van & Storage Co. Parcel Room, which served as a guest locker facility. The facade was modeled after one of the company's first buildings. Parked out front was a ⅝-scale replica of a white horse-drawn Bekins moving van.

unofficial **TIP**
Global Van Lines sponsored the storage facility from 1963 to 1980, and National Car Rental ran the facility from 1980 to 1989.

On the other side of the Emporium were the Crystal Arcade and the Book and Candle Shop. On the corner of Main Street and West Center Street was the Upjohn Pharmacy, a detailed re-creation of an 1890s apothecary shop. Less a retail shop and more a museum, the pharmacy displayed more than 1,000 rare medical and surgical antiques, as well as live leeches in a jar. There was also a display of a human cell. The fixtures were made in Germany in the 1890s, and the 12 leaded-glass chandeliers came from a vintage pharmacy in Kalamazoo, Michigan. Hidden in the back of the store was a showroom of more than 800 then-current Upjohn products. The pharmacy employees, known as Disneylanders or cast members, handed out free tablets of PAC—an old-time headache remedy—and little square bottles of Unicap Vitamins.

Guests continuing down the west side of Main Street soon reached the Carnation Ice Cream Parlor at the corner of the 200-odd block. Sponsored by Carnation Milk Company, the parlor offered a variety of sodas, sundaes, and other snacks "in a red-and-white Gay Nineties setting." Walt liked commercial participants who added to the authenticity of the park. Pete Clark, director of participant development, said, "It is more fun to eat at a Carnation ice cream parlor than the Disneyland ice cream parlor."[21] Next door was Sunny View Farms, selling jams and jellies, and the Puffin Bake Shop.

Penny arcades were a common feature in many 19th- and early 20th-century towns, and Main Street Disneyland was no different. The nickelodeon had vintage penny hand-cranked Moviolas, Mutoscopes, and Cailoscopes (an electrically driven rather than hand-cranked Mutoscope). Music was provided by a 19th-century Welte Sohne Grikeburg I/B Orchestron (a machine that plays music designed to sound like a band by using perforated paper rolls) that Walt purchased from Bud Hurlbut. A week after the grand opening, the Main Street Shooting Gallery opened next door to the Penny Arcade.[22] It contained eight guns with targets consisting of pinwheels, rows of pipes, and moving animation. It closed in 1962.

The Candy Palace appealed to all of the senses. Guests could watch the unusual assortment of candies being made in a display window and smell vanilla and chocolate pumped out of vents built into the facade. At the end of the street was the Coca-Cola Bar, where entertainment was frequently to be found.

On the east side of Main Street, facing town square in the 100-even block, was a temporary structure that was being used as the Maxwell House Coffee Garden. The foyer was decorated as a hotel lobby with an authentic registration desk. Coffee, sandwiches, and pastries were available, and there was indoor and outdoor dining.

The Wurlitzer Music Hall was next door on the corner facing into town square. The store was the official music center of the Magic Kingdom. Sam McKim designed the interior, and the shop featured a rare 1838 harp piano, a 1905 pianino, and the latest products from Wurlitzer. Especially popular was an oscilloscope, which, when operated, allowed guests to "see" a musical note; within six months of Disneyland's opening day, the key had been struck an estimated 3.5 million times. Daily organ concerts were broadcast in town square.

Adjacent to the Wurlitzer shop was the Wonderland Music Co., where guests could purchase music boxes, player-piano rolls, and the complete catalog from Buena Vista Records. The American Indian figure in front of the cigar store signified where the fine tobacco shop was located. Random Parts, Inc., operated the tobacco shop, as well as the jewelry store down the block. The Main Street Cinema featured silent films such as *Tom Mix* and *Keystone Cops,* newsreels, and hand-tinted slides. The people at the Yale & Towne Lock Shop would tell guests that they provided all of the locks in Disneyland and that Walt could open any of them with just one key.[23]

At the corner was the Swift Market House of 1900, a replica of the old-fashioned grocery and butcher shop. Swift & Company was known for its ham, bacon, and other meat products. Dill pickles and cider were available for sale, and guests were invited to take a seat next to the authentic pot-bellied stove and play a game of checkers. On the walls were hand-crank telephones where guests could listen in on a recorded party line call and get a laugh. At the rear of the store was a Seeburg upright grand piano built in 1910.[24] Just outside, on Center Street, was the Disneyland Art Festival, where artists painted pastel portraits of guests.

North of Center Street on the corner, on the east side of Main Street, was the Gibson Greeting Card Shop, with Ellen's Gift shop next door. The Kodak Camera Center, owned by Walt's friend Art Linkletter, was one of the very few shops ready for opening day. In negotiating the deal to host the opening day television show, Art Linkletter suggested to Walt that he would do it for scale, which was a couple of hundred dollars. Walt was certainly pleased with the offer, even when Linkletter upped the ante by asking for the camera and film concession. Linkletter already owned the Royal Tone camera shop in downtown Los Angeles, so he was already familiar with the business. He insisted on paying the same fees as any other lessee. Walt agreed to the deal, and Linkletter operated the shop for 10 years. During the live television broadcast, Linkletter stood on the balcony of his shop and described the parade.

unofficial **TIP**
In the back of the Gibson shop was a stamp shop, a coin shop, and a pen shop.

Other lessees were Blue Bird Shoes for Children and Timex. Offering merchandise for the park's youngest guests was Grandma's Baby Shop. Next door was Ruggles China & Glass. One of the most unusual offerings was the Hollywood Maxwell's Intimate Apparel shop, also known as the Wizard of Bras. This short-lived store sold corsets and lingerie, plus it had a small museum dedicated to the history of ladies' undergarments. It was the only storefront with a porch, which allowed the men a place to wait comfortably while the ladies shopped.

Main Street was a work in progress on opening day. Many of the stores' interiors were not yet completed. To mask the empty storefronts, Harper Goff suggested that artists decorate the windows with signs such as HARPER GOFF WILL BE OPENING HIS STORE HERE SOON. This was the start of a long tradition at Disneyland to honor those who have contributed to the park's success.

Drawing guests to the end of Main Street was Sleeping Beauty Castle. In the movies, a quick jump into a fantasy sequence is sometimes required to advance the story. What could be more of a contrast to the sanitized re-creation of the ideal small town in America than a

TODAY THERE ARE RULES to determine which names are placed on the stained glass windows. According to Disney Legend Marty Sklar, the honor is given only upon retirement; only to those who have earned the highest level of service, respect, and achievement; and only with the agreement of top park management and Walt Disney Imagineering, the successor to WED Enterprises.

medieval castle? The effect was profound and effective. The castle's placement at the end of the corridor acted like a beckoning hand that drew the guests deep into the park.

The Plaza Hub

Just in front of Sleeping Beauty Castle, at the end of Main Street, was the plaza hub. The hub served as the distribution point for the hub-and-spoke layout of the park. Walt said, "The more I go to amusement parks in all parts of the world, the more I am convinced of the wisdom of the original concepts of Disneyland. I mean, have a single entrance through which all traffic would flow, then a hub off which the various areas were situated. The hub gives people a sense of orientation. They know where they are at all times and it saves a lot of walking."[26] The hub was a circular park decorated with olive trees and electric lampposts from Chicago.

USING THE CASTLE to transition between lands was a visual trick Walt called a weenie. According to Disney historian Jim Korkis, during the development of Disneyland, Walt would come home late at night and usually enter his house through the kitchen, which was closer to the garage. He would walk into the kitchen and grab two uncooked hot dogs, or wieners, one for himself and one for his dog. He learned that he could make the dog do just about anything for that hot dog. Korkis said, "By wiggling the treat, Walt could get his dog to go from side to side, around in a circle, jump up and more. Wherever he moved the weenie, his dog would eagerly follow. Both Walt and the dog loved the game and she was finally rewarded with the tasty and satisfying treat."[25]

Each of the gateways into the lands offered weenies. The spinning carousel through the portal leading through Sleeping Beauty Castle called guests into Fantasyland. The stockade gates, the steam bellowing from the *Mark Twain* sternwheeler, and the seemingly infinite horizon beckoned guests to visit Frontierland. Over in Tomorrowland was the Clock of the World and the TWA *Moonliner* ready for launch. Only Adventureland lacked a weenie. It was thought that if guests knew too much, it would not be much of an adventure.

The castle was placed at the center of the park for a reason. "The important thing is the castle," Walt told his team. "Make it tall enough to be seen from all around the Park. It's got to keep people oriented. I've been studying the way people go to museums and other entertainment places. Everybody's got tired feet."[27] He called this "museum feet," a condition caused by walking around forever without any change or orientation, and he knew it was exhausting. "I want a place for people to sit down and where old folks can say, 'You kids run on. I'll meet you there in a half hour.'" Walt pledged that "Disneyland is going to be a place where you can't get lost or tired unless you want to."[28] When the park opened, each of the lands eventually culminated in a dead-end, forcing guests to return to the hub. Nobody could ever get lost.

Like most great public spaces, the hub is at the crossroads, thereby achieving the critical mass necessary to create a lively, functional space. The plaza hub gave families space to regroup and peer into each of the gateways leading to the other lands. It is a remarkable achievement that the Imagineers were able to put a world of fantasy next to a frontier town and the world of tomorrow with a jungle off to the side and have it all make sense. It should not work. However, Walt's commitment to detail and to the rich and familiar background stories from movies and television created an emotional integrity and success.

Overlooking the hub was the Red Wagon Inn, a fine dining restaurant. Walt purchased and dismantled an old Los Angeles mansion in 1955 and used the interior paneling, stained glass windows, staircase, and crystal chandeliers. The restaurant was operated by Swift & Company and could feed up to 500 guests per hour.

Main Street Transportation

The vehicles along Main Street played an important role in the show. They added life to the street and created a way to ferry passengers up and down the corridor. At the start, the modes of transportation included a horse-drawn fire wagon and surreys. Although they were very low capacity per hour, Walt felt they added to the show.

unofficial **TIP**
The fire wagon was retired early and became a permanent fixture in the fire station.

The most popular conveyance along Main Street was the horse-drawn streetcar. Disney historian Michael Broggie said the streetcars were very important to Walt. "He remembered them from his childhood, and wanted them in Disneyland, but there was no money in the budget. He finally just wrote the check for them. They're one of the few things in the Park that have never been changed or replaced. They're still completely original," Broggie said.[29]

The four streetcars were a composite of trolleys from Chicago, Boston, and Philadelphia used as late as 1900. Each trolley could carry 15 guests on a one-way journey of 6 minutes. There was 3,660 feet of track, and a doubletrack midway allowed two cars to pass. The streetcars were pulled by Belgian, Percheron, Clydesdale, and Shire horses. All of the horses went through special training simulating the chaotic environment in which they would be working. While prancing in a circular ring, they were subjected to music, tooting automobile horns, and the sounds of people blasted through loudspeakers. Each horse worked 4 hours a day and five days a week and was given taxi service to the 15-acre pony farm that accommodated the approximately 250 horses, mules, and ponies that the park used every day.[30]

Archetypal Truth

Walt believed that a show needed a strong opening. Take the way he introduced the Disneyland television program each week when "Uncle" Walt would begin the show by opening a beautifully bound volume of fairy tales, picking up an artifact or model, or playing a narrative theme song such as "Davy Crockett." Walt also used Tinker Bell to sprinkle pixie dust on viewers and fly down and around the park in Anaheim. The audience would be hooked and stay for the next hour. Main Street U.S.A. was that opening statement for Disneyland.

The first scene, as described in a 1955 press release, was "America from 1890 to 1910 at the crossroads of an era." It was a place where "the gas lamp is giving way to the electric lamp, and a newcomer, the sputtering 'horseless carriage,' has challenged Old Dobbin for the streetcar right-of-way." Walt promised, "For those of us who remember the carefree times it re-creates, Main Street will bring back happy memories. For younger visitors, it is an adventure in turning back the calendar to the days of grandfather's youth." It was a "nostalgic stroll through the immediate past."[31] Just exactly whose past it might be has been a subject of speculation and myth for decades.

The Main Street U.S.A. segment was directed by Marvin Davis. At one point, 112 men, including Harvey Gillette and Harry Webster from the Disney Studios, were working for him. Webster had a special touch with American Gothic and Victorian details. Wade Rubottom and Harry McAfee from MGM were also on the team. Many of the interiors were designed by set designers Harry Johnson and Emile Kuri. Each artist had to get Davis's approval before starting any work.

Main Street's facades were designed singly and then put into groups according to what would look the most comfortable and the most authentic. What the designers came up with was their own version of Victorian architecture. Many of the buildings were primarily derivatives of the Italianate style with flat facades and relatively simple detailing, all of the signs of a modest but growing Midwestern town.

For many of the designers, this project was a very different experience. Designing sets was one thing. Those buildings were in the background. Designing a building that a guest could stare at was much more difficult. Most of the designers had to teach themselves about the correct architectural details that would create an authentic-looking structure.

Artist Harper Goff was one of the principal designers of Main Street. When asked about the influence of Walt's fabled boyhood home in Marceline, Missouri, Goff's reply was, "Well, that's a good story."[32] Instead, Goff recalled how his own hometown of Fort Collins, Colorado, influenced the design. He said, "It was a very prosperous town. We had banks that looked like banks, you know, and there was a Victorian city hall." Goff showed Walt photos of Fort Collins, and he approved. Goff said, "Disneyland's City Hall was copied from Fort Collins [County Courthouse] . . . so was the Bank building and some of the others."[33]

Architectural critic Beth Dunlop suggested, "By extrapolating familiar approaches to design (among them, the generic late-Victorian style of Main Street), Disney offers up memorable architectural symbols that are much greater than the proverbial sums of their individual parts."[34] John Hench called this the archetypal truth. He said, "You can't paint sunflowers without referring to [Vincent] Van Gogh. He expressed a whole truth. Or take Henry the Eighth. There are many versions of Henry the Eighth. We don't even know what he looked like, but we accept [Hans] Holbein. He owns Henry the Eighth. In much the same way, [Disneyland owns] Main Street, because we expressed the archetypal truth about main streets everywhere."[35] A visit to the park in the first few months felt like a blend of something entirely new that somehow felt immediately comfortable and familiar.

With Disneyland, Walt was able to take his passion for scale-model railroading and miniatures and use storytelling as the unifying factor for every element inside the park. Walt said, "It's not apparent at a casual glance that this street is only a scale model. This cost more, but made the street a toy and the imagination can play more freely with a toy." To achieve this quality, the Imagineers applied another cinematic optical trick called forced perspective. In the movies, forced perspective added depth to the two-dimensional film. In three-dimensional design, it allowed the designers to imply that the buildings were much taller than they really were. Cultural historian John Findlay said, "The overall effect of the built environment was impressive but not intimidating."[36]

The use of plant material also played a part. Main Street was based on a disciplined Victorian formality from Town Square to the Hub. Bill Evans hired a landscape architect by the name of Ruth Shellhorn, who designed this Main Street area for its initial opening. Shellhorn said, "I doubt if this procedure could have been followed successfully on any other project on earth."[37] The street was lined with elm trees, and the landscaping would be maintained to "always springtime" standard.

Color was also important. John Hench would become known as the master of theme park color theory. He said, "We humans have an intimate relationship with color. . . . Color is one of those mysterious elements that awaken our basic survival instinct. Certain colors are reassuring, while others imply action. All of them deliver messages." He noted, "To complement the action on Main Street we introduced a more saturated color throughout. It was an appropriate and stimulating response to the attitude and feeling of the guests. It just seemed to give the place more life."[38] Disney historian Jeff Kurtti describes the results as "a 'storybook realism,' an essence of genuineness and authenticity that is more utopian, more romanticized than the actual environments could ever be."[39]

At a time when the future of retail development was at a crossroads, Disneyland provided a new alternative. Dunlop noted, "With its nineteenth-century architecture, Main Street U.S.A. was a major revelation, and in many ways is one of Disney's great contributions to American life. The small-town sensibility of the architecture reaffirms the beauty and joy of the American streetscape. The buildings represent a pastiche of styles and were built at a scale that reinforces the pedestrian experience."[40] According to architect Robert A. M. Stern, "Ironically, Main Street and the very way the theme parks are designed would probably be, much to Walt Disney's surprise, the actual genius of American Urbanism captured at a time when it had no value to most people, certainly in the architecture and planning profession."[40]

ALL ABOARD!

AFTER EXPERIENCING the Main Street scene, guests could write their own plot for their visit by selecting for themselves which scene to visit next. Just like a movie theater, a preview of coming attractions preceded the main show—except that at Disneyland, the Santa Fe & Disneyland Railroad was the preview reel. The hope was that guests would start their day riding the train. Because the train circled the perimeter of the park, it would enable guests to peer into the park and get a sense of what was there and give them ideas of where to go next. The train tracks were positioned at the high ground, giving the guests a perfect vantage point to take in all of the attractions. Carefully planned vistas were created to showcase the trains, which were the only attractions visible from any location throughout the park.

Walt was very picky about the size of train he wanted. He did not want one of the 12-inch novelty trains that could frequently be found at the local amusement parks. He wanted something much grander. Walt went around to museums and talked with owners of miniature trains. At one point he came close to buying the locomotives that were used at the Panama Pacific Exposition in San Francisco. He even came very close to buying five locomotives from William "Casey" Jones. The trains originally ran at the Venice Pier, on an 18-inch gauge railway (18 inches between rails). Jones purchased the trains in 1941 and built a track on his property in Los Gatos. Walt offered Jones $50,000 but was turned down.

Once Walt saw the trains at Travel Town in Griffith Park and Ward Kimball's Grizzly Flats Railroad, he knew that he wanted something bigger, more realistic, and more impressive. He decided on a ⅝-scale locomotive running on 3-foot narrow-gauge track. A traditional narrow-gauge train made the tracks look narrow as well. But at ⅝ scale, the locomotive looked like a standard gauge. It just looked right. Walt was proud that he was running real live steam trains and did not resort to placing a diesel engine inside like so many other amusement parks. He knew the trains would be expensive to maintain, but that was why "the railroad was Walt's baby. He was going to have a real railroad with steam and they would look full size," according to Kimball. "Walt was very proud of these real working locomotives."[42]

Roger Broggie used the *Lilly Belle,* Walt's backyard locomotive, as the prototype and scaled it up five times larger. Then they built a plywood mock-up and tweaked it until they could fit a 6-foot door for the passenger cars. Once that was settled, the roof and the sides all followed in proportion. They built two locomotives at the same time, with the style of their domes and stacks as the only significant difference. One was a freight engine and one was a passenger locomotive, but their 4-4-0 chassis were the same design. The detail work was fabricated at the Studio, while the wheels, frames, and boilers were done by outside contractors.

The first locomotive was the *C. K. Holliday,* named for the founder of the Santa Fe Railroad. Back in the 1880s, the Santa Fe Railroad operated a train in the Southwest called the *Cyrus K. Holliday.* The locomotive had a distinctive 1873 wood-burning diamond stack with a large headlight, a steel-blue boiler jacket, and a red cab. It had a 33.5-inch boiler with 36-inch drivers and weighed 15 tons. The rolling stock were 1885-style wooden coaches with windows and indoor seating. It was known as the Santa Fe & Disneyland Limited.[43]

The second locomotive was the *E. P. Ripley.* It was named for the 1895 president of the Atchison, Topeka, and Santa Fe Railroad. To set it apart from the other locomotive, the *Ripley* was decorated as an 1890s-era coal-burning engine straight stack, painted in green and black with a light-gray smoke box. The boiler fittings were also different from the *C. K. Holliday,* as was the shape of the cab. The *E. P. Ripley* was based on locomotive #771 of the Baltimore & Ohio Railroad. Built in 1887 by Rogers Locomotive Company, that locomotive would typically pull a load of cattle cars with STANDING ROOM ONLY signs.[44]

The *E. P. Ripley* cattle cars were controversial. Originally the openings between the wooden slats were about 8 inches. Ward Kimball thought this was a horrible idea and suggested that the openings be enlarged to 14 inches. When Walt saw what Kimball had done, he was mad. He said, "I want all the people inside those cars to feel the way the cows feel, looking out through the slats on a real cattle train." A compromise was worked out, and Kimball said, "I think we settled on about 12 inches between boards."[45]

Another problem was the "standing room only" policy. Kimball asked Walt, "What's gonna happen when they accidentally slam on the air brakes and everybody piles up at one end of the car?" Walt replied, "Oh no, they won't slam on the brakes . . . we'll be very careful about that."[46] Broggie heard people complain, "They've got us in here just like pigs."[47] The cattle cars were very unpopular,

unofficial **TIP**
The clicking sound heard from the window of the Main Street station was a telegraph signal sending out the opening day dedication speech.

except very late in the day when people did not mind the crowds as they left the park.

To board the *C. K. Holliday*, guests had to go to the Main Street station. If a guest wanted to ride the *E. P. Ripley*, he or she had to go to the Frontierland train station, which was modeled after the depot in the 1948 Disney film *So Dear to My Heart*. Walt had given Kimball the original building after the film was done. Walt tried to buy it back for the park, but Kimball refused. Fortunately, the blueprints were at the studio.

Walt wanted to demonstrate the old-fashioned way two trains bypass each other. While one train was stopped at either the Main Street or Frontierland station, the brakeman would run over and throw a switch, allowing the oncoming train to move to a siding and leapfrog the stationary train. Not long after the park first opened, a brakeman threw the switch too soon, between the fourth and fifth cars of the train. As the front of the last coach followed the rest of the train on the mainline, the rear wheels went onto the siding. Then the coach went sideways, scraping along the concrete curbs along the tracks. Nobody was hurt and the brakeman walked away, never to return. Because of this, a light/block system was installed, and the trains began to stop at both stations.

THE TRAINS WERE AN IMMEDIATE SUCCESS, and Walt was soon considering expanding his railroad empire. Ward Kimball owned two locomotives, the narrow gauge *Emma Nevada* and the much smaller *Chloe*. Roger Broggie had a picture of the *Chloe* on his workbench when Walt saw it. Kimball said, "He calls me out of bed early on a Sunday morning and says, 'Hey Kimball . . . You don't have any place to really run that little locomotive of yours. Why don't you bring it down here? We need another locomotive because of the crowds in the Park. We could use yours, and we'd pay a nominal fee . . . $1 a year . . . just to make it legal. You could come down here on Tuesday when the Park is closed and you could run it all around and get it out of your system. You'd have all that trackage all to yourself."

Kimball was still groggy with sleep and said, "Walt, the *Chloe* is a woodburner and you burn oil down there . . . you'd need to put in those atomizers and everything." Walt said, "That's all right . . . we'll change it to oil, and you can always change it back to wood when we're through.'" Kimball complained, "NO . . . I've just restored it . . . even though I don't run it all the time, like Disneyland, I can still walk back and enjoy just looking at it." Kimball said, "So we went back and forth, and he finally gave up."

ADVENTURELAND:
You'd Sell That Tree?

THE GUESTS HAD ENJOYED their tour of Main Street and the train ride preview, and they were ready for the next act: one of the four lands. Each land represented one of the major movie or television genres of the day. Professor of art history Karal Ann Marling said, "Each ride is a four- or five-minute segment, slotted in among snacks, trips to the restroom, and 'commercials' in the form of souvenir emporia."[48] When the park first opened, it was a three-dimensional reflection of what people were experiencing on television and in the movies. It was the largest virtual reality project of its time.

Adventureland was every film set in an exotic, foreign local with decidedly foreign indigenous people. It was dedicated to adventure, romance, and mystery. Main Street U.S.A. set the baseline, and every other land was meant to provide a contrast. Adventureland's jungles were about as far removed from Midwestern America as one could get.

Right up to the last moment, the area had been called True-Life Adventureland and would bring to life Walt's nature films. Adventureland was the smallest land, with a total of 3.96 acres and only 1 acre of public space. Once you crossed the bridge from Main Street, the formal gardens gave way to an untamed jungle. There was not much there when the park opened—just a few shops with souvenirs, some fast food, and the Jungle Cruise.

The Jungle Cruise was the signature attraction in Adventureland. In fact, it was the only attraction in Adventureland. Early on it was known as Tropical Rivers of the World or Jungle Rivers of the World. Harper Goff, the principal designer of the attraction, had traveled to real jungles and found them "uneventful and boring." Goff was a big fan of John Huston's film *African Queen* with Humphrey Bogart and Katherine Hepburn. Another influence was the 1955 Disney film *The African Lion*. Goff suggested to Walt that they design a Hollywood jungle, where "exotic inhabitants would appear and perform on cue for each boatload of guests."

Creating a convincing jungle out of an orange grove and doing it virtually overnight was a special challenge for Evans and Goff. The objective was to make it appear as if it was always that way, that nature had run amok. Instead, they were dealing with the reality of time and budgets. Walt became very frustrated when all he could see along the banks were buckets of little saplings. However, it would not take very long for Evans's work to bloom and become the wild environment that Walt wanted.

Bill Evans and Harper Goff drove all over the Los Angeles region looking for trees. For example, they would drive up to Pasadena, which is famous for its street trees, and offer homeowners $200 to carry away a desired tree. Most people just looked at the men like they were crazy.

Fortunately, construction of the Los Angeles–area freeway system was at full throttle. As the construction crews carved the 200-foot right-of-way through residential neighborhoods, hundreds of mature street trees would become available. Evans had his crew monitor the progress and tag trees that were in the way. Disneyland paid $25 for each tree so that the contractors would not take them to the dump or damage them. Then Evans's crew would swoop in, put a 6- by 6-foot box around the roots, pick up the 5- to 10-ton trees, and move them to Anaheim. The Santa Monica, Pomona, and Santa Ana Freeways all yielded trees for Disneyland.

One time Evans and Goff were driving to Beverly Hills to take a look at a great big banyan tree. When they got there, they saw exactly what they were looking for. Goff went up to the homeowner to ask if they would be interested in selling them the tree, and much to their surprise they discovered that the homeowner had been thinking of chopping it down anyway. They were able to make a deal by removing the banyan tree and planting a small replacement tree. The tree was planted toward the back of the hippo pool. It flourished and remains there today.

Evans used imported trees from Australia, New Zealand, China, Japan, South America, and South Africa. To achieve the look of the Amazon Jungle, the first 100 yards featured a lot of native African and Brazilian trees. Walt insisted on using real plant material, so some of the orange trees from the original orchards were turned upside down to look like mangrove roots.

With regard to the landscaping, the challenge for Evans was to find the balance between creating an instant, mature environment and something that would not be completely out of scale in 20 years. Fortunately, for Adventureland and Frontierland, this would not be a problem. Time was on his side. He carefully prepared the ground with vitamins, hormones, peat moss, and a solution of nitro-humus to create this "wonderland of nature's own design." Over time, the jungle became self-perpetuating. Virtually all of the larger trees in Adventureland are original.

Laying out the river was a frustrating experience. During the conceptual stage, Goff and the other Imagineers relied on drawings. When they got to the construction bid stage, contractors were demanding more detailed blueprints. Goff's solution was the jungle jeep. He built a framework that slipped over a jeep that was the length and width of the boats. Before the crew finished digging down or building up an area, Goff would hop into his jungle jeep and drive around and see how much space was needed for the bow and stern. Then they would put stakes down where they thought the banks of the river should be. Finally, the bulldozers would dig out the earth between the stakes. The process gave Goff a good feel for the turns in the river and how fast the boats could travel.

Walt wanted live exotic animals along the banks of the river, but Goff talked him out of it by claiming the animals would generally be asleep and unable to put on a consistent show. Herb Ryman knew, "If some boatload of people see a crocodile, they'll say, 'Oh wasn't that beautiful. We saw a crocodile.' And somebody else in another boat didn't see any crocodile, so they're going to sue."[49] For a reliable show, Goff suggested that they use mechanical animals such as the ones you would see in a movie. They brought in Bob Mattey, the mechanical effects artist who brought the giant squid from *20,000 Leagues Under The Sea* to life. Walt told Mattey to build mechanical animals that looked real. The jungle would be populated by artificial animals, with hydraulic and electronic systems. Mattey divided the figures into three types. The motionless figures were basically statues. The stationary figures had limited movement such as tail wagging. The showcase figures actively performed in some way.

The boat dock area was originally planned as a Tahitian village. Instead, Goff created a jungle outpost atmosphere straight from the movies, blending elements of the Caribbean, progressing through Amazon and South Pacific settings. Early on there was a display area with live baby alligators. After one alligator escaped, the display was removed. Beyond that was a brown river with earthen banks, wild grasses, and clusters of small trees.

The original plan was to have the boats drift through the jungle, pushed by a moving current. Walt was concerned about using gasoline engines that might catch on fire for insurance reasons, but that was deemed impractical. Instead, Goff designed a natural gas fiberglass single-propeller motor launch with white hulls, dark wood trim, brass fittings, controls, and black enameled smokestacks with colorful striped canvas awnings.

The seven explorer launches or safari boats were fabricated by Glasspar. Each boat was 27 feet in length, weighed 2 tons, and was powered by a 40-horsepower marine engine. The boats were free floating and connected to a single guide rail by two guides on each boat, front and rear. The boats were given colorful names such as the *Orinoco Adventurers* from Venezuela, *Ganges Gal* from India, and *Zambezi Miss* from Rhodesia. Originally, there was only one opening to board the boat. George Whitney suggested cutting out a second opening to expedite loading and unloading. Capacity was between 30 and 36 guests per boat; during a typical day, 28–30 boatloads would leave the dock, allowing for up to 24,000 guests a day to explore the jungle.

The journey along the 1,640-foot-long river took 7 minutes. Guests would leave from the two-story Victorian boathouse, which had an observation level for the ride foremen. For many guests, the most memorable part of the trip would be the explorer guide, or skipper. The original script was straightforward and meant to be educational. The skippers were nicknamed "Jungle Bunnies" because they wore white yacht caps, black turtleneck sweaters, and white pants.

The first destination was Burma's Irrawaddy River with a "rain forest" made of a vine-covered steel structure dotted with real orchids. At the first bend, guests encountered the first of the 39 mechanical creatures and natives, including hippos, and the crocodile Old Smiley. The Mekong River featured the Cambodian ruins with a statue of Buddha, and small monkeys hung from tree branches. Walt noted, "We tried real monkey skins. They get ratty. We found nylon's better."[50] To add a sense of realism, the banks were lined with 24 recordings providing a soundtrack.

Around the next corner was the Nile River, with baby rhinos running circles around their mother and two bull elephants on either bank. The most prominent physical feature was Schweitzer Falls, designed by Goff. He took advantage of a natural grade change. Walt suggested it should be named after someone famous and Goff decided to dedicate the falls to Albert Schweitzer. Guests got a near miss with the waterfall and then got a chance to see the back side of the water. At first, Walt was opposed to the gag as he did not want the guests to get wet. So Goff and Sam Hamel designed the boat hull high enough so that water never splashed in. People would scream and duck down to avoid the water, but it was designed so they would always miss the waterfall.

Even with Mattey's expertise and overtime fabrication, the attraction opened with fewer mechanical figures than Walt or Goff wanted. Along with the two giant elephants, seven hippos, eight crocodiles, and two giraffes were a vulture, a python, monkeys, lions, and some rhinos. The lions, busy eating the zebra, roared with their approval, and the giraffes nodded as the boats passed by. While the average depth of the river was 5 feet 6 inches, it dropped down to 8 feet at the hippo pool. Just beyond the hippos were the Native Village and then another crocodile pool.

Original Disneylander Dick Nunis recalled a time when Walt called him over while standing on the dock. "Dick, what is the trip time for this attraction?" Walt asked. Nunis knew Walt already had the answer, "Well, sir, it is seven minutes." Walt replied, "Well, I just had a four-and-one-half–minute trip and went through the hippo pool so fast I couldn't tell if they were hippos or rhinos. How would you feel if you paid to go to the movies and they cut the center reel out of the picture!"[51]

On another occasion, Walt was riding the Jungle Cruise and the crocodiles' mechanical effect was not working. This sort of breakdown was common in the early days. Walt turned to his team and said, "I know damned well these things work. I saw it on television." The next few times Walt decided to take a ride on the Jungle Cruise, two maintenance men would hide behind the bushes and manually operate the crocodiles. It did not take Walt long to catch on to this ruse.

FRONTIERLAND:
Ingenuity of the Pioneers

Invigorated by the Jungle Cruise, the guests might next head for Frontierland, which symbolized "America's westward march from revolutionary days through the taming of the Great Southwest." Walt wanted Frontierland to depict America from 1790 to 1876. The dedication plaque read: "Here we experience the story of our country's past . . . the colorful drama of Frontier America in the exciting days of the covered wagon and the stagecoach . . . the advent of the railroad . . . and the romantic riverboat. Frontierland is a tribute to the faith, courage, and ingenuity of the pioneers who blazed the trails across America."

Guests entered through a log stockade and found themselves in a frontier town straight out of the movies or television. The logs for the stockade were cut in the Arrowhead mountain region of Southern

California and then shipped to Disneyland, where specially trained men with experience in shipbuilding hewed the logs by hand. At the end of Frontierland's main street was the Rivers of America.

On a trip to Jackson Hole, Wyoming, Walt found a pile of gnarled pine posts. They were diseased tree trunks. He bought them all and had them shipped to his house in Holmby Hills and then moved to the Burbank studio. At the time, he did not know where he was going to use them, but they found their way into Frontierland.

Once past the stockade gateway, guests found a single block of storefronts with a boardwalk on the south and rustic buildings and a horse corral made of logs on the other side. Continuing west, a footbridge crossed an open stream between Adventureland and Frontierland. Swift's Chicken Plantation House was the farthest destination and was separated from the rest of the park by the footbridge. Symbolically, on one side of the bridge was a bustling frontier town and on the other side was the countryside.

Swift's Chicken Plantation House was Walt's reply to the incredibly successful chicken restaurant at Knott's Berry Farm in nearby Buena Park. The building was unique because it displayed two different architectural styles. Depending on your point of view, it was an antebellum mansion (from the Frontierland side) or a Spanish colonial home that belonged in Mexico (from the train).

The Rivers of America was the centerpiece of Frontierland. In the Walt Disney Archives is a napkin with Walt's sketch of the river pretty much the way it is. The 350,000 cubic yards of dirt that was excavated for the river formed the 8- to 15-foot berm that surrounded the park and the island in the middle of the river. Walt wanted to create a typical Midwest river of the 1840s.

To create the illusion that the river had always been there, Bill Evans lined the banks with California and Aleppo pines, silver maple, sycamores, and junipers. The shore was lined with wild European irises to prevent erosion of the banks from the wake of the *Mark Twain*.

When the river was first filled, all of the water drained overnight. The porous Anaheim soil was great for farming but not great for a fake river. So a blend of clay was trucked in from the Los Angeles River basin, and liquid cement was placed as a liner.[52] Over the years, the clay was gradually replaced with concrete. Because it was an artificial waterway, maintenance crews had to dump 12 pounds of brown or green dye a couple of times a week to color the river. It took approximately three days to mix the water to the proper color. The dye helped to hide the tracks below the water.

At the center of the river was a hilly island barely covered in plants. The river held 6,159,510 gallons of water and lost 30,000 gallons a day in evaporation. At its most shallow point, it was 4 feet deep; at its deepest, 8 feet 2 inches. Behind the berm was a Disney-owned well that reached down 137 feet 4 inches.

"To Walt Disney, the *Mark Twain* and the Disneyland trains were like the seventh and eighth wonders of the world," said Ward Kimball.[53] Walt had a passion for live steam technology and its historic importance. The riverboat and the railroad would bring that experience to others.

QUEEN OF THE RIVER

THE S.S. *MARK TWAIN* RIVERBOAT was the "Queen of the River" and the first authentic stern-wheeler packet steamboat built in more than 50 years. Inspired by the *Little Rufus* and the *Natchez*, the *Mark Twain* was typical of the boats that plied the Mississippi in the 1870s. The ship was a ⅝-scale model built to strict, historically correct specifications. Walt spared no expense and used the highest-quality materials. Standards from the American Bureau of Shipping were used for all castings and forgings. The deck planking was Douglas fir, and the railings and window framings were made of mahogany. The ship was a showcase of beautiful woodwork and gingerbread trim painted bright white. The paddle wheel was made of oak bracings and Douglas fir paddles. It cost $150,000 to build.

The Disneyland ship had three decks (Main, Promenade, Texas), plus the Wheelhouse. In one way, the *Mark Twain* was unlike any other riverboat. The intimate scale of the ship was further reinforced when viewed from various angles. From the side, the decks appeared spoon shaped instead of flat. From the bow or the stern, the superstructure was slightly slanted inward on both sides, making the Texas Deck smaller than the Main Deck.

The hull was constructed in one piece at Todd Shipyards in San Pedro, and then trucked overland in the middle of the night to Disneyland, where a crane lifted it over the berm and placed it into Fowler's Harbor. Fowler's Harbor was one of those pesky infrastructure details that Walt had initially thought to be a waste of money. Joe Fowler insisted that a dry dock facility be built along the river to maintain the

Mark Twain. Finally understanding Fowler's insight, Walt named the dry dock in honor of his colleague.

The upper decks and details, such as the doors, posts, and the bar, were fabricated in Burbank. Other components were built by the Disneyland mill shop inside the Opera House on Main Street. Final assembly was done in Fowler's Harbor in May 1955.

The *Mark Twain* was 105 feet long, 28 feet high, and 26 feet 6 inches wide. The draft was only 2 feet 3 inches. It had a displacement of 150 tons and could carry 350 passengers, plus freight. Top speed was 1.3 knots. The custom-built propulsion system was on the Main Deck. The stern wheel ship was powered by two single-cylinder long-stroke steam engines connected to the paddles by a rod. The diesel-fired boiler was controlled from the engineer's cage on the Main Deck. There was a Johnson Bar floor lever, brass fuel and steam pressure gauges, and a large steam valve that was opened and closed with an iron wheel the size of a plate. This was the throttle valve and controlled the actual speed. The *Mark Twain* was fitted with a number of automatic devices that control such things as water levels (from a matched pair of steam-operated feedwater pumps), a fire-eye that fires the boiler when necessary, and a periodic blowdown of the boiler to remove any sediment that may have accumulated. Unlike locomotives, which blowdown dramatically, shooting steam sideways a great distance, the *Mark Twain* vents this steam quietly downward into the river. If you see smoke coming from the crown stacks, then something is wrong. The steam is vented through the small vent stacks to the rear.

The second level was the Promenade Deck. Here guests could get stern-wheeler mint juleps and listen to Dixieland jazz from the bandstand. The upper level was the Texas Deck. It was said that passengers on riverboats that used to ply the Rio Grande would climb to the top deck to get the best view of the north shore and Texas. At the very top were the wheelhouse and the captain's quarters, where the river pilot rang the bells, blasted the steam whistle, and manned the ship's wheel.

The attraction opened with a crew of four. The captain worked from the wheelhouse and watched over the river ahead, and the other crew members included the engineer, a deckhand who assisted passengers in boarding, and the fireman. The fireman position would be eliminated when the diesel boiler was automated a few years later. The *Mark Twain* was restricted to a 2,450-foot-long guide rail. The trip around the river took approximately 15 minutes. The appearance that the ship was free-floating was all an illusion. Under the water was a system of wheels and guide rails that simulated the natural look of a rudder's action.

The ship left the Frontierland landing and traveled clockwise around the island. Along the shore was Frontierland Park, with an anchor that had been found in a New Orleans antiques shop. Rumor had it that the anchor was 200 years old and that it had once served Jean LaFitte's pirate ship. However, the plaque also warned, "Don't believe everything you read." Also along the banks were the Oaks Tavern sandwich and snack shop and Shanty Town. The Dixieland bandstand would frequently be filled with live entertainment. Fowler's Harbor was on the portside before the ship set off for the wilderness.

Walt wanted an American Indian chief mounted on a horse waving to the guests on the *Mark Twain* and on the trains, and he asked sculptor Blaine Gibson to work on the project. They hired actor Wood Strode, and Gibson had him lay flat on his back to cast a mold of his body. Then he used the casting with different heads for the figures in the friendly American Indian village.

On opening day, actress Irene Dunn christened the ship with a bottle containing water representing all the major rivers across the United States, thus the name Rivers of America. When she completed her task on live television, she was heard to exclaim, "We're listing!" The *Mark Twain* was also designed to operate as a piece of firefighting equipment with water pumps and fire hoses.[54] Walt loved it. He told Joe Fowler, "When things get hectic, we can always get on the *Mark Twain* and just ride around our Rivers of America."[55]

THEY WILL APPRECIATE IT

IN FRONTIERLAND, the main attraction was the Painted Desert and the Indian Country of the Old West. Guests could access this area by catching a ride on the Disneyland Stage Lines, taking the reins of one of the Pack Mules, or hopping aboard a Conestoga Wagon. In front of the loading area were the Miniature Horse Corral and the office of Willard P. Bounds, Blacksmith and U.S. Marshal. Bounds was a distant in-law of Walt's wife.

The Disneyland Stage Lines was the first attraction completed. In keeping with the rest of the park, the ride featured "fully equipped Concord Coaches" at a smaller-than-full-size scale. They were built by animal trainer Owen Pope and pulled by miniature horses. Like everything at opening-day Disneyland, the ride reflected Walt's attention to detail. John Hench recalled a discussion with Walt that had taken place while the coaches were being fabricated. He asked the boss, "Why don't we just leave the leather straps off, Walt? The people are never going to appreciate all this close-up detail." Walt looked right at Hench and replied, "You're being a poor communicator. People are okay, don't you ever forget that. They will respond to it. They will appreciate it." Hench said, "We put the best darned leather straps on that stagecoach you've ever seen."[56]

As the Disneyland Stage Lines made its way back into Indian Country, they were frequently held up by "robbers." Robbers weren't the biggest challenge for the guests, however. Because the guests were still full size, the diminutive coaches had a tendency to tip over, and people got hurt. The horses would get frightened by the train whistle and would bolt. One driver was hurt badly during one accident and that led to the early demise of the attraction.

The Pack Mules were the most popular option. The idea for a burro ride, along with a steam train and a carousel, were in the earliest plans for a park. There were 30 mules in the Disneyland stable. Fifteen mules would be out on the trail at any one time. When they were finished with their shift, the mules were relieved of their saddles and blankets, which were then placed on the other 15 mules. Waits for the pack mule rides could be very, very long.[57]

The mule train had seven or eight mules of varying sizes and a trail boss on a large mule or horse. The youngest mules were 2 years old and were ridden by the smallest guests, those whose feet could not reach the stirrups. They were placed up front so that the trail boss could keep his eye on them. The adults and taller children rode on the larger mules to the rear. For many children who had never been this close to a large animal, the Pack Mules were a big thrill. However, there were some problems. Cast members had to deal with angry parents who refused to ride in the back because they wanted to be near their children.

Because of the special skills necessary to manage the mule trains, only professional animal handlers were allowed to be trail bosses. The park hired ex-jockeys and real cowboys who worked exclusively on this one attraction, unlike other cast members who were interchangeable. Mules, being mules, were cranky and would frequently bite the guests. Even with all of these troubles, the attraction was a favorite of Walt's because he felt it added to the richness of the background and a touch of authenticity.

The Disneyland Stage Lines and the Pack Mules were both available to the opening-day guests, but the Conestoga Wagons did not open until August 16. The wagons followed the same trail as the stage coaches. Bill Martin summed it up by stating, "The Wagon Train was a dumb ride . . . it was slow motion, and we had some Indians out in the sand dunes there. Walt never cared for that stuff."[58]

The highlight of the trip for many, regardless of the travel mode, was a visit to the Painted Desert. Evans and his crew went out to the desert and imported some Joshua trees and various kinds of cacti. Because most of these plants thrived at several thousand feet elevation, they resented being at sea level and in the amount of humidity found in Anaheim. Disneyland was having to replace them every two years. Evans did find some piñon pines out in Arizona with very short needles and planted them throughout Frontierland.

The Indian Country of the Old West segment could only be described as very spare. The trail for the Pack Mules was an out-and-back loop with a dogleg to the right at about the halfway point. The Disneyland Stage Lines and Conestoga Wagons circled around the outside. The interaction of the coaches, wagons, and pack mules only added to the fantasy.

Along Frontierland's main street was the Pendleton shop where Lillian Disney was a regular patron and bought clothing for their daughters and bolts of yardage. Pendleton manufactured Walt's casual blue blazer that became a part of his image. When the company was first approached about participating in Disneyland, they thought a small display might be the way to go. Because of Walt's passion for their product, he convinced them to take over a large part of Frontierland's retail space. It was perfect timing for the company, as they were trying to expand their brand from shirts alone to sweaters, slacks, and women's clothing. Anytime a customer bought an item, the store would send half of the profits of the sale to the customer's hometown dealer.[59]

The first Indian Village was located between the Golden Horseshoe Saloon and the Frontierland train depot. Guests had to cross over a bridge where there was a big dance circle and a few tepees. Sam McKim had put fake human scalps on top of the tepee poles, but Walt asked him to remove them. McKim argued with Walt that this was a realistic representation of life in the Wild West, but Walt was still opposed. Walt told his team that sometimes it was possible to overdo the realism, breaking the fantasy he was trying to provide. He suggested that there were other aspects of American Indian life that he wanted to share with the guests. Walt hired Bill Wilkerson, a full-blooded Cherokee Indian, to be the proprietor of the Indian store, which was made up of 7-foot poles tied together with leather straps.[60] American Indian artists made sand paintings, and dancers performed for the audience.

FANTASYLAND:
Not Needed But Necessary

THE GUEST'S FANCY now fully engaged, he or she might next want to visit Fantasyland, the land that Walt intended to be "the world of imagination, hopes, and dreams." In a bold move, Walt put at the center of his park a tribute to a film that would not be released for another four years. Sleeping Beauty Castle was the gateway to Fantasyland, and it would become the most recognizable and photographed element in all of Disneyland. Walt knew that a "castle is fantasy in any language."[61] To support the fanciful illusion, Bill Evans surrounded the castle with plantings that were fun, unrestrained, and had a bit of whimsy. He used lacy elm trees that sparkled when lit by twinkle lights tied to the branches.

Walt had put artist Herb Ryman on the project in 1953. The design was inspired by Neuschwanstein Castle in Bavaria in southern Germany. Harriet Burns made several small models (6–8 inches tall) of the castle and had Ryman and Eyvind Earle paint them. Earle's version was trimmed in black, red, and gold. The turrets were different colors: orange, black, pink, red, purple, and yellow. In Ryman's version, the turrets were all blue like slate. It was felt that Ryman's castle would look better against the blue sky.

At some point during the design process, Walt had told Ryman that his interpretation was a little too realistic. Still Ryman continued on his own course. When the team gathered for the final design sign-off meeting with Walt, the model was as realistic as it had been when Walt had expressed his concern. At the very last minute, just before Walt joined the meeting, Ryman removed the top of the model and turned it around. Everybody complained that Walt would be mad, but Ryman knew better. Walt took one look and gave his approval.[62]

During construction, Ryman added the Disney family crest above the entrance and placed the castle in a park-like setting. Ryman added also another special touch: 22-karat gold-leafed spires. Walt had authorized the expense while Roy Disney was away on vacation. On a visit to Disneyland many years later, Author Ray Bradbury saw a spire on the side of the castle that he described as "a duplicate of the convoluted and beauteous spire Viollet-le-Duc raised atop Notre-Dame 100 years ago." Bradbury called John Hench and asked, "John, how long has Viollet-le-Duc's spire been on the side of Sleeping Beauty's Castle?"

Hench replied, "Thirty years." Bradbury remarked that he had never noticed it before and asked who put it there? Hench said, "Walt." When asked why, Hench said, "Because he loved it." Bradbury said it was "something not needed but needed, not necessary but necessary."[63]

Just beyond the drawbridge was the Fantasyland courtyard. Bill Martin placed the carousel in the center with the Teacups and Pirate Ship to the back. The rides were placed in two 60- by 100-foot prefabricated show buildings to each side. Because they were working with a budget, Martin had the Masonite facades painted like tournament tents, creating a festive carnival flavor. Below the pastel-colored awnings were signs made of shields, ticket booths inside of striped tents, and flags and banners hung from lance-point flagpoles. The overall tone was heavily influenced by Earle's drawings for the film *Sleeping Beauty.*

The castle seemed to have a power of its own. John Hench suggested, "If you walked up and asked a guest WHY he likes the castle, WHY it is worth photographing? He could never tell you. He'd probably stammer out something like, 'Because it's just beautiful.' And yet, when he gets back home and shows his pictures, the feeling will never be the same that he experiences simply standing there."[64] Hench explained, "The fact is, as we stand here right now, there are literally hundreds of stimuli etching an impression and an experience in our minds through every one of our senses."[65]

He noted that the most obvious was the sense of sight, but the experience runs even deeper. "There is a static nature about the castle structure itself that makes you think it's been standing there for centuries," said Hench. "And yet there is motion. The motion of those flags, and the trees around us made by the wind. The movement of people, vehicles and boats, water, balloons, horses, and the white clouds passing by overhead."[66] He also suggested standing in front of the castle was "the best stereo or quad system in the world" with "an ever-changing background." The rock work, the horses, appeal to the guest's sense of touch, and the flowers are real and one can smell them. Finally, "That popcorn, you can go over and taste it." The result was that "every one of our senses are coming into play," said Hench. "This is total involvement. You can never capture this moment and take it home with you in a camera or tape recorder. You can only take this experience home in your mind."[67]

Ray Bradbury said, "In Disneyland, Walt has proven again that the first function of architecture is to make men over, make them wish to go on living, feed them fresh oxygen, grow them tall, delight their eyes, make them kind."[68] He proclaimed, "Disneyland liberates men to their better selves. Here the wild brute is gently corralled, not used and squashed, not put upon and harassed, not tramped on by real-estate operators, nor exhausted by smog and traffic."[69]

ALL JUMPERS

AT THE CENTER OF THE COURTYARD and the heart of Fantasyland was the King Arthur Carrousel. As far back as 1939, a merry-go-round was included in the plans for the park. Walt greatly admired the one in Griffith Park and asked then-owner Ross Davis if he could find one just like his for Disneyland. Davis told Walt that his was a one-of-a-kind machine built in 1926 from Spillman Engineering and it was the last one in existence with four-abreast jumpers. The carousel was brought to Griffith Park in 1937.

Most carousels featured different types of horses, classified by their body positions. A listener is posed with one ear forward and one ear back. A star gazer holds his head back, eyes upward. The top knot pony has a heavy forelock, which seems blown straight up by the wind. Most prized of all were jumpers, with all four feet off the ground. Walt Disney wanted only jumpers for his carousel.

Ross Davis found a carousel at Sunnyside Park in Toronto, Canada, that had been built in 1922 by William Dentzel of Philadelphia. The original was a menagerie-style carousel with horses, cats, deer, and giraffes. The ride was so finely balanced that one person could make it spin. Walt wanted to heavily modify the carousel for Disneyland. He wanted it to be four abreast, all horses, and all jumpers like the one at Griffith Park, so he hired Davis to repaint and repair the horses. In exchange, Walt gave Davis the unused figures.

Arrow Development did the engineering, including new crankshafts to operate the four rows of horses. Things were moving along until they hit a road bump. They ran out of jumpers. Luckily, Davis found some in storage beneath the Coney Island pier designed by Charles I. D. Loofa and some others from George Whitney's Playland in San Mateo, California.

The King Arthur Carrousel featured 72 horses, all considered outside horses. That meant they had a highly detailed right side, considered the "romance" side because it faces out to the public. They were the very best, and they were interchangeable. The horses were painted a variety of colors. Guests had a choice of black, tan, brownish red, or gray.

When they first started the carousel, they discovered that the electric brake would stop the ride too quickly, and one day they broke the gear teeth out. They could not find any replacement gears, so they asked Bud Hurlbut if he could help. He had a similar Dentzel machine at Knott's Berry Farm that was delivered without the bull gears, so he had fabricated a set himself. He found an old machinery handbook and figured out the tooth pattern. As it turned out, these were exactly the same gears that were needed for the Disneyland carousel.

Imagineer Bruce Bushman designed the high-peaked canopy, which hid the outer rim and showed off the horses at a distance. Although the 70-foot canopy appeared to be made of fabric, it was actually made of aluminum. The band organ came from a collection of 50 such machines that Walt purchased through Hurlbut in 1954. The collection of horses grew to 85 so that a "four on, four off" maintenance schedule could be maintained.

Right behind the King Arthur Carrousel was the Mad Tea Party. It was a basic carnival spinner ride; guests sat in a teacup and turned a wheel at the center to spin. In spite of frequent bouts of motion sickness, guests loved the spinning teacups because they had no brakes, so there was no limit to the speed that guests could spin the cups. The ride was originally a maintenance nightmare. Every morning crews would be ordered to spend the first 2 hours welding cracks. It was reengineered late in 1955, and the maintenance issues abated.

unofficial **TIP**
In 2004 maintenance crews came up with a new brake system that greatly slowed down the speed of the turning cups, but the outcry from guests persuaded the crew to reverse the modifications.

Opening-day guests were disappointed to miss several attractions that opened later in the summer. Casey Jr. Circus Train, which opened on July 31, was originally going to be Disneyland's thrill ride, but it was tamed down when things did not work out as planned. For example, up-stop rails were immediately added to mitigate the locomotive's tendency to rear over backward while it tried to go up Impossible Hill. Bob Gurr designed the two locomotives, and the rolling stock came primarily from the elements being removed from the Dentzel carousel in Fantasyland.

Also in the courtyard was Dumbo the Flying Elephant, which opened on August 16. It was originally called The Pink Elephant Ride after a sequence in the 1941 Disney film *Dumbo*. The attraction was a common carnival spinner ride re-themed. Walt said, "There's many ways that you can use those certain basic things and give them a new decor, a new treatment."[70] Artist Chris Mueller sculpted the flying elephants. Each of the elephants weighed 700 pounds and had mechanical ears that flapped when they worked, which was rarely. The ears kept shaking the mechanism to pieces and were soon disabled. They also had to cut an opening in the side to allow smaller guests easier access.

On the central hub stood Dumbo's best friend, Timothy Q. Mouse. Blaine Gibson carved the figure at home over one weekend based on a drawing from Bruce Bushman. It was Harriet Burns who had to paint it while it sat on top of the ride. "I have acrophobia and I hated that," she recalled. "I said to myself, 'I'm going to do the best job I've ever done so I'll never have to do it again!'"[71] The attraction was featured on a float during the 1955 Pasadena Tournament of Roses Parade. This was the start of a long tradition of participation between the park and the Parade.

On August 27, the Mickey Mouse Club Theater opened next door to Snow White. The theater was also known as the Fantasyland Theatre. While the Main Street Cinema was dedicated to the silent classics, in Fantasyland guests could enjoy "All Talking and Singing Sound Films" in air-conditioned comfort. The initial program consisted of Disney shorts, including "Lambert the Sheepish Lion," "Out of Scale," "The Big Wash," and "Squatter's Rights."

One of the most prominent features in the Fantasyland courtyard was the Chicken of the Sea Pirate Ship. The Van Camp Seafood Company sponsored this "gay Spanish galleon which provides a poop-deck for a different view of Fantasyland." The ship was best known for its tuna fish sandwiches. Sculptor Chris Mueller worked on the mermaid for the bow, but Walt did not like it, so he asked animator Marc Davis to take a shot. Davis used Tinker Bell (Margaret Kerry) as the prototype, and Mueller translated Davis's drawings into three dimensions.

unofficial **TIP**
In the summer of 1969, Disneyland took over operations of the restaurant from the Van Camp Seafood Company. The park renamed the facility Captain Hook's Pirate Ship and changed the figurehead from a woman to painted scrollwork.

Intertwined with the Casey Jr. Circus Train were the Canal Boats of the World, which opened on September 19. The initial concept had guests floating in a metal tub past landmarks from the countries of the world. After another European trip, Walt changed the tubs into canal boats. The advertising copy promised a ride on the "Boats of Holland, France, England, and America" and "travel through canals [that] pass the fabulous sights of Fantasyland." The reality was a fleet of boats with loud diesel outboard engines mounted inboard that slowly moved through barren canals embellished with signs featuring the Latin names of the weeds. Most of the time the engines would just burn up and the boats had to be towed back in. Dick Nunis named it The Mud Bank Ride, and the employees went out of their way to dissuade guests from wasting their tickets. They actually placed signs at the entrance that said, "This ride is not complete." However, they still wanted to go for a ride.

DRAMA, HUMOR, AND BEAUTY

MORE THAN VIRTUALLY ANY OTHER attraction in the park, it was the Fantasyland dark rides that set Disneyland apart from other parks. Before Disneyland, the typical dark ride would be something like the Tunnel of Love, where boats followed each other through a canal. Coats felt "the big improvement we made over what had been done before was the way we left people with a little two-minute experience within a certain story that they had known from our animated films. Now they got to see it in a more dimensional way, and these were interesting ways of doing it."[72] Walt wanted each ride to represent a different emotional experience. He wanted drama, humor, and beauty.

The process started with the source material, the animated films. The Imagineers used the original 4- by 8-inch storyboards and concept sketches. Claude Coats credits Ken Anderson with finding a way to make it work. Anderson drafted storyboards that highlighted key elements of the story but focused more on creating the right mood. Then Anderson and Coats designed the interior sets. Fortunately, both Anderson and Coats worked on the films and knew the material well. Once they finished, Bill Martin would make modifications to fit the shows inside the buildings.

The Imagineers pioneered the use of ultraviolet paints. At the time, black light was considered a novelty. When it was used at an amusement park, it was usually limited to scary rides. Because the spaces within the dark rides were not very large, the use of black light created a better illusion than incandescent light. Working at the Burbank studio, Coats and Anderson applied black light paint on plywood flats.

Martin was proud of what his team created for Fantasyland. "Ours were the first dark rides as such. It's my feeling that our first three rides in 1955 were original and kind of breakthrough. When we went back East to visit all those amusement parks, all we saw were the 'iron rides' and midway attractions, but no dark rides like we were planning, using 'black light.'"[73]

Peter Pan and Mr. Toad were mocked up at the Studio first while the ride show buildings were still under construction. Snow White was an exception. Because they were just trying to copy the film, the look and the key scenes had already been established. Martin did the track layout, and Anderson started to paint the theatrical flats himself. Guests would travel through Snow White in little mining cars; the cars would be moving quickly, so there was very little animation.

The dark rides shared many elements. For each, guests queued up in front under a shaded canopy with a mural previewing the attraction. The murals were created by Anderson and Coats, who could execute the paintings quickly because they had worked on the source films. Walt was big on giving people previews.

All the Fantasyland dark rides shared another trait. The guest was supposed to fulfill the role of the lead character. For example, when a guest rode Snow White, they were supposed to be Snow White. The attraction was designed with that point of view in mind. You were the girl that was being threatened. At one point, George Whitney reported to Joe Fowler that guests were getting confused because they did not see the main character. He suggested that the image of the featured character be added to the rides. His advice was set aside for more than 25 years.

The rides were also all illuminated with incandescent light instead of black light for the opening and closing scenes. For example, Peter Pan starts off in the Darling children's bedroom and Mr. Toad in the grand hall of his home. This made for a more natural transition from the outside.

The most dramatic and scary dark ride was Snow White. In Snow White, guests boarded 1 of 13 mine cars that were built by Arrow Development. They were meant to look like ore cars hand carved by the dwarfs. They ran along a single-rail guide track. The cars had no lap bar, just a rope hooked across the door of the vehicle.

Guests traveled through the Dwarf's mine, past Dopey as he opened the jewel vault door with precious gems glowing, and then deeper into the mine. The Witch made an appearance before guests were confronted with a choice: to head for the cottage or go to the castle? With vultures looming over the cottage, the ore car turned toward the castle. Suddenly, the guests were being chased by the witch. Coats remembered, "We got some letters about the witch scene in that ride. Walt never seemed to mind. He thought that children would sometimes have to learn that things were scary, you know."[74]

Guests frightened by Snow White found reprieve in Mr. Toad's Wild Ride, where humor was in abundance. Inspired by the Wind in the Willows segment in the 1949 animated film *The Adventures of Ichabod and Mr. Toad,* the ride featured J. Thaddeus Toad, who was described as "a disturbing factor, a reckless adventurer, having a positive mania for fads while never counting the cost." The ride would become the closest thing to a thrill ride at Disneyland until the opening of the Matterhorn Bobsleds in 1959. In fact, Bruce Bushman's original idea for the Mr. Toad ride was a roller coaster with the cars following a downhill track towards obstacles that would move out of the way at the last minute. Walt thought it might be too rough and suggested it be toned down.

It was decided that the Mr. Toad ride would be best served not by telling the plot of the film but to focus on Toad's motor mania as he might have experienced it from behind the wheel. Once again, the guests were asked to take an active role and to become the lead character.

While Coats and Anderson were working on the content, Martin was busy working on the layout. He knew the size of the floor space available and that the ride was supposed to last about 1½ minutes. This helped him determine how many cars he could fit on the track and the interval of loading. From there he could figure out the timing and spacing of the bumping doors. The vehicles had a minimum turning radius of 4 feet, which was very fast. Initially, only some of the swinging doors between scenes were automatic. They were closed as the car approached, and it looked like you were going to hit them. When the ride first opened, sometimes you actually did.

While drafting the layout for Mr. Toad, Martin was limited in the amount of space he had to work with. Peter Pan was placed along the long side of the building, while Mr. Toad was pushed into the end of the building. That limited the number of cars to only nine, compared to Peter Pan's 11 boats. There was so little space out front.

Once the track configuration was determined, the team would meet and talk about gags. Martin said, "I remember the meeting when we thought of the 'train coming at you' idea. That was a 'catch-on' gag, the last effect at the end of the ride that sends you to Hell. That idea of going through the Devil's mouth, through the Jaws of Hell, was okay with Walt at the time, too."[75]

The little cars were an in-stock item at Arrow Development. Disney bought 12 cars with 9 online at any time. Each vehicle weighed 200 pounds and was made of fiberglass and sheet metal. The cars were powered by a ¼-horsepower electric motor with a small guide wheel in front, following a single "T" rail installed along the floor of the ride corridor. The bodies were modified to look like Bushman's concept drawings. Each car leaned slightly backwards. Along with the twisted fenders, it gave the car a wacky look. The cars were some of the first pieces of equipment to be delivered to the park.

The cars were named after the primary characters, including Mr. Toad, MacBadger, Moley, Ratty, Cyril, Winky, and Weasel. Every 11 seconds, guests would get behind the wheel and be whisked away past the fireplace in Toad Manor and then crash through a window out toward the Hammy Hamlets: Woostershire, Outinshire, Notsoshire, and Nowhere In Particular.

Although Mr. Toad escaped from prison in the movie, the ride was mostly about his bad driving habits. This is one reason why there are so many policemen throughout the ride. The show was filled with gags, making the ride seem out of control. The cars raced through the backstreets of London before coming in contact with a train in RR Tunnel No. 13. As guests passed through the Jaws of Hell, the moral seemed to be if you play, you pay. Martin took advantage of the 4-foot turning radius of the vehicles to make a twisting track with quick turns.

When it came time to install the attraction at Disneyland, Coats and Anderson found themselves on the short end of the stick. Peter Pan and Snow White were painted by Grosh Studios, but they were too busy to work on Mr. Toad. Fortunately, Coats had worked on the original film and was able to bring the project together quickly.

Next door was Peter Pan's Flight. Based on the 1953 animated film, Peter Pan was different than the other two dark rides. In Snow White and Mr. Toad, guests were chased by the wicked witch or their own inner demons, leading them to hell. The scenes were based on the films' negative plot elements and the vehicles maneuvered through tight dark corridors. Only when the vehicles came out to the sunlight was the guest able to breathe a sigh of relief. Even though it included some adventure scenes, Peter Pan had very little of the tension guests experienced in Snow White and Mr. Toad. Peter Pan was certainly the most positive of the Fantasyland dark rides. It was the ride with the most beauty and wonder.

To begin the ride, guests boarded one of nine flying Spanish pirate galleons and were whisked over London to Never Never Land. The galleons were based on a small model made by Bruce Bushman. The little model was lacking in detail, so sculptor Chris Mueller stepped in to do much of the detail work for the full-size prototype.

Each boat was 7 feet long and 4½ feet wide. They were made of fiberglass and weighed 250 pounds. They were suspended from a track system built by the Cleveland Tram Rail Company and powered by a one-horsepower electric motor with a gearbox located forward of a wheeled trolley carriage. The ships used friction drive, with a "pinch drive" wheel system to permit the vehicles to climb or descend as the track plan dictated. The sails blocked the view, hiding the track ahead, and encouraging guests to look down toward the sets. The keel holds the boat steady for loading and unloading. The original track rail system was not reliable and soon had to be rebuilt.

The overhead track started at 8 feet 9 inches in the loading area and quickly rose 2 feet as the ships entered the nursery. Once they exited the bedroom they gained another 4 feet. The highest point over London was the pass over Big Ben, which was 16 feet 9 inches from the floor. The boats then dropped a foot as they approached Never Land Island.

The scenes within each of the rooms strongly reflected the animated film. As guests fly above London, they see little lights down below. The flight over London used forced perspective. Big Ben was tapered upward, for example. The flight over Never Never Land was also strongly influenced by the film. The island was 15 feet long and set on a platform 2 feet above the floor. In the last room, the ships appeared to pass through the left eye socket of Skull Rock. Standing on a boulder was Captain Hook, ordering Smee to shoot down the guests. Nearby was the crocodile.

Animator Frank Thomas said, "One of my biggest memories about the Peter Pan ride was when the ride first opened at the Park, and one of the flying boats broke down. This elderly couple was riding in it, and they were up there in the little sailboat. They were flying along and they came to the place in the ride where Captain Hook is yelling, "Shoot them down, Smee . . . shoot them down!" and all of a sudden . . . POW . . . the car mechanism broke and down they came, and it spilled them out on the ground. So they came out of the ride building, rubbing their hips and saying, 'That's the greatest ride you have here. It's so realistic!' And the park people asked, 'Are you all right? Are you hurt?' And they said, 'No, no . . . we loved the ride . . . can we go again?'"[76]

TOMORROWLAND:
Science-Factual

The dedication plaque for Tomorrowland promised "a vista into a world of wondrous ideas, signifying man's achievements . . . a step into the future, with predictions of constructive things to come."[77] Walt hoped it would be a "living blueprint of our future." However, that was not the case at the grand opening. The project was put on hold in late 1954 and only restarted after the first of the year. Gabriel Scognamillo was assigned to be the art director for Tomorrowland and struggled to manage the project. On opening day, the land was not up to the standards found in the rest of the park.

The theme was a "science-factual" projection of America in 1986 AD, the year of the return of Halley's Comet. A press release proclaimed Tomorrowland was "not a stylized future, but a scientifically designed projection of future technology." The chairs, benches, umbrellas, and other amenities could not be modeled after any particular period, so the Imagineers had to devise their own street furniture that seemed futuristic. To provide for shade, they built giant hairpins made of aluminum tubing and illuminated the area with futuristic lights attached to aluminum tripods. The exhibit and show buildings were touted as "advanced architectural design."

How the landscape would look in the future was a big question. Bill Evans had very little in the way of reference materials. Other than science fiction movies that were set on Earth, very little time was spent outdoors, and Evans wanted to avoid creating a Martian landscape. With what little money he had, he used a palette of bold, gutsy plant materials that could compete with the stylized structures.

The Clock of the World, sponsored by Timex, marked the gateway to Tomorrowland. A promotional piece asked, "Do you want to know what time it is in Tokyo, or New York? Paris or Cairo? Walk around its stately column, and you can read the time of day in any city in the world." The U.S. Time Corp. built the clock based on French urn clocks of the late 17th and mid-18th centuries. The clock had an hourglass shape and stood 17 feet 2½ inches tall.

On top of the clock was a half-sphere gold-anodized aluminum sun and silver crescent moon with a stylized Man in the Moon face. This element rotated clockwise to make one full revolution per day. At night, lights from within the sun illuminated the moon face. Herb

Ryman designed the sun, and Blaine Gibson sculpted the moon based on Ryman's design.

Below the rotating sun and moon was a stationary roof of Italian glass mosaic tile rimmed by a 24-hour plastic dial revolving counter-clockwise. The dial was lit from behind and featured black numerals on a white background during the day and white numbers on a black background at night. Below the dial was the globe projected around the conical pedestal. Major cities, such as New York, Los Angeles, Madrid, Moscow, Casablanca, Paris, Buenos Aires, and Chicago, were marked. Even Disneyland was included on the map.

To figure out what time it was, the guest would line up the city of interest with the hour indicator dial. A small, aluminum globe with a digital display counted out the minutes. The base was made of the same blue Italian glass mosaic tile used on top but flecked with silver tiles, representing the stars in the heavens. When the Court of Honor was moved in front of the clock in 1956, a flagpole obscured the view from the hub, and the icon lost some of its drama.

Although the Clock of the World was supposed to be the thematic icon for Tomorrowland, it was the TWA *Moonliner* that seemed to capture the public's imagination. The spacecraft was designed by John Hench based on conversations with rocket scientists Willy Ley and Wernher von Braun. That may be why the spaceship resembles a V2 rocket. The ⅓-scale model stood at 76 feet tall and was easily seen from the hub. It was placed prominently in front of the Rocket to the Moon.

Walt Preston did the engineering and had the spacecraft fabricated just like a boiler. It consisted of three sections. The largest section was the 60-foot main cabin at 9 feet in diameter; the nose added 16 feet, and the three legs were 22 feet long. It was covered in 15,000 square feet of Kaiser aluminum. The rocket was built quickly, and this caused problems. The interior structure was made of wood. The exterior was aluminum. When the aluminum started to expand as the sun hit it, the rocket would make a tremendous bang. As the day went along and the rocket started to cool, it let out yet another loud noise.

At a time when the first satellite to orbit the Earth was still a couple of years away, Walt thought it would be fun to give guests a bird's-eye view of the world from a "platform in space." That was the concept behind *Space Station X-1*. Claude Coats and Peter Ellenshaw painted an aerial view of the United States based on the first photograph from space, which was taken on October 24, 1946, from an altitude of 65 miles. In this case, they moved the perspective up to 90 miles in space and painted the scene on a doughnut-shaped canvas. Guests stood along a railing and looked down at the painting. The lighting changed from daytime to nighttime, and the painting was illuminated in black light. The platform moved from the East to West Coast in 3 minutes.[78] Over the years, the name would be changed to the *Satellite View of America,* but that was not enough to draw guests, and it closed on February 17, 1960.

The big draw in Tomorrowland was another space journey, the Rocket to the Moon. Due to technical glitches, it opened on July 22, 1955. The attraction was developed by the Imagineers and was subsidized by Trans World Airlines (TWA). The attraction was based on the upcoming "Man in Space" segments for the *Disneyland* television program. The programs were inspired by a series of articles first published in *Collier's* magazine from 1952 to 1954 by space experts Willy Ley, Heinz Haber, Wernher von Braun, and illustrator Chesley Bonestell. This approach is what Walt called science-factual.

At the end of Tomorrowland's "main street" was a show building that sported two large domes with fins, giving the building the appearance of an observatory. As guests entered the lobby, the hostesses reminded them that this was a spaceport terminal in the year 1986. They would be called to enter the Briefing Room, where they were to stand along aluminum railings, look up at a large screen, and view a short film explaining the history of space flight and the mission. The film was shot in 16 millimeter and projected from behind. The time spent in the lobby and the Briefing Room was 15 minutes.

Once the preshow concluded, the guests were escorted to the Control Center. A cast member would point to a model and explain some of the details of a space vehicle much like the one they were about to board. Guests also watched a short film of a rocket launching. The loading ramp to the launching pad was a narrow 24-foot corridor made of Neotex and aluminum on a spring-mounted ramp. The ramp was built in three sections so that it appeared to telescope tighter as guests moved forward. Just out of view, the guests could hear workmen doing final checks on the spacecraft. Although the story line suggested there were two different rockets, the *Star of Polaris* and the *Star of Antares,* everybody was led to the *Polaris.*

The rocket interior was a domed room with seating for up to 102 guests. The smooth plastic seats were arranged on three levels. The facility was rather barren with the exception of a few details, such as dials, rectangular speakers, and little fins that suggested a vision of space travel from the movies in the 1950s. The dials would change throughout the show, verifying the spacecraft's conditions. Two large screens mounted on the wall and two circular "scanner screens" placed on the floor and the ceiling allowed guests to monitor their trip.

At launch, the entire theater would vibrate for 25 seconds. Each seat was fitted with an air jack. Once past the "sonic barrier," the captain would direct guests to look up at the ceiling screen to see space station Terra. Wathel Rogers built the model "space wheel." A moment later, the captain would tell the guests, "Now, in the upper screen, the first glimpse of our goal . . . the moon."

At this point, some guests might have wondered why they were not floating about the cabin due to the lack of gravity. On the ascent, it was assumed that the forward motion had created artificial gravity. The captain explained, "As we approach the moon we must decelerate. The deceleration is another way to generate the artificial gravity necessary to keep us in our seats." He directed the audience to view the upper screen and watch a similar ship make a turn-around maneuver. Then the *Polaris* did the same trick with the Earth on the lower screen and the moon on the upper screen. Soon, the two heavenly bodies traded places. Outside of the cabin were noises that seemed to substantiate the flip-over move. German rocket scientist Willy Ley, whom the Studio had hired as a consultant, suggested this element of the show. Ley also suggested ideas such as the Earth receding and the moon growing larger in the view screens to suggest movement. As the spacecraft approached the moon, Halley's Comet flashed by as a reminder that the show was set in 1986.

As the rocket approached the dark side of the moon, the captain told the guests, "While we're in [the moon's] shadow, flares will be launched so that you may see more of the surface." Ward Kimball added the faint image of an ancient civilization on the back side of the moon, visible only in the flash when the flares were lit. He said, "Wernher von Braun was against doing this, but I said, 'We can't just go around the moon. We've got to have a little mystery . . . at least some evidence that might look like an ancient civilization that has crumbled away.'"[79] The idea came from the television program that he was producing.

After completing the orbit around the moon, the rocket headed back to Earth. On the trip home, guests learned about the new moon colony and the elimination of California smog in 1971. As Earth approached, the same flip-over maneuver was executed. Suddenly, just as the ship penetrated the atmosphere, something went wrong. Warning lamps flashed, sirens screamed, and chaos ensued. The sound of debris hitting the hull of the spacecraft added to the confusion. The captain explained, "We've just passed through a shower of meteor-oids, sometimes called shooting stars." Once back on track, the space-craft landed and guests exited past the TWA *Moonliner.*

The Rocket to the Moon was the last major attraction to get the green light. In April 1955, the production schedule was accelerated and some of the first drawings were completed. Artist Peter Ellenshaw shot most of the film himself. The film was made up of a number of truck-in shots to simulate movement toward the moon and back to Earth. He used clouds and interference on the screen to mask the edits. To see if the effect would work, Ellenshaw set up a little mock-up at the Studio.

The attraction was not ready for opening day despite all the effort. The control systems were not working and had to be rewired. Then a disgruntled electrician sabotaged the electrical work. The team worked all night to get the attraction ready for opening day, but they could not seem to make it work. Walt walked in and said he liked the interior but knew the show was not ready for the public. He decided to show excerpts from the films instead. It took another four days to get things right. Once they did get things up and running, they ran into a different problem. The preshow area was exposed to the outside. Guests would stop, watch the film, assume that was the attraction, and move on.

The rest of Tomorrowland was made up of corporate-sponsored exhibits. Walt had a team, including C. V. Wood, who would contact companies, present ideas, and bring in Walt to close the deal. Walt was a very charismatic salesman and knew how to wow the money men. The idea was much like a World's Fair: companies could showcase their products to millions and build goodwill.

Kaiser Aluminum & Chemical Corporation sponsored one of the exhibits, which opened on October 19, 1955. Guests passed through a telescope fabricated from aluminum that measured more than 40 feet long by 8 feet in diameter. Once inside, they learned how "alumi-num has mushroomed in a relatively brief period from a rare, precious metal to the servant of man it is today." They even had their own mas-cot acting as host—KAP, the Kaiser Aluminum Pig. The climax was a life-size statue of the goddess Venus, historic symbol of beauty, draped in "the inherent beauty" of aluminum yarn and colored lights."[80]

Monsanto Chemical's Hall of Chemistry was another corporate-sponsored exhibit. Monsanto was a diversified chemical manufactur-ing company headquartered in St. Louis, Missouri. Their exhibit was called "Where Chemistry Works Wonders for You," and it featured a display of eight huge shining test tubes called a Chemitron. Each one contained the "natural materials from which all chemicals are made" and "from which Nature forms all materials." In 1965, a display was added that compared "Fashion and Fabrics" from centuries ago with today's "fabrics produced through chemistry." More than 30 million would visit the exhibit before it closed in October 1966.

Later in 1955, the Society of Motion Picture Art Directors sponsored a display of artifacts from films such as *Giant, High Noon, Forbidden Planet, Rear Window, Guys and Dolls,* and *The Egyptian.* Disney was represented by artwork from *Pinocchio, Song of the South,* and *Sleeping Beauty,* plus models used during Disneyland's construction. Other corporate exhibits included National Lead's The Dutch Boy "Color Clock" paint exhibit, Richfield Oil's "The World Beneath Us" film, and American Dairy's "Today's Food Builds Tomorrow's Man" exhibit.

ONLY TWO CARS RUNNING

WHAT WOULD TURN OUT TO BE one of the most popular rides in the park was the miniature highway known as Autopia. Freeways were new and futuristic to Americans in the mid-1950s. In Southern California, work had already started on a promised network of highways that were within 5 miles of every residence. Indeed, Disneyland's success would be dependent on access from a freeway.

Walt wanted young people to grow up to be responsible drivers, so he felt that a "training" freeway would be educational as well as fun. Marvin Davis did the first layout. He outlined a single street, 1 mile long and wide enough for two cars. The drivers went counterclockwise on the loop. Probably the most exciting element was the three-sided cloverleaf. To add a touch of authenticity, two billboards for sponsor Richfield Oil dotted the landscape. That was about it. By the time construction started on Autopia, Bill Evans had exhausted his landscaping budget and only had 5-gallon trees left for Tomorrowland. The queue was a simple modern awning with bent pipe arch supports.

Bob Gurr began work on the Mark I Autopia cars after Hartmann Engineering left the project. Walt considered a prototype given to him from a German importer. Gurr took a look and said, "The car I'm talking about had a kind of Studebaker front end. It was the ugliest green and pale yellow car, but it did have 'Disneyland' painted on it." His assessment was, "I couldn't believe that [the Germans] were serious. It took me about a week to come back with the sketches for our car."[81]

The Mark I was a sleek futuristic car patterned "after the Ferrari," according to Gurr. Gurr used fiberglass for lightness, strength, and flexibility. The bodies rested on a 64-inch wheelbase chassis and weighed 475 pounds. They were powered by a 7.5-horsepower, one-cylinder engine with a top speed of 25 mph, but mechanically limited to fewer than 11 mph. For safety, the cars had foam-covered dashboards, a padded black rubber "deep dish" steering wheel on the left side, safety belts, and wraparound soft aluminum bumpers. Guests sat on bench seats covered in vinyl, and the cars were outfitted with two accelerator pedals, one for shorter legs. There was an automatic braking system, so when the guest let up on the accelerator, the brake came on. At first, the cars also had working headlights, but they became problematic and were the first things removed. The Tomorrowland area was so brightly lit, they were deemed unnecessary.

Walt saw the first full-size mock-up in a garage in North Hollywood in January 1955 and gave his approval. An order was placed for 40 cars. The bodies were fabricated by the Glasspar Company in Costa Mesa from a clay mock-up, and Mambo Engineering in Newport Beach did the final assembly and testing. As a 12-year-old, Michael Broggie helped to test the cars; he later recalled, "I was given the job to find a way to break them. I'd go over to the Studio to run the prototypes, which were literally lined up out there, and this was something that needed to be done."[82]

Bob Gurr did prepare one very special car just for Walt. Unlike the standard cars, "Walt's Car" was painted metallic maroon with red and off-white leatherette interior, a plastic windshield, and spun wheel covers. The front bumper came from a 1953 Pontiac upper bumper bar that Gurr sliced, re-welded, and re-chromed to look like a new bumper.

The attraction opened with no center rail, and the cars were allowed to pass one another. However, accidents were common when cars would jump the curbs, spin out, or block the roadway. Cast members had to be positioned around the road to escort the biggest offenders from the attraction.

To keep order, two black-and-white "squad" cars were built with Sheriff's insignias on the hood. They did not have a speed governor and were capable of speeds up to 25 mph. They were outfitted with a siren and a flashing light and were frequently used to give small children rides. At the first, the regular cars' speed was limited to 11 mph, but the engines would get so hot that the governors would quit and the cars would be able to go much faster.

The cars were untested and constantly breaking down. Because there were maintenance issues throughout the park, Autopia was given a low priority and Bob Gurr tried to do what he could. At one point, on one very hot day, only two cars were running while the rest were sitting in a side lot. Thankfully, two mechanics arrived to help Gurr out and the three began to make headway.

Gurr described the development process. "We had two budgets: one to develop the project and another to make changes once it went into operation. Roger [Broggie] would just wave his hand when the job was pretty well done and he met his budget and then send it out to the field to get 'adjusted' and then billed to the park."[83] Gurr added, "The Mark I went through a number of changes. There were design details that evolved from day one."[84] They included parts made of sheet metal, for instance, which had to be replaced with stronger castings. We had changed to smoother-running Wisconsin engines because the Gladden was so rough." This was the beginning of the Mark II model and "designing park devices that could take the kind of use they got at Disneyland." Gurr said, "We knew we had to take a really hard look at the cars, and design a car that didn't need constant repair."[85] The original Mark I cars were retrofitted with the new technology.

At one point Walt toyed with the idea of building a bus to ferry smaller guests. Gurr drew up a preliminary design based on the 1952 General Motors Scenicruiser. A driver would sit in front with several rows for children behind. Gurr said, "Instead of the well-known greyhound dog painted on the sides, I used a dachshund dog." He said, "This [bus] idea did not make much sense to the operations folks."[86]

One attraction that was an immediate failure was the Tomorrowland Boats, which opened on July 30. On August 16, they would be renamed the Phantom Boats. The 9-foot-long fiberglass motorboats were turquoise or pink with futuristic jet engine air scoops and huge shark fins like a Cadillac. Each of the 14 boats sat two guests and had a driver. The boats were designed by Bruce Bushman, and the fiberglass bodies were duplicated from a sculpture by Imagineer Chris Meuller. Although the boats looked sleek and fast, they rarely worked. Breakdowns were frequent. Typically, the outboard engines that were mounted inboard would just burn up. They only lasted six months. They made a brief return in summer 1956 before being retired permanently.

The park was looking for ways to replace the Phantom Boats. Walt really wanted some sort of futuristic water transportation system on display. Admiral Joe Fowler suggested an airboat ride on Tomorrowland Lake. The idea went so far as to merit the development of a prototype, and Walt placed a billboard announcing them as a coming attraction. Concerns about guest safety forced the idea to be put on the shelf.

WHALE OF A TAIL

WALT WAS DESPERATELY TRYING to fill space in Tomorrowland, and an employee suggested that he bring some of the sets and props from the popular 1954 film *20,000 Leagues Under the Sea* down to the park. Ken Anderson was pulled away from his work in Fantasyland in the last two weeks before the park opening to work on the show. He said, "I was up all night with two other studio artists just before opening day painting the giant squid. Walt was supposed to be at a party his wife, Lillian, was giving for some VIPs at the park, but he was too nervous about everything being ready on time to stay there. He went around from ride to ride and exhibit to exhibit, checking work, helping out. He even came into where we were painting the squid, put on a mask, and did a little painting himself." [87] John Hench also joined in.

The walk-through display opened on August 5, 1955. Guests entered the exhibit through a 40-foot mural of the *Nautilus* and the giant squid. Originally, costumed guides would have provided a tour, but that idea was scrapped in favor of a prerecorded narration track voiced by Thurl Ravenscroft (possibly best-known for Tony the Tiger's, "They're grrrreat!" for Frosted Flakes). As the guests entered the exhibit, the movie's theme song, "Whale of a Tale" played in the background while they peered through portholes to see a model of the *Nautilus* in its final resting place. The guest's point of view was from the stern window of a sunken ship with treasure chests spilled out in the sand in the foreground and the upper deck of the submarine in the distance.

Next, guests passed through a full-size interior of the wheelhouse, designed by Harper Goff for the film. Throughout was ironwork that was Victorian in feel but without the frivolous ornamentation. Goff called this "sewing machine Gothic." A spiral staircase led to the chart room and Professor Pierre Aronnax's cabin, where his writing desk could be seen from the passageway.

The salon was completely furnished and included the famous pipe organ from the film. Through the view port, guests could see the scary giant squid moving closer. The prop was hung on cables and animated. In the pump room was a bank of lights that were cleverly made out of the bottoms of glass salad bowls. From there, guests moved into the diving chamber with the equipment hanging in the fitting chamber. The original diving suits were made of rubber, which rotted, and the diving helmets were dressed-up Japanese sponge diving helmets. Occasionally, a bubble would pop from the water at the bottom of the diving chamber. Once past the power supply room the guests got another glimpse of the *Nautilus*.

Based on the Jules Verne story set more than a century earlier than Tomorrowland's 1986, the 20,000 Leagues Under the Sea attraction may have seemed an odd fit in Tomorrowland. When asked, the Disneyland publicity department would explain that the submarine was powered by atomic energy; therefore, it fit in perfectly.

THE 20,000 LEAGUES UNDER THE SEA attraction had been slated to run six months but stayed until August 1966. Over the years, the park replaced the original rented props. In the early 1960s fiberglass castings replaced the original rotted diving suits. When the attraction finally closed, the pipe organ was reused in the Haunted Mansion and the glass curio cabinets were installed in the One-of-a-Kind shop in New Orleans Square.

OPENING DAY:
The Public Is My Subsidy

IF THE GUESTS COULD HAVE gone behind the scenes on opening day, the Disney magic might have been diluted by the planning details. Industrial labor relations expert Van France speculated that July 17, 1955, was selected as the date for the grand opening because of the production schedule of the television show rather than the construction schedule on the site. He said it would take one year to plan and execute such a complex show for an expected audience of 90 million. They were limited to a day that the Disneyland television show was scheduled to be broadcast, and mid-July was the last possible date for capitalizing on the summer tourist season.

Opening day's "Dateline: Disneyland" was broadcast on ABC and became one of the most viewed television events in history. The 90-minute show was hosted by Walt's good friends Art Linkletter and Ronald Reagan, along with Bob Cummings. A beaming Walt rolled into the ceremonies at the throttle of the *E. P. Ripley.* The locomotive was chosen because Mr. E. P. Ripley, grandson of the 1895 president of Santa Fe, was in attendance. California Governor Goodwin Knight and Fred Gurley, president of Santa Fe Railroad, were also in attendance.

The guests did not need to know about the rushed planning to know that the opening day experience was not all magic and joy—although Walt was not aware of the chaos surrounding the park. The traffic was backed up for 7 miles on the Santa Ana Freeway. Originally, 15,000 tickets had been handed out to studio employees and other invited guests. But counterfeit tickets led to a crushing crowd of 28,154 people on an 87° day, one of the hottest July days on record in Anaheim. Most of the rides broke down, and refreshment stands were running out of food and drink. By early evening, the Anaheim police had assisted 15 lost children. One guest believed his car had been stolen until police found the car right where he left it in the huge parking lot.

Opinions varied as to the success of the opening day ceremonies. Marvin Davis, who laid out the park, said, "I think we were pleased with the overall Park plan, the way the single entrance street worked, and the hub. The general flow of traffic was as we expected, and it worked. People saw everything we wanted them to see."[88]

Animator Frank Thomas attended as a member of the Dixieland band Firehouse Five Plus Two. He recalled, "We were out there, sinking down into that fresh asphalt, hour by hour. They had just put that stuff in, I think, that morning. I was on a chair by the door to the Main Street Firehouse, sitting around with some of the other guys in the band. I was leaning back in the chair, reading a copy of the *Police Gazette*. After I'd been there a while, I tried to straighten up, and the chair wouldn't straighten up. It had sunken into the street."[89]

Among the many problems that day, probably the biggest scare was a small gas leak somewhere under the castle. Blue flames were spotted along the base of the structure near Merlin's Magic Shop. It was determined that somebody on landscaper Bill Evans's crew had dug up a pipe with a backhoe. At the time, Bill Martin did not know what was going on and pulled out his pipe to have a smoke when, suddenly, the fire chief came running out of the castle, grabbed him by the arm, and dragged him toward the hub.

At one point during the festivities, Fess Parker and Buddy Ebsen went up to Walt's apartment above the fire station to have a drink. Walt was beginning to relax, changed into a sport shirt and one of his signature hats, and stood out front chatting with guests. Parker noted,

"There's a way that people look when they've reached a certain goal. Walt was in that kind of elevated state on that day."

Animator Ollie Johnston was there and remembered being stuck in one of the infamous cattle cars. He said, "Kids were crying and suffocating and I was about to quit the Studio at that point." Anaheim City Administrator Keith Murdoch said, "It was such a mess I went home and watched it on television."

The opening day press was not very kind. In the halls of Disney, the day would become known as Black Sunday. Headlines such as "Disneyland Keeps Local Police Busy" and "Walt's Dream a Nightmare" did not make a good first impression. As stated in the annual lessees' report, "Editorial comment on Disneyland's opening was, in many cases, sharply critical and contrasted unfavorably with the publicity which appeared prior to July 18th." In the first two weeks, most of the complaints centered on incomplete exhibits and rides, temporary lack of public facilities due to construction schedule, and commercialism.

The public grand opening was the following day, July 18. Guests began to arrive the night before, and a 2-mile-long line of cars on Katella waited to park at dawn. The gates opened at 10 a.m. and more than 50,000 walked through the turnstiles. Throughout that first summer, the park was open six days a week and closed on Mondays. A general admission ticket cost $1 for adults and 50¢ for children. Ride tickets were purchased at a ticket booth near each attraction and the cost ranged from 10¢ to 50¢. Even with a disastrous start, only 52 days later on September 8, 1955, 5-year-old Elsa Bertha Marquez became the 1 millionth guest.

To overcome the press's initial skepticism, Walt began a campaign of reaching out and inviting them to return with their families for private tours. The reporters got a chance to see the park as Walt intended without all of the fuss caused by the television broadcast. The program worked. Disneyland was a hit.

1. Randy Bright, *Disneyland: Inside Story* (New York: Abrams, 1987).
2. "Planning the First Disney Parks," *The "E" Ticket*, Number 28, Winter 1997, 8–19.
3. Charlie Haas, "Disneyland Is Good for You," *The New West Magazine*, 4 Dec. 1978.
4. Ibid.
5. Ibid.
6. Ibid.
7. Bright, *Inside Story*.
8. Ibid.
9. Jack Boettner, "Disney's Magical Little Park After Two Decades," *Los Angeles Times*, 6 July 1975.
10. "A Disneyland Discussion With Dave Smith," *The "E" Ticket*, 1988 Annual.
11. Tim O'Brien, *Ripley's Legends: Pioneers of the Amusement Park Industry*, Vol. 1 (Nashville, TN: Ripley's Entertainment, 2006).
12. John Hench, *Language of Vision* (Anaheim, CA: Walt Disney Productions, 1975).
13. Ibid.
14. Walt Disney, WED memorandum, 22 June 1955.
15. "Disneyland Art Director Bill Martin," *The "E" Ticket*, Number 20, Winter 1994–95, 10–19.
16. "Your Guide to Disneyland" (San Francisco, CA: Bank of America, 1955).
17. Anne K. Okey, "Room With a View," *Disney Magazine*, Spring 1995.
18. Boettner, "Disney's Magical Little Park."
19. Ibid.
20. Michael Broggie, *Disney's Railroad Story* (Pasadena, CA: Pentrex, 1998).
21. Tom Self, "Disneyland: Commercial Participants Say It is The World's Greatest Showcase," *The Executive*, Nov. 1977.
22. Disneyland Operations Department Group II, *Background Information: Adventureland, Frontierland, New Orleans* (Anaheim, CA: Disneyland, 26 Jan. 1970).
23. Disneyland University, *Welcome to Main Street* (Anaheim, CA: Disneyland, 1972).
24. "Offering Guests a Glimpse of the Past," *Disneyland Line*, 27 March 1992.
25. Jim Korkis, interview with the author, 2 Dec. 2012.
26. Disneyland University, "The Dream is a Reality" (Anaheim, CA: Disneyland, July 1975).
27. Bright, *Inside Story*.
28. Ibid.
29. Broggie, *Railroad Story*.
30. Linda Brickley, "Gentle and Tireless . . . the Disney Horses," *Orange County Register*, 6 July 1978.
31. Disneyland, "A Visit to Disneyland," press release, 13 May 1956.
32. "An Interview with Harper Goff," *The "E" Ticket*, Number 14, Winter 1992–93, 4–11.
33. Bruce Gordon and David Mumford, *Disneyland: The Nickel Tour* (Santa Clarita, CA: Camphor Tree, 2000).
34. Ibid.
35. Haas, "Disneyland Is Good for You."
36. John Findlay, *Magic Lands* (Berkeley, CA: University of California Press, 1992).
37. Ruth Shellhorn, "Disneyland: Dream Built in One Year Through Teamwork of Many Artists," *Landscape Architecture*, April 1956.
38. Wendy Lefkin, ed., *Walt Disney Imagineering: A Behind the Dreams Look at Making the Magic Real* (New York: Hyperion, 1996).
39. Jeff Kurtti, *Disneyland: From Once Upon a Time to Happily Ever After* (New York: Disney Editions, Inc., 2010).

40. Beth Dunlop, *Building a Dream: The Art of Disney Architecture* (New York: Abrams, 1996).
41. Ibid.
42. "On the Track to Disneyland," *The "E" Ticket,* Number 12, Winter 1991–92, 20–31.
43. Steve DeGaetano, *Welcome Aboard the Disneyland Railroad!* (Winter, CA: Steam Passages Publications, 2004).
44. Ibid.
45. "On the Track to Disneyland," *The "E" Ticket.*
46. Ibid.
47. "Roger Broggie," *The "E" Ticket,* Number 10, Winter 1990–91, 26–27.
48. Karal Ann Marling, *Designing Disney's Theme Parks: The Architecture of Reassurance* (New York: Flammarion, 1997).
49. John Stanley Donaldson, *Warp and Weft: Life Canvas of Herbert Ryman* (Las Vegas: Incanio Press, 2010).
50. Walt Disney, interview with Peter Martin, *Saturday Evening Post,* Summer 1956.
51. Disneyland University, "The Dream is a Reality."
52. Disneyland, "Building a Dream," press release, 13 May 1956.
53. "On the Track to Disneyland," *The "E" Ticket.*
54. Disneyland Operations Department Group II, *Adventureland, Frontierland, New Orleans.*
55. *The Spirit of Disneyland* (Anaheim, CA: Walt Disney Productions, 1984).
56. Wendy Lefkin, ed., *Disney Insider Yearbook: 2005 Year in Review* (New York: Disney Editions, Inc., 2006).
57. Disneyland Operations Department Group II, *Adventureland, Frontierland, New Orleans.*
58. "Disneyland Art Director Bill Martin," *The "E" Ticket.*
59. Self, "World's Greatest Showcase."
60. Disneyland Operations Department Group II, *Adventureland, Frontierland, New Orleans.*
61. Disneyland University, "The Dream is a Reality."
62. Lefkin, ed., *Behind the Dreams.*
63. Ray Bradbury, "Disneyland, or Disney's Demon for Happiness," *Modern Maturity,* March/April 2002.
64. Hench, *Language of Vision.*
65. Ibid.
66. Ibid.
67. Ibid.
68. Ray Bradbury, "The Machine-Tooled Happyland," *Holiday*, Oct. 1965.
69. Ibid.
70. Gordon and Mumford, *Nickel Tour.*
71. Pam Burns-Clair and Don Peri, *Walt Disney's First Lady of Imagineering Harriet Burns* (Virginia Beach, VA: Donning, 2010).
72. "Prototypical Imagineer," *The "E" Ticket,* Number 31, Spring 1999, 4–15.
73. "Disneyland Art Director Bill Martin," *The "E" Ticket.*
74. "Prototypical Imagineer," *The "E" Ticket.*
75. "Bill Martin," *The "E" Ticket.*
76. "Peter Pan, Captain Hook and Frank Thomas," *The "E" Ticket,* Number 26, Spring 1997, 26–40.
77. Walt Disney, Tomorrowland plaque located at the entrance to Tomorrowland near the flagpole (Anaheim, CA: Disneyland, July 17, 1955).
78. J. S. Hamel and C. M. Cutler, "Disneyland," *Light Magazine*, July/Aug. 1956.
79. "Disneyland's Rocket to the Moon," *The "E" Ticket,* Number 24, Summer 1996, 4–17.

80. "Giant Telescope Kaiser Exhibit in Disneyland," *Anaheim Bulletin*, 5 July 1955.
81. Bob Gurr, *Design: Just for Fun* (Togging, CA: APP-Gurr Design, 2012).
82. Broggie, *Railroad Story*.
83. Bob Gurr, interview with the author, 20 June 2012.
84. Gurr, *Just for Fun*.
85. Ibid.
86. Ibid.
87. "Ken Anderson," *The "E" Ticket*, Number 11, Summer 1991.
88. "Planning the First Disney Parks," *The "E" Ticket*.
89. "Peter Pan, Captain Hook and Frank Thomas," *The "E" Ticket*.
90. Ibid.
91. "A Conversation with Ollie Johnston," *The "E" Ticket*, Number 19, Summer 1994, 3–16.
92. Boettner, "Disney's Magical Little Park."

CHAPTER 3

LEARNING *to* WALK: 1955

▍YEAR ONE

JUST AS AN INFANT'S FEATURES and personality quickly evolve, the "face" of Disneyland transformed throughout its first year. In the early days, the park was not populated by the familiar cartoon characters. Roy was very protective of Mickey Mouse and the other major characters, and he did not want them tainted if the park idea failed. Instead, people were hired to create characters that embellished and enhanced the various themes. These types of atmosphere characters were commonplace and very popular at nearby Knott's Berry Farm.

Street sweeper Trinidad Ruiz was the best known of these characters. He was personally selected by Walt. Trinidad was a turn-of-the-19th-century whitewing who swept up after the many horses that made their way up and down Main Street. He wore a spotless white costume with a tall white hat. He quickly became the most photographed man on Main Street.

The one-legged Captain Guy Exon and his parrot, Paco, were the Fantasyland characters. They could usually be found at the Chicken of the Sea pirate ship restaurant. He had lost his leg in World War II and was the first one-legged man to travel over the Pan-American Highway.[1]

Frontierland was the site of frequent gunfights between Sheriff Lucky, the white-hatted hero, and Black Bart, the stereotypical Hollywood Western bad guy. Sometimes Golden Horseshoe Saloon comedian Wally Boag would join the battle. After the smoke cleared, Sheriff Lucky and Black Bart would act as greeters and help provide security.

unofficial **TIP**
Sheriff Lucky was named after retired Los Angeles police officer Lucky Fauntz, who originated the role.[2]

Tomorrowland had Space Man K-7. The costume was oversize, very heavy, and very hot. The actor had his head inside of a plexiglass dome with only a small hole for ventilation. It has been said that one spaceman actor became very popular because he snuck a battery radio inside the suit and kept everyone informed about the latest summer baseball scores. He was frequently joined by Space Girl.

For many, there was one more character: Walt Disney. Walt spent a lot of time in the park. He had his apartment above the fire station. He insisted on standing in the lines with paying guests. He could frequently be found talking with children to gauge their reactions. Before he would leave his apartment above the fire station, he would sign a bunch of photo cards to pass out along his walks.

When the park first opened, each guest bought a general admission ticket at the main gate and individual tickets for each attraction. The constant reaching into the pocket gave many families the impression that Disneyland was an expensive place to visit. When an Associated Press reporter criticized the park, Walt angrily replied, "We have to charge what we do because this Park cost a lot to build and maintain. I have no government subsidy. The public is my subsidy."[3] He added, "I mortgaged everything I own and put it in jeopardy for this Park. Commercial? How have I stayed in business all my life? The critics must know a newspaper exists on advertising. They're crazy!" Walt reminded the press, "We have a lot of free things in the Park. No other place has as high a quality. I stand here in the Park and talk to people. It's a most gratifying thing. All I've got from the public is thank-yous."[4]

To simplify the guests' expenses, the park made available the Day at Disneyland ticket book starting on October 11, 1955. The cost was $2.50 for adults and included one general admission and eight attraction coupons in three price categories, A–C. The ticket categories reflected the prestige or cost of the attraction. An A ticket would be good for a ride on a Main Street vehicle while a C ticket would allow you to board the Jungle Cruise. The ticket books had many benefits. They helped distribute guests throughout the park, helped in forecasting attraction capacity, and gave cast members an opportunity to interact with guests as they passed over their tickets.

At the end of the year, guests got a chance to ride on a real piece of Hollywood with the opening of the Mike Fink Keel Boats. The *Gully-whumper* and *Bertha Mae* were the actual boats used in "Davy Crockett's Keelboat Race" (November 16, 1955) and "Davy Crockett and the River Pirates" (December 14, 1955) segments of the Disneyland

IN 1965, the wood Mike Fink Keel Boats were replaced with fiberglass boats, which were considered to be five times stronger than the wood ones and about half the weight. There was also no steel in the hull to rust. Douglas fir wood was used for the deck. The boats were powered by a natural gas, 70-horse-power, four-cylinder marine engine. Starting in 1994, the keelboats were run only occasionally. On May 17, 1997, the keelboats were retired for good after one flipped into the Rivers of America with a boatload of guests. The *Bertha Mae* was put up for auction on eBay and sold for $15,000. The *Gullywhumper* was used as a prop in the Rivers of America until it was removed in April 2009.

television show. The *Gullywhumper* opened on December 25, and the *Bertha Mae* came online in May 1956.[5]

The two seaworthy boats were 38 feet long and made entirely out of wood. They were powered by a four-cylinder diesel motor and had a top speed of 15 knots. Each boat cost $27,500—nearly $240,000 in 2013 dollars. Walt brought them down to the park mostly for show rather than economic profit. They made the river more alive and gave guests another way to experience the Rivers of America environment. The boats could carry 32 guests. Twelve guests could sit inside in the lower deck and 18 on the upper deck on the roof. Two guests could sit on the coveted bow seat. A cast member gave a live spiel during the 11½–minute trip, and the boat was free to wander from shore to shore as the boat was not attached to a guide rail.

For Walt Disney Productions, Disneyland was a smash hit. The first-year revenues came to $10 million, one third of the total gross of the entire Studio.[6] The park was designed to handle 60,000 visitors. Guests who toured every land walked 1.4 miles. Guests had 20 restaurants from which to choose. During that summer, the park employed 1,000 people.

For the surrounding community, the project was an even bigger hit. When the park opened, there were only 60 motel-hotel rooms in the Anaheim area. After only two months, businesses reported increases exceeding 21%. Travel patterns had changed. The owner of the Golden West Motel, one of few lodging establishments in the area, said, "People used to wait until late afternoon to come in but now the units are filled by noon every day, with some people coming in as early as 6 a.m. to reserve rooms." Disneyland general manager C. V. Wood said, "The Customer Relations staff who interview people in the park each day report that we receive as many as 800 requests a day from visitors who are asking where they can find hotel and motel accommodations in the area."[7] On October 5, 1955, television producer and entrepreneur Jack Wrather opened the first phase of the 104-room Disneyland Hotel across West Street.[8]

WORLD'S LARGEST STRIPED CIRCUS TENT

IN 1952, *THIS IS CINERAMA* was the highest-grossing film in the United States. By using a then-novel three-projector format, producer Lowell Thomas was able to immerse viewers in a way never before seen. What was even more remarkable was that the movie was only shown in one theater in New York.[9] Walt also wanted to find a film technology that would fully immerse the guest into the experience, something that would add depth without requiring viewers to wear special glasses. He wanted guests in the middle of the action. His answer was Circarama, a 360-degree format developed in-house by Ub Iwerks with help from Roger Broggie. The system used 11 16-millimeter cameras. The team used 11 screens placed in a circle and separated by small spaces, with a projector placed between the screens, to project across the space to the opposite screen.

unofficial **TIP**
In 1967 Cinerama sued Disney, claiming the name of the attraction was too close to its trademark, so Disney changed the name of its system to Circle-Vision 360.

The early results were not promising. When the films were first projected on the 11 screens, many viewers suffered from eyestrain and dizziness. What they discovered was having all of the cameras facing outward from center mount meant they did not share the same nodal point. The solution was to aim the cameras up toward mirrors so that they could be aimed and focused at the same central nodal point. The first presentation was "A Tour of the West," with the camera mounted on top of an American Motors Rambler driving past natural wonders. The 15-minute show was sponsored by American Motors.

Another early experiment did not turn out as well: the November 11 opening of the Mickey Mouse Club Circus. Walt always loved the circus and thought that was something the park needed. The world's largest striped circus tent was set up at the far north section of the park just behind Holiday Hill, which was the pile of dirt from the Sleeping Beauty Castle moat. The tent was heated. There was a separate fee for the circus. C. V. Wood tried to talk him out of the circus entirely. He argued that the Disneyland visitor came to see the park and would not want to spend a couple of hours seeing something that they could see anywhere else. This criticism merely made Walt more determined.

Ads for the 1-hour show proclaimed the circus to be "personally produced by Walt to introduce his Mouseketeers to the public." Members of *The Mickey Mouse Club* television show performed circus stunts, accompanied by the March of Toys with all the famous Disney characters along with Santa Claus, Bob-O (the Disneyland Clown), and Serenado the Wonder Horse. The most thrilling act was Prof. Keller and His Feline Fantastics, "an exciting and educational experience with 13 of the World's most deadly killers!" At one point, the llamas escaped and made it to the Main Street station, and a panther attacked a tiger during a parade.[10] Bill Martin complained, "You couldn't tell the animals what to do, though, and Walt wanted more control. That's why we went to Audio-Animatronics later."[11] The circus left town on January 8, 1956, deemed a commercial failure. C. V. Wood had been right. Joe Fowler said, "That was the first time that we learned this lesson. People came to Disneyland to see Disneyland."[12] The area that had contained the circus was reshaped in preparation of the Junior Autopia.

Attractions weren't the only thing changing that first year; Walt was also changing his team. A *Billboard* magazine article on January 28, 1956, was brief and it gave only the slightest details: C. V. Wood was out as vice president and general manager of Disneyland as of January 1956 and would be replaced by a committee headed by Jack Sayers starting on February 1. Wood's original contract was for one year; it would have expired on July 16, 1956. A Disneyland spokesperson told the magazine the obvious: that Wood was leaving "five months ahead of schedule." Walt Disney and C. V. Wood Jr. were two supreme salesmen with larger-than-life personalities and reputations. For many who worked for the two men, the news did come as a surprise.

Although his contribution is rarely acknowledged in official Disney histories, C. V. Wood's leadership had been critical in getting Disneyland built. He took care of the messy details that came up in any major construction project. Unfortunately, he also tried to build a team within the Disneyland organization that was loyal only to him. Perhaps he forgot that Disneyland was Walt's production; in any event, Wood certainly underestimated the man. "In one week, Wood was holding his regular meetings as usual, with an office crowded every minute of the day," Van France said. "Just about overnight, he was out. On the day of his departure, his usually busy office was empty. The sycophants and favor seekers were gone."[13]

France continued, "Walt had read the maxim 'divide and rule,' and didn't mind friction between individuals. However, he would never accept this kind of disloyalty."[14] Wood said of Walt, "Oh, hell you know Walt. He'd throw his arms around you and kiss you, one day, and he'd look right through you, the next."[15] Wood left with a healthy parting bonus and would sell himself as "The Master Builder of Disneyland" until Walt Disney Productions sued him and won.

France noted that Walt "didn't like pretentious, status-seeking, title-happy people, or stuffed shirts. He either put them down or got rid of them. I liked that."[16] France also noticed that Walt did not like organization charts. "I don't know the reason for his dislike of these lines and boxes," France said. "My guess is that he felt they inhibited team work and created little empires. I loved that." Finally, France said Walt "could dream dreams, but he could also be realistic."[17]

With the park open, the management team had recommended that an administration building be built. As a reflection of Walt's values, he immediately opposed the idea. "I don't want you guys sitting behind desks," he said. "I want you out in the Park, watching what people are doing and finding out how you can make the place more enjoyable for them." He wanted them to "stand in line with the people, and for god's sake, don't go off the lot to eat like you guys have been doing. You eat in the Park and listen to people." He reminded them, "The public isn't coming here to see an administration building."

Sayers's and his team's top priority in 1956 was fixing what did not work and adding attractions as quickly as possible to absorb the ever-growing crowds. To that end, Disneyland had embarked on a $1.5 million expansion program that included new attractions in almost every land: the Astro-Jets, the Storybook Land Canal Boats, the Skyway, the Rainbow Mine Train, and Tom Sawyer Island. This meant closing the Pack Mules, Stagecoaches, and Conestoga Wagons on February 1, 1956, to make room for the new additions.

The first new ride to open was Tomorrowland's Astro-Jets on March 24. The ride was a Dumbo-type spinner for older guests. Just like the Fantasyland ride, guests could adjust the altitude of their rocket, with the biggest difference being that it spun faster, higher, and in the opposite direction. It was designed to give guests "jet-age thrills, as they broke the sound barrier" and "a thrilling spin through space."

With the park's immediate acceptance by the public, Tomorrowland's corporate sponsors became more confident and quickly added new exhibits. On April 5, Crane's "Bathroom of Tomorrow" opened and featured the next generation of bathroom fixtures and a launderette, all done in citrus yellow. The bathroom was equipped with radiant heated floors and a Crane central air-conditioning system. Other displays included a mural depicting the history of sanitation in the home and a "Tear Drop" exhibit featuring the "dramatic story of valves in the industry." The American Dairy Association updated their opening-day exhibit by adding the "Dairy of the Future," with cows watching color television while milkmen deliver milk with helicopters on their backs. Another new exhibit was the WenMac "Hobbyland," which featured the Thimble Drome Flight Circle, where guests could watch a 20-minute demonstration of model planes in flight and fast-moving model speedboats jetting around a circular fenced enclosure 200 feet in circumference. Occasionally, they even flew miniature jets. Walt had visited a hobby show in Los Angeles and became interested in these models. The Art Corner moved out of its temporary tent on Main Street and found a permanent location in Tomorrowland. Guests could buy original Disney animation cels for only $3.95. "No two are alike . . . a picture which will never have an exact duplicate."

unofficial **TIP**
The spinner was renamed the Tomorrowland Jets in August 1964 due to pressure from United Airlines. As a new Disneyland sponsor it did not want to see an attraction named after the jets used by competitor American Airlines.

Main Street U.S.A. also saw some changes. As guests entered the park they were greeted by another movie tradition: the oversize upcoming attraction poster. The 36- by 54-inch posters were hand-produced, silk-screened, and printed on high-quality heavy paper stock. Some of the posters, such as the one for the Art of Animation, used traditional four-color printing; others, such as the 20,000 Leagues Under the Sea exhibit poster, were more complex, with as many as 11 colors.

Mounted at varying heights on a wall in Town Square were Kodak Stereo II viewers displaying full-color 3-D slides of the scale model of the proposed International Street. Guests could peek at the plans for a new land to be located behind Main Street just off the Plaza Hub. Guests would cross over a scale reproduction of the London Bridge with little barges passing underneath. From there they could visit an English cottage with a waterwheel grinding grain, a reproduction of the French Quarter, the Italian area, and the German/Bavarian compound. The rides would have included a taxi cab through Paris and a cog-railway that would travel up and down the street.

To get to the north end of Main Street, guests could hitch a ride on the new red, six-passenger 1903-style Horseless Carriage with a fringed canvas top. The automobile made its maiden Disneyland run on May 12. The Horseless Carriage was designed by Bob Gurr and became known as a Gurrmobile. The automobile was meant to look old and rickety, but it was made of modern (1950s) mechanics, including the drive train, suspension, rear ends, and springs. This car used a Jeep rear end, a Ford Model A front end, brakes from a 1952 Mercury, and steering from a 1950 Chrysler Imperial. It had a two-cylinder Hercules water pump engine, selected for its durability, and the right sound of a vibrating motor under the bonnet. The "wood" spokes were actually aluminum castings. The brass lamps were built at the Studio. It took 7½ minutes to travel the 1,987 feet at an average speed of 4 mph. When one staffer was concerned that the car might be vandalized, Walt said, "Don't worry about it. Just make them beautiful and you'll appeal to the best side of people. They all have it. . . . All you have to do is bring it out." [18]

GET *a* BIT LOST

OVER IN FRONTIERLAND, Magnolia Park opened on May 31, 1956. The New Orleans–themed area was located near the Swift's Premium Chicken Plantation House Restaurant. Guests would be able to attend band concerts shaded by magnolia trees. Along with the park, the banks of the Rivers of America were finished and more parklike. New paved walkways were added, along with more fences and plantings.

The Disneyland publicity machine was gearing up for the park's first full summer. A 10-foot billboard was erected at the *Mark Twain* dock announcing the June opening of Tom Sawyer Island. The press release promised that "great names from American folklore and history will be brought alive this summer with the official opening of Tom Sawyer Island. The island, until now inaccessible to Disneyland visitors, will provide a slice of living Americana."

In early concept drawings, the island at the center of the Rivers of America was a display of scale-model reproductions of famous American buildings. There would be replicas of river towns such as New Orleans, Natchez, and Mobile. Other buildings would include Mount Vernon and West Point. However, once the park had opened, Walt saw a different need. He knew that children needed an opportunity to run free and play, to use their own imaginations, and to create their own personal stories. With the island, he had the opportunity to combine control with the chaos.

Tom Sawyer Island opened on June 16. The island was named after "the most famous youngster in American folklore" and modeled after Jackson's Island in Hannibal, Missouri. Walt was personally responsible for drawing the dog bone–shaped island that was 12 times longer than it was wide, approximately 800 feet from top to bottom. The plump ends measured approximately 250 feet to accommodate the turning radius of the *Mark Twain,* and the narrow middle was approximately 50 feet to conserve space. Overall, the island was approximately 3 acres. From above, the island looks somewhat like a catfish.

It would be a "playland out of a youngster's dream" and "an island built just for FUN!" according to a Disney spokesman. The project cost $250,000. Tom Sawyer Island had trails built on three levels in most places, providing variety and ways to elude others. Time spent on the island was different than time spent anyplace else in the park. There were no lines, very few rules, and no limit to the amount of time a visitor could stay. Kids had choices to make. Leon Janzen of *The "E" Ticket* suggested, "Tom Sawyer Island is big enough to get a little bit lost, and unsupervised access to caves, bridges, escape tunnels and secret passages lets each kid script his or her own exciting story."[19] Bill Evans was responsible for the landscape design.

Access to the island was by raft. Two rafts, the *Huck Finn* and *Becky Thatcher,* boarded at a dock near the *Mark Twain* and headed to Tom's Landing between the Old Mill and the Fishing Pier. Both rafts were free floating. The original 14- by 24-foot rafts were made of timber logs and powered by Gray Marine engines. Each raft could carry as many as 45 guests. The rafts would soon be rebuilt with built-in flotation tanks and powered by a four-cylinder engine. Before 1958, guests could occasionally take a raft all the way around the island when the *Mark Twain* was out of service.

Once on the island, guests could wander anywhere. Many headed toward the Old Mill with its flume-driven Grist Mill. Or they would go to the Huckleberry Finn's Fishing Pier where a small area was stocked with 15,000 catfish, perch, and bluegill. Guests could "borrow one of Huck Finn's bamboo poles and a can of worms." Walt was the first to try to catch a fish. When a reporter asked if he had any luck, Walt replied, "I caught one a minute ago but he got away before

I could land him." At Smuggler's Cove, they could cross over a Suspension Bridge on their way to Lookout Point, a hill made up of the fill from the Rivers of America.

Many a young child would spend all day working up the nerve to enter Injun Joe's Cave, "a romantic interpretation of the cave in the Samuel Clemens story" and "where Tom Sawyer and Becky Thatcher wrote their names with candle smoke."[20] Flaming torches marked the entrance to the 120-foot cave. The cave was built at grade and then buried under dirt. Inside was the Chamber of the Bottomless Pit, which was actually only about 7 feet deep. Skeletal fossils were embedded along the walls. A two-room shack stood near the exit of Injun Joe's Cave.

At the northern end of the island was Fort Wilderness, an "authentic log-built fort" at the edge of "hostile Indian territory." The fort had been built at the warehouse backstage, disassembled, labeled with brass tags, and floated, log by log, across the river to be reassembled.[21] Inside of "Regimental Headquarters" were the full-size wax figures of Davy Crockett and Georgie Russell, which had been moved from the Davy Crockett Arcade in Frontierland. In case the fort was "attacked," guests could escape through a "secret" escape path in a tunnel just to the right of the back stockade gate. Behind the fort was a graveyard. Tom Sawyer Island was a chance to exercise guests' bodies and their minds.

The grand opening celebration featured contest winners Chris Winkler and Perva Lou Smith from Hannibal, Missouri, who came in costume as Tom Sawyer and Becky Thatcher. They christened a raft with a jug of Mississippi River water and planted a box of soil from Jackson's Island, Huck Finn's Mississippi River island. After the ceremony they boarded a raft and made their way to the Plantation House for an "old fashioned fish fry" with 38 pounds of authentic river catfish flown in from the Mark Twain Hotel in Hannibal.

Bill Evans said the illusion was so real "we used to get letters, in the early days, from guests who complained that 'junior' got poison oak while running around on Tom Sawyer Island, and why didn't we remove such dangerous plants? Well, obviously we didn't plant poison oak, but these people believed they were in a completely natural wilderness."[22]

In Adventureland, a large open dining patio was opened with a view into the Jungle Cruise where the *Tiki Room* sits today. The Adventureland Bazaar was expanded with the Hawaiian Shop, the Mexican Mart, the Island Trade Store, the Tropical Tiki Shop, and the Here & There Imports.

NEW WORLDS
of ENCHANTMENT

JUNE 16, 1956, WAS THE DEBUT of the Mickey Mouse Club Theater in Fantasyland and the premiere of the 27-minute *Mickey Mouse Club 3D Jamboree*. Guests could relax in air-conditioned comfort and watch the new Mouseketeer film, as well as a 30-minute reel of cartoons. Another new addition to Fantasyland was The Storybook Land Canal Boats, which were a direct descendent of Walt's Mickey Mouse Park project. A gravity-flow canalboat ride was in Walt's very first plans for the park across the street from the Studio. Model builder Harriet Burns said, "Walt came in and he said he had seen miniature cities, both in Canada and in England, and he was most impressed with the one in England. He recalled how charming it was, and how kids and families could walk along the roads and between the buildings. It really intrigued him."[23] Walt called on "all the genius available at the Studio to re-create, in miniature, three-dimensional scenes from the world's great folk tales" and enter "new worlds of enchantment." The $200,000 project opened on June 18.

The Storybook Land models were scaled 1 inch to 1 foot and were made primarily of plywood covered in fiberglass. Walt wanted the sets to be designed as if the characters were just out of sight. He had seen how effective this type of staging was when he saw the Thorne Collection of Miniatures on display at the 1939 San Francisco Golden Gate International Exposition.

Miniatures were one of Walt's passions, and he was obsessed with the details. As part of the Storybook Land Canal Boats, he wanted a miniature church with a stained glass window. Harriet Burns was assigned to the project, and she began work on a window designed by artist Frank Armitage. Burns had been working on the complex project that contained more than 360 pieces of lead when Walt stopped by the model shop as he frequently did. Without thinking, he picked up the window before Burns had a chance to solder it together, and all of the pieces scattered on the floor. Burns did not let it bother her, as she was used to Walt wanting to play with the models.

It would have been simpler to create a window out of celluloid placed behind plexiglass, but Walt expected more. For example, Moley's House had hand-hammered locks and pulls, and the gutters were made of copper. Burns said, "Nobody could really see it, but Walt knew it was there—that was the good part."[24]

Guests rode in newly designed Dutch Canal boats built by Robert Dorris Boat Works. The old gas outboard motors were replaced with quiet electric motors that were individually powered by direct chain drive from the propeller shaft to a General Electric motor. There were five different styles of canal boats: some with teapots on the roof, another with two tillers, while another had miniature stairs. The boats were 16 feet long and were guided on a rail like the Jungle Cruise. The initial fleet of 12 boats would soon grow to 14, and they floated in a canal that held 465,000 gallons of water. Bill Martin was responsible for weaving the Canal Boats and Casey Jr. Circus Train together.

A little lighthouse was used as the ticket booth. Guests would queue up in front of Monstro the Whale. He would occasionally blink his eye and blow his whistle, and if guests were not paying attention it was easy to be startled. When the boats left the loading dock, they passed through the whale's mouth. Although this was not consistent with the story in the *Pinocchio* film, Walt decided that he was spending a lot of money to build the whale and he wanted to make sure that everybody got a good look.

One of the standout environments was Geppetto's Village. Geppetto's shop had tiny toys hanging from the windows, and Pinocchio had his own mailbox. The backdrop was the Swiss Alps, which helped hide the Casey Jr. train. From Geppetto's Village was a bridge that led to Pig Island, which was adorned with miniature oak trees and three little houses. The setting was staged so that it appeared that the Big Bad Wolf was nearby. Dividing the canal was Peter Pan's London Park with fully mature miniature trees and a gold statue of Peter Pan. Artists used bushes and fine grasses to create the miniature flora. They did not use bonsai trees. Instead, they created stunted trees by putting them in small pots and never letting the root systems expand.

Along another stretch of the canal was a collection of structures from *Alice in Wonderland,* including Alice's Cottage, the Old Mill, the Rabbit Hole, and the church with the stained glass window that Walt had played with in Burns's studio. Not far from Alice's world is Toad Manor, home of Mr. Toad.

Farther along the canal was the home of the Seven Dwarfs, with their diamond mine nearby. To get the right look for the Black Forest, Bill Evans tracked down a particular type of evergreen tree that is only found in Van Damme Beach State Park in Northern California. The trees were more than 150 years old and were naturally dwarfed. Because Evans could not buy the protected trees from the government, he found some on an adjacent property and brought those back to Disneyland.

The tallest visual element within the attraction was Cinderella's Castle. The castle was more than 15 feet tall, and designers had used forced perspective to make it appear even taller. The spires and roof were covered in gold leaf. A large area along one bank was covered with a patchwork of plants that resembled a quilt blanket. The original proposal included a giant's head and shoulders as if he were resting under a blanket. The giant would have limited animation, including his head gently rocking from side to side and his eyes moving. Walt decided against the idea because he felt it would spoil the tranquil feeling of the ride.

Just beyond the Giant's quilt were three old windmills. Walt suggested that tulips be planted in front of the windmills, so the Imagineers hired a horticulturist from the San Francisco Bay Area to locate miniature tulip plants that would fit the scale of the windmills. They found what they were looking for in New Zealand. The only problem was that the plants had 18-inch stems. This meant they had to be buried and hidden. In the end, the landscapers could not keep the plants alive, so they were removed.

According to Harriet Burns, Walt considered the Storybook Land Canal Boats as a placeholder attraction until he could develop something even grander. He said to Burns, "We can do this little ride, and it will be filler for the moment. Later on we can take it out and put something else there."[25]

The Skyway to Tomorrowland was another part of the expansion and opened on June 23. Like the steam trains that circled the park, the Skyway was a conveyance that provided guests an unobstructed preview of all four of Disneyland's realms." It helped guests orient themselves and plan the remainder of their day. The Skyway also gave "camera fans exceptional angles for their snapshots" and "treat[ed] riders to a unique aerial view of the Magic Kingdom," according to the publicity materials.

The Skyway gondola ride was the first of its kind in the United States. The cable and drive mechanism came from ski-lift builder Von Roll Company of Berne, Switzerland. The system installed at Disneyland consisted of new components as well as used equipment from the 1955 Rotterdam Fair and the German Federal Garden Show at Karsel, West Germany. The stranded cable extended 1,250 feet to connect Tomorrowland and Fantasyland. It was supported by four cross-braced towers. The tallest tower was 60 feet. The most prominent tower was the one on Holiday Hill.[26]

Imagineer Dick Stine designed the 42 spun-metal gondolas. Publicists promised that the "giant aluminum baskets" would "soar high in the air between these two lands, over Holiday Hill and the Tomorrowland Lake." Each gondola sat two guests on patio chairs that were bolted to the floor. The number of "buckets" could vary from 18 to 44, depending on the need. A one-way trip took 3½ minutes. In tribute to the ride's country of origin, the Fantasyland station was modeled after a Swiss chalet surrounded by a lush alpine garden; the Tomorrowland station was a modern "sky-station."

STALACTITE *and* STALAGMITE CAVERNS

IN A YEAR FILLED WITH AMAZING NEW ATTRACTIONS, the Rainbow Caverns Mine Train promised to be one of the most spectacular. At a reported cost of $500,000, it was also the most expensive addition. The attraction opened on July 2. Harper Goff worked on the original concept, and Bill Martin had begun serious planning right after the park opened. He had the difficult job of integrating the Pack Mules, the Stagecoaches, and the Conestoga Wagons into the same 7 acres.

The publicity materials spoke of guests boarding a "cinder-spouting mine train" for a journey around Rainbow Mountain, and then passing through Rainbow Desert into beautiful Rainbow Caverns and Fluorescent Waters. Guests would be treated to unusual natural features, such as the Underground River with flecks of gold and the Stalactite and Stalagmite Caverns, which featured "an unforgettable spectacle of multicolored waterfalls deep inside the mysteries of Rainbow Caverns." All of this, the materials promised, would be "presented with the world famous Disney touch." The Rainbow Caverns Mine Train was Disneyland's first "D" ticket attraction.

Instead of the promised "cinder-spouting" locomotives, these trains actually used electric motors powered by batteries stored in the tender car. The four locomotives were designed by Roger Broggie and painted green with wooden cabs. Walt wanted to use live steam locomotives, but he was stopped by Orange County officials, who were upset that Walt had three unlicensed steam engines already on the property. Apparently, nobody had pulled permits for the two Disneyland Railroad locomotives and the *Mark Twain*.

The mine trains were part of the Rainbow Mountain Mining and Exploration Company (R.M.R.R.). They were patterned after an early 1900s industrial steam engine but made to look older because of details like the wood-burner smokestack and the large box headlamp. They ran on 30-inch narrow-gauge track and measured 11 feet in length and 4 feet 4 inches in width.

Each locomotive pulled six ore cars. The ore cars were 8 feet 6 inches long and 4 feet 6 inches wide and could seat up to 10 guests on benches along the sides with a door and a jump seat. There was a little round speaker so guests could hear the live narration done by either the Engineer in the locomotive or the Brakeman in the rear. The train traveled more than 1,700 feet of track in a long figure eight. The ride took 7 minutes.

The backdrop for the loading area was the "little mining town" of Rainbow Ridge, a reproduction of a typical California mining town of the gold rush days, designed by Martin. He used forced perspective to re-create a frontier town with miniature facades for the Last Change Saloon, the El Dorado Hotel, and the Rainbow Ridge Clarion. Lillian Disney was fond of the set and could frequently be found walking along the pathway with her husband when they spent the night in the park.

The Mine Train's first destination was the Rainbow Desert, described in a brochure as "the most active desert region man has ever traversed." The trains passed by Coyote Rock, Elephant Rock, Natural Window Rock, and Inscription Rock. They saw the trail to Horse Thief Canyon and Dead Man's Spring. The most prominent feature was the Natural Arch Bridge. As the trains passed underneath the arch, guests frequently saw the Pack Mules crossing overhead. When the mules were within range, the trains were not allowed to blow their whistles for fear that they would scare the animals.

The Rainbow Desert was filled with gags. There were cactus characters, including one who wanted to "hitch a ride" and seven more that looked like the famous Disney dwarfs. There were sandstone buttes with tiny pueblos on top. The Devil's Paint Pots is where the train, Pack Mules, Conestoga Wagons, and the renamed Rainbow Mountain Stagecoaches crossed paths. This layering of attractions was a signature design element of Martin. The trains passed underneath the treacherous Balancing Rocks teetering precariously overhead.

The next destination was the Rainbow Caverns, designed by Claude Coats. He used ultraviolet lights similar to the Fantasyland dark rides, along with special effects using water and fountains to create a 2-minute grand finale. Walt was always on the lookout for anything that might be useful in his park. At some point, he learned of new fluorescent dyes that could go in water. He was already thinking about the mine train ride at the time, and this idea really captured his imagination. He thought it might be fun to have a mine train enter a mountain and inside would be a spectacular cavern filled with fluorescent waterfalls. He had the dye company come out to the Studio and turned to Coats because of his experience using black light in the Fantasyland dark rides. Coats began with sketches and storyboards. He made a mock-up with wood, just to find out how to handle the water and make it go into desired shapes, such as a witch, a cauldron, or an angel.

The interior of Rainbow Caverns was pitch black. The only illumination came from carefully hidden black lights reflecting upon the fluorescent materials. The room was filled with different colorful waterfalls and rivers. Coats had come up with many special effects that had never been tried successfully before. He was working on the grand finale called Rainbow Falls, where he wanted all six primary colors falling side by side in one big wide waterfall. He thought he could make the water flow in separate troughs; when it hit the bottom, he wanted to have them as close together as he could.

Working at the studio at the time as consultants to the "Man In Space" segments of the Disneyland television show were mathematician Heinz Haber and German rocket scientist Wernher von Braun. Haber took a look at Coats's waterfall and said that it was statistically impossible. No matter how hard Coats could try, the splashing between the waterfalls would make the water gray within a week. Coats told Walt what the mathematician said, and the boss simply replied, "Well, it's fun to do the impossible," and then he left.

Each waterfall had a name that reflected its special quality. Staircase Falls was all one color and shaped as a flight of steps. At Bridal Veil Falls, the waterfall seemed to outline a slender figure. Rainbow Falls was a spectacular colored light display. Others included Angel Falls, Paint Pot Falls, Geyser Grotto, Dance of the Seven Sisters, and Witches' Cauldron. A female choir accompanied by a theremin performed a haunting soundtrack for the ride.

The addition of the Mine Train meant changes to the original Frontierland attractions. The loading areas were arranged so that the Mine Train and Rainbow Ridge would be to the east, the Pack Mules were in the middle, and the Rainbow Mountain Stagecoaches and Conestoga Wagons shared the same loading area to the west. Because the show elements were primarily pointed toward the Mine Train, a trip on the Pack Mules or the wagons gave a whole different perspective.

The Pack Mules promised to take riders past frontier settlements into wilderness. They would follow Dinosaur Trail over Natural Bridge to Rainbow Mountain. In anticipation of larger crowds, 45 mules were added to the pack at a cost of $50 each. To increase capacity and minimize turnaround time, there were enough saddles and blankets on hand for every mule. The Rainbow Mountain Stagecoaches and Conestoga Wagons would go across the valley, under Natural Bridge into Rainbow Desert and return via Indian Territory and Wilderness River with a view of Tom Sawyer Island.

Disneyland celebrated the Fourth of July with a completely new Indian Village. The attraction was moved from its original location between the Golden Horseshoe Saloon and the Frontierland train station. A tunnel was built near Fowler's Harbor to create a transitional passageway and to set the Village apart from the rest of Frontierland. From the Indian Village, guests could see a demonstration of American Indian culture, watch the *Mark Twain*, Indian War Canoes, or the Mike Fink Keel Boats pass by, or glance over at the activity on Tom Sawyer Island at Fort Wilderness.

"When we worked on the films, we designed environments in a way so that a certain 'action' could happen," said John Hench.[27] "Everyone would work to support this, and avoid any element that would contradict the action, at the very least. We brought this ability to the designing of Disneyland, and we found that the 'action' was people enjoying themselves . . . having a great day . . . we wanted to create an environment that would support and enhance this."[28] The Indian War Canoes provided such an opportunity. They provided a rare chance for guests to roll up their sleeves and become part of the show.

The canoes were manufactured by the Old Town Canoe Company from Old Town, Maine. They were 30 feet long and made of varnished wood with a textured birch bark appearance. Electric motors were originally installed, but with the canoes loaded down with the weight of the passengers and the batteries, the batteries would run down, stranding guests in the middle of the river. The canoes were docked diagonally, which meant a relatively slow loading process. The 2,300-foot journey took approximately 10 minutes.

Each canoe sat 18 guests and was piloted by "real" American Indian guides at each end, known as the bowman and the sternman. Van France remembered, "We made quite a deal of our Indian Village.

Unfortunately, regardless of what you may have read in history, our Indians didn't know how to paddle their own canoes. They required special training."[29] The guests were treated to an exclusive look shared only by the *Mark Twain* and the Santa Fe & Disneyland Railroad of the new Chief Big Thunder figure making his debut on the Rivers of America. He was able to shift direction so that he could wave to both the paddle wheeler and the train as they passed by.

"One day Walt and his granddaughters wanted to go on a canoe ride, so we set off," said cast member Ray Van De Warker. "A child in a neighboring canoe shouted to us, 'Let's race!' Walt said, 'Sure.' We won the race, but by the end, Walt was soaked. When he got out of the canoe, he was grinning from ear to ear; his granddaughters had splashed him more than paddling the canoe did."[30]

The park celebrated its first anniversary on July 17, 1956, with a cumulative attendance nearing the 4 million mark, making it "the largest single private enterprise attraction in the Western Hemisphere."[31] About 41% of the guests had come from outside California. This was a remarkable achievement, considering the difficulty of transcontinental travel. The park claimed that guests from 64 nations had also visited that first year.

1. "Pirates Are Real in the Land of Fantasy," *Disneylander Magazine,* June 1958.
2. "People and Places in Disneyland," *Disneylander Magazine,* June 1957.
3. Randy Bright, *Disneyland: Inside Story* (New York: Abrams, 1987).
4. Ibid.
5. Disneyland Operations Department Group II, *Background Information: Adventureland, Frontierland, New Orleans* (Anaheim, CA: Disneyland, 26 Jan. 1970).
6. John Taylor, *Storming the Kingdom* (New York: Ballantine Books, 1988).
7. "Tourism Demands Increase," *Anaheim Bulletin,* 15 Sept. 1955.
8. Donald W. Ballard, *Disneyland Hotel: 1954–1959, The Little Motel in the Middle of the Orange Grove* (Fremont, CA: Magical Hotel, 2011).
9. *Cinerama Adventure,* dir. by David Strohmaier (Van Nuys, CA: C. A. Productions, 2002).
10. "Disney Disaster," *Los Angeles Times,* 23 Nov. 1994.
11. "Disneyland Art Director Bill Martin," *The "E" Ticket,* Number 20, Winter 1994–95, 10–19.
12. Bright, *Inside Story.*
13. Van Arsdale France, "Backstage Disneyland: A Personal History" (unpublished manuscript, 1980).
14. Ibid.
15. Ibid.
16. Ibid.
17. Ibid.
18. Disneyland University, "The Dream is a Reality" (Anaheim, CA: Disneyland, July 1975).
19. "Tom Sawyer Island," *The "E" Ticket,* Number 37, Spring 2002, 14–28.
20. Disneyland Operations Department Group II, *Adventureland, Frontierland, New Orleans.*
21. Ibid.
22. "Tom Sawyer Island," *The "E" Ticket,* Number 37, Spring 2002, 14–28.
23. "Flair and Versatility," *The "E" Ticket,* Number 44, Summer 2006, 28–41.
24. Ibid.
25. Ibid.
26. "A Bird's-Eye View of Fantasy and the Future," *Disneyland Line,* 4 Dec. 1992.
27. John Hench with Peggy Van Pelt, *Designing Disney: Imagineering and the Art of the Show* (New York: Disney Editions, Inc., 2008).
28. Ibid.
29. France, "Backstage Disneyland."
30. "A 'Beary' Peaceful Land Makes a Splash," *Disneyland Line,* 13 March 1992.
31. Disneyland, Annual Report to Lessees, 17 July 1958.

CHAPTER 4

HANDS-ON:
1956–1958

SOMETHING
WE DON'T HAVE

THE AUTOPIA MINIATURE CARS had turned out to be one of Disneyland's biggest moneymakers. It seems every child wanted to drive on the little freeway, and parents were happy to ride along. To increase capacity, the freeways were reconfigured as a double ride with an A side and a B side. A second loading platform was also built.

There was only one problem: the lack of reliable cars. Assigned the task of fixing his design, Bob Gurr started with the updated Mark III model with a Continental engine, a Ballock clutch, and an all-new gearbox. That worked—sort of. He continued to refine the cars based on the knowledge gained from the daily operations. The Mark IV model used a Kohler engine and a Dorris gearbox but retained the same body style and the removable drive unit with engine and driver's axle all in one unit.

Another way the Disney team built ride capacity was the quick addition of the Junior Autopia, which opened on July 23, 1956. It made sense to build on the Autopia's momentum, so Disney built a temporary attraction that would target younger, smaller guests. They found a dead area behind Fantasyland that had been used for the by-then-defunct Mickey Mouse Club Circus. The space was near the Main Street Omnibus stop, the Fantasyland train depot, and the always-troublesome Phantom Boats. Forty Mark II Autopia cars were modified with extender blocks on the pedals and booster seats. The steering was placed on the left side, and the cars drove counterclockwise around a one car–wide, dog bone–shaped roadway. It was the first ride where adults could not accompany their children.

A week later, the Mineral Hall opened in Frontierland. Guests could look at rocks glowing under ultraviolet or black light. This use of black light was considered novel at the time, and Mineral Hall is one of the few places in America where guests could buy one.

The attractions just kept coming online during the summer of 1956. At the turn of the previous century, many cities across America had an amusement park or beer garden at the end of the trolley line. Disneyland would be no different. On August 18, 1956, the Carnation Plaza Gardens opened at the end of Main Street, adjacent to Sleeping Beauty Castle. A dance floor was sheltered by a large red-and-white canopy. There were sandwiches, snacks, and ice cream, as well. During the day, guests could enjoy band concerts, while in the evening, the dance floor provided another reason for guests to extend their visits. (The Carnation Plaza Gardens was closed in 2012 and was rebuilt as the Fantasy Faire, a meet-and-greet location for the popular Disney princesses.)

On August 24, traffic on Main Street got even more congested with the addition of the Omnibus. Among Walt's massive collection of miniatures was a red model bus from Dinkie Toys of England. In May, Walt went to Gurr and suggested that Main Street needed an Omnibus. He sent Gurr to Travel Town in Griffith Park, where they had an omnibus on display. Gurr was especially pleased with this task, as his father and uncle both worked for the Los Angeles Transit Lines omnibuses.

The challenge was to get full-size adults into a double decker bus that had to fit the miniature scale of Main Street. Gurr started with a chassis from International Harvester that would typically be used for beer trucks. This allowed for a low inside center aisle. The truck weighed 8,500 pounds and was powered by a six-cylinder "in line" motor with a three-speed transmission. The two-level bus was beautifully detailed with leather and oak and painted by the Crown Coach Company. He used the same decorative tooling that was applied to the horse trolley cars. In the early days, the Omnibus would drive past the Plaza Hub, past Holiday Hill, and all the way to the Fantasyland train station.

At 222 Main Street at the northeast corner facing the hub, the vacant space became the INA Carefree Corner in September. It was sponsored by the Insurance Companies of North America and would become Disneyland's official guest registration and information center. The interior resembled a hotel lobby, where young ladies waited behind the registration desk and invited guests to sign one of the visitors' books with a quill pen. Guests could also pick up a guidebook. Other changes on

Main Street included the addition of the Jemrocks store and the glass blower in the Crystal Arcade; The Silhouette Shop replaced Grandma's Baby Shop. In December, Hollywood–Maxwell Intimate Apparel Shop, also known as The Wizard of Bras, closed. Pete Clark, who worked in the Disneyland merchandising department, said, "Nobody comes to Disneyland to look at corsets." On December 9, 1956, a second Horseless Carriage joined the fleet. This one was painted yellow and was a stretch version of the red car.

When the park opened, it had both pay and free toilets. This was common practice at the time. Rolly Crump recalled, "Walt went into the bathroom and noticed that all the free toilets were in use, but the paid ones were completely empty. [Walt] checked his pockets, and he didn't have a dime to get into one of the paid ones."[1] The next day, a frustrated Walt asked the maintenance team why there were both free and paid toilets; he was told, "Walt, people expect to pay for toilets because they're cleaner." He told them, "The thing that's going to make Disneyland successful is that our toilets are always going to be clean, and they're always going to be free."[2] Crump said, "They had already paid to get in; he didn't want them to have to pay to use the restrooms as well."[3]

Attendance had been a staggering 3.8 million in the first year. By October 3, 1956, the 5 millionth guest had arrived. Walt wanted a park that appealed to all ages, and he got it. For every child who visited there were four adults. The average guest spent an unheard of $2.37 on parking, admission, rides, amusements, and souvenirs. Since opening day, the park had added seven new rides and doubled the number of free exhibits. The most popular rides were Peter Pan, the Jungle River Boat Ride, the Santa Fe & Disneyland Railroad, and the Autopia Freeway. When surveyed, 98% of guests said they would recommend Disneyland to their friends and families and that they would come back.[4] Walt had a hit on his hands. Once again, he had read the moment right and made the bold decision as so often he had done before. Could it last?

On November 11, the park announced a major expansion slated to open in 1959. According to Walt, Liberty Square "will authentically bring to life the America as it was when this nation was founded. It will show the Founding Fathers as they lived and breathed, what they thought and meant when they created our republic." The main attraction would be "This 'Hall of Presidents,' or something like it." He said, "I feel very strongly about this. I'm afraid the American people today have forgotten what a land of opportunity this is, what a God-given heritage we've got here. When a poor boy like me can get as far as I've got, I know what it means. The American people today are spoiled. They're never satisfied."[5]

The area would have been a cul-de-sac extending northeast from Town Square. Themed to Colonial America, various craftsmen, such as silversmiths, weavers, and a blacksmith at work, would have been on display. The big attraction would be One Nation Under God. Inside would have been a Hall of the Declaration of Independence and the Hall of Presidents. Walt wanted the presidents "to be modeled life-size like a wax museum, and one at a time they would get up and through recorded actors' voices would recite something like the Gettysburg Address or an appropriate speech. But this idea is still in a development stage. It may not end up like this at all." He was determined. "If it costs $60 million to do it, we'll get the money from somewhere, somehow . . . the kids of this country ought to know." Walt told biographer Bob Thomas, "I'm trying to interest big companies to sponsor it, because I want the attraction to be free."[6]

A GOOD SYSTEM

"I CAN NEVER STAND STILL. I must explore and experiment. I am never satisfied with my work. I resent the limitations of my own imagination," Walt said.[7] He was always looking for ways to improve the park, and he began to have regular Saturday morning walks with his team in 1956 and 1957. This was Walt's way to look for new opportunities, fix things that were not right, and to keep in touch with his management team.

The walks would begin about 9 a.m. in Joe Fowler's office, downstairs in City Hall. The group usually consisted of Walt, Fowler, John Hench, Dick Irvine, Tommy Walker, Bill Martin, and Truman Woodworth, who was in charge of construction. They would walk through each land before the park opened and meet with each area manager of operations.

The group knew that Walt already had ideas floating around in his mind before the walks began. As they walked, he would point out things he wanted added or changed. He would suggest ideas and see what type of reaction he could get. The men would take notes. And sometimes they would bring along Marty Sklar and a cameraman from the Publicity Department. They would be shooting pictures of the things they saw and talked about. When they were done, everybody would go to Harvey's Lunchwagon and have hamburgers around noon.

The group would work on the suggestions and bring Walt some drawings after a day or two. He would then provide direction by saying, "Well, let's go a little farther with this" or "Let's change it to something like this." It was a good system and a testament to the remarkable achievements made by such a small number of people.

One of the ideas that Walt was already toying with was a replacement for the Storybook Land Canal Boats, just six months after its debut. Walt Disney Productions owned the rights to the Oz books by L. Frank Baum, with the exception of the most-famous first book, *The Wonderful Wizard of Oz*. Under development at the Studio at the time was a film called *Rainbow to Oz*. Walt wanted to find a way to exploit the property inside the park and asked Claude Coats to develop a new boat ride that would be larger than the Storybook Land Canal Boats and would incorporate the Casey Jr. train. He wanted to call the attraction Rock Candy Mountain.

As the boats entered the mountain, the guests would have been surrounded by a beautiful cavern and one of WED's first interactive scenes. Coats said, "Guests would have to come up with a password before the boat could view the miniatures inside the mountain. Password spoken, the guests would see beautiful scenes of Princess Ozma's birthday party."[8]

Artist and animator Rolly Crump built the first model. Crump started at the Studio in 1952, and this was his first assignment with WED. Coats liked Crump's ability to create kinetic sculptures. Crump started to build the large model, reportedly 8–10 feet long, with trees and rock outcrops made of chocolate, and marshmallow sauce for snow. As Crump continued to work, a consensus was growing at WED that it did not look very good. They decided it might be the materials Crump was using. Somebody suggested they use real candy and see what happened. That is what they did.

The Imagineers made a list of every kind of candy Walt loved as a child, and Coats went to the Toluca Mart and cleared out the shelves. They began to apply the candy to a huge clay model. Harriet Burns recalled that model builder "Fred Joerger had a sweet tooth and he'd say, 'One for you, one for me' [speaking to the mountain]!"[9]

Hench remembered, "The more candy we piled on this thing the worse it looked. It finally got nauseating, and even Walt got sick."[10] He added, "We learned a lesson . . . that you can't stand oversized food. If we had a 60-foot pumpkin pie, we'd hate it. We quit the thing right there, and Walt agreed with us." The (exterior) model was wheeled out to the parking lot and "left for the enjoyment of the local birds."[11]

BLOODMERE MANOR

WALT WAS ALWAYS LOOKING to the future and coming up with ideas to keep his people busy. He was getting interested in doing something with pirates or ghosts. In 1957, he asked artists Bruce Bushman and Duane Alt to draft some sketches for a pirate-themed wax-museum walk-through attraction. Both of the men took their work to Claude Coats for further refinement. This was the beginning of 10 years of development for one of WED's greatest achievements, The Haunted Mansion.

In early 1957, Walt told Ken Anderson that he wanted to build a haunted house. However, this would be no ordinary haunted house but something that had never been seen before. Walt told Bob Thomas, "I'm told I'm not supposed to scare the public, but shucks, people like to be scared."[12] He wanted to set the haunted house in New Orleans.

Anderson realized after this meeting that this was a one-man project at this point, and his job was to get the ideas started. Walt did not give him much direction at first, so Anderson started by visiting haunted houses in Louisiana.

As the men worked on ideas, they considered using actors James Mason or Peter Lore as the narrator but decided that the best host would be Walt himself. Walt even suggested a story line. As the guests arrived, they would find a wedding taking place inside the house. They even considered using some of Universal Studios' famous monsters such as Dracula and Frankenstein.

Anderson envisioned the house as a large antebellum mansion, out in the Louisiana bayou, all rotten and moldy. Because Walt had a fetish for cleanliness, he figured he could place the house on a back street behind a grove of trees. Once they passed through the iron gates, they would see the mansion. Along the path shaded by magnolias and southern oaks would be a graveyard. Suddenly, they would see a big moss-covered haunted house with faces that seemed to appear in the upper windows. Walt did not approve. He wanted his haunted house to be as clean and pristine as the rest of his park.

Anderson drafted an elaborate backstory to support the attraction on February 1, 1957. As the story goes, the mansion belonged to Captain Bartholomew Gore, a wealthy sailing merchant, who built the

Southern antebellum home for his young bride, circa 1810. They called the home Bloodmere. After moving into the home, the wife discovered her husband's secret identity—that of a bloodthirsty pirate. The husband killed his bride in a rage, and her ghost haunted the house, eventually driving the pirate to suicide. Together, the newlyweds walk the halls of the Haunted Mansion. The reason the "mansion" was moved to Disneyland intact was that Walt felt "it was such a fine example of early architecture from that section of our country." Run down, the Disney staff started restoration right away but "strangely enough . . . the work of each day was destroyed during the night . . . and the night watchman reported that when he had passed the house he'd heard eerie screams and weird lights." Guests were supposed to try and solve the mystery of the bride and groom as they walked through the house.

The prerecorded Walt tells visitors, "The house has proved too dangerous to be lived in, but we have succeeded in making it safe enough for a visit . . . it mysteriously remains always night within the house . . . the night in which all ghosts are condemned to exist . . . we recommend that you stay close together during your visit, and please, above all, obey your guide's instructions." Guests would be grouped into parties of 40. Researchers were sent to the Winchester Mystery House in San Jose to study traffic flow. To get an idea about timing, they tested moving groups of 20–40 people using the *Zorro* television sets in October.

In the proposed attraction, a guide dressed as a butler walks the groups of 40 through seven rooms loaded with special effects. Guests would see portraits that would change, trophy busts with movable eyes, a ghost that would follow you in the mirror, and weird theme music as you moved from room to room. The guide would disappear through secret panels and appear in the next room. Sometimes a guest would be invited to do the same. The overall atmosphere was a house that was moldy and filled with rats and bats. The floors would creak and give the impression that they are so rotten and unsafe that the guests might feel like they are about to fall through the floor to the bayou below.

The tour groups would walk into a room "with famous ghosts in attendance, such as Anne Boleyn's decapitated head, the ghostly groom, the Lonesome Ghost, and the Headless Horseman" preparing for a wedding ceremony. Next was a two-story room with a balcony overlooking a "great hall" where ghosts were at a banquet table with a wedding cake. There would be an "invisible ghost playing a pump organ." The bride would appear with glowing eyes and a visible beating red heart.

In December 1957, Anderson, along with Bob Mattey, filled up a sound stage at the Studio just as if it were to be transplanted to the park. The expectation was that each group of 40 would move through each room in 1½ minutes. That way, over a 10-hour day, up to 16,000 guests could experience the attraction. After the test, it was determined that there was no way they could get that many people to walk through within the time allowed and to enjoy all of the effects.

Anderson went back to the drawing board and came back a week later with the suggestion to gather people on a porch, then enter a room and have the guests board a "temporary" vehicle that looked like it was made up of two-by-fours and painted with primer. This was the only vehicle the ghosts would allow inside the building. The cart would descend into the basement and then move through the attraction. At the time, the technology was not available. This would be a reoccurring theme at Disneyland. Often the ideas surpassed the existing technology but became the motivation for innovation.

Some of the other special effects described in Anderson's draft survived all the way to the final show, such as a ghost granny rocking in a chair, the "Ghost Host," the changing portraits, the bride, and the hanging corpse in the stretching room. The stretching room was an elevator that brought guests to a basement and a tunnel, which then led to a show building on the other side of the berm, where the attraction was going to be placed. The fact there are two stretching rooms is a reflection of a time when they were going to build two haunted houses to increase capacity. The sticking point was the exterior appearance of the mansion and the way to move people through the attraction. The project was put on hold.

unofficial **TIP**
In tribute to Ken Anderson's original story contributions, the weathervane on top of the Haunted Mansion is a sailing ship.

THERE WAS SOMETHING MISSING

THE PARK NEEDED TO ADD even more capacity fast, so they purchased an off-the-shelf amusement ride from Arrow Development, called it the Midget Autopia, and opened the attraction on April 13. They were not like the other Autopia cars where the driver was in control. The Midget Autopia cars were simple four-wheel dark ride cars that followed the electrical bus bar down the center of the pathway. They ran on 24 volts of direct current on an open bus bar, and the cars picked up electricity with a single shoe arrangement, underneath. That's the same technology used on almost all dark rides.

The track was mostly level, with a low hilltop that went over a 30-foot tunnel. The track went counterclockwise. As the little cars approached a garage, the doors would swing open. The staff disliked working at the attraction because they had to bend over all the time. The attraction was only open in the summer and on weekends.

Most guests did not realize that Sleeping Beauty Castle was empty. It was just a shell, a stage set made of wood and fiberglass with only one piece of steel in the whole thing. It was not always meant to be that way. Bill Martin recalled a time when he wanted to install a camera obscura in the highest tower of the castle so that people could see the whole park from that vantage point. Walt had Eustace Lycet, the head of the Studio Camera Department, go to Santa Monica to see their camera obscura along the coastline. When he reported back, he said there was not enough light for the 40-foot throw, so the tower became just a tower.

unofficial **TIP**
A December 27, 1956, memo outlined a children's-only area called Mouseatopia, with a helicopter ride, a boat ride, and the Midget Autopia. Only the car ride was built.

One day, Walt, Ken Anderson, and set designer Emil Kuri decided to peek into the castle to see what could be done. Kuri was in a white suit, and when they opened the door they found dozens of cats. Within minutes Kuri's white suit was black with fleas. All three men turned around and ran. The park found homes for all of the animals.

It was decided to build a walk-through attraction. Anderson started by modifying the castle exterior to fit in the attraction because the structure was not originally designed to be occupied. The two retail shops flanking the castle were reduced in size and the ceilings lowered. Windows were moved and doorways were cut into the walls. Most notably, the arches that had been open on opening day were enclosed to house the room with the Goons.

Anderson worked alongside artist Eyvind Earle to create the new attraction. Earle had a very distinctive style, and Walt had turned over much of the design of the animated film *Sleeping Beauty* to Earle, so Walt could concentrate on Disneyland. The quality that Walt was striving for in the film was a moving tapestry, and Earle was the one artist with the vision to accomplish that goal.

Guests entered a new door carved into the side of the castle. At the entrance was a beautifully hand-engraved storybook in the unique style of Earle. As guests walked through the castle, there were little dioramas made primarily of plywood and using forced perspective and special effects to add depth. Each of the displays was about the size of a closet, and guests would walk up, one at a time, and peek through a window. The dioramas were developed well before the movie was completed, and a number of the scenes did not match the story the public would see when the film was released in 1959.

Many of the special effects that Anderson utilized would be later adopted in other Disneyland attractions. It was the first use of the Pepper's Ghost effect at Disneyland, which would be used throughout the Haunted Mansion. The gag was based on a Victorian-era illusion called "Pepper's Ghost" that used reflective glass and special lighting effects to make objects seem transparent. According to Rolly Crump, Yale Gracey learned of this trick while reading *The Boy Mechanic*. The Waltz of the Spinning Wheels appeared to be set in an endless chamber of countless spinning wheels much like the Haunted Mansion's endless hallway.

Gracey would become legendary at WED. Bob Gurr said, "Of all the people at the Studio, Yale was always just there. He would literally sit in his room and fiddle with his stuff, and occasionally invent something . . . and Walt was totally happy with that. Yale always puffed on a little pipe and was very quiet. He often had a little smile on his face, and if you got near his room he'd say, 'Hey Bob, you want to see something?' He'd show you what he had going, and take the pipe out of his mouth, give a little puff and wait for your response. That was the setting around Yale Gracey."[13]

Using reflective glass, Crump and Gracey came up with an illusion for one sequence where the goons are dancing around in the smoke. The goons scene was a particular favorite. Originally, the plan was to allow guests to stand on the balcony on the backside of the castle overlooking Fantasyland. It was felt that this would cause congestion problems, so the team came up with a better solution: As guests peeked through little holes, they were startled to see someone staring right back at them. They were looking at a reflection of their own eyes through the use of dozens of tiny mirrors carefully aligned toward the peek hole.

Another fun special effect could be found at the bottomless pit. Guests could lean into a shallow area that seemed infinite due to mirrors above and below. They were able to hear their own words repeated due to a custom-made recording mechanism with a continuous loop passing over one recording and several playback heads giving the illusion of an echo.

Wathel Rogers prepped the show for Walt's inspection. He said, "When we did the final scene in the Sleeping Beauty Castle Walk-Thru, I had all the effects going—the birds were flying, the music building, the moonbeam sparkling. But Walt felt there was something missing." Walt said, "Make her eyelids open as she's waking up." So that is what Rogers did. After the attraction opened, Rogers said, "I stood in the shadows watching the guests, and they never said a word about the birds or other effects. To their delight, they did notice her eyes actually opening."[14] The attraction opened on April 28, 1957. Shirley Temple was the guest of honor at the grand opening, and guests were given a full-color, 12-page, fold-out booklet describing the exhibit.

An INNOVATOR *and a* THINKER

MONSANTO HAD BEEN ONE of the original lessees and had been happy with the initial response to the Hall of Chemistry. In 1956 Walt called John Hench about a new Monsanto exhibit called the "House of the Future." Walt learned of a project that began in 1953 between Monsanto and Architects Richard Hamilton and Marvin Goody of Massachusetts Institute of Technology (MIT) Department of Architecture, as well as engineer Albert G. H. Dietz of the Plastics Research Laboratory, MIT Department of Building and Engineering and Construction. The project was sponsored by Monsanto's Plastics Division.

The chemical giant wanted to expand its presence in the home construction industry. The goal for the project was to design a house that would explore the maximum structural and aesthetic use of plastics as a material for home construction. The team was given one rule. They were not to substitute plastic for standard materials—for example, no fiberglass two-by-four studs or polyester roofing shingles.

The Monsanto "House of the Future" opened on June 12, 1957. This was exactly the type of exhibit Walt wanted for Tomorrowland. To ensure the largest possible audience, the attraction was free. This would be a chance for guests to really test-drive the future. "Walt was a firm believer in experience," said Hench. "He said that experiences were the only thing that you really own. They were yours. The example he would talk about was with apples. He said you could see pictures of apples, but you didn't know what an apple was until you sank your teeth into one. Then it was a matter of experience." Hench believed the attraction "gave people that kind of experience . . . they could come in and walk through and sit in a futuristic idea, rather than just hearing about them, or seeing pictures of them."[15] Walt was a big believer in the power of American free enterprise and technology. He used his fame to allow his Imagineers to visit major corporations and see what they were up to. It was important to Walt that Tomorrowland reflect his optimism.

The 1,280-square-foot house was placed in a prime undeveloped area to the left of the entrance to Tomorrowland. The design was a white cruciform with four curved wings cantilevered from a 256-square-foot central core. The central core also housed the air temperature control units. A cruciform was chosen because it ensures full daylight for every room, reduces inter-room noise, and provides added privacy for various family activities.

The modular structure was made of polyester reinforced with 10 layers of hand-laminated fiberglass. The material and methodology were similar to those developed by Charles Eames and Eero Saarinen for molded plastic chairs in the 1940s. Each wing was 8 feet tall, 16 feet wide, and 16 feet long. The house had three bedrooms, two baths, a living room, a dining room, a family room, and a kitchen. The house reflected what *Architectural Forum* magazine predicted the future would look like, with "new forms as graceful as spiderweb suspensions, giant seashells, the branches of trees and soap bubbles" made possible with the new building materials that will become available.[16] Engineer Albert Dietz said, "The 'House of the Future' was designed for a jam-packed cocktail party in a howling windstorm during an earthquake." Monsanto described it as "strangely graceful."[17]

It was estimated that if the homes had been mass produced in a central factory, the average cost would have been $15,000 to $18,000 in 1957, the equivalent of $125,000 to $150,000 in 2013. The house was virtually indestructible. Because it was set on a 16- by 16-foot pedestal, the house could be placed almost anywhere. The house was designed to be expanded if necessary. The bottom was a compression member, and the top had a tension ring that the modules hooked on to and hung from. You could just hang more pairs of them as needed. The design also solved many problems of traditional housing, such as termites and flooding, and problems like the foundation settling.

Guests entered the house through the dining and family room. All of the furniture was ultramodern, made of plastic materials with an anti-gravity aesthetic featuring lots of nylon wires, thin metal legs, and painted supports for the built-ins. The laminates and plastic finishes were done in turquoise, salmon, and ivory. Walt proudly proclaimed, "Hardly a natural material appears anywhere in the House." According to *The "E" Ticket* Disney fan magazine, "Veteran Monsanto House attendants would bet new employees that they could predict whether the next guest through the door would be male or female. To the puzzlement of the novice, the other was always right. The secret . . . on a certain step on the stairway entrance, men would invariably rap on the side of the plastic exterior just to see if it was built solid."[18] The result was a spot that got worn and dirty every day and required regular touchups with plastic-based exterior paint from the National Lead Company. Women also had their predictable behavior. They reached over the rope to touch the clothes in the closet so often the clothes would get worn. It wasn't long before the clothes were wrapped in plastic sheeting.

The Atoms for Living Kitchen was designed by the Kelvinator Division of American Motors Corporation. It was a "step saver" kitchen where many of the appliances either dropped from cabinets or popped up from the counter. The dishwasher used ultrasonic waves to clean and was also the storage unit for the plastic dishes. Instead of one large refrigerator freezer unit, the house featured three cooling units called "cold zones" that lowered from ceiling cabinets: one zone for regular refrigeration, one for frozen, and one for irradiated foods. Even the storage shelves lowered from the ceiling unit with the push of a button. The microwave oven was hidden in a counter. The Armstrong Cork Company provided foam-backed plastic floor covering embedded with pearl flakes with controlled resiliency and noise-reducing properties. Sylvania Electric Products Company provided adjustable lighting behind polarized plastic ceiling tiles to light the room. Bell Telephone installed the push-button speakerphone with "preset" dialing. The climate control system allowed for different temperatures in different zones within the house. There were even buttons the occupant could push to release the scent of roses or the ocean into any room.[19]

Next was the children's room. The room was divided in two by a sliding accordion panel, one side for the boy and one for the girl. Plastic allowed for "tough durable materials that are easily washable." The children shared a bathroom, which had a movable sink that rose and fell at the push of a button.

The master bedroom and bathroom were the next display. For the lady, there was a vanity with a push-button speakerphone. The master bath was modeled in two pieces and inspired by inventor, designer, and futurist Buckminster Fuller's all-metal, one-piece bathroom unit. It was amoeboid in shape and made efficient use of the space. There were a built-in electric razor and toothbrush plus another hands-free push-button phone mounted on the wall. This phone contained a closed-circuit television so the occupant could see who was at the front door. The ceiling lighting was adjustable and had Panelescent panels, which acted as a night-light. There was even a sound system in the shower.

The spacious living room featured a giant, non-operational, wall-mounted television screen and built-in stereo system. The linear furniture "hovered" above a striped Acrilan carpet. John Hench designed the "Alpha" chair, the first contoured chair that adjusted automatically, as well as a phone and music system with built-in speakers. Facing Sleeping Beauty Castle were ceiling-to-floor thermal-pane picture windows featuring decorative laminated safety glass. At night, when the home would glow with all of the lights on, it added a special magic to the area. Malibu lights adorned the garden.

The Monsanto "House of the Future" represented Walt's vision for Tomorrowland. This was an opportunity for the average person to experience the leading edge of technology and to not fear the future. He was so excited about the project he suggested to his daughter Diane and her husband Ron Miller that they should consider living in one. The Millers decided that it was not for them.

TWO HEADS
for ONE *of* YOURS

The Santa Fe & Disneyland Viewliner made its debut on June 21, 1957, in Tomorrowland. Originally called the Blue Streak Express Train and dubbed the Train of the Future, the two streamlined trains were patterned after the Aerotrain, an experimental train built by General Motors in Pontiac, Michigan. Three Aerotrains had been produced and leased to the Rock Island, Pennsylvania, and New York Central Railroad lines. They were designed to travel at an average speed of 100 mph. Santa Fe had tested one in 1956 and was considering adding them to their fleet. Both the railroad and Disneyland saw this as an opportunity. The theme park version would be built at ½ scale.

Bob Gurr was assigned the task of designing and engineering the two trains. They were built at the Studio and ran on a 30-inch track, which was narrower than the Santa Fe & Disneyland Railroad's narrow-gauge track. There was a locomotive, four center cars, and one observation car all wrapped in a sleek aluminum body. The train was powered by a Chevrolet Corvette engine and could travel at speeds up to 30 mph. The train was difficult to operate due to the wheel spin from the eight-wheel drive system.

There were two stations. The Red train ran out of the Tomorrow-land Station, and the Blue train used the Fantasyland station. Two streamlined trains ran on a continuous loop in Disneyland's northeast corner. At one point, the track paralleled the Disneyland Railroad, creating quite the contrast.

The Aerotrain turned out to be a dud for the railroads and never met expectations. They were plagued with problems, right-of-way issues negated any speed advantages, and the public was not impressed. By 1957, the New York Central and Pennsylvania railroads returned their trains, and Santa Fe never moved forward with their project. By this time, Walt was done with the Santa Fe & Disneyland Viewliner. He already had his eyes set on a monorail, something he had wanted from the very beginning. The ride lasted just over one year.

When the attraction was dismantled, Walt tried to give the 1,100 railroad ties to Ward Kimball, but Ward did not need them for his backyard railroad. Instead, animator Ollie Johnston took them home for his backyard railroad. Disneyland tried to donate the trains to be used as parking lot trams for the proposed Los Angeles Dodger stadium in Elysian Park and as a way to connect the stadium to Griffith Park. Neither plan was realized, and the trains were scrapped.

The Motor Boat Cruise was another addition that opened in June. The little boats were a lot like a Fantasyland dark ride where the guests had no control over their vehicle, they just went for the ride. The boats had a bench seat big enough for two adults and one or two small children. The kids could play with the nonfunctional steering wheel placed in the middle of the dashboard. There was a gas pedal, but it mostly made for a louder sound and not a faster ride. The boat was on a track, and Joe Fowler insisted that the propeller be in front and the engine in the back for safety reasons. There was nothing to look at other than glimpses of the steam trains and the Santa Fe & Disneyland Viewliner.

Just outside the berm, along West Street, was the first new "land" since the grand opening. Holidayland was a corporate playground designed by Sam McKim. It opened on June 16. Walt wanted to have a place where large groups could meet and then enjoy the park. Facilities included a large circus tent, a baseball diamond, and picnic grounds. There was also a separate entrance that let guests enter via Frontierland. (Holidayland closed in the fall of 1961.)

Disneyland was performing well financially by 1957. With Roy's confidence finally firmly in place, Walt Disney Productions increased its ownership in Disneyland, Inc. to 65.52% on June 1. They exercised options to the selling shareholders Walt Disney, WED Enterprises, and Western Printing and Lithographing, Co.

The Jungle Cruise was about to get some enhancements. Walt was frustrated that the jungle did not look jungly enough for the first three years. Bill Evans tried to overcome this limitation by adding a tropical rain forest with brilliant orchids ablaze with color. They added a couple of gorillas, more native dancers, and a war party trying to attack the boat. Also, Trader Sam, the "head" salesman, made his first appearance.

Not everything made it off the drawing board. Sam McKim worked on a gag that had a chimpanzee tossing coconuts over the heads of the guests to another chimpanzee. The target chimpanzee would duck at the last second and not get hit. Then he would pick up a coconut and toss it back. Walt took one look and just said no.

Frontierland was also seeing changes. Starting on July 1, guests could access Tom Sawyer Island from two new rafts, the *Becky Thatcher* and the *Injun Joe,* departing from the Indian Village and arriving at Huck's Landing. The two original rafts could be found by the Plantation House near the Frontierland bridge. The extra rafts were needed because of all of the new elements that had been added to the island. Herb Ryman and Claude Coats designed a barrel bridge. A tree house was built on Lookout Point. A giveaway map drawn by Coats proclaimed the tree house "the highest point in Disneyland." Children could climb Castle Rock or crawl into the Castle Dungeon. Merry-go-Round Rock was very popular, as was the Pontoon Bridge.

Young gunfighters could test their skills at the new Frontierland Shootin' Gallery starting July 12. The attraction, which replaced a corral of ponies, started as an outdoor gallery but soon was placed indoors. Guests could choose from 16 guns. The unique air guns were manufactured by Mac Glassine Guns and had power comparable to a .22-caliber rifle. The extra-soft lead bullets imported from Australia were sold in tubes of 14 shots.[20] Because they were using lead pellets, the Sam McKim–designed shooting range had to be repainted every night. This was another example of the maintenance attitude in Disneyland that would become one of the park's trademarks.

Another addition to Frontierland was not so obvious. One of the things Walt loved to do was to add little surprises throughout the park that guests could stumble upon. They were known as interstitials, events between the major events. One example was the petrified tree in Frontierland.

In July 1956, Walt and Lillian had driven through Colorado, near Pike's Peak, just outside of Colorado Springs. Walt saw a sign for PET-RIFIED TREES FOR SALE at Pike's Petrified Forest. He pulled in and told Lillian to wait in the car. She was not happy with the detour and was starting to get agitated. When her husband returned, he proudly proclaimed that he had just bought her anniversary present; a petri-fied tree stump. The 5-ton stump was still in Colorado on their 31st anniversary on July 13, 1956. When she said that it was too big for the mantel, Walt brought it down to Disneyland. On Walt and Lillian's 32nd anniversary, July 13, 1957, the 10-foot tree stump was installed next to the Rivers of America.

The park was also reaching out to serve its guests in unexpected ways. The Disneyland Baby Station on Main Street made it easier for parents to change diapers, prepare formulas, and feed their infants. Ken-L-Land, a dog and cat "motel" adjacent to the main entrance, could house up to 160 pets.[21] For 25¢, pets were placed in an "airy" individual enclosure and given food and water. Over the years, the kennel would see a whole menagerie of animals, including rabbits, chickens, pigs, mice, and birds. At one point, a guest left a cricket in a bamboo cage. Even more exotic animals, including skunks, mountain lion cubs, snakes, and even a horse, have found their way there.[22]

Changes along Main Street U.S.A. included the addition of The Merv Taylor Magic Shop in the 100-even block, taking over the spot from Wonderland Music Company. Across the street, the Imported Candy store opened, taking over from Sunny View Farms. The Art Gallery also opened. Disneyland's Christmas present to itself was a second Omnibus for Main Street. When there was only one Omnibus, it would leave Main Street and drive all the way back to the Mickey Mouse Club Circus. The practice was stopped for safety reasons when the second Omnibus was added, and it was determined that the path-way was too narrow for two vehicles. Another consideration was an Omnibus did not fit the theming of Fantasyland.

As the year closed, on December 21, 1957, the 10 millionth guest walked through the gates. Annual attendance grew to 4.3 million.

WILD TURKEYS

THE *FRED GURLEY* joined the Disneyland and Santa Fe Railroad fleet on March 28, 1958. Locomotive #3 was named after the 1958 chairman of the board of the Santa Fe Railroad. While the *Ripley* and *Holliday* locomotives were scaled-up versions of Walt's backyard railroad, "They started that way because they didn't know better at the time," said animator and train buff Ward Kimball. "I remember that it cost $50,000 each just to make the frames for the engines and now it would be an enormous amount of money. Later it was decided, for this reason, to look into the locomotives that were being sold down in the South, at lumber companies and so forth. The decision was made to buy those that were 3-foot gauge and just throw away everything but the frames, save all that money, and get a locomotive for a fraction of the cost of starting from drawings."[23] The *Gurley* was the first narrow-gauge industrial engine to be rebuilt for the park.

Jerry Best, a railroad historian and associate of the Studio, found an 1894 Baldwin 4-4-0 Forney that ran in New Orleans on the 24-mile-long LaFourche, Raceland & Lockport sugar plantation railroad. In 1910, the locomotive was moved to the Godchaux Sugar Co. in Reserve, Louisiana, where it ran until it was retired in 1956. Best found the engine at a storage shed owned by C. W. Witbeck. Roger Broggie paid $1,200 for the locomotive, loaded it up in a boxcar, and had it shipped back to Los Angeles for refurbishment.

The locomotive was disassembled and rebuilt at the Studio shops. A boiler was fitted with both a new water tank and an oil tank. A "pony truck" was installed in front—thereby converting the engine into a 2-4-0—and an old-fashioned curved-window cab was added. Much of the work was done by Arnold Lindberg.

Along with the new locomotive were new rolling stock and a new destination. The brand-new five-car train was inspired by the open-sided Narragansett cars used during the summer months for rides in the country and at mountain and seaside resorts. The seats faced toward the inside of the park, giving guests a much better show and making loading and unloading quicker.

Starting on March 31, 1958, guests were invited to take a trip through the *Grand Canyon Diorama,* the world's largest three-dimensional scenic display. The attraction was based on the 1958 Disney CinemaScope film *Grand Canyon.* At a cost of $435,000, artists took "more than 80,000 man-hours of design, painting, and construction to complete the first 'reproduction' of Arizona's famed Grand Canyon," according to an early press release. The 306-foot background was painted on a seamless, handwoven canvas prepared especially for the park. The palette included 14 colors, and more than 300 gallons of paint was used.

The *Disneyland Gazetteer* said the attraction "portrays the famous Grand Canyon of the Colorado River at early morning, as the sun sets and during a thunder and lightning storm. Even the seasons vary from Spring in an adobe village of Pueblo Indians to Winter snows covering the trees and wild animals."[24] The soundtrack was Ferde Grofé's "Grand Canyon Suite."

Walt got the idea for the diorama while visiting museums in Los Angeles and New York. He found Bob Sewell, who worked at the Los Angeles Museum of Natural History for 10 years, to help out. Claude Coats also got involved. "Walt sent me down to the Grand Canyon to get the right look of it, and what it should be like," he said. "We did storyboards once again, and Walt liked pretty much all of it."[25] Coats added some wild turkeys roosting in a tree and Walt said, "They don't have wild turkeys in the Grand Canyon." Coats disagreed with his boss and told him that he saw some in a museum.

Later, when Walt was showing the storyboards to a guest, he asked, "Do you know they have wild turkeys in the Grand Canyon?" The guest replied, "Gee, no I didn't know that." Feeling confident, Walt turned to Coats and asked again, "Are you sure they've got wild turkeys in the Grand Canyon?" Coats was ready. Prior to the meeting he called the park superintendent responsible for the Grand Canyon. "Yes, and the flocks are on the increase!"[26]

Emile Kuri directed the taxidermy staff. The diorama included mountain lions, deer, desert-mountain sheep, other birds and animals native to Arizona, and wild turkeys. All of the natural materials had to be treated with flame retardants. The project would prompt a new policy at Disneyland. One day Walt was giving a tour at WED when they walked into Bud Washo's shop. Walt opened up the freezer and saw a frozen carcass of a skinned coyote, left there by the taxidermist. The diorama would be the last time that real animal skins would be used in an attraction. Walt did not want to get the reputation that Disneyland killed animals for the rides.

Another BIG BOAT

"THE *MARK TWAIN* and Tom Sawyer Island Rafts were running, but the *Columbia* wasn't there yet," recalled Ron Dominguez. "That was one of the things Walt Disney wanted. He liked to see the Rivers of America busy, and when it opened, it was just the *Mark Twain*. He'd sit up there at the Chicken Plantation House and do some of his dreaming about expansion and he wanted the river busy and exciting."[27] Walt asked Admiral Joe Fowler to look for a second ship, and Fowler went around to various maritime museums to find the right one. He recommended the *Columbia,* the first American ship to circumnavigate the globe. The original had been built in Plymouth, Massachusetts, in 1787. At lunch, Walt asked renowned ship builder Ray Wallace to come up with a drawing of the *Columbia Redivia,* which Wallace did on a napkin. Then Sam McKim stepped in with some conceptual work.

It was on one of those days at the Swift's Chicken Plantation House when Dick Nunis, who was the manager of Frontierland, met with Walt to survey the traffic along the river. According to Disney biographer Bob Thomas, "The *Mark Twain* was pulling away from the dock, one keelboat was landing at the pier as another departed, two rafts were crossing to Tom Sawyer Island, and three Indian Canoes were racing around the

unofficial **TIP**
Ray Wallace based *Columbia Redivia* on blueprints of the *Bounty,* which was considered very similar.

bend. 'Look at that!' Walt exclaimed. Nunis expected him to complain about the congestion, but Walt said, 'Now there's a busy river! What we need is another big boat.'" When Nunis asked Walt what kind of boat, Walt replied, "Not just another stern-wheeler. This time we need a sailing ship. I think we should have a replica of the *Columbia.* Did you know that was the first American vessel to sail around the world?"[28]

At a cost of $100,000, the *Columbia* sailing ship set sail on June 14, 1958. The ship was a full-scale replica at 83 feet, 6 inches long and 84 feet high above the weather deck. It was the first three-masted windjammer built in the United States in more than 100 years. The ship was made of Douglas fir, oak, and mahogany. It was powered by two 150-horsepower DC electric motors with two 30-inch propellers and a top speed of 1.3 knots.[29] The guide mechanism was the same as the *Mark Twain* and allowed for a simulated "rudder action."

The superstructure was built at the Walt Disney Studios. Walt personally put a dollar under each mast for good luck before it was set. The *Columbia*'s 90-foot flat-bottom hull was built in Todd Shipyards and trucked into the parking lot. From there it was lifted onto three flatcars by the Main Street Station and brought around to the Frontierland depot. The hull was lifted from the train sideways and hoisted into the dry dock at Fowler's Harbor.

The recorded narration track by "Old Salty" was done by Golden Horseshoe favorite Fulton Burley. A full load was 305 guests, and the journey around the river took approximately 16–17 minutes.

DOWN *the* RABBIT HOLE

THE SAME DAY THAT THE *Columbia* set sail in Frontierland, Alice in Wonderland opened in Fantasyland. If the first three Fantasyland dark rides represented drama, humor, and beauty, Alice in Wonderland represented, like the 1951 film, a bit of craziness. Walt put Claude Coats in charge; Alice was Coats's first show design credit. Coats had worked on the original film; he was assisted by Colin Campbell, Blaine Gibson, and Ken Anderson on the attraction. Like many of the Disneyland attractions, this one started out as a walk-through. Instead, it was decided to build a two-story ride above Mr. Toad. Since the ride was designed later than the other dark rides, it was more dimensional, with animated three-dimensional characters in Tulgey Wood. It also had an unusual outside track section.

Coats had plenty of room to play with, and he wanted to come up with a more elaborate queue than the other three dark rides. Some of the early ideas included a scene in the English countryside and Bill Martin's little cottage with Alice's feet sticking out of the windows just like in the film. The exterior became a garden of giant dandelions and stylized blades of grass.

Once the attraction design evolved from a walk-through into a ride, the first proposal was to have guests ride on a deck of cards. Walt did not like that idea and suggested a caterpillar. Coats designed the distinctive two-toned, five-passenger "Caterpillar" cars. Gibson molded a three-dimensional model of Coats's design and then blew that up to a full-size clay model for the fabrication process. Coats later learned that his vehicle design was patented and he earned an additional $10.

Bob Gurr stepped in to help with the engineering. He purchased car frames from Arrow Development and added the caterpillar bodies. The Alice vehicles were longer than the other dark rides, allowing for two rows of seats, and slower (4 feet per second) because they were heavier. Gurr installed the lowest gear ratio he could use to get the caterpillars up the steep incline to the second floor. The 16 cars rode along a 764-foot guide rail with 38 volts. They were powered by a one-horsepower motor.

Like the other dark rides, it was assumed that the guests would play the role of the lead character. In this case, neither Alice nor the caterpillar was seen inside the attraction. Narration was done by Kathryn Beaumont, who voiced Alice in the film. Guests purchased their tickets at a giant mushroom, boarded their caterpillar, and descended down the Rabbit Hole, where a large convex mirror would turn their reflections upside down. When they entered The Upside Down room, all of the distorted dimensional furniture was hung from the ceiling.

The next scene was the Oversized Room. Guests were dwarfed by a 15-foot chair and the Cheshire Cat sitting on a 6-foot footstool. The ramp to the second floor was decorated as the Garden of Live Flowers. Flowers with dimensional heads lined the corridor, singing "All in the Golden Afternoon."

Tulgey Wood was filled with eye candy. In this room, the caterpillar cars rode on top of the Mad Hatter Tea Party table. There were fully dimensional Horn Birds, an Umbrella Bird, a Birdcage Bird, and an Accordion Owl. Bob Gurr and Roger Broggie built pop-ups of the March Hare and the Mad Hatter. Playing in the background was "The Unbirthday Song." The cars left the party and moved into the Shrinking Door Hallway, where they burst through the second-floor door and began to descend back down to ground level and the loading ramp.

40-HOUR WATCH

IT WASN'T LONG before Walt started thinking about another expansion idea. He knew that General Electric was embroiled in a corporate scandal, and he thought the park could help improve its image. General Electric was originally the Edison Electric Company, founded in 1878, and Walt liked the idea that he could celebrate Thomas A. Edison, one of his boyhood heroes.

WED put together a proposal specifically for General Electric. "Edison Square in Disneyland will dramatically present the story of the way in which one invention by Thomas A. Edison has influenced the growth and development of America. The story of that era: the birth, growth, development and future of electricity and General Electric products."[30] It would be the first new land located off the hub. The gateway would be right next to the Red Wagon Inn, with the cul-de-sac hidden behind Main Street. Edison Square would complement Main Street by being "a composite of residential districts of major American cities at the turn of the century."[31]

A paved brick road would lead to an 1890s plaza called Progress Place, enclosed by 500 linear feet of residential facades, including "the red brick houses of Philadelphia, New York's brownstones, the wooden edifices of San Francisco and Chicago and the colonial brick of Boston." At the center would be a life-size statue of Thomas A.

Edison. Some of the Main Street vehicles would circulate in and out, making the area feel "alive and vital."

The big draw would be a show called "Harnessing the Lightning." Inside the 40,000-square-foot horseshoe-shaped show building was an entrance lobby, four theaters, a product room, plus backstage areas. From the lobby, 125 guests would walk into the first theater and see a 3-minute show before moving on to the next theater. Lighting, sound, and entrance/exit doors of each of the four theaters were to be synchronized, ensuring continuity and a controlled progression of guests through the presentation. At the exit would be the product display room. The entire production was meant to last approximately 15 minutes.

In the lobby were full-dimensional dioramas animated with special lighting. The dioramas portrayed the time Edison and his associates tested the first incandescent lamp during the "40-Hour Watch." From there, guests passed through the four theaters, each one a display of household appliances for that time period. The first act is set in an American home in 1898, in days before electrical appliances. An electromechanical man with lifelike movements named Wilbur K. Watt hosted the visit. From there, guests moved forward in time to 1918, 1958, and then to a New York penthouse apartment set in the future of 19?8. (The future time frame is left ambiguous intentionally.) The epilogue was set in the General Electric product room, where "Progress Is Our Most Important Product." The main show would become the foundation for the *Carousel of Progress,* and the project would resurface again in 1963, 1972, and 1986.

Bob Gurr loved fire trucks, and he thought it might be fun if Disneyland had one of its own. One day, he turned to the boss and asked, "Hey Walt, you know what we haven't got? A fire truck!" Gurr waited for a response, but none was forthcoming. In fact, Walt raised his eyebrow, never a good thing, and walked away. What Gurr did not know was that Walt had had a boyhood passion for fire trucks. Harper Goff said, "I remember him describing what it was like to be a kid in his hometown when the fire engines came by. He said he didn't realize, as a kid, that the fire was causing someone to suffer. He just loved the sounds of the engines." Gurr was sure he was in trouble and ran to his office. As he walked through the door, the phone rang and it was the accounting department. They told him he had some money to build a fire truck.[32]

He designed two 1900s-era fire trucks powered by a 12-horsepower, two-cylinder engine. They were red and the space that would traditionally hold the hoses was replaced by bench seats. The bell and siren were authentic, and the trucks were hand-built at the Studio. When Gurr drove one down the Santa Ana Freeway from the Burbank Studio, he had to go so slowly he created a traffic jam. He stopped at one corner, and a small boy yelled out, "Hey Mister, by the time you get to the fire it will be out!"[33] The trucks made their debut on August 16 and quickly became one of Walt's favorite ways to tour the park.

▌ BUILD THIS!

FAR AWAY FROM DISNEYLAND, Walt and Lillian were taking a driving tour of Europe. The couple enjoys traveling in Europe because people really did not know who they were. When they visited Wuppertal, Germany, they had to ride the nine-and-one-half-mile historic monorail train. Wuppertal is a mountain town with a curving river. The train had been put into service in 1901 and was the easiest way to go up and down through this little town. It was a simple system. The track was hung between pylons along the banks of the river. The train swung freely from the track overhead. Walt always wanted a monorail for the park; in Herb Ryman's earliest sketch for Tomorrowland, one just like this was passing over the entrance. However, the swinging of the cars made Lillian feel ill.

As the trip continued, the couple was driving north on an old main road near Cologne, Germany, when a monorail train crossed over their heads from the right to the left. It was going from the factory to the administration building. Walt immediately pulled over to the administration building and learned about the Alweg company, owned by Dr. Axel Wenner Gren, who had made a fortune by investing in ElectroLux vacuum cleaners. He had a lot of money at the end of World War II, but he could not repatriate it back to his home in Sweden, so he decided to spend it on the development of a monorail until all of it was gone. The Alweg monorail was different than the train that had made Lillian queasy; the Alweg train rested on a single beam below instead of hanging from the track. This became known as the "German saddle bag" method of monorail construction. The first prototype had gone online in 1949. Gurr said, "I've often thought that 10 seconds either way and Walt would have driven right by and never have seen that thing."[34] Walt wanted one for Disneyland.

Later that summer, the couple visited Zermatt, Switzerland, for a week to watch the filming of the live action adventure *Third Man on the Mountain.* Zermatt was located in the Pennine Alps on the Swiss-Italian border. The film was based on James Ramsey Ullman's novel *Banner in the Sky,* and it tells the tale of a young Swiss man who conquers the mountain that defeated his father—the Matterhorn, one of the last great alpine peaks to be climbed. Walt had developed a fondness for Switzerland's scenic beauty on earlier trips, but he had never appreciated the Matterhorn as he did on the 1958 trip. He often stopped to stare at its distant peak for as much as an hour at a time, when an idea struck.

unofficial **TIP**
The first ascent of the Matterhorn, made in 1865 by Edward Whymper, marked the end of the golden age of alpine climbing.

Walt loved the Skyway ride, but he thought the tower on Holiday Hill was an eyesore. Walt's vision was to hide the Skyway tower inside of a scale-model mountain. Walt said, "Disneyland is like a piece of clay, if there is something I don't like, I'm not stuck with it. I can reshape and revamp."[35] This was a perfect example. Sam McKim even included a mountain with the tower sticking out of the top in his 1957 map of the park. Walt's infatuation with the Matterhorn inspired a solution.

He could also address a request from his operations staff. They had been clamoring for a thrill ride, and Walt had even included a bobsled ride in the original Disneyland prospectus. This could work. Walt asked Joe Fowler, "Do you suppose we could get some snow and have a toboggan ride here?"[36] Fowler gave it some thought and tried to explain the complexity of maintaining the snow-making equipment. Walt understood and moved on until he heard about Wild Mouse–style roller coasters from Jack Sayers, who saw one in an October 28, 1957, article in *Funspot* magazine.

He sent two postcards of the Matterhorn to the model-making department at WED. Scribbled on the back of each was a simple but intriguing note: "Build this!"[37] The hill was renamed Snow Hill. Others started to call it Mount Disneyland, Magic Mountain, Fantasy Mountain, Echo Mountain, Lookout Mountain, and the Valterhorn. Whatever its name, the mountain was soon to be a reality at Disneyland.

And **THAT WAS THAT**

DISNEYLAND WAS A HUGE HIT, but its success created a wave of pretenders. After C. V. Wood Jr. left the team, he started his own business called Marco Engineering, Inc. and helped build Magic Mountain in

Golden, Colorado, in 1957; Pleasure Island in Wakefield, Massachusetts, in 1959; and Freedomland U.S.A. in the Bronx in 1960. In nearby Santa Monica, a group of investors, including the CBS network and the owners of the Santa Anita Racetrack, spent $16 million in a lavish remodeling of 28-acre Pacific Ocean Park, nicknamed POP. The park opened on July 23, 1958. They hired Hollywood set designers, and everything was converted to fit an Oceanic South Seas motif. There was a gondola ride, a flight to Mars, a safari dark ride, and a train.

It may be a coincidence, but on the same day that POP opened, Walt sent a memo to his staff outlining the roles and responsibilities for the greatest expansion in Disneyland's early history. Dick Irvine would be in charge of the project that would include the monorail, the Matterhorn Bobsleds, and the Submarine Voyage. Claude Coats and Bill Martin would serve as art directors, with Coats working with Bob Sewell on the show's overall design. Martin would handle the track layout and the architectural planning. Roger Broggie and Wathel Rogers were to engineer the animation and effects, and work with Ub Iwerks on projections. Lighting was designed by George Feldcap and Jim Eddy. Civil and structural engineering was overseen by Admiral Joe Fowler. Bob Gurr, working for Roger Broggie, would design the submarine vehicles and their drive system.

unofficial **TIP**

Although Pacific Ocean Park got off to a tremendous start and was known nationally as the occasional backdrop to *The Lawrence Welk Show,* the park fell into decline by 1963 and closed in 1967. The pier on which it sat was knocked down in 1974.

The team got started right away. In preparation for the new attractions, the Santa Fe & Disneyland Viewliner was closed on September 14 and the Junior Autopia closed the next day. A month later, Bob Gurr delivered his first rendering of the Monorail Viewliner. Gurr said, "I made that famous drawing [with the two trains crossing in the air] and brought it to a meeting in the Animation building. I put the drawing up on the wall, and Walt walked in and just looked at it. His eyes lit up and reached out and tapped it and said, 'Bobby, can you build that?' And I said, 'Yeah.' Walt just looked around at everybody and said, 'Okay!' And that was it. End of meeting."[38] Walt sent Gurr and Roger Broggie to Germany in November to start on the monorail development.

Back at WED, Coats continued to work on a pirate ride. The original plan was for a walk-through attraction with about 40 people walking through it at a time. Guests would purchase tickets and then walk onto the deck of the pirate ship. They would go below decks and peek into the Captain's Cabin and then walk on the deck just in time to see sailors repelling boarding pirates. The guests would then leave the ship and step onto the pier. Walking along the pier, they would see the "Sack and Burning of the City" off in the distance. They then would turn a corner and look into the Grog Shop. Quickly turning from the Grog Shop and stepping out onto the beach, the guests would find a group of pirates "Burying Loot." To escape, the guests would make their way to the "Cypress Swamp" and then find themselves right in the middle of the "Battle for the Defense of New Orleans." Finally, they are safe when they spot General Jackson's Headquarters and head for the exit.

The growth of Disneyland and the economic impact on the surrounding community of Anaheim and Orange County was unprecedented. To celebrate the park's third anniversary, the Disneyland Public Relations Division put together an annual report. In just three years, 12,058,071 guests had passed through the turnstiles. Year over year, growth had been a strong and steady 10%. To keep pace with all of the new guests, the park had invested $6 million and gone from 22 attractions to 44. Because of this, the average guest spent 5½ hours in the park, which was more than double the time spent at the typical amusement park.

In order to be a good neighbor, the park adopted a "Buy in Orange County" policy. The growth of the tourism industry brought tremendous potential market for all types of goods and services. Of course, the park had been a leading contributor to both sales tax and property tax revenues. The report stated that the pride of the park was its employees, who were known as Disneylanders. The total number of employees had jumped from 1,280 to more than 3,400 in just three years, with a payroll increase of 57%. A survey of the staff "reveals that the composite average Disneyland employee is married, has 2.4 children, is a member of a church, is active in some type of community organization, owns his home, lives in Orange County, spends the great majority of his earnings in the County, and has been employed at Disneyland for two to three years."[39] Annual attendance remained steady at 4.35 million.

By the end of 1958, Bill Martin had completed the complex master plan for the 1959 expansion. It was no easy task to stack the Submarines, the Autopias, and the Monorails within the same space. On December 4, Walt announced the $5 million expansion to the world. The event would become known as Disneyland's second grand opening. Nothing would ever be the same.

1. Rolly Crump with Jeff Heimbuch, *It's Kind of a Cute Story* (Clearwater, FL: Bamboo Forest, 2012).
2. Katherine Greene and Richard Greene, *Inside the Dream* (New York: Disney Editions, Inc., 2001).
3. Crump with Heimbuch, *It's Kind of a Cute Story*.
4. Disneyland, "Disneyland One Year Old," press release, July 1956.
5. Wendy Lefkin, ed., *Disney Insider Yearbook: 2005 Year in Review* (New York: Disney Editions, 2006).
6. Bob Thomas, *Walt Disney: An American Original* (New York: Disney Editions, Inc., 1994).
7. Disneyland University, *Space Mountain* training manual (Anaheim, CA: Disneyland, 1977).
8. "Prototypical Imagineer," *The "E" Ticket*, Number 31, Spring 1999, 4–15.
9. Pam Burns-Clair and Don Peri, *Walt Disney's First Lady of Imagineering Harriet Burns* (Virginia Beach, VA: Donning, 2010).
10. Bruce Gordon and David Mumford, *Disneyland: The Nickel Tour* (Santa Clarita, CA: Camphor Tree, 2000).
11. Ibid.
12. Thomas, *An American Original*.
13. Jeff Kurtti, *Walt Disney's Imagineering Legends and the Genesis of the Disney Theme Park* (New York: Disney Editions, Inc., 2008).
14. "Sleeping Beauty Castle," *The "E" Ticket*, Number 10, Winter 1990–91, 4–12.
15. Charlie Haas, "Disneyland Is Good for You," *The New West Magazine*, 4 Dec. 1978.
16. Alan Hess, "Monsanto House of the Future," *Fine Homebuilding*, Aug./Sept. 1986.
17. Ibid.
18. "Putting the Tomorrow in Tomorrowland," *The "E" Ticket*, Number 12, Winter 1991–92, 12–19.
19. " 'House of the Future' Demonstrates Way People Will Live Within Decade," *Anaheim Bulletin*, 6 Sept. 1957.
20. Disneyland Operations Department Group II, *Background Information: Adventureland, Frontierland, New Orleans* (Anaheim, CA: Disneyland, 26 Jan. 1970).
21. Disneyland, "News From Disneyland '65 Tencennial Celebration," press release, *Disneyland Gazetteer*, July 1965.
22. Donna Davis, "Beasts Are No Burden at the Magic Kingdom," *Orange County Register*, 21 Sept. 1981.
23. Steve DeGaetano, *Welcome Aboard the Disneyland Railroad!* (Winter, CA: Steam Passages Publications, 2004).
24. Disneyland, "News From Disneyland '65 Tencennial Celebration," press release, *Disneyland Gazetteer*, 17 July 1965.
25. "Prototypical Imagineer," *The "E" Ticket*.
26. Ibid.
27. Randy Bright, *Disneyland: Inside Story* (New York: Abrams, 1987).
28. Thomas, *An American Original*.
29. Disneyland Operations Department Group II, *Adventureland, Frontierland, New Orleans*.
30. Jim Korkis, "A Visit to Edison Square 1959," *USA Today*, 25 Jan. 2012.
31. Ibid.
32. Bob Gurr, *Design: Just for Fun* (Tugging, CA: APP-Gurr Design, 2012).
33. Ibid.
34. Bob Gurr, interview with the author, 20 June 2012.
35. Dave Smith, *Walt Disney Famous Quotes* (Lake Buena Vista, FL: Walt Disney Theme Parks and Resorts, 1994).
36. Jason Surrell, *The Disney Mountains: Imagineering at Its Peak* (New York: Disney Editions, Inc., 2007).
37. Burns-Clair and Peri, *First Lady of Imagineering*.
38. Gurr, *Just for Fun*.
39. Disneyland, Annual Report to Lessees, 17 July 1958.

CHAPTER 5

WALT'S DISNEYLAND: 1959–1966

The COMMITTEE CAR

BY 1959, Disneyland was really coming together. Disneyland was allowing many of the store and restaurant leases to expire in order to take control of the retail and dining locations by replacing them with Disney-owned companies. Disney was also taking charge of most of the backstage functions. Walt had complete control.

Main Street's public realm was enhanced by the addition of the Disneyland Flower Market and The Hills Brothers Coffee House and Restaurant. The Flower Market was a colorful outdoor display with artificial flowers available for sale. The flowers were handmade, so they would look more life-like. Across the street, The Hills Brothers Coffee House offered coffee, sandwiches, and desserts. The interior reflected a Colonial motif, and guests could enjoy their food on an outdoor dining patio.

Hallmark replaced Gibson selling greeting cards, postcards, and party goods. As a sponsor, Hallmark had an unusual agreement with Disneyland. Hallmark was allowed to keep control of its retail space because it generated so much new product and because the large store was used as a promotional tool for its dealers.[1] The Upjohn Pharmacy added a spectacular 6-foot plastic model of the basic cell mechanism of life.

Walt was not excited about sequels when it came to his film productions, but he was smart enough to capitalize on one of the earliest hits at Disneyland, and Autopia was exactly that. The little cars were a big money maker for the park, so Walt decided to double the capacity by adding a brand-new course in Fantasyland.

The Fantasyland Autopia, sponsored by Richfield, opened on January 1, 1959. The Fantasyland version was very similar to the Tomorrowland layout, and the boarding area worked the same. Guests drove new Mark V Autopia cars around the two-lane, multilevel track. At a pine-covered feature called McKim Hill, the two tracks came together. What is most remarkable is the illusion of unity. What many guests do not realize is that they are driving on top of a building. Just below the roadway was the Submarine Voyage. To re-create the countryside, Bill Evans had built 10-foot berms off the edge of the structure and planted pine trees, eucalyptus, maples, and ash. When the cars were driving down the slopes, they were coming off the roof of the Submarine ride building.

This was just one component of an incredible engineering feat. The entire area was a giant jigsaw puzzle where Bill Martin had to layer the Submarine, the monorail, the Motor Boat Cruise, and the Tomorrowland and Fantasyland Autopias all in one area. At the bottom were the submarines and the motorboats. Just above were the two Autopia tracks. Up in the air was the monorail riding on its beam way.

The Mark V Autopia car was introduced as part of the Fantasyland project, and on June 6, 1959, the revamped Tomorrowland Super Autopia opened with a fleet of Mark V cars. It was decided to stop tweaking the earlier cars and to build something new from the ground up. The Mark V had become known as the committee car because of the number of people involved in the design. The park hired consultants and experts who tended to disagree with each other. The new car reflected everything that everybody wanted. It featured a new body style and headlights made partially with 1957 Buick parts.

However, the new car was as unreliable as the earliest versions. It had independent front suspension, a backbone frame, front bumper shocks and a larger body. It was so heavy, tipping the scales at more than 1,100 pounds, that they began to destroy the curbs along the Autopia freeways.

When the park first opened, the Fantasyland dark rides were designed and built quickly with mostly unproven methods and temporary materials. By 1959, many of the special effects had become inoperable, and most of the flat cutouts had been repainted so often that they no longer resembled the original characters. Yale Gracey and Rolly Crump were given the assignment to go through each ride and update the effects. In the Snow White forest scene, they installed mobiles with glow-in-the-dark eyes. Mr. Toad's barrel scene was rebuilt with dimensional barrels.

Peter Pan received an improved volcano effect courtesy of Gracey and a new campfire near the tepees of the American Indian camp. The newest dark ride, Alice in Wonderland, was enhanced with a new water gag that enabled the Mad Hatter to pour the March Hare an endless stream of tea.

Walt was certainly proud of his park. In a May 1959 interview with the *Baltimore News-Post,* he admitted, "Maybe it's because I don't know enough to realize what's impossible. I've found that guys who know too much don't do things." He realized that "I'm not the perfectionist anymore. It's my staff. They're the ones always insisting on doing something better and better, I'm the guy trying to hurry them to finish before they spoil a job. You can overwork drawing or writing and lose the spontaneity." He joked, "I had to borrow on my life insurance to start Disneyland. Now it's Roy who went out and got the $5 million for the Disneyland enlargement that opens in June. Where do you think he got it? From a big life insurance company! A 15-year arrangement. Our bankers nearly flipped." Upon reflection, Walt said, "I could never convince financiers that Disneyland was feasible because "dreams offer too little collateral." In the case of Disneyland, the financiers could not have been more wrong.

Along with the Fantasyland Autopia, Disneyland was about to experience its largest expansion in its short history. Located on 11 acres between Fantasyland and Tomorrowland, guests would soon be able to enjoy five new attractions, including the Submarine Voyage, the Disneyland Monorail, and the Matterhorn Bobsleds. These innovative rides had cost $6 million and were the first E-ticket attractions. At one point, there were so many construction walls at the park that guests were handed a gate flyer proclaiming, "Don't miss the Greatest Construction Show on Earth!"[2]

GIVE 'EM *a* REAL SHOW

ONE OF THE MOST UNUSUAL Disney attractions ever created was the $2.5 million Submarine Voyage, which opened on June 6, 1959. Submarine Voyage was born of an attraction that didn't make it off the drawing board: Dick Irvine's glass-bottom boat ride over a picturesque lagoon in Tomorrowland was similar to the boats that attracted tourists to Catalina Island near Los Angeles. As so often happened, Walt saw the proposal and had a different idea. "No, let's do a real submarine ride. Let's take them down and give them ports to look out of. Give 'em a real show."[3]

The ride was inspired by the United States Navy's participation in the international exploration of the Antarctic for the International Geophysical Year (1957–1958). The event spawned three segments on the *Disneyland* television show: "Antarctic, Past and Present" (1956), "Operation Deep-freeze" (1957), and "To the South Pole for Science" (1957). At one point, the Navy wanted to sponsor the ride, but Walt said no. He did not want to become involved with government bureaucracy. Instead, the sponsor was General Dynamics, a firm closely associated with America's nuclear submarines. According to a press release, General Dynamics provided "technical data advice in building the Disneyland submarine fleet."

Bob Gurr did the initial drawings and adopted the look of the U.S.S. *Nautilus* with a conning tower and portholes. Engineering of the submarines was a challenge. He gathered as much information as he could with the assumption that the submarines would actually submerge 6 feet below the water. Gurr thought he could power the boats using a cable system. He and Roger Broggie traveled to San Francisco to inspect their world-famous historic cable cars. After a day with their operations people, Gurr and Broggie quickly shelved the cable system.

Another part of the development process was the construction of a mock-up of half the submarine out of wood framing and cardboard. They wanted to see how people would board and how they would view the show. What they discovered was that once the show started nobody really cared about the seats. What happened was the guests would slide forward, pushing their faces in the round portholes. With the guests leaning forward, they quickly became unaware of anybody sitting near them. This meant the Imagineers could install flip-down seats with a very short 19-inch pitch and really squeeze everybody together between the spiral staircases at each end. They installed air-conditioning vents in the portholes to simulate breathing in a diving helmet and to provide additional ventilation. The interior was outfitted in military gray, exposed wires, and metal caged lamps.

Once that testing was completed, Walt had his team dig a test pond to test some of the gags in the water. They installed a 40-foot concrete pool of water covered with pipes, planks, ropes, and wires and placed the mock-up under the water behind a plate glass window. That configuration allowed Gurr and Broggie to animate the vinyl figures to create the most lifelike movement. Many of the early animation effects were very simple, usually consisting of fish hanging by wires and circling from turntables overhead. Walt frequently dropped by to see what was happening.

The project called for eight 52-foot, fully air-conditioned submarines, each with enough individual 12-inch portholes for 38 passengers. They were built at the Todd Shipyards in San Pedro at a cost of $80,625 each. The submarines were flat-bottomed and had a hull displacement of 94,000 pounds. The chassis was made of 3-inch steel plate with steel ribs sheathed with steel plate. The fuselage ends were hand-hammered into shape. Guests would enter via one of two spiral staircases. The first of eight submarines were delivered on April 25, and the lagoon was filled for the first time on April 26. Testing ended on May 2, and the rest of the fleet was delivered by May 23.

The sparkling 9 million-gallon submarine lagoon was kept clear by a vacuum system that pulled up to 1,800 gallons of water per minute through filter screens and a diatomaceous earth filter. The water was tested three times a day, and the park claimed that it is pure enough to drink. Once the lagoon was filled, initial testing took place during the daytime, while Bob Sewell and his divers worked overnight for three months installing the seaweed, fish, clams, mermaids, and other props throughout the ride. Fortunately, Sewell and Bud Washo developed a way to bypass the usual sculpting work and cast a plaster mold from the body of a specimen fish. Considering there were 539 stationary figures, 126 animated figures, and 15,000 underwater plants, this meant a huge savings in time and money.

The submarines traveled at 1.8 mph along 1,365 feet of track with 650 feet out front in the lagoon. Because the submarines actually did float, they were connected to two 10-foot guide wires. Each submarine was powered by a German-made MAN (Maschinenfabrik Augsburg-Nürnberg, a mechanical engineering company) 40-horsepower diesel engine that generated electrical current to the 10-horsepower motor. It was selected by Admiral Joe Fowler because it was especially quiet. The sub had a 34-inch, four-blade bronze propeller. Each boat was named after a U.S. Navy nuclear-powered submarine, including the *Nautilus, Seawolf, Skate, Skipjack, Triton, George Washington, Patrick Henry,* and *Ethan Allen.* Walt called it "the World's largest peacetime submarine fleet."

As a submarine pilot, a cast member was responsible for controlling the forward and backward movement as well as the speed. He was responsible for keeping a certain distance from the submarine in front of him by watching the running lights. He also advanced the narration tape. The adventure lasted 8 minutes and 15 seconds.

A lightly themed loading dock was placed underneath the monorail platform. To allow passengers to board the submarine, a ramp was lowered from the dock to the boat, which led to a spiral staircase to reach the seats. The very tight turn of the staircase added to an authentic cramped feeling. Once the guests were seated, the hatch was lowered with a thud and tightened down. For those who were claustrophobic, this was not a good moment.

When the submarine left the dock, a torrent of air bubbles rapidly passed by the portholes, providing the illusion that the craft was descending. All of the sets and effects were a mirror image to serve both sides of the submarine. The combination of floating figures both close up and far away created a sense of great depth. The lagoon was filled with angelfish, bonito, sea bass, and crabs. Guests would encounter lobsters "fighting" and observe a fight between an octopus and a shark. Giant clams like those found in the East Indies and Australia sat on the seabed. A simple visual effect was the kelp beds being stirred up by the passing subs. As the submarines approached the waterfall, moray eels popped out of crevices frighteningly close to the portholes.

The rest of the attraction was placed inside of a huge, hidden, reinforced-concrete parking structure. The roof was almost 1 acre. Bill Evans wanted to landscape the roof to hide the building, so the roof was capped with 5 feet of earth at the center, tapering off to 2 feet at edges for drainage. Guests would not be aware that below the landscape were sea serpents, a giant squid, whales, and the lost ships in the sunken city of Atlantis.

As the ride progressed, the captain suggested that a storm was approaching and reassured the passengers that the sub could dive below the storms; however, the captain pointed out, "Other craft have not been so fortunate." The illusion was enhanced by the roar created by the waterfall that was used to hide the entrance to the show building. The submarine was equipped with sonar hydrophones that allowed guests to "listen in" on the deep sea creatures. The first scene inside the building was the Graveyard of Lost Ships. Remnants of broken Greek, Roman, and Viking ships were scattered amid the coral reef. A group of treasure-seeking divers struggled with a treasure chest lighted by a satellite submarine.

From there, the submarines re-created the historic voyage of the U.S.S. *Nautilus,* which left Hawaii on July 22, 1958, on course for the North Pole. On August 3, 1958, at 11:15 p.m. EDT, Commander William R. Anderson informed the *Nautilus* crew that they had reached the North Pole. As the narrator recounted the story, guests peered through the portholes to see the blue and white glow from the bottom of an iceberg.

As the submarine dove even deeper, the captain explained, "Here, in this realm of eternal darkness, nature has provided her creatures with their own eerie luminescence." Swimming near the boat were fluorescent jellyfish with giant teeth and illuminated hooks dangling near their mouths. If that is not frightening enough, the 50-foot giant squid dragging a killer whale into its mouth did the trick.

As the story goes, there was once a great island at the mouth of the Mediterranean Sea. It was there where man first rose from a state of barbarism to civilization. The Lost Continent of Atlantis was discovered with a satellite sub. What happened? The captain spoke of an undersea volcano as the boat passed over remnants of the crumbled ancient stone city. There were a giant statue of a foot broken off at the ankle and a giant stone head. Suddenly, red lights started flashing and bubbles were seen outside the portholes. The captain told his guests, "This confirms it! That seething mountain still denies rest to the civilization it destroyed thousands of generations ago . . . helmsman, steer clear of the tottering columns!"

Just beyond were three mermaids swimming in a circle, admiring some of the 14,000 beads, jewels, and treasures strewed among the ruins. Blaine Gibson had sculpted the mermaids out of clay, and then they were cast in Duraflex. It was Walt's idea to have the mermaids go without seashell bras.

The final gag was the encounter with a 60-foot-long sea serpent. Before guests saw the mythical beast, they heard the first mate say, "Sir, it looks like a . . . it is! . . . it's a sea serpent!" Then, in between the rocks appeared a smooth green surface, the body of the sea serpent. The payoff was a funny-looking, rather confused sea serpent. "We should enter this into the log, shouldn't we?" asks the first mate. "No, no, no . . . forget it. Nobody would believe it anyway," answered the captain. "I think we've been submerged too long . . . stand by to surface." The submarine passed under another waterfall and then waited for an open loading berth.

For opening day, Walt wanted to have real mermaids to entertain the guests. Disneyland hired professional swimmers who were fitted with flexible lower bodies and tails. Tommy Walker choreographed the mermaids, and they lasted until the summer of 1967.

Due to the ultraviolet light and the chlorine, the paint tended to fade rapidly, so a program was set up for a complete rehabilitation every six years. The attraction would prove to be a maintenance headache.

▌HIGHWAY *in the* SKY

WALT WAS DETERMINED to put a monorail in Tomorrowland. The deal had been sealed in his mind once he saw the Alweg train crossing the road on his 1958 European trip. Bob Gurr was assigned to design the trains, and Walt sent him to Germany to study the Alweg trains. Gurr immediately determined that "we couldn't design anything that looked like theirs. It was ugly." He asked himself, "What in the world am I going to do with this ugly loaf of bread with a slot in the bottom sitting on a stick?"[4] He relied on his training as an auto designer. "I knew that the way you make something look slender is to put some 'tumblehome' (an automotive design term meaning 'tuck it in' or 'curve it' to improve its appearance) on it."[5]

Gurr was a big fan of Buck Rogers and Doctor Zarkov and liked the look of their rocket ship, with its big wraparound windshield, portholes, a big fin along the top, and nozzles out the back. He noticed that the spaceship would land like a sled on runners. He figured out that he could hide the wheel assembly with a skirt like the rocket.

The Mark I monorail was a three-car train with nine compartments. Each compartment could seat eight guests. Five lucky guests could sit in the front and another five in the rear compartment. The total capacity was 82 guests. The body was based on the Viewliner train and made of lightweight aluminum, plastic, and stainless steel. "If you compare the drawings for the Monorail coach and the Viewliner coach . . . the windows, doors, face-to-face compartment seating . . . you'll see that the structures are identical, at least from the floor up," said Gurr.[6] The siding, color scheme, and passenger door mechanisms were virtually the same.

"I made the body pointed (which was a very anti-German approach) and used the 'belt line' to split the shape of the car," Gurr said. "With a wraparound windshield and windows from the Viewliner, along with corrugated metal sides (like the California Zephyr) and some recessed headlights . . . well, that was all there was to it!" He admitted, "The Mark I Monorail was a very simple design, because Lee Adams (the chief electrical engineer at the Studio) was a Westinghouse guy, and he had access to some used Westinghouse DC motors that were really cheap!"[7] It was claimed that the trains were capable of speeds up to 80 mph.

For many, the most identifiable design element of the Mark I monorail was the plexiglass bubble on top for the pilot. Gurr attributed that feature to Walt. As Gurr was working on early drawings for the monorail, Walt stopped by and noticed the shape of the cab. Much like a bus, the driver was in front and a bench was provided right behind for guests. Walt took one look at the drawing and told Gurr, "I don't want any passengers lookin' down the greasy neck of a Motorman."[8]

Gurr was critical of the Mark I monorail, but he needed something to take to Alweg in early November 1958. Alweg was surprised and happy that somebody wanted to actually buy one of its trains. The park originally intended to have a subcontractor of Alweg's from Mannheim, Germany, build the monorails, but the proposed trains were extremely heavy and unattractive. Instead, Roger Broggie and Bob Gurr engineered a train based on parts they could purchase in Los Angeles. In the end, it was decided to proceed with Gurr's design and to do without the Alweg technology. Although Alweg had very little to do with the final design, it claimed that the trains at Disneyland were its. Construction started at Standard Carriage Works, but they got so far behind schedule that the project was pulled, and the trains were built at the Disney Studio.

Building the monorail trains was not the only challenge. There was also a conflict between "engineering people who wanted to go in a straight line forever with no grades, and the Disney art directors who wanted to draw tight turning radii and plot an interesting ride that climbed maximum grades in order to thrill the guests," said Broggie.[9] The prototype did not work very well on the steeply banked turns. Gurr had to work with a train that had a high center of gravity. If it stopped on a turn, it tended to lean over. He engineered a whole new suspension system where the train was only using the wheels that it needed.

The route of the 0.8-mile loop (3,844 feet) took guests across the Submarine Lagoon, wound around the Matterhorn, and passed over the Super Autopia and the Motor Boat Cruise. The beam was built of precast concrete "I" section elevated girders that ranged in length from 32 to 60 feet. The track dipped as low as 5 feet and rose to 31 feet with grades of 7 percent. The typical steel wheel train could only climb a 3 percent grade. There was a "bad beam" on the curve just past the motorboats where the train "bumps and wobbles." At one dramatic point, the beam paralleled the Santa Fe & Disneyland Railroad track.

When the $1.3 million system opened on June 14, 1959, it was "the nation's first practical monorail train system—considered a key to future travel," according to a press release. It would become the first passenger-carrying monorail in the Western Hemisphere to operate daily. The typical trip took 6 minutes and 45 seconds.[10]

First on the line was the Red Mark I Monorail, which was piloted by Gurr on opening day. The first passengers were Walt, U.S. Vice President Richard Nixon, and Mr. Nixon's family. The people at Alweg were amazed. One engineer said, "We never put the public on a train in less than seven years. In six months' time, you Americans put your own vice president on one!" Gurr remembered, "It was then I realized what we did at WED."[11]

Monorail Blue joined the fleet on July 3. The "ultra-modern station" featured a Speedramp, an inclined moving sidewalk developed by Stephens-Adamson Company that carried guests to the loading platform and back down without their walking a step. For the guests, the monorail was an exciting new ride. For Walt, it was a prototype of a new transportation system that he knew could solve real world problems.

The opening-day press release suggested the monorail was "a practical prototype of high-speed interurban transportation systems, which could well be the answer to the growing problems of metropolitan area congestion." Author Ray Bradbury suggested that "the psychology of the monorail is what makes it superior. First of all, it's not an elevated like the old trains in Chicago. It's up in the air, but it doesn't make noise . . . you can hardly hear it. The important thing is that it's above the traffic, and would glide past the traffic." Walt was proud of his monorail. He believed he found the solution to traffic congestion and frequently showed it off to visiting politicians. Sadly, none of the politicians took Walt up on his idea.

The Motor Boat Cruise was also updated as part of the expansion project. To blend in with the rest of the attractions, the ride explored a whole new waterway with two new lakes and a whitewater rapids section. The boats were redesigned, and a new two-sided loading dock was built.

Millions of viewers were tuned to the ABC television network on Sunday, June 14, 1959, to watch *Disneyland '59* to celebrate the park's fourth anniversary and the opening of the Matterhorn, monorail, and Submarine Voyage. The show was much more polished than the 1955 opening-day broadcast, and it featured all of the new attractions. As the show began, Host Art Linkletter asked Walt, "How do you feel?" Walt's reply, "Like any new father, I guess. Nervous but wonderful." The show highlighted a parade with an international theme, the Firehouse Five Plus Two Dixieland Band, a fleet of Mark V Autopia cars, and floats representing each of the new attractions.

Also on the occasion of the park's fourth anniversary, the Stanford Research Institute presented an economic impact report to the Orange County Board of Supervisors. The report was impressive: Since the first grand opening, more than 16,600,000 guests had visited the park. Almost half (48.6%) of the guests were from outside of California. More than 3,650 people worked at the park with a payroll of $10.5 million. Proudly, the park reported 835 businesses within Orange County benefited by supplying goods and services to the park. Local governments also benefited through related taxes, which had topped more than $2 million during the park's first four years. April 1959 saw the 15 millionth visitor come through the gates. For the first time, annual attendance surpassed the 5 million mark.

POETIC LICENSE

THE MATTERHORN BOBSLEDS have become a Southern California landmark and a Disney attraction that has never been duplicated. Harriet Burns was assigned to make the first model of the mountain based on materials such as *Life* magazine, postcards, and the *Encyclopedia Britannica*. The first model was at a 1:1,200 scale, and she remembered, "I made it like a birthday cake, with layers in it, so if I boo-booed, we could just take out a layer and put in a new one." She tried to be as accurate as she could. One day, she heard from an official from the Smithsonian who said the "overhang was a little more than was correct." Her reply, "We told him that it was poetic license for the shadow pattern."[12]

During construction, a detailed model was built to guide the contractors. Because the Matterhorn, the monorail, and the Submarine Voyage were under construction at the same time, the model shop created a reference model on a huge platform with roller skate wheels on it. The model was broken down into three sections and could be combined or separated as needed. The Matterhorn Bobsleds had quickly turned from an idea into an engineering problem never before seen.

The construction firm of J. B. Allen was put under contract, and American Bridge fabricated the steel skeleton. Built like any other modern skyscraper, the structure was like an umbrella with the skin stretched on the steel frame. It was a complex puzzle where none of the 2,175 pieces were the same length. Plywood forms were used to define the rockwork on the upper portion of the mountain. A way to understand the structure was to think of it as an eight-story building. The first four floors were the ride, the fifth floor was a break room and half basketball court for the mountain climbers, and the remaining three floors included a couple of exit doors called "Walt's ledge" and the "Italian door." The structure was built to $\frac{1}{100}$ scale; at 146.5 feet, the Matterhorn would become the tallest structure in Orange County and would retain that crown for many years.[13]

The construction process was complicated by the Skyway. They had to remove the original Skyway support tower and hold the cable in the same exact spot. They did not want to chance moving the cable layout. So they removed Snow Mountain and the main tower, built the Matterhorn Mountain, and put the cable back in the same spot as before. Just prior to the opening, Joe Fowler told Walt, "I think we'll have it finished on time, but next time, when we have to build a mountain, let's let God do it."[14]

Once again, the landscape architecture would enhance the fantasy. Bill Evans decided that the treeline would be about halfway up the mountain. Full-size spruce trees were planted around the base. Dwarf trees were planted on the mountain structure. No artificial trees are planted on the Matterhorn. Evans used Colorado blue spruce trees that have a needle about 1 inch long. The blue cast imparted the illusion of distance. Local pine trees would not work because their needles would be out of scale. They used a crane with a 150-foot extension on it and a cement bucket to install the trees. They would fill the cement bucket with planter mix, add a tree, add a gardener, and haul all three of them up to the top. Then they would plant the trees in reverse order and go down for another load. A drip irrigation system was installed, and the typical life of the tree was from two to five years before being replaced.

Once the mountain was finished, Arrow Development installed the track. This was Arrow's first roller coaster, and its team was led by Ed Morgan and Karl Bacon. The ride design program came with the following conditions: the ride had to have a high ridership capacity, it had to be safe, and it had to be fun. The roller coaster would travel in and around a replica of a real mountain, and the Skyway ride must pass through the middle. After all, hiding the tower is what got this all started in the first place. To achieve these goals, WED and Arrow had to invent a brand-new roller coaster technology.

To achieve the ridership goals, it was important to be able to run multiple bobsleds simultaneously. The solution was to use tubular track with bracing welded to the outside of the rails instead of flat rails along with a computerized ride-control system. The track was made of hollow steel pipe and was pressurized. Sensors could detect any drop in pressure, which indicated wear on the rails.

In an industry first, the Matterhorn Bobsleds permitted multiple dispatch of cars by using a computerized block system. There were three primary block zones, including the loading/unloading platform, the lift hill, and the gravity region. An operating bobsled would occupy two zones at the same time. If another bobsled were to intrude, the system would automatically shut down the roller coaster. The system could be overridden by the control tower. Bob Gurr said, "Designing the Bobsled track plan was probably the hardest project I ever worked on. I had failed Geometry I in high school and had to teach myself trigonometry to design the track."[15]

The 60 bobsleds were made of fiberglass, which allowed them to be light, flexible, and easily molded into the right shape. Up to four riders sat single file in two pairs of double seats. They were protected by molded front and rear cushioned bumpers. They used load-bearing polyurethane wheels on top of the track with guide wheels to control horizontal movement. There were brass "upstops" that restricted vertical movement. The benefit of the upstop design was that the vehicle was connected to the track on three surfaces, allowing for greater twists and turns than ever before and a smoother, quieter ride.

The queue was the mountain itself. Guests lined up around the base until they got to a set of switchbacks where they handed over their E tickets. Painted diagrams above the queue provided instructions on the seating arrangement. There were two tracks: Track A, commonly known as the Tomorrowland side, was 2,126 feet long; and Track B, known as the Fantasyland side, had 2,238 feet of track. The pair of tracks wove in and out with each other, and at times they would be side by side, giving guests the impression they really were racing.

To fit the track inside of the mountain, the chain lift was set at a steep 30 degrees instead of the typical 22 degrees. Anti-rollback ratchet ladders prevented the bobsleds from going backwards. The caverns were not fully realized. Guests could see the steel frame that held up the mountain and the catwalks used by the cast. At the top of the lift were two large holes where guests could see Main Street U.S.A.

Throughout the attraction were booster/brake wheels to maintain the desired speed. Pressurized air brakes were used to slow the sleds down when necessary. The platen relied upon friction, so it was surfaced with automotive brake lining material that could operate in all weather conditions.

Imagineer Randy Bright said, "Joe Fowler was especially concerned about the safety of the bobsleds as they careened down the mountain. He found a water ride in a park outside of London where the vehicles were slowed by landing in a pool of water." Based on that example, the Matterhorn designers included "glacial pools" at the end of the ride to act as an unconventional braking system.[16]

Well before the days of computer simulations, the track was designed with a slide rule, marbles, and daring disregard for personal safety. For the first ride, Roger Broggie turned to his young assistant Gurr and said, "You designed that track . . . now you can be the first to ride it."[17] He and three sandbags successfully made it to the bottom of the hill on the partially completed track.

unofficial **TIP**

In 1961 a 30-foot-high metal star was mounted on top of the Matterhorn, creating a new holiday landmark. The energy crisis of the early 1970s put an end to the tradition.

A MECHANICAL GENIUS

ON JULY 25, the Santa Fe & Disneyland Railroad fleet grew with the addition of Locomotive #4, the *Ernest S. Marsh*. Named after the president of the Santa Fe Railroad from 1957 to 1966, the locomotive was built in April 1925 by Baldwin. It was originally a 0-4-0 saddle tanker used by the Raritan River Sand Company in New Jersey. This meant that it had no wheels on the front or under the last part of the engine, and it had four wheels under the middle part of the locomotive. In 1950, the locomotive had been retired and was acquired by a group of steam train buffs who operated the narrow-gauge Pine Creek Railroad. However, it failed to pass a boiler inspection in 1954, and by 1958 it had been sold as scrap to a junk dealer in Newark, New Jersey. Roger Broggie saw it advertised for sale in a railroad trade publication and bought it for the park.[18]

Ward Kimball helped with the design. His prototype was the *Montezuma*, an 1871 Baldwin 2-4-0 with a four-wheel tender. It was the first engine used on the Denver & Rio Grande narrow-gauge railroad. The locomotive was brought back to the Burbank Studio and disassembled in July 1958. The restoration project took six months. To achieve a period look, it was converted to a 2-4-0 train and gained a new 34-inch boiler, a new four-wheel tender car, ornate sand and steam domes, a new headlight, and a diamond stack as well as a square cab and pilot wheels. The Marsh pulled the newly built "River Train," which had all the seats facing the inside of the park. The River Train replaced the cattle cars that had been so unpopular on the *E. P. Ripley.*

Walt was not ready to rest on the success of the Second Grand Opening additions. He wanted to take Frontierland to the next level. To get ready for the ensuing changes, Walt permanently closed the Conestoga Wagons and the Rainbow Mountain Stagecoaches on September 13, 1959. Both rides were problematic and downright dangerous. The Pack Mules closed temporarily on October 2, and the Rainbow Caverns Mine Train on October 11 to make way for something new.

"On Walt's direction, we took over the back half of one of the second-floor wings at the Studio in Burbank," said Rolly Crump. "During that year, Yale and I developed many of the first versions of the illusions for the Haunted Mansion. To be honest, Yale [Gracey] did about 85% of the designing . . . he was a mechanical genius, and I was 28 years old and just learning. I made the 'boxes' for him, and worked with him and came up with as many ideas, as much imagination as I could." Crump said, "For research, we started reading books on ghosts and went to see movies about them. In fact, we took Walt with us once to see *13 Ghosts,* the film by William Castle. Walt just wanted us to be left alone, and he gave us the freedom to do whatever we wanted."[19]

They developed a number of special effects gags that would ultimately make it into the final attraction. In their version, guests would walk through six rooms. To enter the library, groups of 40 guests would pass through a long hallway where they would be constantly watched by a shelf of "converse busts," an effect used in the final attraction and described in detail later. The portraits on the wall would become active and the marble busts would come alive and start to talk with one another using a face projection system developed by Gracey that would be used in the final attraction as well.

In the Sea Captain's Room, Gracey came up with a concept and had Marc Davis draw up a sketch based on Ken Anderson's original script. Gracey and Crump put together a demonstration for Walt, Dick Irvine, and Roger Broggie. As the story goes, there was an old sea captain who used to live in the house before he drowned at sea. However, before he died, he murdered his wife and bricked her up in the fireplace in the room. While Gracey did the narration, Crump worked the mechanics of the illusion.

They wanted to demonstrate what it would look like when the sea captain periodically came back to his home and was wandering through the mansion. The illusion had the Captain's ghost slowly appearing in the room, gripping the harpoon and lantern, the rain coursing down and streaming across the floor. Then, while everyone's eyes were on the captain, the hideous spirit of the murdered wife seemed to burst through the brick wall, plunging straight at the audience.

To achieve the effect, Gracey ordered an 8- by 15-foot piece of glass and installed it in a room where the audience stood on a small platform and looked down at the action. The figures and mechanical actions were hidden on the sides. Crump said they placed a mannequin off stage covered with seaweed, and an old slicker and raincoat, with a lantern in his hand standing in a pan of water. In the pan were mirrors and they installed a shower above spraying water down over the mannequin at the flip of a switch.

Crump described the scene. "This guy slowly appearing from nothing. And you'd see the water running off of him, and the water would reflect, and you could see it running around on the floor of the room. It was an incredible illusion because then he would slowly disappear, and all the water would be gone! And you could see that it was real water."[20] Then the murdered wife would slowly appear behind her brick wall. "Suddenly she would raise her arms and FLY OUT through the wall towards him in the middle of the room . . . and then she would disappear!" Crump revealed. "We actually built all that . . . we 'jerry-rigged' it out of clothesline and wooden pulley, spit and glue. But it worked and it was wonderful." During the demonstration, Walt and the others reached out and shrieked in disbelief, then suddenly both ghosts vanished. Walt reacted to this by saying, "Gaaaaaaahhhd . . . that's great!"[21]

Using the same set-up, the two came up with a gag that involved a pair of candles with flickering flames (actually lightbulbs) sitting on the fireplace mantel. In reality, only one candlestick was on the mantel; the other one was mounted on a black-painted two-by-four and held by Crump, who was dressed all in black. Gracey would make a "poof" sound, Crump would cover the light with his hand, and it would appear that Gracey had blown out the candle. Gracey would say he could relight it by magic, and Crump would uncover the light again. The pair developed other effects, including pop-up ghosts with two lengths of wire anchored below the opening and extending upward to the ceiling. The ghosts (each one no more than a head with long hair, dressed in a light, flowing gown) were operated with a burst of compressed air that shot the ghost 16 feet straight up into the air.

A FAVORITE
SUBJECT *of* MINE

ANOTHER SPLENDID LITTLE TOUCH would appear on April 9, 1960, on the east side of Sleeping Beauty Castle. Walt had a special affection for wishing wells. He said, "Wishing long has been a favorite subject of mine. Wishes have come true for many of the characters in my motion pictures—and for me, too."[22] The Variety Club of America wanted to sponsor a wishing well in Disneyland and use the money to benefit children's charities around the world. Walt was happy to oblige and came up with the Snow White Wishing Well and the Grotto.

Walt was given a set of exquisite Carrara marble statues of Snow White and the Seven Dwarfs carved by Italian artist Leonida Parma. The statues were modeled after a set of soaps that were being sold at the time in Europe. When the statues arrived, John Hench noticed that all of the figures were the same size. This meant Snow White was as small as the dwarfs. Hench came up with a clever solution. He used forced perspective by placing the Snow White figure at the very top, standing next to a deer that was the right scale. The dwarfs were placed lower and closer to the guests. By applying this solution, the illusion is everything is correct.[23]

In 1960, Sunkist Growers Association joined as a sponsor and opened the Sunkist Citrus House on Main Street. It replaced the Puffin Bakery. Guests could sample fresh-made orange juice, lemonade, lemon tarts, and other treats. The store could also ship Sunkist products back home, a very popular reminder of a trip to Southern California. Also on April 11, 1960, four electric runabouts were introduced to Main Street. They had a curved dash like a vintage Oldsmobile and were steered using a tiller. They did not last long as a way to transport guests and were gone by August. However, Walt loved them and was occasionally found driving around the park in one.

The Jungle Cruise allowed guests to relive the best moments of Disney's exotic True-Life Adventure films. The Submarine Voyage was the next step in virtual reality by placing the guests underwater. On May 28, 1960, the Mine Train Through Nature's Wonderland became the latest of these immersive adventures. Many of the show elements in the Mine Train were influenced by films such as *Beaver Valley* (1950), *Olympic Elk* (1951), *Bear Country* (1953), *The Living Desert* (1953), and *Vanishing Prairie* (1954). The new show took up 7 acres in Frontierland at a cost of $1.8 million.[24] The gateway to the new adventure was an expanded version of the little mining town of Rainbow Ridge. A new opera house and dance hall were added, as well as Snowshoe Miller's Hides and the Rainbow Ridge Outfitters. Recorded sounds could be heard emanating from inside the miniature buildings.

Walt wanted to take guests from a wilderness outpost to the "secluded habitats in the forests of Wyoming, the deserts of Arizona and New Mexico, mountain terrain of Colorado, or the precarious terrain of the Grand Canyon." To provide as realistic a show as possible, the Mine Train was the first Disney attraction to use Audio-Animatronics. The new show featured more than 200 animated animals and birds "performing" for visitors. The goal was to have the animals look as though they were doing their daily activities just before the train would have frightened them off. Some of the figures were animated, and at quick glance, this made the motionless figures come alive as well. It was enough to create a convincing illusion.

A lot of new technology from the military and the space programs was being declassified, and the WED team took advantage of this for the Mine Train. Suddenly, they had new fabrics, plastics, metals, and miniaturized solenoids to play with. New hydraulic systems and smaller servo-mechanisms became available. Building on the knowledge gained during the development of the Disneylandia project, the team had been able to move away from the notched platters and light-sensitive photos used for controlling the characters toward magnetic tape and computer technology. The attraction was described as "the most elaborate and ambitious animation project ever attempted."

The locomotives from Rainbow Caverns were reused, and the trains were painted yellow and expanded to seven cars. Capacity was increased to 74 guests. The track was extended to 2,307 feet, and the updated ride took just under 9 minutes. A prerecorded narration track by Dallas McKennon was also added. Operators had the option of using the prerecorded track or to do the spiel live. It was discovered that one downside to the live spiel was the narrator was in the back of the train and could not see the same thing as the passengers in the front.

As was the practice at WED, scale models were built for many of the key scenes such as Bear Country. Other scenes were created straight from the artist's drawings. The Mine Train would become a life-size outdoor diorama filled with wonderful details—so many details that it would be impossible for the guest to see everything in just one visit. To create a convincing environment, Bill Evans used more than 156 different types of trees and other flora.

Animator Marc Davis got involved in the project and injected a bit of his brand of humor. He had been working at the Studio when studio executives began considering discontinuing making animated films. Walt was a fan of Davis and decided his unique talents could be helpful at WED. Davis's approach was to create storytelling tableaus that could be quickly understood as the trains passed by.

Two of the segments were based on the True-Life Adventure films. Beaver Valley had the animals working hard to build a dam. As the trains passed by, a beaver rose out of the water and then quickly submerged again. In Bear Country, a black bear was scratching his back up against a tree, while other bears were in the water fishing. From there the train entered a tunnel and emerged along the banks of the Rivers of America, passing by and under waterfalls. The guests on the train got a beautiful view of the river, and those playing on the river and on Tom Sawyer Island got something more to look at. This kind of layered interaction also took place at the Natural Arch bridge. That was the one point were the newly renamed Pack Mules Through Nature's Wonderland crossed overhead on the bridge while the train passed underneath.

The Living Desert was reduced in size and improved. The original cactus forest was made from molded fiberglass with indentations but no spines. Bob Sewell knew this was wrong and tracked down a plastic that would not curl up in the sun, so he could add clusters of spines all over them. Old Unfaithful Geyser shot plumes of water 70 feet into the air. Improvements were made to Rainbow Caverns as well, including new lighting, more stalactites and stalagmites, and more color.

Cascade Peak was a new addition. Towering over Frontierland at 75 feet, the mountain replaced a portion of the desert from the previous version of the Mine Train. Bill Martin designed it to hide Bear Country and Beaver Valley from guests traveling on the river. Other than housing the mechanical mountain goats and being a platform for waterfalls, Cascade Peak was basically empty inside. The waterfalls were powered by three pumps (totaling 510 horsepower) that forced 91 tons of water a minute up a huge central standpipe into the pool on top.

WED's first opportunity to participate in a World's Fair had been at the United States pavilion at the 1958 World's Fair in Brussels, Belgium. It produced a new Circarama film, *America the Beautiful,* which took "visitors on a tour of the United States from New York Harbor through giant industries and golden wheat fields, to Washington D.C. at cherry-blossom time, to New England, Glacier National Park, San Francisco's Golden Gate and the Grand Canyon," according to a press release. The film also made a brief appearance at the American National Exhibition in Moscow, Russia, in 1959 before debuting at Disneyland on June 14, 1960. No ticket was required for the 15-minute film.

Late in 1960, the three Fantasyland dark rides received updates with new gags and scenes. For Peter Pan's Flight, Yale Gracey and his team reworked and improved the lighting, the sound system, and scenery and upgraded the animation. Issues with the overhead track were resolved. The Skull Rock effect was changed, and guests no longer went through the eye but merely passed by on their way to the grotto. The London scene gained new life with the addition of rows of vehicles moving below. The illusion was a simple bicycle chain and black light.

For Mr. Toad's Wild Ride, the track layout was reconfigured to create more movement. Additional breakaway doors were added that were electrically activated by triggers along the track. Some of the new switches enabled simple animation effects, such as a policeman who could raise his arm as the cars passed by. When the attraction first opened, the devils were just painted images. When Blaine Gibson got the chance, he sculpted one of the now-familiar cow devils, based on a sketch by Ken Anderson and so-named because of their horns and barbed tails. Snow White was updated with new elements, including tree branches, mine timbers, sound effects of chirping birds, and fluttering leaves. The evil trees were individually lit, and new witch figures were installed.

Walt's commitment to quality was apparent everywhere. Evans suggested, "[Walt] was a stickler for authenticity and for good taste, good quality, good design. Walt wasn't trying to directly educate people about landscape, or architecture, or anything else, but he believed his audience would always know the difference between good and bad. And Disneyland was a kind of gigantic laboratory . . . an adventure in public entertainment."[25] Ray Bradbury agreed and said, "[Walt] wanted an environment of trees. Thousands of trees and bushes were not necessary, but he placed them in Disneyland anyway."[26]

One day, Walt wanted to check out the new Calico Mine Train at Knott's Berry Farm. He went up to the owner, Bud Hurlbut, and said he wanted to go for a ride. Hurlbut said, "At that particular time there were no people in front of the ride, but when we walked back past the trestle, the whole line was full of people!"[27] Walt said, "My God, that's a sneaky thing! There are 200 people in line back here and I didn't know there was anybody!" From this point forward, virtually every Disneyland attraction would open with a hidden queue.[28]

With Davis working at WED, Walt was ready once again to explore a pirate attraction. Walt suggested a walk-through wax museum in a basement in New Orleans Square. Each scene would have been placed behind glass and would light up when the guests entered the room. However, Walt was not ready to commit to the attraction, as he was distracted by other priorities.

In September 1960, Walt started to explore other ideas that would enhance the Disneyland experience. The area around the park was growing rapidly and without any consideration for the beautiful aesthetic he was trying to achieve inside of the berm. WDP controlled 133 acres adjacent to the park. A study by Economics Research Associates (ERA) considered opportunities such as a convention facility with an auditorium, more restaurants, and an idea proposed by Disneyland marketing director Ed Ettinger called California Living.[29]

Postwar Southern California had grown rapidly, and a lifestyle had developed that combined an outdoor orientation and informality. To exploit this trend, the Los Angeles County Arboretum had added two residential garden displays in conjunction with *Sunset* magazine in 1958, and attendance had more than doubled. Inspired by the Arboretum's success, Walt in 1960 was considering a continuing exhibition at Disneyland that represented the best of living in California. The project was described as "a show, an idea mart, and a merchandise mart on themes and products related to the home and leisure pursuits, combined in a comprehensive and integrated exhibition and display." Approximately 8–12 model homes would have been built representing the various regions of the state, including the beaches and the mountains. Guests would experience first-hand the active California lifestyle.

California Living would include more family-style restaurants themed to match the type of food served. The interiors would include dioramas and "other techniques" to enhance the theme. There would be a California Arts and Crafts area with products on display and for sale. Projected attendance was 1 million guests at opening, with an admission charge of $1.50. A 1,000-seat auditorium was also under consideration as part of the project.

In the meantime, a new landmark was added in Fantasyland at the end of the year. Skull Rock Lagoon was inspired by the Disney animated film *Peter Pan* (1952). Many of the rock artists who worked on the Matterhorn were retained to complete Skull Rock Lagoon. It became a picture spot, an eating area for the Chicken of the Sea restaurant, and it blocked the view of the Casey Jr. train, which was not consistent with the pirate ship in the foreground. A waterfall poured through the teeth of Skull Rock.

Walt's third child was growing fast, and annual attendance held steady at 4.9 million in 1960.

UNDAMPED DIVERGENT OSCILLATION

CHANGES WERE HAPPENING in Tomorrowland in 1961. The new four-car Mark II Monorail debuted on June 12. The trains were longer, at 112 feet, and each train could carry 108 guests. One addition that would prove to be very popular was the "double bubble" top. Just like before, Walt wanted to change the cab configuration. As the boss, he had a chance to sit in the pilot's seat of the Mark I cab and loved the view. This time he suggested to Bob Gurr to move the driver and find a place for guests to enjoy the view from the bubble. The electrical system was upgraded as well as the air-conditioning system. The monorail also graduated from a novelty ride to a true transportation system when the track was extended to the Disneyland Hotel. The beam was now 2.5 miles long, and trains cruised along a 43 mph zone between Harbor Boulevard and the hotel.[30]

Gurr was also working on another attraction for Tomorrowland. In 1960, he had been assigned to work on a "duck bump" attraction—a type of water ride popular in the Midwest that Walt wanted to bring to Disneyland. The ride featured boats—actually a large inner-tube—with a pivoting motor in the middle that a guest could pilot around a pond. They wanted to put the attraction in Tomorrowland Lake, which had been vacant since the removal of the Phantom Boats.

One day, a German salesman visited WED with a small propeller-powered hovercraft. Walt asked Gurr to check it out and his assessment was bleak. With a blade spinning at high speed directly below the guest, Gurr figured it would not be long before somebody got seriously injured. Instead, he took a look at a new idea being promoted by his friends at Arrow Development. Their system worked like a giant air hockey table.

Walt told Joe Fowler and Roger Broggie to work with Arrow to develop a prototype hovercraft—which at Disneyland would be called a saucer—at their Northern California shop.

Broggie worked the numbers and determined that they could move a 2,000-pound payload with air being pumped through holes on the floor. Coincidentally, several surplus actuators from the second stage of a U.S. Air Force Jupiter missile came on the market. Disney bought all of them, and they immediately failed. The supplier was confused. The actuators were designed to control pitch on the second stage of a missile and run for 5 seconds. They were overbuilt to be seven times as strong as the typical actuator, so as to not fail during those precious 5 seconds. Arrow and WED needed to find a better solution. The prototype sort of worked, and the attraction was put into hyperdrive.

At Disneyland, the saucers would float on a bed of air produced by four giant blowers mounted below the ground. To maintain the air pressure, a complex 16,000-square-foot network of air ducts with holes and valves was installed. As a flying saucer passed over a valve, the air pressure would become imbalanced and the valve would open. This provided the lift. The constant air pressure would quickly close the valve once the saucer had moved on.

Gurr designed the sleek flying saucers and even received a patent for his efforts. He said, "I was now recognized by the United States government as a 'flying saucer inventor,' a title which placed me in good company with all the other flying saucer crackpots of the time."[31] Sixty-four single-seat saucers were put into production.

Pilots could steer their saucers by leaning one way or another: Lean forward and air would escape out the back of the saucer's skirt, pushing the guest forward. Lean back and the saucer moved back. Move either way too much and the saucer would stall. Also, a heavy person would sit there and sink while a very light child would just bounce around.

Bill Martin came up with an innovative loading/unloading system for the attraction. He got the idea from a boat ride at Riverside Park in Chicago where the boats floated in a rectangular-shaped pond. When the ride time was over, a boom would sweep across the water and gather up the boats. As the boom passed over the water, another group of boats would be released.

The Disneyland flying saucers were placed on an oval arena that was separated into two halves by the loading platform. A movable pier unfolded from each side of the loading platform, cutting the arena into quarter sections. As the piers moved, they swept 16 of the saucers tightly against the loading platform. While this was happening, 16 other pilots would be struggling with their vehicles out on their half of the arena. Each side was operated independently, and the system allowed for 32 saucers loading while 32 saucers were operating at any one time. Martin received a patent for his design.

During installation and testing, the attraction was plagued with problems. The prototype worked well in testing at Arrow Development, but that was due to a plenum that was only 4 feet deep. The plenum chamber housed air at positive pressure, which, combined with the values, held the saucers aloft. The one built at Disneyland was 9 feet deep. Because the air pressure in the plenum is what kept the saucers afloat, it was easy for pressure to rapidly evaporate. Once the pressure dropped, all of the Morgan valves would open at once, releasing the air beneath. The result was a loud boom, and the saucers would drop. It took a long time to regain the proper air pressure. Gurr blamed it on "undamped divergent oscillation."

The new attraction opened on August 8, 1961. Due to the mechanical issues, it was the first Disneyland attraction that failed to open on schedule. The attraction was very popular with the public but continued to be plagued by maintenance issues. The operational issues trumped the ride's popularity, and the saucers closed on September 5, 1966.

Gurr said, "In hindsight, had it gone through several levels of production, it could have become successful. What was needed were electronic controls and high-speed damper doors so that the flow of air in the plenum could have been kept uniform despite the interaction of the bouncing saucers above, and the pressure changes would not have affected the valves."[32] Like some many of Walt's dreams, the technology was not up to the vision. Gurr noted, "This is always the problem with mechanically operated devices versus those that are electronically operated with sensors that feed a processor which makes all the decisions. With a few electronic feedbacks, and a control system which could have worked the doors quickly, the ride could have continued. But this was all done before computerization. With sensor-pressure data, high-speed action on the damper doors and a program written for damping and smoothing . . . the whole thing could probably be operated with one PC today."[33]

The growth of Disneyland and Anaheim was phenomenal. There was only one major problem: Most of the money came in the summer, so cash flow was uneven. In addition, although Disneyland welcomed its 25 millionth guest on April 19—Dr. Glenn C. Franklin[34]— attendance in 1961 was down slightly, to 4.7 million. To flatten out the dips in the off-season, Disneyland became a key player in establishing the Anaheim Visitor and Convention Bureau to promote Anaheim as a tourist destination year-round. Disney's primary contribution was to give the bureau interest-free loans to get the organization started.

SIZZLING TERIYAKI STEAK

IN 1962 WALT TURNED HIS ATTENTION away from the park and focused on the upcoming 1964 New York World's Fair. He had convinced Ford, General Electric, and the State of Illinois to fund the research and development for three new state-of-the-art shows (the Ford Skyway, GE *Carousel of Progress,* and Illinois animatronic Lincoln exhibit) that would appear at the fair and then make their way back to Anaheim. Still, progress continued to be made at the park. Walt needed to make room for the Haunted Mansion and New Orleans Square, so the Swift's Chicken Plantation House was removed on January 7. By April, the train track was moved away from the Rivers of America to prepare for the Haunted Mansion. The original Frontierland train station and water tower were moved to the other side of the tracks, and an antique semaphore signal from the Delaware and Hudson Railroad was installed near the old station. The signal was wired to a switch at the Main Street U.S.A. station and was lowered just before the train arrived in Frontierland/New Orleans Square. The footbridge that separated Frontierland from New Orleans Square was also removed; the waterway was put in a pipe and paved over.

Bill Evans was a genius in understanding how the landscape would mature over the years. He realized that guests were not visiting Disneyland to look at the trees and landscaping. But they would sure miss it if the trees and landscaping were not there at the high standards that Evans set. The result was an audience of three adults to every child.

Adventureland was coming into its own. The jungle had grown quickly, with some of the bamboo stalks along the banks of the Jungle Cruise reaching 30 feet tall. To prepare for the addition of the African Veldt and the Elephant Bathing Pool segments, the river was extended to 1,920 feet. The two-story Jungle Cruise boathouse was removed and rebuilt as a single-story structure. The overgrown jungle made it impossible to see into the attraction, and the observation tower was deemed impractical just as he planned.[35]

Evans cleverly installed important infrastructure elements, such as a hidden sprinkler system high up in the trees. For cold nights, he installed two huge gas heaters that rose up from the ground on the Manhattan and Catalina islands. Because the folks at WED were busy working on the World's Fair, it would take two more years before the animals would be installed.

The jungle became the perfect backdrop to Disneyland's first dinner theater, the Stouffer's Tahitian Terrace, which opened in June 1962 to bring a little bit of South Seas atmosphere to Adventureland. Guests could experience such exotic foods as "sizzling teriyaki steak, savory shrimp tempura, fried almonds in rich egg batter, and raisin ice cream topped with flaming caramel sauce." It was considered by many to have the best food in the park. A popular drink was the nonalcoholic Planters Punch Tahitian. Entertainment was provided by the Royal Tahitians, a fire-knife dance, a daring barefoot fire walker, and the ever-popular hula dancers.

For the Tahitian Terrace, Evans wanted to use a large African coral tree with brilliant orange-red flowers as the dominant feature in the dining patio. However, it was not big enough for Walt; he wanted to use the tree to hold the sound and lighting equipment. Only an artificial would do, so the African coral tree was replaced with a 35-foot-tall artificial tree with 4,075 handcrafted artificial leaves and colorful faux flowers that were always in bloom. When the tree was completed, Walt still was not satisfied. He wanted to optimize the guests' sight lines and asked to have the tree cut in half and raised to the proper height. That is exactly what the team from WED did.

However, it was a much larger tree nearby that would become the big new attraction for 1962: the Swiss Family Treehouse. The attraction was inspired by the 1813 Johann Wyss novel and the 1960 Disney hit movie *Swiss Family Robinson*. When it opened on November 18, it became an immediate hit and appealed to every person who had ever dreamed of living in such an exotic place.

Imagineer Bill Martin began working on the walk-through attraction in January 1962. Artist Jack Ferges crafted a 4-foot model that accurately captured the majesty of the tree house from the film. The engineers used the model to draft the structural drawings. The artificial banyan tree was 70 feet tall and 80 feet wide. The 18-foot-wide tree trunk was supported by 10 concrete pilings, each 2 feet in diameter. Disguised as tree roots, the pilings were buried 42 feet down. The trunk was a hollow concrete pedestal to the height of the first bedroom. The tree was fabricated out of 110 cubic yards of concrete and 6 tons of reinforced steel, and it weighed a total of 150 tons.

The limbs of the tree reached 40 feet and were made of hollow steel tubing. The small terminal branches were also made of steel tubing. Fitted into the tubes were manzanita branches covered with plastic leaves. All the steel work was covered with plastic to look just like a natural tree, including the massive root system at ground level. The 202,250 vinyl leaves were bundled into 20,650 clusters at a cost of $40,000. All of the architectural elements came from either the shipwreck or from the jungle. The budget for the entire project was $254,900. The tree would become known as *Disneyodendron semperflorens grandis*—large, everblooming Disney tree.

Guests climbed 39 steps and reached three landings before viewing the Family Room. Playing in the background was the memorable "Swissapolka" by Disney staff composer Buddy Baker. Eight more steps led to Mother and Father's Bedroom. Just like in the film, there was a thatched hinged opening in the ceiling. Twelve more steps took guests to the highest point in the attraction, the Crow's Nest that acted as the boys' bedroom. From there, guests enjoyed outstanding views of the Jungle Cruise below.

Throughout the climb, guests came into contact with a clever bamboo water wheel system that used a continuous supply of scoops and pulleys to lift 200 gallons of water per hour high into the tree. The system delivered clean, running water to every room. The rope work was installed by Ray Wallace, who also designed and fabricated Frontierland's *Columbia*.

At the base of the tree was the kitchen, with "all the latest innovations," and the library. The park estimated that the average guest would take about 7 minutes to walk through the attraction. The tree house would prove to be an intimate experience with little distraction from projected images or special effects. It was not hard for the guest to imagine what life would be like living in the tree house.

On the other side of Adventureland was the new Safari Game Hunt, which opened on July 24, 1962. The shooting gallery opened with 12 semiautomatic guns using compressed air and capable of shooting 14 shots per guest. For the Disneyland attraction, Sam McKim designed the largest variety of targets of any shooting gallery in the United States. Like the Main Street and Frontierland shooting galleries, the targets were painted each night, requiring more than 37 gallons of paint per week.[36] Ricocheting pellets had the unfortunate habit of hitting the guests; after a number of lawsuits, Disney decided to replace the air guns with technology first developed at Knott's Berry Farm. The new guns used electronic beams to trigger special effects with animated elephants, crocodiles, tropical birds, lions, and hippos.

The Adventureland Bazaar was also remodeled in 1962. Imagineer Rolly Crump was put in charge of the six-week project and given a budget of $38,000. To expedite the process, Crump found items in the boneyard (backstage at Disneyland). He also recycled bits of trim from the Swift's Chicken Plantation House. The results were three intimate shops separated by the floor materials and old ticket booths as cash register stands. Guests could browse the unique items from General Lee's Shop, Guatemalan Weavers, and The Magic Carpet.[37]

According to Crump, when he started working on the project, Ken Anderson took him aside and said, "Now you guys remember that when you're designing anything for Disneyland, you're the gods! You tell them what you want, and you make sure that they do it your way no matter what!" Then Crump met with Walt, who told him, "You gotta remember that there are electricians, there are plumbers, there's air conditioning . . . you've got to work around that . . . they're just as important as you are."[38]

Throughout the park, small improvements were also being made. In Frontierland, the Indian Trading Post opened in the Indian Village on July 4. The structure was constructed of logs and sheltered by a sod roof. The park hired a Chippewa Indian to design the new store and Indian Village. The remodel was patterned after styles typical of the Northwest Plains Indians. There was a "lean-to" refreshment stand nearby, and the Indian War Canoes loading area was reconfigured so that the boats docked horizontally along the riverbank.[39]

Backed up behind the Tahitian Terrace but facing Main Street was the turn-of-the-century Plaza Pavilion restaurant-cafeteria. Guests could dine outside on the dining porches or sit on the umbrellaed terrace. It shared a kitchen with the Tahitian Terrace. Evans recalled that when he planted a pepper tree beside the restaurant, "Walt walked by and made a comment in passing that it was a little too close to the curb." Evans moved the 10-ton tree back a few feet, and "the next day we walked by and Walt didn't say a word. He just smiled."[40]

There were changes in Tomorrowland as well. On July 8, sponsorship for the Rocket to the Moon changed from TWA to McDonnell Douglas. Although the ride remained much the same, the iconic *Moonliner* rocket out front got a new look. Renamed the McDonnell Douglas *DC-78*, the rocket was repainted, and it never looked quite as impressive again. By using forced perspective, the original paint scheme had made the spaceship seem much taller than it really was; with the repaint, that illusion of height was shattered.

During the summer, the 20,000 Leagues Under the Sea exhibit was transformed every evening into a bandstand featuring rock music. Big-name artists were invited to perform for the teenage audience members, who were known to sometimes get out of hand and crowd the stage.

By the end of the year, the scaffolding that had been hiding the Haunted Mansion was removed. The exterior design of the Haunted Mansion was based, in part, on the 1857 Evergreen House in

Baltimore, Maryland. The house's exterior design had long been the source of controversy at WED. During the initial design phase, artist Ken Anderson had imagined a decrepit house set back from Disneyland's pristine public realm, but Walt opposed that idea and the project got put on the back burner.

When Harriet Burns got involved, she "built three models, two 'haunted' and one the way it looks now. We kept pushing that one back, and Walt kept picking it. When we asked why, he said, 'Because I want everything in Disneyland to look good.' He was always right."[41]

Then Walt assigned Marc Davis to work on the project. Davis said, "I couldn't understand why they wanted this plain-looking building there" and asked Walt, "What do you want us to do to the outside? Do you want to do Charles Addams or what?" Walt replied, "No Marc, I don't agree with that. I think that everything in the Park should look like we take very good care of it. I don't want to see a shabby building there. I want it pristine and clean on the outside. I want the lawn mowed, I want beautiful flowers. I want people to know that I have a clean park and they can bring their families and they can come." With that said, Walt did tell Davis, "When you get inside, then you can do anything you want." Davis got the hint. "I took that to be a very definite instruction to me, and it meant we could be scary inside the ride if we wanted to." Claude Coats thought this was a very clever idea. He said, "Everyone expects a residence for ghosts to be run-down. But Walt was always looking for the unexpected."[42] The house would remain empty for six years as guests peeked through the wrought iron fencing, fueling dozens of rumors.

Once again, attendance jumped. In 1962, more than 5.1 million guests visited Disneyland.

The BIRD SHOW

SINCE THE VERY BEGINNING, Disneyland depended on mechanical creatures to enhance and embellish the story. The first generation was based on the Project Little Man of Disneylandia days that used a mechanical cam and lever system. The second generation was the electronic hydraulic pneumatic approach, with the cam lever principle used also used in the Jungle Cruise and Mine Train Through Nature's Wonderland. These were pretty simple mechanical effects. Effects changed dramatically in 1963, when guests were treated to the next generation: Audio-Animatronics.

It began as a Confucius-type character in a restaurant for Center Street, next to the Market House in October 1959. At the push of a button, the robotic character would come to life and an actor could answer questions from the audience, mixed with his own sayings, all orchestrated by a live emcee. Comedian Wally Boag was recruited to provide the voice for the mechanical character. In addition to the central character, two comedic dragons on either side would also be able to talk.

Model maker Harriet Burns started working on a model for the Chinatown addition. "It was wonderful," she said. "So I had all this wonderful little filigree on the Chinatown to show [Walt] when he came in on Monday morning. He came in and he didn't even look at it." Walt told her, "We're not going to do Chinatown." He said, "San Francisco and L.A. have Chinatowns—there's no need for one at Disneyland."[43] Walt killed the project because he had a different idea. "Why can't we use what we've learned to create one of the presidents?"[44]

Around 1959, Walt had started toying with the idea of a Hall of Presidents as the big attraction in Liberty Square. He assigned Wathel Rogers to work with animator and sculptor Blaine Gibson. This was one of Gibson's earliest projects at WED. Walt asked Gibson to sculpt a bust for each of the presidents, but then the concept was reduced from The Hall of Presidents to *Great Moments with Mr. Lincoln*.

Walt figured he would start with animating his favorite president, Abraham Lincoln. Burns described a time when "In the shop, we had an early version of the head for Lincoln." She said, "I recall several of us were sitting around the plywood table discussing it. There was John Hench, Dick Irvine, Fred and myself. Walt said, 'Hmm . . . we can call it . . . anima . . . anima . . . Animatronics! We can combine electronics, and animation! It will be called Animatronics.' And everybody was mumbling all these words together. Then Vic Greene said, 'Yes, but there's sound in there too.' Walt said, 'Well, that would be audio.' And so they added the word Audio to Animatronics. Walt liked that! But I remember all of them saying all these funny words together and combining them. Then Walt said, 'and we can have Lincoln be our first Audio Animatronic character!' "[45] Walt thought that Audio-Animatronics would become the grand combination of all the arts because the technology included the three-dimensional realism of fine sculpture, the vitality of a great painting, the drama and personal rapport of the theater, and the artistic versatility and consistency of the motion picture.

However, it would not be a former president who would debut the new technology. Instead, it would be a flock of talkative birds and singing flowers. Hench found the perfect opportunity to use Audio-Animatronics for the first time: Stouffer's wanted to sponsor a second restaurant, and Hench suggested one that could feature a choir of tropical birds. Hench showed Walt drawings of several colorful birds that were perched directly above the tables. Walt said, "I'm not too sure about this idea, John. The birds will be pooping on the tables." Hench said, "He didn't want 'dead birds' either." Hench laughed, and responded, "These aren't real birds, Walt. These are all animated!"[46]

An early Disneyland press release read, "For the first time in his entertainment career, Walt Disney is creating a restaurant. And just as his full-length animated films, True-Life Adventures, and Disneyland pioneered in their fields, Walt's creation may alter the course of many full-course meals." Originally, the show was going to be called *The Enchanted Tiki and Bird Room featuring Disney's Legends of the Enchanted Tiki Show.*

After testing the show with audiences, it became very clear early on that the restaurant concept was not going to work. People in the test audiences never wanted to leave. Walt decided he wanted a faster turnover, so the idea was scrapped well into the design process. Because the original intention was to serve food, the show building was designed with public restrooms, and the tables they bought were moved into the Tahitian Terrace.

On June 23, 1963, *Walt Disney's Enchanted Tiki Room* opened adjacent to the gateway to Adventureland. It was the first fully Audio-Animatronics show. When it opened, it was sponsored by INA Insurance. Guests had to purchase a special ticket that was more expensive than even the 60¢ E ticket: Admission for adults was 75¢, while admission for children cost 50¢.

unofficial **TIP**
United Airlines took over sponsorship of *Enchanted Tiki Room* in 1967 until Dole took over in 1975.

As guests arrived, they waited in a small lanai. Artist Rolly Crump was put in charge of designing this area. He researched Hawaiian culture and then prepared a number of drawings of potential tiki gods. The tiki culture was very popular in America at the time. Many soldiers who had served in the Pacific theater during World War II brought back fond memories of Polynesia. Crump took his drawings to Walt for his approval and then went to sculptor Blaine Gibson for fabrication. Gibson looked at Crump and said, "Rolly, I don't have time." Crump asked who was available to do the work and Gibson replied, "You are." When Crump revealed that he had never sculpted anything in his life, Gibson joked, "You're gonna sculpt now."[47] And sculpt he did; Crump created a 10-minute preshow with seven animated figures and two static figures.

Guests entered the 240-seat theater and sat on chairs originally intended for the restaurant. Marc Davis had worked on the interior because he had a long-standing interest in Oceanic art. He was also responsible for the design of the birds. Bob Sewell assisted Davis with research in the bird study collections at the Natural History Museum. For awhile, Sewell collected a large number of tropical bird skins, but it was decided to discard them because they did not want to get a reputation that they had to kill wild birds for a Disneyland attraction.

Walt felt an Audio-Animatronics show worked best when it gave flashes of things within the subject matter. Also, the show must unfold before the guest, becoming a place of great discovery for people. Throughout the presentation, there must be unexpected surprises. In the case of the *Enchanted Tiki Room,* that surprise would first come from the talking bird, then the glee club, and finally the entire room coming to life.

Racks of sensitive electronic equipment were stored beneath the showroom. The entire show ran off a single tape drive. The cast members placed a guest book down there because they were showing it off to so many VIPs. One unintended guest benefit was that the *Tiki Room* would become the first air-conditioned non-theater attraction. Due to the very hot high-tech equipment in the basement, the building had to be air-conditioned.

Rogers developed a control system that used a joy stick. The system made an appearance on *The Disney Story* television show episode that featured Walt making José the macaw move. The joy stick system was made to control and program the birds for the *Tiki Room* attraction itself.

Programming the crude machinery was not easy. Wathel Rogers was responsible for programming the 225 birds, or personalities, directed by a 14-channel magnetic tape feeding 100 separate speakers and controlling 438 separate actions.[48] The tape recorder that they were using was the same type used in the Polaris Submarine. He programmed all the macaws with the same movements. He did the same for the other groups of birds. In one of the early tests, much to their surprise, the flowers were singing the birds' tracks, the tiki poles were singing the flowers' tracks, and the lights were flashing on and off sporadically. It was a mess.

The vocal cast was first class and included Boag (as José), fellow *Golden Horseshoe* cast member Fulton Burley (as Michael, the Irish bird), Ernie Newton (as the French Pierre), and the talented Thurls Ravencroft (as the German Fritz). Boag helped write the script. The original show was 16 minutes and 8 seconds long and was performed three times an hour.

The project was a constant challenge. Crump remembers, "When we got everything installed, and the drummers were beating their drums, I looked up there and thought, 'Those drummers look dead.' I went up there with a screwdriver and some screws and put those little sparkle things in each one of their eyes so their eyes twinkle."[49] Yale Gracey designed the climatic rainstorm.

Walt turned to his star music writing team, the award-winning Richard and Robert Sherman, to compose a song that tied everything together. The resulting theme song, "The Tiki Tiki Tiki Room," provided the necessary commentary. To give guests a preview of the unique attraction inside, the Imagineers came up with a "barker bird" named Juan (José's cousin). His job was to give the guests a preview of what was inside. He was voiced by Boag and was so impressive that he created a huge traffic jam right at the entrance to Adventureland. He was soon removed.

Walt was a huge fan of the show and would stop by frequently when he was in the park. On September 26, 1963, Walt said about the use of Audio-Animatronics characters, "Well it's another door that's opened for us. You see our whole 40 some-odd years here have been in the world of making things move. Inanimate things move, from a drawing through all kinds of little props and things." As he looked to the future, he said, "Now we're making these human figures ... dimensional human figures move ... we make animals move ... make anything move through the use of electronics ... it's just another dimension in the animation we have been doing all our life. It's a new door ... and we hope we can really do some exciting things in the future."[50]

With Autopia being one of the most popular attractions in the park, something had to be done about the constant breakdowns. The first step was for Arrow to install a center control rail just like the one that had been in use since 1960 at Six Flags Over Texas. This change meant there was no need for a side bumper anymore. Another solution was the new Mark VI car. Joe Fowler hired Arrow Development to design and build the "ultimate car" that wouldn't break up the curbs and roadways. In

1963, 160 all-new Mark VI cars from Arrow (80 for each Autopia) were delivered to the park. They had Kohler engines, Mercury clutches, and lightweight frames. Gurr worked on the Mark VI body design but did not work on the mechanics. The Mark VI had fenders and fins like the Mark V, but had an oval front end like the Mark IV. They weighed about 600 pounds.

There was only one problem with the "ultimate car." They ultimately did not work very well and were prone to frequent breakdowns. The clutch blew up on a regular basis, the light frame would get bent or break due to the crashing from the front and the back, and because they were supplied by an outside vendor, maintenance was becoming a nightmare for the operations people.

Attendance jumped 10% to 5.6 million in 1963.

▌WE'RE SELLING HAPPINESS

NOT ONLY DID DISNEYLAND CHANGE the way people experienced the built environment, it also changed the use of language in the service industry. One day early on, Walt was standing on the rail platform and he noticed a surly railroad conductor. He pulled the manager over and said, "See if you can't give that fellow a better understanding of the business we're in. Try to cheer him up. If you can't, then he shouldn't be working here. We're selling happiness. We don't want sourpusses around here."[51]

Walt quickly learned he needed complete control of every aspect of the Disneyland environment. "The first year I leased out the parking concession, brought in the usual security guards, things like that," Walt recalled. "But I soon realized my mistake. I couldn't have outside help and still get over my idea of hospitality. So now we recruit and train every one of our employees," Walt said. "I tell the security police, for instance, that they are never to consider themselves cops. They are there to help people. The visitors are our guests."[52]

Much of that training was developed by Van Arsdale France, who created the Disneyland University just before the park opened. Walt knew that "You can dream of, create, design, and build the most wonderful place in the world, but it still takes people to operate it."[53] Early on, the park was very particular who it would hire and what role they would play in the show. For example, they would not hire people who worked at an amusement park or a circus. African Americans were only hired in backstage or performer positions. There was a strict dress code and grooming standards that were adhered to. To remind the cast members what their role was in the show, the slogan "You'll Create Happiness for Others" was born.[54]

It was a tradition at Walt Disney Productions that everybody went by their first names. Walt enjoyed the informality of first names, and in an early training manual, there was a reminder "that within the berm, we don't use the Mr., Miss, or Mrs. It's Walt, or Roy, or Jack or Jane."[56]

unofficial **TIP**
Van France worked out of one of the old homes on West Street where the Disneyland Hotel is now located. Dick Nunis was his first assistant and went on to become the head of Disney theme parks.[55]

Early employees were called Disneylanders, then hosts and hostesses who work at "a gigantic outdoor show with the sky as the backdrop" and then finally cast members, for each has a role to play. Everyone who worked at the park wore a costume, not a uniform.[57]

To stand out from amusement parks, every visitor was a guest, not a customer. Guests had been invited to visit Disneyland and they were all VIPs. There were no rides, rather attractions, adventures, or experiences. A group of people were an audience, and they did not stand in lines—they waited in audience waiting areas.

The areas accessible to the public were onstage, while the areas where the show was planned and prepared was backstage. Landscaping played an important role in the show by separating the guests' areas from the backstage without destroying the illusion.

SPREADING THE SUCCESS

DISNEYLAND WAS A SMASHING SUCCESS, not only for Walt Disney Productions but also for the surrounding community. Disney had invested $46 million in the facility by 1964. The multiplier benefit to the community topped $560 million, according to ERA. Disneyland was the largest employer in town and the number one property taxpayer.

Not only was the park an economic success, it was becoming an American cultural icon. In 1965, Architect Charles Moore called it "the town square of Los Angeles"[58] and the "most important single piece of construction in the West in the past several decades."[59] Town builder James Rouse told an audience of planners and architects at Harvard in 1963 that "the greatest piece of urban design in the United States today is Disneyland."

Urban sociologist Mark Gottdiener said in 1982, "Disneyland definitely establishes a contrast to the surrounding urban life. That kind of environment is all but lost in the Los Angeles area." He noted, "It's always been the case that the best examples of urban design have come from visionaries who occasionally have been given the opportunity to produce environments that make people happy. Disneyland is an example of that." Most recently, architecture critic Beth Dunlop said, "Urban planners study Disneyland to understand ideas of proportion and perspective and to learn, more technically, about the flow of pedestrians and the placement of public spaces. Disneyland simply changed the way we think."[60]

John Hench saw the impact of the park outside the berm. He said, "Today, there is almost an endless variety of 'theme experiences.' Dining experiences, ranging from Old English Taverns to Roman gardens to World War I Air Bases, and much more. 'Shopping experiences' in the form of environmentally controlled malls in almost every major community across the nation. And there are new forms of 'recreation experiences.' For example, dreary, museum displays of fish life in conventional aquariums have evolved into oceanographic shows and seagoing experiences in parklike settings. And there is a new generation of planned residential community and municipalities consciously avoiding some of the visual contradictions so prevalent just a few years before."[61]

OTHER WORLD ILLUSION

DUE TO ESCALATING LAND COSTS in the immediate Disneyland area, some developers thought about building up instead of out. The Disneyland Hotel set the precedent when, in September 1962, they completed an 11-story tower, the tallest inhabited structure in Orange County. In planning the hotel, a tall building was not a foregone conclusion; Walt did not want any buildings outside of the park to be visible to guests inside the park. According to Edwin Ettinger, Director of Marketing for Disneyland, the Wrather Corporation performed a balloon test to convince Walt that the tower could not be seen from inside the park. New Orleans Square was strategically placed to help screen out the new hotel tower.

Even with the success of Disneyland, Anaheim struggled to attract national brand chain hotels. In late 1963, it looked like things were about to change. Sheraton-West had submitted a plan to the City of Anaheim to build a $15 million, 22-story, 780-room hotel at the northeast corner of Ball Road and West Street. The hotel tower would have a penthouse restaurant that would look right into the park.[62] If it were successful, the thinking was other chains would follow.

May 1964 brought another high-rise proposal. Entrepreneur Leo Freedman wanted to build a ten-story office tower, a five-story bank building, and a public plaza with fountains right across the street from the park's entrance.[63] Freedman was known for Melodyland, a theater in the round at Freedman Way and Harbor Boulevard that he had built in 1963. The *Anaheim Bulletin* described the project as "virtually in the afternoon shadow of Disneyland's Matterhorn."[64] Although it was considered the first legitimate theater in Orange County, Melodyland lasted only a few years before being converted into a church.

Disneyland management was committed to Anaheim's success but did not fully embrace Freedman's high-rise proposal. They were becoming increasingly concerned about the threat of outside buildings encroaching on the park's carefully planned vistas; in June 1964, they asked the City Council to consider adopting height limits. In a rare moment, Walt personally "asked councilmen to help preserve the worlds of illusion which he and his artists have worked to create in Disneyland." He wrote in a letter, "I find it hard to understand how anyone willing to make such an investment can fail to see or comprehend the importance of Disneyland's basic concept, to their own best interests as well as ours."[65] With a new $10 million Anaheim municipal auditorium and convention center dependent on Disneyland's economic sustainability, Walt's influence was staggering. He reminded the City Council, "I don't want the public to see the world they live in while they're in the park. I want them to feel they're in another world."[66] Maintaining this illusion was part of the magic formula for Disneyland's long-term success.

To back up his assertions, Walt presented the expert testimony of his landscape architect, Bill Evans, who explained, "I think it is important to point out that the landscape scene, an integral and essential element of the Disneyland image, was never conceived to be a wall or a king-size hedge around the Park, but rather to create, insofar as possible, the illusion of another land, limited visually only by a natural backdrop of varying trees silhouetted against the sky." To preserve this effect, Disney officials said they had spent more than $100,000 on screening since 1957.

The Disney team prepared a map that outlined potential development zones. Inside the park was the area where Space Mountain would
eventually be built. On property they owned outside the park, the
backstage area to the north of the railroad tracks was also slated for
development. Across West Street, west of Frontierland, was another
area under consideration. The park frontage along Harbor Boulevard
was set aside for new backstage service areas. From this baseline map,
the team also created a visual-intrusion contour map that presented
zones with recommended height limitations. [67]

The permit review process was moving forward, and the Planning
Commission approved the Sheraton-West project in July, contingent
on some required changes. The building height was reduced from 22
stories to 14, but the penthouse restaurant with a view into the park
could remain in the plans.

Then in August, Anaheim received yet another proposal for a
high rise: a group of developers wanted to build the Angel Spire,
a 750-foot tower modeled after the Seattle Space Needle. The project
budget was $6 million and included a revolving restaurant, cocktail
lounge, observation tower, and storage facilities. It would be located
on 4 acres near the proposed municipal baseball stadium. There was
no doubt that this project would be visible from inside the park.

By this time, Disney was beginning to gain traction with city officials with its height limit proposal. At a joint City Council and Planning Commission meeting in August, the Disney team proposed a
sliding scale, dependent on the distance from the Plaza Hub. The goal
was to preserve the "in another world" illusion that Disneyland and
its visitors cherished so much. Properties adjacent to the park were
limited to a 75-foot height. A structure 1,800 feet from the Plaza Hub
could rise to 100 feet. At 2,200 feet from the Plaza Hub, a building could reach up to 125 feet. At 2,600 feet, approximately one-half
mile, a hotel could build a tower of 150 feet. With a unanimous 6-0
vote, the City Council sided with Disney.

Not everyone in Anaheim agreed with the height-limit vote. The
community was politically conservative, and many leaders felt that
Disneyland had no right to dictate what property owners did with
their own land. The *Anaheim Gazette* said the park was "neither
a sacred shrine nor a natural resource." The newspaper emphati-
cally stated, "It is called a park in the sense of 'amusement park,' not
'national park.' "[68]

HUMOR DOESN'T HURT ANYBODY

ONE DAY EARLY ON, Walt was standing in front of the Jungle Cruise, watching and listening to his guests as he usually did. As a couple passed by, one was heard to say something like, "Oh, we've been on that. We don't need to go again." Right then and there he was reminded that he always had to keep the show fresh, and the concept of plussing was born. He said, "We can't be satisfied . . . even though we'll get the crowds. We've always got to give 'em a little more. It will be worth the investment. If they ever stop coming, it'll cost 10 times that much to get 'em back." Walt felt, "Whenever I go on a ride, I'm always thinking of what's wrong with the thing and how it can be improved."[69]

In that spirit, Walt thought it would be fun to have little vignettes representative of each land as a special treat for riders of the Santa Fe & Disneyland Railroad, so he asked animator Marc Davis to visit Disneyland and see if he had any ideas. The hope was the guests would see something they liked and would be encouraged to visit that attraction.

Davis first visited Disneyland in 1960 and was not very impressed. He felt it was as stale as most World's Fairs and certainly lacked a sense of humor. In animation, Davis was brilliant at capturing the maximum humor out of the least amount of movement, and he would be revolutionary in applying those talents to theme park attraction design.

Davis came up with all sorts of gags, including members of a trapped safari who have climbed up a post with a rhinoceros close behind. Walt was so impressed he decided to forgo the preview tableau and to put the scene in the Jungle Cruise. Davis continued to generate memorable gags, such as the African veldt, where a wide variety of animals are watching a pride of lions guarding over their prey, and the sacred bathing pool of the elephants described below. For the first time, humor was the foundation of an attraction. Davis said, "You want to take your family down there and have some fun and be entertained, and humor doesn't hurt anybody."[70]

Humor may not hurt anybody, but not everyone on the team was laughing. "There were some square people working down there." Davis concluded. "You know, Joe Fowler couldn't stand me, originally, because he was basically running the whole thing . . . sort of the overall manager. And everything I did involved a change, or something, down there. He wasn't very happy with that."[71] The new elements would have to wait until the [1964 New York] World's Fair projects were done.

When the Jungle Cruise closed and reopened in 1964, it was a very different ride. John Hench said, "[The Jungle Cruise] began in 1955 at Disneyland as an adaption from our True-Life Adventure films. We created an attraction where all the things that you might see on a jungle river journey actually do happen. The truth of the matter is, you could probably spend two years on a real journey like that before you'd see everything."[72] With Davis's influence and contribution, the tone had changed from the serious to a comic journey through the jungles of the world with a touch of fantasy. A good example was the Sacred Bathing Pool of the Elephants. As Hench pointed out, "Our guests know that real elephants wouldn't lurk under the water and then rise up to squirt the boat. And they know that a real herd of elephants wouldn't be quite so happy with a strange boat in their midst." He noted, "Real elephants would have either retreated defensively into the jungle or smashed the boat to pieces." The Disney difference is "we've programmed in a Utopian realism, added a touch of fun and fantasy and the guests love it."[73]

Sculptor Blaine Gibson had not worked on the original version of the Jungle Cruise, and he was not fond of the attraction's animals. Gibson's job was to translate Davis's "wonderful little sketches and concepts" into scale models. Gibson built a model of the entire Jungle Cruise layout. One day Walt stopped by to look at the model and started to act like an elephant reaching for a branch, like in the True-Life Adventures. Gibson grasped what Walt was trying to do immediately and added a figure to the model.

Gags could come from anywhere. During a preliminary walk-through with Walt, the group ended up at the Trapped Safari scene, where a rhinoceros had run an expedition team up a tree. Imagineer Bob Sewell said, "Walt put on a riotous verbal description of what the action would be, with the bottom hunter getting 'goosed.' One of us had a high, funny laugh. Walt heard it and said, 'That's it, let's have all the hyenas laugh like that!'"[74] All of this new fun demanded that the length of the ride be expanded from 7 minutes to 9 minutes.

Walt enjoyed the addition of humor to the park, but he also continued to include educational accuracy in his attractions. For example, Frontierland's *Columbia* had fulfilled Walt's desire to create a more active waterfront, but he also wanted to use the vessel as a way to teach. Opening February 22, 1964, the lower deck was outfitted as it would have appeared in 1787, when the commercial ship set sail to circumnavigate the globe, traveling 41,899 miles in three years. On display were eight bunks, a galley, a sail and rope-making display, officer's quarters, bilge pump, cargo bales, navigation charts, and a mess table. Guests could walk below deck and imagine what life aboard ship might have been like.

THIS STUFF IS REALLY WEIRD

ANOTHER PROJECT that Walt wanted to get started on was updating Tomorrowland. At lunch with Walt one day, Ray Bradbury asked, "Walt, why don't you hire me to come in and help you with ideas to rebuild Tomorrowland?" Walt replied, "Ray, it's no use . . . you're a genius and I'm a genius . . . after two weeks we'd kill each other!" Bradbury was flattered, "That's the nicest turndown I've ever had, having Walt Disney call me a genius."[75] Bradbury never got to work on Tomorrowland, but Walt did like bouncing ideas off of his friend. During the lunch, Walt began to talk about an indoor attraction that combined the thrills of the Matterhorn Bobsleds with the experience of space travel.

The haunted house was also on Walt's mind, and he returned to the project in July. The idea had been brewing for a long time, and he decided to get Marc Davis involved. Davis successfully brought his unique sense of humor to the project. One of the ideas that Davis developed was the stretching pictures for the elevators that would take guests down to the basement. He would frequently show them off to visitors at WED.

Among Davis's bag of tricks were paintings that would slowly morph from one image into another. Davis was filled with ideas for this illusion. In one, Henry the VIII first appears alone; then Anne Boleyn joins him in the image holding her own head. She then turns to Henry and tells him off. Davis also conceived a great white hunter who is killed by the tiger he is looking for. Ever the deep thinker, Davis even came up with a portrait of Faust selling his soul to the Devil and the Devil collecting.

Walt also assigned Imagineer Rolly Crump to the haunted house project. Crump looked at the previous efforts and described them as the "Cat and the Canary" kind of haunted house similar to a 1940s-era spook house film. For example, as guests walked through the house, they would find secret panels and portraits on the walls with eyeholes. Crump felt that the reliance on such movie clichés would not be very interesting and wanted to explore different ideas. He had been influenced by Federico Fellini and the foreign version of *Beauty and the Beast* and wanted to use the human body as the basis for architectural elements. For example, Crump envisioned a light scone made of a human arm holding a torch.

Even with Davis and Crump on the job, Walt wanted more ideas. In October, he brought in his senior people, including Davis, Claude Coats, Chuck Miles, and Dick Irvine. He gave each 45 minutes to pitch their ideas, and the meeting went on for about 4 hours. When all of the designers had finished their presentations, Walt asked about some objects he had seen on Crump's bench. Crump replied, "I'm not sure what they are, Walt, but I feel that unless we put something in that's different, the Haunted Mansion is going to be just the same old thing." Walt replied, "This stuff is really weird, Rolly! What the hell are we going to do with that?" Crump could only answer, "I know it's weird. That's why I did it!" Walt paused and then said, "Well, that's it!" and left.[76]

The next day, Crump arrived very early at work and found Walt sitting on a stool, wearing the same clothes as the day before. Walt told the young artist, "You son of a gun! I couldn't sleep last night! All that stuff you showed me yesterday, it drove me crazy all night. But I know what we're going to do with it!" He decided that a Museum of the Weird would be a perfect addition to a spill area for guests entering and leaving the mansion. Walt and Crump talked until 9:30 a.m., when the rest of the senior team arrived. Walt turned to them and announced that Crump would be heading up the project.[77]

In November, just outside the berm, construction started on the building pads for Pirates of the Caribbean and The Haunted Mansion. The future of Disneyland was being built. Attendance was 5.9 million in 1964.

SET *on the* SHELF

AS DISNEYLAND REACHED ITS 10TH BIRTHDAY in 1965, it was preparing for a major growth spurt, and the *Anaheim Bulletin* described Disney's third child as a "teenage giant." The park dubbed the occasion the "Tencennial," and Walt was certainly proud of his baby. The success of his 1964 New York World's Fair pavilions had given him the confidence to reach even higher. Over 10 years, the Disney organization had poured more than $53 million into the park. Annual attendance jumped from 3.8 million in 1955 to more than 6.4 million in 1965. All of this took place within the 65 acres surrounded by the berm. Walt Disney Production's confidence in the project was cinched, and on February 2, they purchased WED Enterprises.

Since his meeting with Walt in late 1964, John Hench had been toying with the idea of a "spaceport" for Tomorrowland. "Walt didn't call it Space Mountain at that time but he felt we needed an attraction in Tomorrowland that would present the future through space travel."[78] In *Designing Disney*, Hench said, "Walt wanted to build a roller-coaster style ride, but in the dark, which no one had ever done before. He wanted to have precise control of the lighting and to be able to project moving images on the interior walls."[79] He added, "Walt had a prophetic ability and knowledge of how to bring different experiences together in a perfect blend, and he knew Space Mountain would be an attraction that would enrich the guest's experience one step farther."[80]

By February, Hench had drafted the now-famous image of a futuristic cone with the hopes that the attraction could make it into the plans for the Tomorrowland update scheduled for 1967. "Space Mountain begged to be cone shaped," said Hench. "It wanted to echo the expanding spiral of the ride inside. The form housing the ride follows its movement, so that the center of the structure is naturally elevated, like the peak of a mountain being pushed up from the pressure below."[81]

Hench proposed a layered environment that would permit multiple experiences just like other areas in the park. The big draw would be a roller coaster with four separate tracks inside (and outside) of the show building. Also, inside of the cone would be space for pedestrians on one level and for the continuous motion of the proposed PeopleMover trains on another. He completed the plan in 1966, but there was only one problem. At the time, ride control systems were not sophisticated enough to have multiple rockets rolling down the track in the dark at the same time. The project was put on the shelf. Hench's image of a space dome was so compelling that it would be reproduced on souvenir maps many years before the attraction actually opened.

On June 9, Vic Greene began preparation for the building that would house It's a Small World. The massive building was one-third larger than the New York World's Fair facility and covered 1.5 acres (114,600 square feet). The building was prominently placed at the north end of the berm. To make room, the Midget Autopia and the Fantasyland train station were removed.

Installation of the Small World building meant moving the rail-road tracks back approximately 75 yards, with significant change to the park's largest berm at the north end of the park, which had been designed to block the noise from the interchange of Harbor Boulevard and the Santa Ana Freeway. This would be a constant at Disneyland. When Walt would come up with new ideas, Evans would have to readjust the landscape, just like putting another notch in a belt.

The trees along the berm had matured since the park's opening and were very large. They would have also been very expensive to replace. Bill Evans devised a plan to transplant the trees. His solution was to bore 1-inch holes through the trunks of the trees, about 4 feet above the grade, put a case-hardened steel pin through each hole, and place four guy-wires into the branches of the tree. The arborists would then hook the pin to a crane and lift the tree out of the dirt. They did not box the roots. Then they would move the tree to the new location. Once it was replanted, they removed the steel pin and inserted a piece of hardwood treated with a fungicide. After a couple of years, the hole would not be noticeable. Their success rate was approximately 85%.

New to Main Street and overlooking the Plaza Hub was the Plaza Inn. The dining facility opened on July 18 at a cost of $1.7 million and replaced the Red Wagon Inn. Designed by John Hench, the Plaza Inn was a plush Victorian restaurant with specially made bevel-leaded glass windows and abundant mirrors. It featured two dining rooms with 18th-century crystal chandeliers, two lighted-lamp dining porches, and two dining terraces with slightly elevated seating areas to encourage people watching. Also new to Main Street was the new Mr. Lincoln show in the State of Illinois Information Center, located in the Opera House. Guests could also find the shoe shine stand nearby. It was "one of the last 10-cent shine parlors in the country with dancing shine boys to entertain as well as turn out polished shoes."[82]

WE'RE JUST GETTIN' STARTED

AS PART OF THE 10TH ANNIVERSARY CELEBRATION, Walt gathered the remaining cast members who had participated in the Grand Opening day. The event took place at the Magnolia Room in the Disney-land Hotel on July 15, 1965. It was an important moment for Walt. He was with the people who made his dream come true, and it was a chance for him to reflect on the past and to project his ideas for the future.

He began with a humorous story on how he had found comedian Wally Boag, the star of the long-running *Golden Horseshoe Revue*. Even though the show had been running 10 years, Boag quipped, "We're still in rehearsal, Walt." Walt replied, "Yeah . . . That's my tag line." Then he turned his attention to Admiral Joe Fowler. He said, "We had to have somebody that could take ahold of this thing and really make it work. So we were told about this retired admiral that had run the San Francisco Navy Yard." Walt had initially hired Fowler as a part-time consultant, but "little by little we got him sort of trapped into the thing."[83]

As Walt reflected on the problems of launching Disneyland, he recalled how everybody had asked, "What the Hell's he want that damn amusement park for?" Walt's only explanation was, "I wanted it." He described how the NBC and CBS television networks had fought him and how ABC had profited from the relationship. Shortly after the park opened, the bankers had told Roy that they would not lend the brothers any more money. Roy, not one to mince words, had told them, "Well, if you're gonna start runnin' our business, we're goin' out and find some other place we can borrow money." Walt told the audience, "By gosh, they finally gave him the money."[84]

"If we could have bought more land, we'd have bought it," Walt said. He would have "control and it wouldn't look too much like a second-rate Las Vegas around here." However, the brothers ran out of money and "by the time that we did have a little money, everybody got wise to what was goin' on and we couldn't buy anything around the place at all, you know."[85]

Walt and Roy were grateful to the cast members who had "been a part of making this thing come across." He said, "It's just been a sort of dress rehearsal and we're just getting started." But he warned them, "If any of you start to rest on your laurels, I mean, just uh . . . forget it."[86]

Just to prove his point, Walt touted Dick Nunis, who was running the park at the time. Walt related how Nunis would tell him, "You know, we've got to take care of these people." For Walt that meant "trying to enlarge the park to take care of the extra millions [Nunis] thinks we're gonna gain every year." Nunis showed Walt "a graph where you started here with 3 million and the way he's got it going it's goin' up to 10 million and he may be right." Over the years, Nunis would prove that he knew what he was talking about.[87]

"We do have plans to expand [the park] . . . to open up areas that will . . . it's like a sponge," Walt said about the future. "You have to have these areas to absorb the people, you know." He talked of the new Tomorrowland, New Orleans Square, and the Haunted Mansion. Maybe even a new Fantasyland in 1966 (the addition of It's a Small World). He promised "forty plus million dollars' worth of stuff planned out for the next five years" if he could secure the money. "Thank God," he quipped to this inside audience, "for [the 1964 Disney film] *Mary Poppins* out there."[88]

With confidence, Walt told his cast members, "You know my office is above my brother's and I look down and when I see him walking on the ceiling . . . you know . . . That's the time I go down and say, 'Let's put another $10 million in Disneyland.' And lately he's been walking all around that ceiling." He ended with, "As I say, we're just gettin' started, you know."[89]

LINCOLN'S OWN PEN

THE *TIKI ROOM* HAD JUST BEEN THE START—*Great Moments with Mr. Lincoln* would take Audio-Animatronics entertainment to a whole new level. The show debuted at the 1964–1965 New York World's Fair. It was the featured attraction at the State of Illinois pavilion and was a huge hit. Just to be safe, WED built two custom Mr. Lincolns. A slightly more advanced second figure was installed at Disneyland. The show would open in the Opera House on Main Street U.S.A. on July 18, 1965. Bringing Mr. Lincoln to life was estimated to have cost $1.5 million.

For Walt, the Lincoln project was very personal. He said, "Most Americans will agree with me that no man has had more of a positive impact on a nation than Abraham Lincoln has on our country. He is venerated not only in our land but in many other parts of the world. Yet I have always felt that too few people realize that Lincoln's concepts and philosophies are as useful, as necessary, as applicable today as they were when he pronounced them a century ago."[90] Walt was impressed with "his analysis of freedom and its true meaning, his approach to justice and equality, his own courage and strength—all are as vital in the 1960s as they were during the mid-1800s."[91]

He noted, "There were many fine statues of the great Civil War President and an even larger number of Lincoln portraits and photographs. Many of us have spent memorable moments in theaters as some of our best actors have brought him to life on the stage or motion picture screen." Plus, "Hundreds of volumes have been written about the man Lincoln, and some of his speeches and writings are still among history's most often quoted passages."[92] But Walt wanted to find some new way to convey the complexities of the man and the strength of the message.

Walt felt Audio-Animatronics was the solution. "Such a medium, I realized, would have to offer the three-dimensional authenticity created by a talented sculptor, as well as the color and life left on canvas by the genius-painter's brush," Walt said. "The drama and personal rapport of the theater were indispensable. This technique must have the artistic versatility and consistency of the motion picture. From the best literary sources must come the proper atmosphere which this medium must create. And, finally, Lincoln's own pen must supply the most important element of all . . . the message."[93]

Marty Sklar remembered, "Walt said that Audio-Animatronics would not replace human beings but there was no way of doing some of the shows if he had to provide coffee breaks every hour and have somebody do a perfect show time after time from 8 a.m. to 1 a.m." John Hench agreed, saying that the issue was even "more important than coffee breaks." He said, "Human beings, you know, have family fights. Really, their performances are different every day. [Walt] wanted to have the best performance. So whatever we did, we rehearsed it until we got it the way Walt wanted it. Then we recorded, and the performance was the same from then on. The same enthusiasm and gusto as the first time. That's something you can't expect from humans."

Some of the Imagineers had reservations. "The Lincoln show certainly didn't appear to some of us the right thing to do," Blaine Gibson said. "It seemed that we were getting into areas that were competitive with acting, something that could be done much better by live performers."[94] He added, "I thought at the time that we'd be fooling with something that the American people considered to be almost sacred, historically. I just couldn't see us doing it in an acceptable way, but we went ahead." [95]

As work continued, Gibson realized what Walt was trying to achieve. He said, "No matter how great the actors were they usually didn't have the physiognomy to be believable. I suspect that Walt was hoping that we could, for the first time in history, really make Lincoln look like Lincoln. Something that an actor could never do, and something that a makeup man could never do."[96]

Ray Bradbury was fascinated with the project. He wrote, "I watched the finishing touches being put on a second computerized, electric- and air-pressure-driven humanoid that will 'live' at Disneyland from this summer on (1965). I saw this new effigy of Mr. Lincoln sit, stand, shift his arms, turn his wrists, twitch his fingers, put his hands behind his back, turn his head, look at me, blink and prepare to speak. In those few moments I was filled with an awe I have rarely felt in my life."[97] He claimed, "Only a few hundred years ago all this would have been considered blasphemous, I thought. To create man is not man's business, but God's, it would have been said. Disney and every technician with him would have been bundled and burned at the stake in 1600." Bradbury declared, "Disney is the first to make a robot that is convincingly real, that looks, speaks, and acts like a man. Disney has set the history of humanized robots on its way toward wider, more fantastic excursions into the needs of civilization."[98]

Gibson sculpted the figure based on a life mask from 1860 and a treasure trove of historic photos from Mathew Brady, a 19th-century Civil War photographer. Gibson was lucky. Because Lincoln was alive during the early years of photography, he had to take poses that he could hold for a long time. Looking through archives, Gibson was aided by multiple side views, front views, and three-quarter views.

One of the things Walt insisted on was having a fully operable mouth on the figure, which would be able to shape the sounds A, E, I, O, and U. He assigned this task to Wathel Rogers, who worked with some of the guys in the machine shop to create something that had never been tried before. Their solution was to place little actuators at the corners of the mouth, which was a solid technical solution, but there was only one problem. Rogers called Blaine Gibson and asked him if he could sculpt Lincoln's head bigger than life size to fit all of the primitive electronics inside. To make it work, Gibson made the entire figure larger than the president's 6-foot 4-inch frame. Once they accomplished that, they focused on animating the actual figure.

The *Great Moments with Mr. Lincoln* show ran 12 minutes and was free to guests under the age of 17. It began in a foyer decorated with a knotted-pile carpet reminiscent of a 19th-century White House reception room. On one wall was a picture window overlooking a model of the White House that was 11.5 feet long and 4.5 feet tall. From the foyer, guests moved into the preshow theater, which was decorated with 900 yards of Rovana-Verel blue draperies. On a 28-foot screen was a slide show called *The Lincoln Story*.

Sam McKim recalled unveiling the preshow to Walt. "They were all set up and they ran these slides, one after the other, and they were timed with full music and narration, and the voice of Lincoln. Everything except the final painting, and I had the original right there." Walt turned to McKim and said, "Sam, you did a good job!"

THE FIVE SPEECHES used for Abraham Lincoln's address in *Great Moments with Mr. Lincoln* were his address at Sanitary Fair, Baltimore, Maryland, on April 18, 1864; his speech at Edwardsville, Illinois, on September 11, 1858; his address before the Young Men's Lyceum in Springfield, Illinois, on January 27, 1838; his eulogy to Henry Clay in Springfield on July 6, 1852; and his address at Cooper Institute in New York City on February 27, 1860.

Imagineer Jim Algar took McKim to his office and said, "You know, Walt just complimented you, and I want you to know something. In all my 46 years here, Walt has complimented me twice. You remember this. It doesn't happen very often."[99]

The 500-seat main theater was fitted with red Stellar-series theater seats. Adorning the stage was 150 yards of red draperies. When the curtain rose, the guests would see Abraham Lincoln seated at the center of the stage. The creative team decided against Lincoln giving the "Gettysburg Address." They felt it was famous enough and it did not meet the purpose, "an in-depth, fresh presentation of Lincoln's principles, ideals, and philosophies." Instead, they edited together statements from five of Lincoln's speeches, the first in 1838 and the last in 1864. Actor Royal Dano was personally selected by Walt to portray the president.

The impact was immediate. "A new door opened for us," Walt said. "Our whole 40-some years here have been in the world of making things move. Inanimate things move from a drawing board through all kinds of little props and things. Now we're making these dimensional human figures move . . . animals move . . . anything move through the use of electronics. It's all programmed . . . predetermined. It's another dimension in the animation we have been doing all our lives. It's a new door . . . a new toy . . . and we hope we can really do some exciting things in the future."[100]

Gibson remembered being in Disneyland and watching the show. Sitting up front was a person crying. Gibson said, "This was after the show, after the flag and the choir singing, and I thought, 'Well, how wrong can you be, Blaine . . . and how right can Walt be?' It was clear who had the vision around there."[101]

TOO MANY GOOD IDEAS

WITH THE WORLD'S FAIR OUT OF THE WAY, Marc Davis was able to return to one of Walt's obsessions, the pirate walk-through museum. Davis's approach initially was to explore the possibility of using real pirates in the show. He studied H. C. Pyle, who was known to have defined the image of the pirate that most people know today. However, as he dived deeper into the material, he began to realize that these characters were not the sort of people you would expect from Disney. He learned that they were not very glamorous, rather unlikable, and very few died in battle. Instead, many succumbed to venereal disease or other ailments. Davis decided to move away from using historical figures and started to create something that was more humorous. This decision gave him the freedom to make the attraction funny and entertaining.

When it was time to show the boss his ideas, Davis recalled, "the funny thing was, Walt was never quite ready to look at these drawings [the walk-through version]. He'd come into my room and not look at the walls and boards. He'd come in and he'd talk to me about pirates, but he would deliberately not look at the storyboards." Davis added, "It was annoying as hell to me, because I knew I had some work that I thought was pretty good, and also, I wanted to know what he thought about them."[102] Of course, what Davis did not realize was that Walt had other ideas.

By this time, construction of the basement that would house the attraction had already been completed. However, nothing happened. The hole would sit vacant for a couple of years while Dick Nunis pushed for something with greater capacity. With the knowledge and experience gained from the World's Fair, Walt agreed.

They mocked up the attraction as a quarter-inch model. Walt was staring at the model one morning and said, "We've got to go under the railroad track and build a great big building. There are too many good ideas. We have some good effects and everything. We should start all over again. We'll just make a grotto out of this part in the front."[103] Davis now knew why Walt hesitated to look at his walk-through drawings. The walk-through was a thing of the past, and now Walt wanted a grand show placed in a building outside the berm.

*un*official **TIP**

MAPO Inc. was the manufacturing arm of WED Enterprises. It was named after the hit movie *Mary Poppins*.

Claude Coats turned to the master of attraction layouts, Bill Martin, to reroute the track underneath the berm to the show building. Martin had to work with the existing basement, which was designed for the walk-through attraction and was a very tight, confined space. Making things even more difficult were structural columns that were already in place and could not be moved. Martin had to figure out how to move the boats around efficiently with their limited turning radiuses in this space and then had to build a tunnel underneath the railroad tracks to a much larger show building outside the berm.

Davis had been working a walk-through attraction. With the changes, everything that he had been working on had to be reconsidered. All of a sudden, they had more room than they ever imagined. The first challenge the Imagineers had to deal with was what to do with the big hole in New Orleans Square. They had to fill it up with something. They pulled out the 1963 drawings of coastal caverns done by Collin Campbell, and Marc Davis suggested the skeletons.

Adding guest capacity was the primary goal. Even the very popular Skyway underwent a major refurbishment that increased the capacity by incorporating Bob Gurr's square-shaped, four-passenger gondola made of fiberglass. It is possible that the park's 50 millionth guest, Mary Adams, took a ride during her visit on August 12. More than 6.4 million guests visited the park in 1965.

A LITTLE BOAT RIDE

IN FEBRUARY 1963, an official from UNICEF (United Nations International Children's Emergency Fund) had approached Joe Fowler and asked if WED could build them a ride for the 1964–1965 New York World's Fair. Fowler told them no, they were already working on three very complex shows and could not handle another one. When Walt heard this, he reminded Fowler who made the decisions. On February 15, Walt committed to the UNICEF project and, with very little time to spare, he turned to his already overworked staff and said, "There's one more piece of real estate left at the Fair, and we can have it if we want it. Pepsi-Cola is willing to sponsor whatever we do and it'll be a salute to UNICEF . . . I've got an idea for a little boat ride."

Rolly Crump said, "That's how it went, from the day Walt had said, 'I've got an idea for a boat ride' to the opening of it's a small world nine months later! We didn't have time to think this out . . . we designed it, built it and installed it in nine months, and that included Walt's approval, before we shipped it to New York."[104] Crump speculated "that Walt kind of liked that last-minute crunch, and the spontaneity that came with it." Walt did say, "Everyone needs deadlines. Even the beavers. They loaf around all summer, but when they are faced with the winter deadline, they work like fury. If we didn't have deadlines, we'd stagnate."[105]

Walt had initially turned to Davis for some ideas, but he was not satisfied with the results. Crump said, "Marc Davis did a real nice rendering, but when Walt looked at it he smiled, turned to Dick Irvine and said, 'What's Mary Blair doing?'" Artist Mary Blair had worked on the Christmas sequence in *The Three Caballeros,* and Walt felt her unique style captured much of the same spirit he was seeking for his boat ride. Crump suggested that Walt "liked the two-dimensional style she used when doing her Little Golden Books. Mary chose that style, of positive and negative shapes, and she went to a new level with her work on small world."[106]

Blair was put in charge of the overall design of the attraction and the color styling. Campbell and Coats assisted with the initial show design for the sets. Crump and Jack Ferges worked from Blair's paintings and collages to create the three-dimensional set pieces and toys. Alice Davis designed the costumes and her husband, Marc, did the sketches of the figures he called "rubber heads."

Walt wanted something simple, something innocent. He did not want a story. Nor did he want a commercial or political message. The ride has been described as "purposely unsophisticated." He just wanted his guests to be immersed in the sense of innocence and pure joy that comes with children united in happiness. The attraction would be a collage of stylized cultural figures, sounds, and backgrounds featuring cultural landmarks.

It was up to Blaine Gibson to turn all of this two-dimensional art into three-dimensional figures. It was not easy. Gibson struggled with Blair's very specific style, but he inevitably caught the essence of her concepts and Marc Davis's drawings. For the eyes, Gibson and Imagineer Orlando Ferante went to every doll eye manufacturer in Los Angeles and bought everything they could find.

As the figures were being sculpted, Alice Davis began to design the costumes and asked Walt for the task's budget. Walt raised his eyebrow and said, "I have a building over there filled with book-keepers that find the money. I want the most beautiful costumes that every little girl, no matter what age she is, would love to have to play with. So you make the most beautiful costumes you can make."[107] One of Davis's innovations was the development of a pattern book that contained swatches of every material used on each garment. The book served as a guide so that anyone could properly maintain the elaborate costumes. She would use this technique with other attractions as well.

The original idea was to have each set of dolls sing the national anthem of their country as guests floated past. It did not work. It was chaos. Walt turned to his studio composers Richard and Robert Sherman. Walt told the songwriting duo, "What we need is a simple little roundelay . . . you know, like 'Row, Row, Row Your Boat.'"[108] The brothers gave it some thought, and Richard Sherman said, "There was a big problem here and it really had to do with the children in the show. Everybody knows that kids grow into adults, and it's adults that keep getting the world messed up. But in the small world of children, everybody loves each other. Then we thought of a concept. Why can't we all just be together, we only have one world to live on?"[109] The theme song, "It's a Small World," would become one of the most rerecorded songs in history. (Ironically, it may also be one of the most ridiculed songs in history.) Throughout the attraction, the song is played in the style and language specific to each culture on display as the boats pass by.

The New York version debuted on April 22, 1964, to rave reviews, and soon it became one of the most popular attractions at the Fair. More than 10.3 million visitors saw the show during its two-year run in New York.[110]

At the Fair, the attraction was housed in an ordinary industrial building. Walt wanted something playful that he could put out front that would become an icon. Rolly Crump suggested "a childlike Tinkertoy approach" with 100 spinning, swiveling, oscillating elements, propellers, and a carousel. The 120-foot "Tower of the Four Winds" would become the world's largest mobile. Walt liked the entrance mobile, but it was deemed too expensive to dismantle and to ship back to California, so, unfortunately, it was destroyed after the fair. (The Federal Sign Company in New York estimated the cost to dismantle and ship the tower back to California would be $80,000.) Instead, Walt put Mary Blair in charge of designing the entrance to the Disneyland version of the ride. She spent two and a half months on the project before giving up in frustration. With every suggestion, Walt had told her, "Mary . . . I don't think that's it."[111] Crump felt Blair struggled with working in three dimensions and could not interpret her own designs. Crump offered to take over the project but said, "I didn't want to answer to anybody but Walt." Irvine said, "No problem, Rolly." Fred Joerger and Crump modeled the facade layout out of black and white cardboard. They worked quickly and completed the model in only seven days. As they were building the model, they set a tray full of little trees on top of the show building. Walt stopped by and said, "You know what I really like about what you did here? I like the idea that you put the trees on the roof. That way, nobody will now there's a building there." Trees were planted on the building.[112]

The building's 300-foot-wide facade would become an irresistible marquee. The structure was a geometrical montage suggestive of architecture from many nations, including France's Eiffel Tower, Italy's Leaning Tower of Pisa, and India's Taj Mahal. The Staff Shop at Disneyland was getting pretty sophisticated when it came to the life cycle and maintenance costs of the Imagineers' designs, and they decided to fabricate the facade out of fiberglass. This meant the facade did not need to repainted as frequently. Soft blue tones were added to enhance the third dimension. This would be the first attraction specifically designed with nighttime lighting in mind, with a blend of pastel shades of lavender, green, and pink. They also used gold-leaf for the decorative elements. A lot of gold-leaf. Crump estimated that they used up all the gold leaf in the United States and had to order more from Germany. The result was a facade that required very little maintenance.

On Walt's European trip in 1958, he had seen some topiary plantings. When he asked Bill Evans about them upon his return, Evans told him, "Walt, most of what you saw over there probably took 20 years to produce, and will last for a century or more!" Walt's reply was, "That's fine . . . I want some in two years!" Evans "found some fast-growing plants to use, and after that we called it 'Short-order topiary.'" Some of those topiary plantings found a home along the canal in front of the Small World attraction.[113]

Walt still wanted something out front to replace the Tower of the Four Winds, and he decided he wanted a clock. Once again, Crump built a model. As he was inspecting it, Walt said to Crump, "Roland, you've got the characters coming out the side door and going in the side door . . . they should come out the front." He then asked, "Roland . . . how many hours are there in a day?" Rolly Crump said, "24." Walt suggested, "Let's have 24 characters coming out of that clock."[114] The toy characters were designed by artist T. Hee. When it was time to approve the final model, the team ran the clock once, and Walt just stood there with no expression on his face. Then he asked them to run it again. Dick Irvine was getting very concerned about Walt's reaction and started to consider replacing Crump with Marc Davis. Then Walt said, "I like it exactly the way it is." Walt wanted to see it run once to study it and a second time to enjoy it. Irvine had not been aware that Crump and Walt met frequently, and the boss was well aware of what was going on.[115]

The clock stood 30 feet tall and chimed every 15 minutes. On the second level, the clock's hands and a huge smiling sun began to rotate, an hourglass turned over while flowers spun, seaweed patterns moved in and out, and gears on the center panels began to turn and grind. A ringing bell added to the mounting volume of merriment as numerals moved in and out while the two doors—one on each side of the clock—opened. Then, as abruptly as it began, all movement stopped, and there was total silence. After a moment there was a brief roll on snare drums and a trumpet fanfare was sounded by six toy soldiers assembled in military formation at the two doors. The first doll represented Greenwich, England, the prime basis of standard time throughout the world.

It's a Small World featured a breakthrough high-capacity ride conveyance system. Guests boarded a small, free-floating, flat-bottomed boat that was pushed by hidden water jets just beneath the water line. The 120,000-gallon trough was 1,515-feet long. The 72 boats were quiet, reliable, and able to carry 20 guests each. When the attraction was relocated to Disneyland, Crump suggested that they could create a more natural feeling by extending the water canal all the way to the edges. "Rolly, we already own the trough . . . we're not going to put water to the sets," was Walt's reply.[116]

unofficial **TIP**
When It's a Small World opened on October 1, 1971, at the Magic Kingdom in Orlando, Florida's Walt Disney World, Rolly Crump's idea to extend the water canal all the way to the edges was implemented.

Because the Disneyland show building was at least one-third larger than the New York version, the Imagineers had more room to play. It allowed them to open up the sets and reduce the irritating or conflicting elements. In general, the set pieces were in roughly the same order as the East Coast show. At the New York fair, the ride started with a Hello Room, followed by the countries organized into five geographical categories: Europe, the Orient, Africa, South America, and the South Pacific. Those regions were further subdivided into six cultural subgroups: Europe, Middle East, India, Asia, Africa, Latin America, and South Seas Islands.[117] New areas included a North Pole area and the Islands of the Pacific. The North Pole area was known as the Hello Room and was meant to resemble a pop-up book.

The attraction featured 302 lifelike children and 209 animated toys. The dolls were very simple mechanically. Many used cam-lifted shafts, pendulum pipes, rotating tube steel turntables, and 50 PSI air solenoid motor-activated valves. More than 100 nations were represented within the attraction.[118]

The show began with the Scandinavian Opening. Here, two new scenes had been added that were not in the New York show: the North Pole and Denmark. In Denmark, the children were playing in Tivoli Gardens. From there, guests floated past Western Europe. That area included a tribute to Mary Blair. Rolly Crump said, "Mary always wore wild outfits, with a poncho and black tights, and high black boots . . . she was from New York, and she had short blond hair. So we decided to include a Mary Blair doll for the ride."[119] High up on the Eiffel Tower was a doll with Blair's distinctive look. Europe East was next, followed by On to the Middle East. The Asian Holiday, Africa at Its Best, and South American Fiesta were the next three rooms. The South Pacific Islands room was also brand-new for Disneyland.

The finale was designed to hit all of the right emotional keys. With all of the dolls dressed in white and all of the children singing in English, the finale suggested that all boundaries between peoples had at last been removed. In this room, the dolls were moved very close to the boats, and they were positioned on pedestals. This was also the only place where guests saw figures that represented the United States: a cowboy and an American Indian.

Upon reflection, Crump said, "Walt's intended audience with it's a small world was everybody. Everything Walt did was for everybody, even his movies . . . he said so, and it was very true at Disneyland. He was always saying that there should be something in Disneyland for everybody." He said, "It's easy to criticize the ride today, because of all that's happened over the past four decades. It's a small world is the same ride now as it was when it opened in the 1960s, but we're not the same people."[120]

Opening day for the Disneyland It's a Small World was May 28, 1966. The huge ceremony included costumed children from 16 ethnic groups, officials from 36 consulates, and more than 800 members of the press. Water samples from the "seven seas and nine lagoons" had been deemed by Walt as mandatory. The water was poured into the trough by child ambassadors, and then 100,000 balloons were launched. Walt and Louis B. Lundborg, the chairman of sponsor Bank of America, took the first ride. Their journey around the world took 12 minutes.

When asked in 1996 why It's a Small World has remained so popular for so long, Rolly Crump said, "The key to the success of it's a small world was that in creating it, we all remained faithful to the mood and feel of Mary's [Blair] design."[121]

DISNEY REALISM

"DISNEYLAND HAS ALWAYS had a big river and a Mississippi stern-wheeler," Walt said. "It seemed appropriate to create a new attraction at the bend of the river. And so, New Orleans Square came into being—a New Orleans of a century ago when she was the 'Gay Paree' of the American frontier."[122] New Orleans Square opened along the banks of the Rivers of America on July 24, 1966, at a cost of $15 million. It was the first new land since the park opened and the first time that the Imagineers were challenged with creating an environment that was a representation of a specific place at a specific time: romantic, pre–Civil War New Orleans in 1850, when it was the most cosmopolitan and diverse city in America.

In an early press release, the Imagineers proclaimed that the Disneyland New Orleans was "a city of contrasts. Magnificently gowned ladies, genteel and gracious, strolled past benign Indian squaws selling sassafras root. Iron-lace balconies seemed even more delicate when compared with stretches of ashed walls. Intimate courtyards were lazy counterpoints to crowded markets." This new section of the park would "be as exciting as a pirate treasure hunt, as colorful as a Mardi Gras ball, as memorable as a visit to the French Quarter." [123]

John Hench described New Orleans Square as "Disney Realism, sort of Utopian in nature, where we carefully program out all the negative, unwanted elements and program in the positive elements. In fact, we even go beyond realism in some cases to make a better show. The streets were much cleaner than New Orleans had ever experienced." He noted, "Frankly, if we created a totally perfect, authentic themed experience where we had complete realism, it would probably be ghastly for contemporary people."[124]

Guests could easily spend an entire day at New Orleans Square. The French Market Restaurant offered buffet-style dining and a terrace with live Dixieland music. It was the largest restaurant in New Orleans Square and was decorated in old brick with accents of core and green, black iron furnishings, and a quarry-tile floor all under an antique pressed-tin ceiling. The domed "skylight" had two tile murals portraying the ceremonies for the Louisiana Purchase in 1803.[125] For a quick drink, the Mint Julep Bar offered nonalcoholic mint juleps, lemonade, and fritters. For those in need of an ice cream or coffee, there was the Sara Lee Cafe Orleans, complete with a 19th-century espresso machine acquired by Walt during a trip to Milan.[126]

At Crystal D'Orleans, guests could watch the glass blower at work and purchase fine Spanish crystal and decorative glassware. The silversmith at Leaflet's Silver Shop made jewelry to order and performed minor repairs. Guest could purchase a hat or film at Le Chapeau Hat Shop and kitchen accessories and spices from Le Gourmet.[127] Custom stained glass and wrought iron could be found at Le Forgeron. Over at Mlle. Antoinette's Parfumerie, guests could blend custom fragrances. The shop kept records so that guests could return and reorder the exact fragrance they had previously selected.[128]

Walt personally wanted an antiques shop in the park. The One-of-a-Kind Shop was meant to emulate a walk through a favorite grandmother's attic. Every square inch was covered in merchandise. Items ranging from old maps to fireplace fixtures to door knockers were available. Some of the most valuable items for sale included a Gregorian Chant Book dated 1607 and old negatives that turned out to be pictures of the Wright Brothers flying in Paris. In spite of such treasures, the store was never about making money, only adding a sense of authenticity.[129] Other touches included tucked-away little spaces like Le Grand Court, with its spiral staircase and ornate gas lamps. At times, an artist would be available to paint watercolor portraits. Throughout the land were carts appropriate to the period, selling flower baskets and candy and Louisiana pralines, mints, and pecans.

Sam McKim was put in charge of designing the Pirate's Arcade (also known as the Rogues' Galerie). Walt wanted him to reconfigure existing arcade games into pirate-themed machines. McKim designed games with names like *Free Booter Shooter*, *Captain Hook*, and *Blackbeard*. Dick Nunis helped McKim build 16 machines. McKim was proudest of one particular machine, Fortune Red, a machine that stamped out pirate tokens. As the mold for the tokens, McKim used a piece of eight coin from an ancient Spanish galleon that had sunk in the Dutch East Indies.

"You know, those arcade machines were played for 10 cents for years . . . I even had some 5 cents machines in there," McKim said. "We were following Walt's philosophy about this. He didn't even want them to raise the price of parking, which stayed at 25 cents for years. He didn't mind making money off the Park, but he didn't want to make money off the parking. He wanted to give the public a good deal."[130]

New Orleans Square was blessed with a mature tree canopy, giving it an instant authenticity. In 1962, Bill Evans had discovered that the City of Los Angeles was doing a remodel of Pershing Square in downtown.

He drove by and noticed that there were about 30 small ficus trees at the edges of the park and another 8 very large ones in the middle. This was too good of an opportunity to pass up. He contacted the contractor and learned that they were going to box up the smaller trees to be reused elsewhere and destroy the large ones. In fact, they had already disposed of one of the large trees. Evans quickly moved in to acquire the remaining trees. He boxed them up and cut off the top 15 feet of the trees as required by the California Highway Patrol.

Walt asked Evans where he was going to plant these trees. Evans had no idea, but he knew this was a good find. He suggested storing them behind the Haunted Mansion area. Within a year, Bill Martin started on the New Orleans Square project, and the seven trees found a home. In addition, six Italian cypress trees that had been used to delineate the entrance to Tomorrowland were moved in front of the Haunted Mansion when construction started on the Tomorrowland area in 1967.

When Walt died, in 1966, he had seen the New Orleans Square area and he'd seen the mock-ups for the Pirates of the Caribbean, but he did not see the ride open. At the grand opening of the new land, Walt joked with New Orleans Mayor Victor H. Schiro how much cleaner his version was compared to the real thing.

A TIME TUNNEL

ONE OF THE HIT SHOWS at the 1964–1965 New York World's Fair was Ford's Magic Skyway, created by the team at WED Enterprises. Visitors got to ride in one of 50 late-model Ford convertibles and go back in time to visit with cavemen, dinosaurs, and other exotic creatures. The cars were propelled by a new ride technology that would later prove important to Disneyland. More than 15 million people saw the Ford show at the Fair. When it was time to bring the attraction back to Disneyland, Walt was not satisfied with the animation of the caveman figures, and Ford did not want to spend the money to improve it—so only the dinosaurs, which Walt did like, were brought back to Anaheim.

When the Santa Fe & Disneyland Railroad reopened on July 1, 1966, it passed through a new destination called the Primeval World, a display inspired by the animated film *Fantasia*. The trains left the Tomorrowland depot and passed by the Grand Canyon Diorama, just as they had done since 1958. A new covered bridge provided street access to the backstage area, and the dark space acted as a time tunnel that took guests 300 million years into the past. The first scene was dressed as a tropical rain forest abundantly filled with giant prehistoric plants, reptiles, and insects. The scene was bathed in a mysterious half-light, suggesting that this was the early stages of life on the planet.[131]

Moving forward about 150 million years, the guests encountered a group of brontosauruses feeding on plants and also witnessed the comical birth of happy triceratops babies. Near the window was a vulture-like pteranodon. This was life in transition; the set was adorned with specimens of the first flowering plants and primitive conifers. As time and the train moved forward, the environment changed to a drought-stricken plain. Three ornithomimuses were trying to drink from a water hole while a 22-foot-tall *Tyrannosaurus rex* was in a perpetual battle with a stegosaurus near flowing lava. There were 46 Audio-Animatronics figures in the display.

To handle the expected crowds, the Santa Fe & Disneyland Railroad added three new trains, called Deluxe Holiday Specials. Holiday Red had seven cars with side-facing seats and a caboose. Holiday Green and Holiday Blue had five cars each, also with side-facing seats, and were topped with striped canopies. This type of rolling stock was typical in the late 19th century for open-air excursions and sightseeing trips to mountain and seashore resorts.

The Flying Saucers, which had been a troubled ride from the very beginning, closed on August 5. It had a poor operational record and rarely worked for long periods of time. Bob Gurr said, "People have talked a lot about this over the years, but when it went out of service, everybody breathed a sigh of relief."[132] More than 5.3 million guests went for a ride.

On August 19, 1966, the park received an interesting glimpse into its own history when the First American Title Insurance & Trust Company gave the park the Chain of Title tracing Disneyland's Main Street from the original land grant to the present. Disneyland was located on parcels of land in the Rancho San Juan Cajon de Santa Ana, which had been under the jurisdiction of the King of Spain in 1769. After becoming part of Mexico, the area was given to Juan Pacifico Onti-veras in 1837. He later sold 1,165 acres at $2 per acre to the founders of Anaheim. Many years later, Walt would pay almost $1,000,000 for approximately 244 acres to create Disneyland.[133]

On August 28, as the summer season wound down, the 20,000 Leagues Under the Sea exhibit ended its extended run. Rolly Crump joked that the walk-through attraction "actually out-earned the

Submarine Voyage ride one year!" He said, "It was because it cost a fortune to maintain the Submarines while there was zero maintenance on the Leagues Exhibit. Once in a while they would replace a couple of light bulbs in the exhibit . . . while the goddam Submarine ride cost them a million dollars every year to run."[134]

A few days later, on September 5, Tomorrowland was boarded up, and wrecking crews were brought in to begin demolition so construction could start on a new Tomorrowland. The Art Corner and Art of Animation closed. The Hall of Chemistry closed after more than 30 million visitors passed through its doors. The *Moonliner,* the defining icon for the land since the park had opened in 1955, was removed. To make sure the rocket did not end up in somebody's garden, Disney required the demolition team to produce a certificate of destruction. Disneyland's childhood was fading as the park began to prepare for a great big beautiful tomorrow.

In November, there was a flurry of rumors of Disneyland's pending sale to Litton Industries, a diversified corporation dealing in defense, space, industrial equipment, and other enterprises. "We continue to get offers of merger or acquisition by big companies in steel, food, merchandising, technical companies, and conglomerates like Litton," Roy Disney said of the talks. "If we accepted such an offer, it would mean dominance by outsiders. We know our operation; we've been selling entertainment for over 40 years. We don't need anyone to tell us how to do it."[135] Both companies denied the rumors, but offers from the "big company" demonstrated how much respect Walt had earned from corporate America since the park's opening.[136] Disneyland was no longer Walt's folly, as some early critics had proclaimed. Attendance grew to a record 6.7 million in 1966.

A **HAPPY ACCIDENT**

WHILE DEATH HAD BEEN A MAJOR THEME in many Disney films, Walt Disney himself was very hesitant to talk about the subject, and he did not want to hear about it from others. One day, Marty Sklar showed Walt a film that he had produced with other team members, *The Disney Image.* Sklar recalled, "At the end of the first screening for Walt there was absolute silence for what seemed like an eternity. Then he slowly got up and made just one comment as he left. 'I feel like I've just seen my own eulogy.' "

Walt told Sklar, "I'm not Walt Disney anymore. Walt Disney is a thing. It's grown to become a whole different meaning than just one man." Ward Kimball said, "I really feel that Walt, after a certain time, had a date with destiny. Even though he was building something that was fun to him, he never lost sight of the fact that it was all Walt Disney. It was a worldwide name. After the park, and after the TV show, he was assured a niche in history."[137]

Upon reflection, Walt said, "I think by this time my staff, my young group of executives, and everyone else are convinced that Walt is right. That quality will out. And so I think they're going to stay with that policy because it's proved that it's a good business policy. Give the people everything you can give them. Keep the place as clean as you can keep it. Keep it friendly, you know. Make it a real fun place to be. I think they're convinced and I think they'll hang on . . . if . . . as you say . . . well, after Disney."

Walt Disney passed away on December 15, 1966, at 9:35 in the morning. He was 65 and succumbed to lung cancer after a lifetime of smoking unfiltered Lucky Strike and Gitanes cigarettes.

Edith Efron from *TV Guide* declared, "He is one of the few men in show business whose name stands for something significantly larger than their work. To say Walt Disney is to pay subtle compliment to the human race." Journalist Eric Sevareid maybe said it best, "He was an original, not just an American original, but an original, period. He was a happy accident, one of the happiest this century has experienced." He added, "But what Disney seemed to know was that while there is very little grown-up in every child, there is a lot of child in every grown-up. To a child, this weary world is brand-new, gift wrapped. Disney tried to keep it that way for adults."

Ray Bradbury recalled a time when Walt told him "Nothing has to die." He wrote, "Walt was right. Nothing has to die. Just rebuild it. Steamboat America, lost? Carve a river bottom, flood it, and send your *Mark Twain* paddle wheel down the riverway. Victorian train travel, gone? Nail up a rococo scrimshaw station, steam in the 19th-century locomotive, carry passengers from Civil War territories through African jungles into AD 2000."[138] Disneyland was a way to live forever.

Roy O. Disney stepped in and said shortly after his brother's death, "All of the plans that Walt had begun, will continue to move ahead without interruption."[139] His confidence was placed in the company that the two built over a lifetime. Roy O. Disney said of his brother, "He was the damndest planner I ever saw. He loved planning things that might be three, five, even ten years in the future. That was what was so unusual about the fellow. He could take care of matters at hand while dreaming for the future." He reminded everyone, "The Disney organization now has more than 4,000 employees. Many have been with us for over 30 years. They take great pride in the organization which they helped to build." He declared, "Only through the talent, labor and dedication of this staff could any Disney project get off the ground. We all think alike in the ultimate pattern."[140]

Things didn't quite work out as Roy O. Disney predicted. Disneyland was such a personal project. Could it survive when its "father" and guiding light was lost? Science-fiction novelist Cory Doctorow noted, "Walt's genius was that he would come up with incredibly novel, innovative things that could only be imitated after a couple of years. Meanwhile, he would have this very healthy margin until his competition figured out what he was doing and drove the price down to a competitive level. Then he would do the next thing." He concluded, "When Walt died, they just stopped doing that. They just started doing the same thing. They basically built a twin of Disneyland in Disney World, but bigger."[141]

Disneyland was the vision of one man who had the remarkable ability to get others to go along with him on his personal journey. He found talented artists who could visualize and implement his ideas. The park reflected one man's tastes and choices. He made all the decisions. That made Disneyland unique.

After Walt passed away, it was obvious that an organization that was going to be run by the rule of the committee was going to have a tough time adjusting. His team could do virtually anything the man wanted. That was their strength. With Walt gone, they were initially unprepared for the new reality. Walt's role in the show was all important and no understudy could fill his shoes in his absence. He would not let them. That was his job.

Now what?

1. Tom Self, "Disneyland: Commercial Participants Say It is The World's Greatest Showcase," *The Executive*, Nov. 1977.
2. Disneyland, "Submarine Voyage, Matterhorn, Monorail Await Visitors in Brand New Disneyland," press release, June 1959.
3. Randy Bright, *Disneyland: Inside Story* (New York: Abrams, 1987).
4. Bob Gurr, *Design: Just for Fun* (Tugging, CA: APP-Gurr Design, 2012).
5. Ibid.
6. Ibid.
7. Ibid.
8. "Early Days of the Monorail," *The "E" Ticket*, Number 36, Fall 2001, 10–25.
9. Bright, *Inside Story*.
10. Disneyland, "Disneyland-Alweg Monorail System," press release, 1960.
11. Gurr, *Just for Fun*.
12. Pam Burns-Clair and Don Peri, *Walt Disney's First Lady of Imagineering Harriet Burns* (Virginia Beach, VA: Donning, 2010).
13. Adam Townsend, "Mountain Turns 50," *Orange County Register*, 20 June 2009.
14. Wendy Lefkin, ed., *Disney Insider Yearbook: 2005 Year in Review* (New York: Disney Editions, Inc., 2006).
15. Gurr, *Just for Fun*.
16. "The Matterhorn—At the Pinnacle of Popularity," *Disneyland Line*, 19 Aug. 1994.
17. Gurr, *Just for Fun*.
18. Steve DeGaetano, *Welcome Aboard the Disneyland Railroad!* (Winter, CA: Steam Passages Publications, 2004).
19. "Museum of the Weird," *The "E" Ticket*, Number 9, Summer 1995, 24–32.
20. Rolly Crump with Jeff Heimbuch, *It's Kind of a Cute Story* (Clearwater, FL: Bamboo Forest, 2012).
21. Ibid.
22. "Discovery in Detail," *Disneyland Line*, 9 April 1991.
23. Ibid.
24. Disneyland, "Disneyland Announces Plans for 'Nature's Wonderland' Attraction," press release, 25 March 1960.
25. "Creating The Disney Landscape," *The "E" Ticket*, Number 23, Spring 1996, 4–15.
26. Ray Bradbury, "Disneyland, or Disney's Demon for Happiness," *Modern Maturity*, March/April 2002.
27. Christopher Merritt and J. Eric Lynxwiler, *Knott's Preserved* (Santa Monica, CA: Angel City Press, 2010).
28. Ibid.
29. Economics Research Associates, "A Study of Land Use Alternatives For Disneyland Periphery Property," prepared for Disneyland, Inc., 16 Sept. 1960.
30. "Disneyland Monorail," *Anaheim Bulletin*, 26 May 1961.
31. Gurr, *Just for Fun*.
32. Ibid.
33. Ibid.
34. Sarah Tully, "Disney history: Mouseketeer rides in parade," *Orange County Register*, 15 April 2012.
35. Disneyland Operations Department Group II, *Background Information: Adventureland, Frontierland, New Orleans* (Anaheim, CA: Disneyland, 26 Jan. 1970).
36. Ibid.

37. Crump with Heimbuch, *It's Kind of a Cute Story.*
38. Ibid.
39. Disneyland Operations Department Group II, *Adventureland, Frontierland, New Orleans.*
40. "Creating the Disney Landscape," *The "E" Ticket.*
41. Libby Slate, "Model Maker Harriet Burns," *Disney News,* Spring 1992.
42. "Disneyland's Haunted Mansion," *The "E" Ticket,* Number 16, Summer 1993, 16–27.
43. Neal Gabler, Harriet Burns, Alice Davis, Blaine Gibson, and Richard Schickel, "The Life & Legacy of Walt Disney," panel discussion, Annenberg School for Communication, University of Southern California, 15 Nov. 2006.
44. Ibid.
45. Burns-Clair and Peri, *First Lady of Imagineering.*
46. John Hench with Peggy Van Pelt, *Designing Disney: Imagineering and the Art of the Show* (New York: Disney Editions, Inc., 2008).
47. Crump with Heimbuch, *It's Kind of a Cute Story.*
48. Disneyland Operations Department Group II, *Adventureland, Frontierland, New Orleans.*
49. Crump with Heimbuch, *It's Kind of a Cute Story.*
50. Dave Smith, *Walt Disney Famous Quotes* (Lake Buena Vista, FL: Walt Disney Theme Parks and Resorts, 1994).
51. Disneyland University, "The Dream is a Reality" (Anaheim, CA: Disneyland, July 1975).
52. Jeff Kurtti, *The Magic Begins with Me* (New York: Disney Editions, Inc., 2005).
53. Smith, *Famous Quotes.*
54. Frank Rich, "Who Killed the Disneyland Dream?" *Los Angeles Times,* 25 Dec. 2010.
55. Van A. France, "A Birthday Worth Remembering," *Los Angeles Times,* 24 Feb. 1985.
56. WED Enterprises, *The Disneyland Dictionary,* employee manual (Anaheim, CA: Disneyland, 1968).
57. Disneyland University, *Our Disney Terms,* training book (Anaheim, CA: Disneyland, 1974).
58. Paul Goldberger, "Mickey Mouse Teaches the Architects," *New York Times,* 22 Oct. 1972.
59. Charles W. Moore, *You Have to Pay for the Public Life* (Cambridge: MIT Press, 2001).
60. Beth Dunlop, *Building a Dream: The Art of Disney Architecture* (New York: Abrams, 1996).
61. Charlie Haas, "Disneyland Is Good for You," *The New West Magazine,* 4 Dec. 1978.
62. "Disneyland May Ask Council for Height Limitation on Hotel," *Anaheim Bulletin,* 28 Dec. 1963.
63. "Disneyland Official Sees No Protest to High Buildings Near Melodyland," *Anaheim Bulletin,* 18 May 1964.
64. Ibid.
65. Disneyland, "Walt Disney Presents Views on High-Rise Proposal," press release, June 1964.
66. Smith, *Famous Quotes.*
67. Jerry Teague, "Planners Eye Height Limit," *Anaheim Bulletin,* 6 July 1964.
68. "Council Should OK Hotel Despite Disneyland Row," *Anaheim Gazette,* 9 Jan. 1964.
69. Smith, *Famous Quotes.*
70. "Designing Disneyland with Marc Davis," *The "E" Ticket,* Number 7, Summer 1989, 4–17.
71. Ibid.
72. Haas, "Disneyland Is Good for You."
73. Ibid.
74. "Model Shop," *The "E" Ticket,* Number 29, Spring 1998, 4–13.
75. Mary Susan Herczog and Steve Hochman, "What Would Walt Say?," *Los Angeles Times,* 24 Dec. 1995.
76. Crump with Heimbuch, *It's Kind of a Cute Story.*

77. Ibid.
78. Disneyland University, "Making Mountain Out of Dreams: Space Mountain" (Anaheim, CA: Disneyland, 1977).
79. Hench with Van Pelt, *Designing Disney.*
80. Ibid.
81. "Disney's Space Mountain," *The "E" Ticket,* Number 30, Fall 1998, 30–41.
82. Disneyland, "News From Disneyland '65 Tencennial Celebration, press release, *Disneyland Gazetteer,* July 1965.
83. Walt Disney, "Tencennial Celebration" (speech, Disneyland Hotel, Anaheim, CA, 15 July 1965), transcript, Anaheim History Room, Anaheim Public Library, Anaheim, CA.
84. Ibid.
85. Ibid.
86. Ibid.
87. Ibid.
88. Ibid.
89. Ibid.
90. Robert Jackson, "Profile: Great Moments with Mr. Lincoln," WED Enterprises press release, 1964.
91. Ibid.
92. Ibid.
93. Ibid.
94. "Walt Disney's Sculptor," *The "E" Ticket,* Number 21, Spring 1995, 14–25.
95. Bright, *Inside Story.*
96. "Walt Disney's Sculptor," *The "E" Ticket.*
97. Ray Bradbury, "The Machine-Tooled Happyland," *Holiday,* Oct. 1965.
98. Ibid.
99. "Visualizing Disneyland with Sam McKim," *The "E" Ticket,* Number 18, Spring 1994, 8–21.
100. Jeff Kurtti, *Walt Disney's Imagineering Legends and the Genesis of the Disney Theme Park* (New York: Disney Editions, Inc., 2008).
101. "Walt Disney's Sculptor," *The "E" Ticket.*
102. Ibid.
103. Jason Surrell, *Pirates of the Caribbean: From the Magic Kingdom to the Movies* (New York: Disney Editions, Inc., 2005).
104. Crump with Heimbuch, *It's Kind of a Cute Story.*
105. Ibid.
106. Ibid.
107. Alice Davis, "Marc Davis Centennial Celebration" (speech, Club 33 event, Disneyland, Anaheim, CA, 7 March 2013).
108. Stacia Martin, "Walt Disney and the 1964 World's Fair" (New York: Walt Disney Records, 2009).
109. Ibid.
110. Robert Jackson, "It's A Small World," WED Enterprises press release, 1966.
111. Crump with Heimbuch, *It's Kind of a Cute Story.*
112. Ibid.
113. Patrick Mott, "Topiary Slowly Adds Life to Gardens," *Los Angeles Times,* 27 Feb. 1993.
114. Crump with Heimbuch, *It's Kind of a Cute Story.*
115. Ibid.
116. Ibid.

117. Robert Jackson, "It's A Small World," WED Enterprises press release, 1966.

118. Ibid.

119. Crump with Heimbuch, *It's Kind of a Cute Story*.

120. Gurr, *Just for Fun*.

121. Wendy Lefkin, ed., *Walt Disney Imagineering: A Behind the Dreams Look at Making the Magic Real* (New York: Hyperion, 1996).

122. Bruce Gordon and David Mumford, *Disneyland: The Nickel Tour* (Santa Clarita, CA: Camphor Tree, 2000).

123. Robert Jackson, "Profiles on New Attractions for Disneyland," WED Enterprises press release, 1966.

124. Haas, "Disneyland Is Good for You."

125. Disneyland University, *Food Division Training Manual* (Anaheim, CA: Disneyland, 1974).

126. Disneyland Operations Department Group II, *Adventureland, Frontierland, New Orleans*.

127. "Les Gadgets, Les Gizmos—Le Gourment!" *Disneyland Line*, 17 May 1991.

128. "Nouvelle Orleans," *Disneyland Line*, 28 April 1995.

129. "At the One-of-a-Kind Shop," *Disneyland Line*, 22 Oct. 1991.

130. "Visualizing Disneyland with Sam McKim," *The "E" Ticket*.

131. Gurr, *Just for Fun*.

132. "Chain of Title Given to Park," *Anaheim Bulletin*, 20 Aug. 1966.

133. "Evolution of a Designer," *The "E" Ticket*, Number 38, Fall 2002, 4–15.

134. Bob Thomas, "Disneyland Sees Broken Attendance Record," *Los Angeles Times*, 17 June 1967.

135. "Disneyland Sale Rumors Denied," *Anaheim Bulletin*, 10 Dec. 1966.

136. "Ward Kimball," *The "E" Ticket*, Number 12, Winter 1991–92, 12–19.

137. Ray Bradbury, "Why Disney Will Live Forever," *Mickey Is Sixty!* (Santa Barbara, CA: Joshua Odell Editions, 1988).

138. Roy O. Disney, letter to Walt Disney Productions employees, 15 Dec. 1966.

139. Ibid.

140. Dylan Tweney, "Q&A: Cory Doctorow," *The San Francisco Chronicle*, 23 Jan. 2003.

CHAPTER 6

MOMENTUM: 1967–1969

■ IT'S LIKE *a* COCKTAIL PARTY

FROM THE BEGINNING, hosting Disneyland was a complex relationship between Anaheim, Orange County, and Disneyland. Back in the 1950s, Orange County had a small planning staff that reflected the county's agricultural outlook. There were no building codes for the type of buildings and attractions that Disney wanted to create. The creation of Disneyland was the largest land use variance ever processed at the county at the time.

In January 1967, the City of Anaheim began to take steps to preserve Disneyland's "in another world" effect with the creation of a 1,000-acre commercial-recreation zone. The park was then zoned for agricultural use, and the creation of a special district "would be a significant step toward the orderly ultimate development of the area," according to a Disneyland spokesperson.[1] The district concept would help protect the height restrictions that had been put in place in 1964.

However, Anaheim policy makers were not persuaded and decided against the proposal. This meant growth would continue to be regulated on a case-by-case basis. The City Council felt the current policy gave them the greatest control. Anaheim city planner Ron Thompson said of the 1950s approach, "After all, you've got to protect the goose that lays the golden egg."[2] In general, Disney management publicly stated they were "satisfied" with the surrounding development but were quick to add "maybe they could have been a little less intense." Without a master plan on the part of the city, the march toward blight would continue in the area that was getting the reputation as "Las Vegas West."

Inside the berm, things were much brighter. Disneyland was about to experience its most significant physical transformation since 1959 in the form of a new major attraction. Walt Disney had been working on a pirates ride since the mid-1950s. Through its series of fits and starts, the project had passed through a lot of hands. It had evolved from a simple walk-through wax museum to an elaborate boat ride with dozens of Audio-Animatronics figures. Pirates of the Caribbean, a landmark attraction, opened on February 14, 1967, at a cost of $5 million.

Walt had pulled together an all-star team to create Pirates of the Caribbean. Marc Davis was in charge of planning out what the pirates were, and what they were doing, and what they looked like. Claude Coats was in charge of the backgrounds and the layout. The project benefited from Coats's background in architecture. His sets supported Davis's animated character studies and gave the characters proper space and light to work in.

Blaine Gibson was responsible for sculpting the three-dimensional reference maquettes and full-size figures. Gibson would begin with Davis's characters, but he had the liberty to make adjustments. In most cases, Gibson took the original idea and pushed it further. However, he was faithful to Davis's brilliant comedic ideas.

Both Davis and Gibson knew they only had a few seconds to say something that could be understood from a distance. Therefore, everything was exaggerated, especially the facial features. The characters' expressions quickly established who the good guys were and who the bad guys were. Like a well-executed caricature, the Pirates of the Caribbean would embellish on reality in order to get to the truth.

Gibson was challenged by what he deemed Davis's "crazy concepts." His job was to make the drawings seem believable in three dimensions, and he worked with Davis to pick heads that would fit certain characters. The two men came up with about 30 different heads, including a number of "repeat heads." If guests look carefully, the characters repeat. Gibson also sculpted all of the animals. Gibson's creativity was constrained by budget limitations, and he sometimes had to make aesthetically distasteful compromises. For example, Gibson sculpted one chicken that was used over and over. Gibson had grown up on a farm, and he "kind of resented making a rooster out of a hen, but we did it anyway and all the chickens are duplicate."[3]

Alice Davis designed and fabricated the costumes. She started work on the pirates ride immediately after finishing It's a Small World and later joked, "I graduated from 'sweet little children' to 'dirty old men' overnight." It took more than a year and a half to complete all of the costumes, and it didn't always go smoothly. Alice and Marc Davis recalled a conflict that she had with the sculptors, who, she said, were from "the classic school and they were sculpting male figures just the way God made them."[4] This meant she had to do extra work to "drop the crotches down so there was more room." The Pirate Auctioneer was the first figure completed, and he wore a vest that came almost to his knees. Walt wanted to see the figure in action. According to Marc Davis, after the figure was turned on, "He looked terrific and everything worked just great until he went back with his arm and he leaned back and said, 'How much am I bid for her?' . . . and his classical sculpting became apparent through the vest. Everybody said, 'Oh my God! What are we going to do?' Alice said, 'You need to get a hack saw and cut it off.' I never had to have another discussion with the sculptors again."[5]

Alice Davis also had to fight with the bookkeepers. She felt it was important to make more than one costume for each figure, but the number crunchers said no. She quickly realized that they did not know much about sewing and that she could easily double up on her fabric orders and make duplicate costumes, with the bookkeepers being none the wiser.

It was a good thing that Alice made the second set of costumes. A few weeks after the attraction opened, a fire broke out—ironically, in the Burning Town scene. The fire suppression system activated, and all of the pirates' hats were ruined. Dick Irvine, who was in charge of Disneyland at the time, ran to Alice to ask how long it would take to remake the hats. Alice told him that it would normally take about one week, but she had a surprise for him. She then showed him where she had hidden a second set of costumes. From that point forward, the need for two sets of costumes was never questioned again.

As she had done for the It's a Small World costumes, Alice Davis made loose-leaf notebooks with a photo of every figure with swatches of materials, buttons, thread, and everything else used, so the costumes could retain the same quality in the future. At first management fought her on the extra cost, but today the notebooks are used to maintain the three costumes for every figure. Upon reflection on her career at WED, she said, "I think it's interesting that the work for which I will be most remembered is men's tailoring in Pirates and children's wear in small world . . . the two subjects I didn't like in school."[6]

The Pirates script was written by Imagineer Xavier Atencio. One day, while walking through the attraction mock-up and listening to the soundtrack, Atencio turned to Walt and said, "Gee, I guess it's pretty hard to understand them." Walt replied, "Don't worry about it. It's like a cocktail party. People come to cocktail parties, and they tune in a conversation over here, then a conversation over there. Each time the guest comes through here, they'll hear something else. That'll bring them back time and again!"[7]

Atencio was responsible for the lyrics to "Yo Ho (a Pirate's Life for Me)," the attraction's theme song. He worked with Studio composer George Bruns to craft a song that would tie all of the visual elements together and give guests something to whistle on the way out. The verses of the song had to be written so that everything made sense no matter where you entered the song. It is a song without a beginning or an end.

Although Walt never got to see the attraction installed in New Orleans Square, he did see a huge, 40-foot-long scale model of the attraction. The layout of the model wound around just like the ride, and Fred Joerger put the model up on stilts so that it would be at eye level. The model gave the Imagineers a chance to experience the same view of the scenes as the guests. This allowed them to adjust the staging of the scenes for the maximum effect. Blaine Gibson had sculpted the delicate little clay model figures. Although the development model was destroyed, some of the figures remain at the Disney Archives.

According to Marc Davis, Walt also "saw a little bit of the 'auctioneer' pirate moving. I don't know how many of the other characters."[8] Walt also visited the construction site in Anaheim just before he passed away. "The Pirates building was up, and the water channel was walkable, all the way through," Davis recalled. "Walt, myself, and a half dozen other guys did a walk-through of the ride. There wasn't much scenery up in there, just some frameworks here and there. You could tell where you were, and Walt's reaction was very favorable."[9]

The Imagineers came up with a clever way to create realistic rocks. They took two layers of PyroKure, a flame-proof wrapping for insulating pipe with aluminum foil inside, crumbled it up, and tied it to rebar using hog rings. Then they sprayed the paper with paint to give it texture and color.

The Pirates attraction was housed in two show buildings totaling 112,826 square feet. Inside, each of the 46 flat-bottomed boats, called *bateaux* in the Creole language of New Orleans, carried 22 passengers along a 1,838-foot-long canal at 2.5 feet per second. The 2-foot-deep canal held almost three-quarters of a million gallons of water. When things ran as planned and each boat was loading passengers every 20 seconds, the capacity of the attraction was 3,600 guests an hour.[10]

DEAD MEN TELL NO TALES

GUESTS ENTERED THE PIRATES OF THE CARIBBEAN through the front door of a stately antebellum mansion overlooking the Rivers of America. Once they were inside the mansion, guests were greeted by other guests still riding in their boats, happy, excited and on their way to the unloading dock. As those in line moved forward, daylight seemed to fade into perpetual night. The guests boarded their *bateaux* from Laffite's Landing and were launched into the bayou. Along with the sights and sounds of the bayou was the smell of food coming from the Blue Bayou restaurant. It was now evening, and it was as if guests were being lulled to sleep.

Adding to the illusion were mechanical fireflies, invented for the ride by Imagineer Yale Gracey. He confessed to archivist Dave Smith that he had never actually seen a real firefly. Rolly Crump described the trick, "It's an incredible, wonderful little illusion. And so damn easy it's incredible! All Yale did was take a 'grain of wheat' bulb, on its own wire, with a little piece of black tape on one side of the bulb and a 'squirrel cage' fan underneath to blow it around. When it blows so that the tape covers it, you don't see it."[11]

Just beyond the settler's cabin with the aspiring banjo player, the waterway tightened and the space grew very dark. This was the first time on the attraction that guests were placed in very tight quarters, a trick used again and again. What the guests saw next must surely have been a dream: A talking skull, dressed in a pirate's head scarf. Voiced by Xavier Atencio, the skull bellows out a series of warnings. Best to listen, because the guests soon encountered two waterfalls. The first drop was 52 feet long and in complete darkness. The second drop was 37 feet long. Both drops were at an angle of 21 degrees. At first, the Imagineers were having a lot of trouble keeping the boats from filling up with water at the drops. They changed the angle, but that only helped a little. People were still getting splashed, so shields were installed.

The drops served as a practical way to get guests to the caverns in the basement below, where the original walk-through attraction was planned. They also added some tension to the ride. Guests did not know what was in the mysterious area beneath New Orleans

Square. A grotto filled with skeletons set within comic tableaus was something unexpected and special.

The boats gently glided past five waterfalls, Deadman's Cove, and the Hurricane Lagoon. In the Crew's Quarters, just over the bar, was a painting by Marc Davis of the lounging Redhead after she had experienced "years of happy marriage to the pirates." The boat passed by a skeleton Captain in his bed in his elegant "apartment," focused on a treasure map. One more turn and guests headed straight for the Treasure Cache. What seemed like millions of gold coins and gold religious idols guarded by a greedy skeleton were actually plastic or pressed out of foil.

Guests entered another very tight and dark space known as the transition tunnel. The tunnel went under the Santa Fe & Disneyland Railroad to the show building outside the berm. Atencio took advantage of the space for story development with a haunting voice bellowing the memorable, "Dead men tell no tales."

As the boats exited this confined corridor, they entered the middle of Bombarding the Fort scene. With pirates on the *Wicked Wench* firing toward the fortress on the other side, guests found themselves helpless in the crossfire. To make the scene feel even more realistic, the Imagineers created the illusion that cannon balls were passing over the heads of the guests and splashing into the water. Wathel Rogers developed cannons that worked with a blast of air. There was a light and then a blast of fog from a water jet. In the water was a cuplike device which was coordinated to create a splash as the "cannon ball" struck the water. The battle scene was the first time that guests saw the "real" pirates.

Pirates of the Caribbean opened with 130 animated figures consisting of 76 humans and 54 animals. All of the animated characters were controlled by a computerized reference system with individual codes that each directed a specific movement such as an arm waving, a head turning, or the eyes blinking. The more complex the figure, the more coded elements controlled its actions. Some of the more complex figures, such as the captain on the *Wicked Wench* in the Bombarding the Fort scene, had 11 functions. Most of the pirates had about seven or eight functions, with some as few as four.

Turning the corner, the guests entered the village and witnessed the mayor being dunked into a well. The mayor's wife screams, "Be brave, Carlos! Don't leesten to heem!" while the captain commands, "Pipe 'im aloft again, matey . . . by gum, he'll talk or do a fine dance at rope's end . . . be that clear, señor?" Yes, family entertainment at its finest.

Just past the mayor in distress was the Auction Scene. In this case, the goods being auctioned were the fair ladies of the village. On one bank were the auctioneer and the brides up for bid, and on the other shore were an equal number of men doing the bidding. There were more than 50 animated figures in this scene, including two goats and 34 chickens. The Auction Scene was not without controversy.

Claude Coats noted that the scene had been a late addition. Walt came to Coats one day and asked, "This will be all right, won't it?" Coats noticed, "He was just a little doubtful of auctioning off the girls. Was this quite 'Disney' or not?"[12] The solution was to add some signs that suggested the scene was a special event.

With 25 movements, the auctioneer was the most complex figure in the Pirates attraction. Marc Davis recalled that Walt had the opportunity to watch the character in action. "We had made the Auctioneer pirate so sophisticated that you could watch him move, and it was as good as watching Lincoln. He had all the little mouth movements and all that, and I mentioned to Walt that I thought it was a 'Hell of a waste.' Walt said, 'No Marc, it's not a waste . . . we do so much return business down here, and the next time people come in they'll see something they hadn't noticed before.' "[13] Davis added, "That was a good example of the kind of input Walt had to these attractions." The rest of the pirates were set up to run in cycles of 2 or 3 minutes in duration. The Auctioneer was so important to the show that the operating procedures required the attraction to be closed down if that character was not functioning properly.

Leaving the auction, the boats passed under a bridge and were confronted by the Lusty Pirates. As a frightened maiden popped up from a barrel, a pirate very close to shore confided to the guests, "It's sore I be hoist me colors on the likes o' that shy little wench . . . keep a weather eye open, mateys . . . I be willin' to share, I be!" Four other pirates were chasing the women of the village. The effect was simple: Two figures with limited animation were mounted on a turntable. On the fifth turntable a "stout fierce village woman" was chasing a bald pirate. On the final turntable were four chickens chasing each other.

To make the scene work, some of the figures were downsized to give the illusion of distance. This is another example of forced perspective. Blaine Gibson had to make a reducing glue mold based on another pirates head. The water-based material used in the mold shrank from evaporation, with the result being a smaller casting. Gibson repeated the process multiple times.

Following the chase scene was the spectacular Burning Town. Yale Gracey created the fire effects after toying with crinkly Mylar and a hubcap. Marc Davis said, "I tried to put some humor all the way through there, even in the burning town scene, because you could scare the Hell out of people with all that fire. I think it works, and nobody is terrified that they are going into a burning room."[14] Nobody, that is, except the Anaheim Fire Department. The effect was so real that they were concerned that they wouldn't be able to tell where the real fire was if it got started in the ride. A system was installed to turn off the special effects in the event of a real emergency.

The Burning Town was filled with Davis's characters, including three singing pirates accompanied by a mule and a dog, a suspicious guy hanging on a pole with a torch, two pirates propping one another aloft, and the memorable pirate with one leg draped over the bridge as guests pass underneath. There was even a pirate sleeping off his rum with three little pigs.

To escape the burning town, the boats floated into a narrow tunnel—but was it safe? They were still surrounded with the threat of fire as they entered the unforgettable Jail scene. Motivated by the approaching fire, the pirates are anxious to escape, but their fate rests with a dog's generosity. Continuing along, the boats entered the Burning Timbers room, a constricted, almost claustrophobic space. It is at this point that the boats are passing underneath the railroad tracks and reentering the park. Yale Gracey's special effects once again put the guests at (safe) peril. The fires continue to haunt the guests, creeping closer to the boats until they reach the town's arsenal.

The finale is the Arsenal Scene, which is as close as a guest could get to an Audio-Animatronic figure in motion. While guests waited to move up the exit ramp, they could try to follow the cause-and-effect actions taking place all around them. The pirate on the cannon fired his pistol and recoiled backward, while the bullet hit something on the other shore. All of the pirates, pistols, barrels, and props were coordinated with split-second timing.

Because most of the attraction was at the basement level, the boats needed to be lifted back to the loading and unloading area. Walt's solution was to let guests "fall up" a waterfall. The boats were pulled up a 90-foot ramp at a steep 16 degrees, a sore spot for Davis. "I don't like the fact that when the ride is over, you have to sit at the bottom of that ramp and then go chug, chug, chugging up this hill and then out, wondering what the Hell you're going to do next."[15] What they were going to do next was to get back in line and take a trip to an amazing place and an adventure they couldn't get anywhere else.

HIS PRIVATE DINING ROOM

GUESTS RIDING ALONG THE BAYOU in Pirates were treated to a glimpse of "the newest restaurant . . . the beautiful Blue Bayou Terrace, where visitors enjoy Southern-style delicacies as they dine in the evening— all day long!" In a large show building designed to simulate perpetual nighttime, the Blue Bayou was an opportunity to dine in the shadow of an antebellum mansion along the banks of the Blue Bayou Lagoon under oak trees draped in Spanish moss. The mansion facade was a near-copy of the Swift's Chicken Plantation House. A balcony acted as a stage for jazz and Dixieland performers. Wrought iron furnishings and candlelight seating greeted the guests. The entrance foyer along Royal Street had a terrazzo and marble pattern floor with brass inlay and paneled walls. Up to 210 guests could dine at one time. The restaurant was considered the finest dining establishment within the park.

Right next door to the Blue Bayou restaurant—at 33 Royal Street, New Orleans Square—was Club 33, which opened on June 15, 1967. For many years, most guests were unaware that there was a private club that served food and alcohol above Pirates of the Caribbean. Walt had not wanted to serve alcohol at the park, but in 1965 General Electric forced his hand. In negotiations to sponsor the *Carousel of Progress* after it moved to Disneyland, the giant corporation demanded that the park provide a hospitality lounge that served alcohol like the one at the World's Fair General Electric pavilion. Reluctantly, Walt agreed to build "an elegant, exclusive club for Very Important People, a place for conversation, and in turn a conversation piece in its own right."[16]

Walt decided to make the best of it. According to the sales brochure promoting Club 33 memberships in 1967, Walt had wanted to create "a private show within a public show" where "Everything—from plush furnishings to crystal chandeliers, from original paintings and sketches to a personalized Audio-Animatronics show for members and guests only—has been chosen or specially created for Club 33." Membership was very limited, with "the desire to create an exclusive private club service for top level VIPs and their important guests." Reportedly, there were only 400 original members, and that number increased only slightly over the years.[17]

Members entered with a personal key card. Once inside the small lower lobby, guests were escorted by a hostess to the Victorian-age French-style cage elevator. The park claimed that "it is one of perhaps a half a dozen that still exist in Southern California." The elevator ascended to Lounge Alley, which served as a cocktail lounge, art gallery, and a venue "where businessmen may discuss the day's events while watching the passing parade of people." A hand-painted harpsichord was soon added. The first art display featured the work of cartoonist Heinrich Kley from Walt's personal collection.[18]

The entire club was designed by artist Dorothea Redmond. The Banquet Room was done in the Napoleonic style; working with interior designer Emil Kuri, Walt and Lillian Disney purchased many of the dining area's furnishings while on trips to New Orleans. The intimate space sat 78 guests. Tall French doors led out to small balconies where guests could enjoy an "adult beverage" while appreciating the view of New Orleans Square and the Rivers of America. Disney executive Ron Dominguez said, "It is a different experience because it is so quiet. There is fine linen, china, and glassware. It's different to have that right in the middle of the theme park." [19]

The second Club 33 dining area was the Trophy Room, which was designed to be a more masculine environment, evoking a British men's club. Forty-two guests sat at "pub-like natural oak tables." On the cypress-clad walls were gifts given to Walt over the years, including a stuffed mountain goat, a stuffed African antelope, native spears, masks, and a 9-foot-long, solid ivory mammoth tusk.[20]

It would be other animals—an owl, two magpies, a raccoon, and a vulture—that captured the attention of the guests, however. Microphones installed in the light fixtures listened in when "the tall tales are spun back and forth across the Trophy Room," and the Audio-Animatronics characters responded just like the "talented Macaws in the *Enchanted Tiki Room,* and as talkative as 'Mother' in the General Electric *Carousel of Progress.*"[21] The show was short-lived; predictably, some executives felt uncomfortable with the eavesdropping capability, and the microphones and speaker were disconnected.

Sadly, Walt never got to experience the club, as it opened seven months after his death.

 A **WORLD** *on the* **MOVE**

IF THE OPENING OF PIRATES of the Caribbean was not enough in 1967, Tomorrowland was about to reemerge as a shining vision of an optimistic future. This would be the Tomorrowland that Walt had always wanted but could not afford in 1955. "Tomorrowland was something very dear to Walt's heart," said Roy Disney. "The old Tomorrowland had always been a source of annoyance to him because he never really accomplished what he was trying to do . . . he was involved in great depth in the New Tomorrowland until the day he died."[22]

From the start, Walt's intention had been that Tomorrowland be "a vista into a world of wondrous ideas, signifying man's achievements, a step into the future, with predictions of constructive things to come."[23] Walt had high hopes for Tomorrowland, but the final product was constrained primarily by a lack of time and money. "When we opened Disneyland, outer space was Buck Rogers," Walt said. "And since then has come Sputnik and our great [United States'] program in outer space. So I had to tear down my Tomorrowland that I built 11 years ago and rebuild it to keep pace." He added, "The only problem with anything of Tomorrow is that at the pace we're going right now, tomorrow would catch up with us before we got it built." [24]

For the most part, the original Tomorrowland was a collection of exhibits from consumer-oriented companies such as Monsanto, Crane, and Kaiser Aluminum. This was at a time when major appliances would go through frequent model changes. When Walt got the chance to freshen up his stale version of Tomorrowland, he jumped on it.

Walt took advantage of his fame and had his Imagineers visit as many laboratories as they could. Organizations such as AT&T, General Motors, and Ford, as well as NASA, were happy to show them around as long as they swore to secrecy. Then the Imagineers would return to Glendale and figure out which of the technologies could be used within the park. Walt's vision of the future would become known as A World on the Move. It opened on July 2, 1967, and for more than three years, WED worked on the $23 million expansion. At 5 acres, Tomorrowland would be twice as large as the original version.

The Imagineers wanted to create something that looked fresh and futuristic. The stark white buildings were a reflection of America's fascination with space travel and Walt's optimistic spirit. The gateway to Tomorrowland was framed by water fountains and the upthrust facades made of sculpted reflective surfaces for *America the Beautiful* on the left and Adventure Thru Inner Space on the right. The beamway for the WEDway PeopleMover transportation system swept over the entrance with the "constant movement in keeping with the ceaseless activity of a futuristic city." The beamway and multilevel "theme" building were the most prominent architectural features.

The 85-foot tower, designed by Imagineer George McGinnis, was the embodiment of A World on the Move, and it became a piece of kinetic art all its own. At the top were the 12, two-passenger, Apollo-style Rocket Jets flying 60 feet overhead. The rockets were mounted on 18-foot-long control arms. Guests entered the spinner ride by using one of two gantry elevators to the upper level.

On the second level was the WEDway PeopleMover, a ride that performed the same function as the Disneyland Railroad by providing guests a preview of the attractions. In June 1964, Walt had directed his team to develop some sort of conveyance that would tie all of the elements within the land together. He suggested an elevated system that would speed up or slow down. Walt temporarily referred to the system as the People Mover, with the hope that somebody could come up with a better name. However, the name stuck.

The WEDway PeopleMover was a direct descendent of another Disney attraction, the Ford pavilion ride system and Magic Skyway show at the 1964–1965 New York World's Fair. When Ford Motor Company hired WED to develop an attraction, the goal had been to allow guests to ride in one of their new vehicles, as they had at the 1939 New York World's Fair. In 1939, guests entered the vehicle and a driver took them around a track. This time, Ford wanted to automate the ride system and eliminate the need for drivers.

In preparation for the 1964 World's Fair, the Imagineers toured a Ford steel plant in Detroit, Michigan, where they found their solution. John Hench said, "We watched them handle this steel ingot . . . the way they would shape it, squash it, and finally make sheet steel out of the thing. It was moved around to different areas within the plant, and the whole process was done on a track of rollers." He noticed, "When this great red hot ingot was finally pressed out, it came back and it was sent streaking on this long run, and when it reached the end of the run, it went through these shapers which curled it."[25]

The WED team was inspired. "Here was all this weight, this mass, and it ended up in a compact roll," Hench said. "[Walt] saw flexibility of how that ingot was turned around, carted back and forth, and he could hardly wait to get back and talk to Roger Broggie about it." Walt asked, "Do you think we could put some kind of seat on that type of conveyor, or some kind of arrangement for people to ride on . . . do you think this thing would handle it?" Roger Broggie's response was, "Sure . . . we'll just put a platen on the bottom of the vehicle."[26] Broggie's solution was to embed 500 electric motors in the track, each with a rubber tire that would press up against a fiberboard platen on the bottom of the vehicle and push the train forward.

The 1967 WEDway PeopleMover was not originally intended for Disneyland. Instead, the attraction was being developed for Walt's proposed Experimental Community of Tomorrow (EPCOT) in Florida. Marc Davis said, "Walt was always looking ahead. He was very interested, in the '60s, in city planning. He had his PeopleMover and he talked about taking a city like Los Angeles and having the People-Mover connecting stores and business and so forth, but all at the second-story level. He was always ahead of things . . . he seemed to get bored easily, so he was always out on the edge."[27]

Walt was using the development of the 1967 Tomorrowland as a way to test ideas for his larger EPCOT concept in Florida. With the WEDway PeopleMover, Walt now had "a silent, all-electric completely automatic intermediate transportation system designed for variable speed, point-to-point shuttle transportation service," as a press release described the system. It went on to explain that the WEDway PeopleMover was "a series of vehicles that never stop moving even when passengers are boarding or debarking. Silent trains that glide along at predetermined varying speeds, automatically spaced vehicles that can't collide. Motorless cars that eliminate the chance of one vehicle stalling all the others. Compartment doors that slide open and close by themselves. A transportation system on which passengers never have to wait for the journey to begin."[28]

The Goodyear Tire & Rubber Company sponsored the attraction, which also featured a VIP lounge located on the back side of the Plaza Inn. The system consisted of 62 continuously moving, fully automatic four-car trains. Each train was silent and motorless and could travel at varying speeds—up to 12 mph—up and down substantial grades. The track was 3,250 feet. Each car had a speaker for the prerecorded narration. The system had a remarkable capacity of 4,885 guests per hour.

Guests loaded the trains via a continuously moving platform. Bob Gurr had been responsible for this part of the project. He started working on a grooved turntable, where the cars would come around on the outer rim while the guests boarded from the moving platform. He was proud that he designed a high-capacity, low-speed loading system, and he rushed over to Walt's office to show him. Walt had just gotten back from Europe after attending the Lausanne Exposition in Geneva, Switzerland. He took one look at Gurr's drawings and told him he had already seen the same type of platform at the exposition. So Walt sent Gurr to Geneva on July 4, 1964, with a 16-millimeter camera. Gurr's approach was validated.

unofficial **TIP**

Over the years, the WEDway PeopleMover trains would be repainted from the original pastel colors at opening to a white- and blue-striped version. On August 21, 1995, the attraction was closed so that the Rocket Rods XPR, a new high-speed thrill ride, could take its place.

The WEDway PeopleMover provided the overview of Tomorrowland that Walt had been seeking. As the trains left the loading platform, they glided along the guideway toward the Tomorrowland entrance. Guests got a chance to preview Adventure Thru Inner Space as the train passed behind the Mighty Microscope, and passengers enjoyed another view as the train passed high above the postshow area. The journey continued through the Character Shop and back outside toward the Tomorrowland bandstand.

Returning indoors, guests passed by Flight to the Moon's Mission Control and the impressive scale model of Progress City inside the *Carousel of Progress*. The trains went outdoors once again and wound over, under, and along the monorail beamway. Guests also got a peek at the Submarine Voyage and Autopia. At times, the WEDway PeopleMover guideway reached a height of 34 feet. The final preview was the preshow area for the CircleVision theater.

John Hench, assisted by Disney sculptor Mitsu, designed the supports for the WEDway PeopleMover beam from the pedestrian perspective as "tree branches" that were "organic." He said, "I had an idea of a type of architecture which was kind of cartilaginous, at least that's what I called it."[29] The design featured structures with soft symmetrical shapes and arches, which he felt contributed to the guests' sense of comfort. Rolly Crump designed environmental elements such as ticket booths and The Mad Hatter store in the same style. The circulation site plan was carefully thought out to minimize the distance a guest had to walk: A stroll around the perimeter going door to door to each attraction measured one-half mile. Even the landscape architecture was specially designed to enhance and embellish the experience as seen from above, as many guests would be riding the monorail, the PeopleMover, and the Skyway.

Walt was not alive when the new Tomorrowland opened, but he had been involved and had influenced every part of its development. He had said, "Science and technology have already given us the tools we need to build the world of the future. If we use them right now, we won't have to wait to know what tomorrow will bring. I believe we will prove with new Tomorrowland that today is the future."

The star attraction was the *Carousel of Progress*. It had been imported from the 1964–1965 New York World's Fair where it had been a huge hit for General Electric's Progressland pavilion. Bringing the show back from New York was one of the big reasons for the entire redesign of the land. Adventure Thru Inner Space, the WEDway PeopleMover, and Bell Telephone's *America the Beautiful* were added to the attraction lineup. Marc Davis restaged a number of scenes in the Submarine Voyage, and McDonnell Douglas's Flight to the Moon received updates. Some of the original Tomorrowland attractions remained to entertain guests: the monorail, the Skyway to Fantasyland, and Autopia.

Opening one week before the other attractions was an all-new version of *America the Beautiful* in 360 CircleVision. The free show was sponsored by the Bell System, American Telephone and Telegraph and Associated Companies, and hosted by Pacific Telephone. The new CircleVision projection system used 9 35-millimeter cameras instead of 11. The technology was a huge step forward from the original Circarama. The theater was also larger. The screens and projectors were arranged above head level, and lean rails were provided for viewers to hold or to lean against while standing and viewing the film. This version of the film took the viewer from Hawaii to Alaska and "reveals the wide range of natural beauty to be found throughout America." The preshow featured such high-tech wonders as Picturephones, where guests could connect with a person in "Chicago"; Voice Mirrors, which played back prerecorded images; and "small fry" phones for children to talk with their favorite cartoon characters. *America the Beautiful* was staffed with female Bell Telephone employees who worked in the park on six-month breaks from their official Bell positions. As many as 3,000 guests per hour could enjoy the show.

AMERICA THE BEAUTIFUL was updated in 1976 for the American bicentennial. The Bell Systems sponsorship of the Circle-Vision 360 film *America the Beautiful* ended on September 11, 1983, due to the breakup of the telecommunications monopoly. Pacific Telephone became the local stand-alone company, and it declined to renew the sponsorship. In 1998 the show building closed and served as the queue for the PeopleMover replacement for the 1998 redo of Tomorrowland.

BACK *on* VISUAL

MONSANTO'S ADVENTURE THRU INNER SPACE was one of the most unusual Disneyland attractions every conceived. Monsanto, the industrial chemical company, had been a sponsor at Disneyland since the very beginning. When the park first opened, the Monsanto Hall of Chemistry was one of the few exhibits in Tomorrowland, the first of four Monsanto exhibits. Next was the long-running and popular Monsanto House of the Future. Over the years, Walt and Dr. Charles Allen Thomas, Chairman of the Monsanto Company, became close friends. Dr. Thomas said of Walt, "I came to respect the fact that he was an extraordinary educator, in addition to being one of our century's greatest showmen."[30]

unofficial **TIP**

During development, Monsanto's Adventure Thru Inner Space show was also known as Adventures in Science, Micro-World, and The Magic Microscope. The name Adventure Thru Inner Space was approved on January 27, 1967.

Right after the opening of the Monsanto House of the Future in 1957, Walt started thinking about "a protozoa ride that would take patrons into a drop of water as seen through a microscope," according to Disney biographer Bob Thomas. Walt felt, "There's a great urgency today to interest young people in science as a profession."[31] During this period, space exploration was all the rage, and Dr. Thomas felt that the other sciences were being ignored. Naturally, he wanted people to get excited about chemistry and the work being done at Monsanto. He felt that the products they were producing were more relevant and immediate to the day-to-day needs of the public. He wanted to remind the public that molecules were just as important and interesting as asteroids. "The astronaut in his space suit may cut a more glamorous figure than the scientist in his lab coat, but we are hoping the excitement generated in our attraction by the creativity of many Disney artists will bring alive the excitement of Inner Space," Dr. Thomas said.[32]

Dr. Thomas wanted people to really see what was going on at the microscopic level. "The quantum mechanical description of a molecule cannot be pictured in any satisfactory physical model. There was simply no way to duplicate the nucleus of an atom within the capabilities of our natural world . . . it is almost unimaginable."[33] Walt enjoyed the challenge of achieving the unimaginable, and he put Claude Coats in charge of the project. In addition to Coats, Xavier Atencio, Yale Gracey, Ed Johnson, and others applied their creative talents. Although Walt never saw the final attraction, Coats said, "Walt had seen most of the development of Inner Space."

Dr. Thomas's goals for the attraction were focused on educating the guests. "Has the exhibit brought the viewer closer to an understanding of the matter at hand? Has something been presented here which hasn't been presented so effectively before? Have we achieved an additional step toward understanding?" The idea of guests traveling through a molecule came pretty quickly. The big question was what kind of molecule?

The Imagineers first looked at Monsanto products; after considering Monsanto polymers, acrylics, and polyethylenes, they felt it would be too difficult to make sense of such complex molecules. Then the Imagineers turned to water, something very simple and relatable, a "substance most basic to man's existence." The simplicity of the water molecule made it the easiest way to engage the guests, and the fact that a water molecule looked a little like Mickey Mouse did not go unnoticed. Dr. Thomas admitted, "We have avoided paths which, however intriguing to the scientist, interfere with understanding by the general public. In the process, we have probably oversimplified certain areas." He hoped the attraction would be "an entirely new method of learning complex scientific fact by immediate experience."

To achieve the desired guest capacity, the Imagineers had to invent an entirely new ride conveyance. One day, Bob Gurr was relaxing in John Hench's office as they were reviewing what they had learned from the New York World's Fair. They started talking about the need for a "continuous chain" ride car when Gurr noticed a red plastic apple sitting on Hench's desk. Gurr picked up the apple and started to twirl it around by the stem. It suddenly occurred to him that he could design a vehicle that could rotate like the apple. The Omnimover was born.

The name Omnimover is derived from the PeopleMover. It was a train system of vehicles that were linked together by a tow bar in an endless loop. Each vehicle could rotate 180 degrees to the right or the left, rock backward, turn and point in specific directions. Gurr designed the clam-shape vehicles with built-in speakers and a restricted point of view. The Omnimover allowed the Imagineers to manipulate the guests' point of view like they would a movie camera. Guests would be focused on the best part of the illusions. The guests would be isolated into small groups, and their movements would be under complete control. The timing of each scene could be precisely mapped out.

Adventure Thru Inner Space would be the first application of the Omnimover technology, and the vehicles would be called Atomobiles. The 123 Atomobiles traveled at 1.2 mph along a hidden 682-foot loop and were driven by 16 electric motors from General Electric through cam-like activators along the track. The trip took 6 minutes. Each Atomobile carried two passengers and loaded every 3 seconds from a revolving turntable. The ride's capacity was a staggering 3,275 guests per hour. The system was built by longtime Disneyland supplier Arrow Development.

The ride was placed in the same 21,733-square-foot space that was home to the original Hall of Chemistry. Guests entered through a 40-foot-high facade that "symbolized the world of tomorrow." A water fountain of abstract forms "symbolized inner and outer space." For adults, there was no need for a ticket. The attraction was free. To prevent unsupervised children from riding the attraction, they could only enter by using the free ticket inside of the Junior and Child ticket books. Monsanto had a VIP guest lounge adjacent to the loading area.

As guests meandered along the curving ramp toward the loading platform, they passed eight "display pods" that previewed the ride ahead and learned that the objective was to shrink down to the size of a water molecule using the Atomobile. Along one wall was a giant multicolor Snowflake Tracking Screen that identified where the other ride vehicles were located. Along another wall was the Mighty Microscope, the most impressive and memorable display in the queue area. Gliding behind the Microscope was the WEDway PeopleMover.

The Mighty Eye Microscope was 12 feet high and 37 feet long and was designed by Imagineer George McGinnis. Guests would watch Atomobiles entering one end of the microscope only to become visible once again, at a much smaller size, in a transparent barrel at the other end. The vehicles appeared to shrink even further and then blasted into the snowflakes in the "laboratory slide." The illusion was very successful; reportedly, many guests became frightened thinking that they would not return back to normal size.

Guests boarded the Atomobiles by stepping on a loading turntable with the vehicles running along the outside edge, much like the PeopleMover. The park learned that they needed to slow the loading turntable down 10% because, while guests had a tendency to hurry to board, they were much slower to exit.

Inside of each Atomobile were speakers for guests to listen to the narration by character actor Paul Frees, who was well known for his voice-overs for Pirates, Haunted Mansion, and other Disney attractions. The story line was enhanced by the narrator who filled in the blanks. External speakers along the route with the voices of the tracking crew augmented the sound. The result was a very intimate experience. All of this was accompanied by the futuristic soundtrack composed by Buddy Baker.

The Atomobiles glided into the microscope for the first act. They entered a dark room and then rotated backward, disorienting the guests. Soon, the guests would be surrounded by projections of snowflakes. As they moved forward, the snowflakes would change from projections to large dimensional sculptures. Continuing along, the scale of snowflakes would continue to change until the shapes became increasingly vague, furthering the illusion that the guests were continuing to shrink.

In the second act, the attraction was mostly dimensional. The Omnimover could move in very close to the sets, adding a sense of drama. However, the Imagineers would learn that sometimes the sets were too close to the vehicle. The sets were being ripped to pieces. Bold children, isolated in groups of two, reached out and grabbed whatever they could touch. This planted the seed for a new ride design consideration called the "envelope of protection."

During the third act, the Atomobiles continued to shrink until they reached the threshold of inner space. The room was filled with moving, spinning projections of Mickey Mouse–shaped spheres that represented water molecules. Eighty-five projectors were used throughout the attraction to create the illusion. Then the Atomobiles entered a room surrounded by three large molecules, wrapped in fluorescent beads and thrust along with air pressure. The water molecules became three-dimensional objects spinning from the ceiling. Guests were now as small as a water molecule and about to enter the subatomic realm.

By this time, attentive guests may have noticed that the tracking crew were beginning to express concern that they no longer had a signal from the Atomobiles, that the Atomobile had gone missing. A flashing shower of lights simulating electrons added to the tension. Drawing the Atomobiles forward was the pulsing nucleus of the atom. The nucleus was actually a ball rotating on a motorized mount and lit by a strobe light, and it appeared to look like a miniature sun.

In the final act, the snow suddenly started to melt, and the guests could sense that the Atomobile was dropping. The narrator reassured the guests that everything was okay and that they were "back on visual." They looked up to see a giant mechanized human eyeball peering down at them through a microscope. As the Atomobiles approached the unloading turntable, they passed the Fountain of Fashion, a two-story hourglass of glycerine oil flowing down hundreds of

> BEGINNING DECEMBER 15, 1972, Adventure Thru Inner Space was no longer free and required a C ticket. Five years later, on September 30, 1977, Monsanto's sponsorship ended. For the first time, the chemical giant did not have a presence in the park. Attendance diminished, and the ride closed on September 2, 1985, to make room for Star Tours.

monofilament strands surrounding mannequins dressed in the latest polyester fashions. "Miracles from Molecules," the bubbly and infectious theme song written by Richard and Robert Sherman, played in the background. The entire Adventure Thru Inner Space ride experience had lasted less than 6 minutes.

The postshow area featured a new version of the Clock of the World. For Adventure Thru Inner Space, the clock is based on a projection of the world as seen from the North Pole. A revolving disc allowed guests to note the time anywhere in the world. There were also display cases inset along the postshow walls.

Adventure Thru Inner Space provoked a wide range of reactions. Leon Janzen of *The "E" Ticket* magazine said, "This attraction was one of the last rides completed with the message that 'science is our friend.' While Inner Space was generally pleasant and non-threatening, the ride was ahead of its time in hinting that there was scientific trouble ahead, and this ominous atmosphere helped the ride's emotional impact."[34] Disney archivist Dave Smith was less kind when he admitted, "I was very much for getting rid of Adventure Thru Inner Space. It amazed me to find out how many people thought that was their favorite attraction at Disneyland!"[35]

GREAT BIG
BEAUTIFUL TOMORROW

WALT WAS A FAN OF THE PLAY *Our Town* by Thornton Wilder and had seen it at least three times when it ran in Los Angeles. He decided to adapt the play's successful format to his Edison Square idea, which had been brewing since 1958. Walt wanted to present "four warm and humorous families welcoming guests into their homes of the 1890s, 1920s, 1940s, and today [post-1960s]." That scenario became a foundation for General Electric's *Carousel of Progress,* which had been a huge hit in the General Electric Progressland pavilion at the 1964–1965 New York World's Fair.

In New York, the show was presented in an innovative revolving theater that had a capacity of more than 3,600 guests per hour, and more than 16 million people saw the show over the two-year New York run. Actually, the *Carousel of Progress* was only one part of a pavilion with multiple attractions, including a VIP guest lounge on the second floor. Architect Welton Becket designed the exterior of that structure. The need for a rotating theater was originally driven by the 32 crude Audio-Animatronics characters that needed substantial backstage support. It made sense to leave the non-portable robot actors in place and bring a new audience to them every few minutes. The 83,000-square-foot Carousel Theatre in New York was a technological marvel all its own. The 200-foot-wide structure contained six 240-seat auditoriums mounted on a giant turntable with steel flanged wheels moving along a hidden rail. It was powered by six 20-horsepower DC motors.

Forbes magazine said of the New York version of the show, "A delightfully done soft sell . . . all sell, but soft, interesting, clever . . . a wonderful 25 minutes." Disney historian Jim Korkis described the *Carousel of Progress* as "a vision filled with optimism that progress was not to be feared but embraced. This attraction was a physical representation of Walt's personal philosophy that people with all their foibles were basically good and that life was good in any era and would only keep getting better." When Disney surveyed the New York audience, 99% of the attendees said the attraction was "good or excellent." Walt used these figures to convince General Electric to bring the show to Disneyland. *Carousel of Progress* was the only one of the four WED-designed Fair attractions to come to Disneyland with the same sponsor.

Carousel of Progress was the star attraction of the 1967 Tomorrowland. By the time the show was moved to Disneyland, the Audio-Animatronics had been greatly improved. Just as they had done for the New York show, guests entered a theater with seating that revolved around six stages. Every version of the *Carousel of Progress* script started with, "Now most carousels just go 'round and 'round without getting anywhere. But on this one, at every turn we'll be making progress. And progress is not just moving ahead, it's dreaming, and working, and building a better way of life." After the prologue, guests experienced the strange sensation of the moving platform they were sitting on. Once the theater stopped rotating, time had shifted and the guests were back in "The Gay '90s."

The first act was a demonstration of what life was like before electricity was supplied to homes. It was springtime, just before the turn of the last century. Guests were greeted by an Audio-Animatronics host, voiced by actor Rex Allen. According to Blaine Gibson, "A guy named Preston Hansen was the model for the figure (of father)." Some of the artifacts guests saw in action included a wind-up gramophone, an ice box, coal stove and water heater, a hand-cranked washing machine, a kitchen water pump, and gas lamps.

While Father sat in the middle of the stage, guests would meet the rest of the family in short vignettes presented at the left and right side of the stage on turntables hidden behind scrims. Mother, Daughter, Son, Grandma, Grandpa, and the dog became familiar characters as the show progressed. Walt was the one to come up with the dog gag. In each scene, the dog's name would change. In the first act, he was known as Rover.

The theater rotated again, and guests entered summertime in the 1920s, when there were so many electronic gadgets that extension cords were strung everywhere. As a demonstration, they all came to life at the flick of a switch and chugged along until the fuse was blown. Some of these modern marvels included a coffee percolator, a toaster, a waffle iron, an electric stove, and a refrigerator. Junior was playing with an electric phonograph while Cousin Orville was taking an "air-cooled" bath, courtesy of a block of ice and a fan. The Orville gag had been a Walt idea; to make sure the team understood what he wanted, he had crawled into a bathtub to demonstrate. Orville was the only time that Mel Blanc, the famous Warner Brothers cartoon voice actor, performed in a Disney production. Once again, close to the edge of the stage, is a dog—named Buster.

Another rotation and guests were in the 1940s. The season was autumn, and the theme for this act was how all of the new electric appliances could help with the hard work around the house. Some of the household wonders included a refrigerator with an ice maker, an electric washing machine, hearing aids, and a black-and-white television. Mother was trying to hang wallpaper using a cake mixer turned into a paint mixer, with disastrous results, while Sport the dog taunted the audience.

Finally, guests entered a world that was sometime in the near future. It was the Christmas season, and the family was enjoying their General Electric Medallion Home with the glass-enclosed electrically heated patio, a fully automated electronic kitchen that featured a self-cleaning oven, and a dishwasher. In the living room was a color television and a video recorder, and the room was illuminated by programmable Coloramic lighting. In this scene, Grandma and Grandpa have moved to a retirement village, and guests are told the children are at the airport retrieving their grandparents for the holiday festivities. Queen the dog guards the house.

A new element added to the Disneyland show was the tower from Progress City, which could be seen out the window in the background. The significance of this became readily apparent as the theater made its final rotation. Unlike the New York show, the final act was an invitation for guests to board a Speedramp and travel to the second level to visit the model of Progress City that had made its first appearance in the previous scene. As the host said, "And now, a new springtime of progress awaits you . . . spring up out of your seats and head for the doorway to the future . . . please keep moving . . . don't stand in the way of progress."

The model was an amazing display that covered 6,900 square feet and measured 115 feet across and 60 feet deep. Guests viewed the model from one of three terraced rows. The model was scaled ⅛ inch to 1 foot. At the center was a soaring, modern 30-story tower designed by architect George Rester. At its base was a domed city. The attention to detail was remarkable, with more than 20,000 trees and shrubs, 1,400 working streetlights, more than 4,500 structures that were lit from within, and 2,450 moving vehicles.

The city was complete with schools, stadiums, shopping centers, and a small amusement park. All of these destinations were connected by working models of the vast transportation network, consisting of monorails, PeopleMovers, automobiles, and trucks. There was even an airport and a General Electric nuclear power plant. Each of the community amenities was highlighted during a 4½-minute presentation from Mother and Father. According to them, "Looks like tomorrow is already here . . . we'll always come back to Progress City . . . and we hope you folks will come back too . . . everything you've seen here in our all-electric city is really possible today . . . tell 'em about General Electric's Progress City."

What most guests did not know was that Progress City represented Walt's intention for the 27,443 acres that he and Roy had purchased in Central Florida. This was his vision for EPCOT, Experimental Community Of Tomorrow. Disney Legend Marty Sklar said, "That model almost exactly matched all our planning for EPCOT. I think Walt got a kick out of doing the model, without having to say that he was going to build this big city, but it was all there for anybody to see."[36] Sklar added, "He was planting a seed through the show in the Carousel of

Progress in Tomorrowland at Disneyland. There was 'Progress City' visible out the window in the final scene of the *Carousel,* and then you went upstairs and there was Walt's own model city."[37]

Much of the attraction's buoyancy was driven by Richard and Robert Sherman's theme song "There's A Great Big Beautiful Tomorrow." Richard Sherman had suggested that the song embodied the spirit of Walt Disney and was their private tribute to Walt. The attraction was a phenomenal success. Over its six-year run at Disneyland, it was viewed by more than 31 million guests.

Throughout his lifetime, Walt Disney had believed that imagination, hard work, and a confidence that technology, especially American industry, could solve just about any problem. In the *Carousel of Progress,* Walt and his team combined all three values to create something never seen before. Relentlessly upbeat and optimistic, the attraction was Walt's showcase of enthusiasm for the wonders of science and technology. He wanted guests to embrace the future and welcome it.

STINGRAYS

TOMORROWLAND REALLY WAS A WORLD ON THE MOVE: Skyway buckets high above, Rocket Jets on top of the tower just below, and the WEDway PeopleMover just below that. At the pedestrian level were the cars of Autopia. Below grade were the Submarines with only their conning towers peeking over the lagoon. Even the buildings moved when the *Carousel of Progress* theater spun every 3 minutes and 15 seconds.

unofficial **TIP**
This underground corridor from CircleVision to the *Carousel of Progress* was the forerunner to the underground Utilidors at the Orlando, Florida, Magic Kingdom.

During the day, the Tomorrowland Terrace stage appeared to be a colorful, modern planter. With a push of a button, the planter became a canopy for a stage that rose from the ground. The musicians would already be in place, so there was no need for a curtain. Guests could rock the night away on the 3,000-square-foot dance floor. The high-tech dining facility featured climate-controlled terraces without walls and a high-tech kitchen with infrared broilers and automatic cooking devices. Designers also built an underground corridor connecting the stage to the CircleVision theater, and over to the *Carousel of Progress.*

On August 12, 1967, another original attraction received a significant update. The Flight to the Moon had been on the cutting edge when

it opened in 1955 but needed a new look. In the 1967 version, the journey began in Mission Control, the "nerve center of Disneyland's spaceport." The attraction's show building was moved to accommodate the
new element. Guests entered Mission Control and stood in long rows.
Behind the glass was a crew of eight Audio-Animatronics technicians
from "space operations" studying their display consoles. They were
being supervised by Mr. Tom Morrow, the control center director, who
was barking instructions to his crew. The host interrupted Mr. Morrow,
and the two began a 4½-minute, tightly scripted dialogue. This would
be the first time a Disney attraction combined Audio-Animatronics figures with a live actor. At one point, the tour was distracted by a way-
ward bird. Finally, the boarding was called for Flight 92, and the guests
moved into the Lunar Transports.

The Lunar Transports' capacity had been increased from 102 to 162
persons. The seats were arranged in two sections with four rows. Like
the original version, the 1967 transports each had two large screens
on the wall, one screen on the floor, and another screen in the ceiling.

The story line remained pretty much the same, but a couple of new
elements were added. The additions included a conversation with an
astronaut working on the surface of the moon and new motorized
seats. The new seats had a movable lower cushion that would drop
upon takeoff, giving the illusion of increased g-forces, and rise once
guests were in orbit to simulate weightlessness. The entire journey to
the moon and back took 12 minutes.

Autopia also got an upgrade. The Mark VI, also known (ironically, as it turned out) as the Ultimate Car, was breaking down even
more frequently than the earlier versions. Early in 1967, it was
decided to let Bob Gurr try to design something that would actually
work. Gurr took under consideration all of the problems that the
Autopia cars had suffered from since 1955, with the goal to find a
reliable solution. To accomplish this goal he began developing the
Mark VII Autopia car.

The primary goal for the Mark VII development was to design a
car that could actually survive. Unlike a conventional car, the Mark
VII avoided using any cantilevered structures. Because the cars were
restricted by the guide rail, Gurr designed a frame that was able to
be compressed, front to rear, and set at the height of the bumper.
That put the driver inside of the frame. The new car was so strong it
could survive a platoon of five moving cars hitting a platoon of five
parked cars. The cars were powered by a Kohler engine, a MAPO

clutch, and a Dorris gearbox. They weighed 830 pounds. One hundred and sixty Mark VII cars were built for Disneyland.

The cars became known as stingrays. Gurr said of his design, "That car came out before the 1968 Corvette Stingray, and I designed the surface development for the '67 Autopia car without ever seeing the Corvette."[38] Henry Haga, an old friend of Gurr's, was the principal designer behind the 1968 Corvette. When Gurr showed Haga the artwork, "I flipped when I saw his Corvette, and he flipped when he saw my Autopia car. These were two separate designs which looked exactly the same, right down to the cut-off spoiler on the back end." The cars did what they were supposed to. Many years later, they would undergo another update, but the Mark VII chassis would remain. "I never guessed, back then, that the Mark VII Autopia car would last this long," said Gurr.[39]

As far as Walt was concerned, all of this activity did not mean Tomorrowland was done. Also on the list was "a towering structure of futuristic, uninhibited architecture containing new rides and exhibits, including an exciting journey into the depths of outer space and return aboard a special Disneyland re-entry vehicle in a ride equaling the thrills and excitement of the Magic Kingdom's Matterhorn Bobsled run." There was also talk of a new version of the Flying Saucers.[40]

Not all of the action was in New Orleans Square and Tomorrowland. Over in Adventureland, the Jungle Cruise would continue to get updates, with new dancing natives and a village and two new gorillas. On Main Street U.S.A., the Arribas Brothers' glass cutter shop opened after Walt, who had appreciated their work at the 1964–1965 New York World's Fair, had encouraged them to bring their craft to Disneyland.

On November 20, 1967, Disneyland sought and got approval from the Anaheim Planning Commission to expand the borders of the park to the north and south on land they already owned.[41] They were going to need the extra land to accommodate their guests. By the end of 1967, more than 7.9 million guests had visited the park, bringing the total attendance to 67 million. Since opening day, the park had more than doubled the number of attractions, from 22 to 52. The total investment had exceeded $95 million. The Disneyland complex had grown to 70 acres, with an additional 115 acres for parking and backstage services. The impact of the park's economic success on the surrounding community was enormous, having led to the construction of the Anaheim Stadium, opened in 1966 as the home of the California Angels baseball team, and the futuristic 9,100-seat

Anaheim Convention Center, opened July 12, 1967. Anaheim motel-hotel accommodations had grown from 60 rooms in 1955 to more than 6,500 rooms in 1967. Because of Disneyland, Anaheim and Orange County had become a world-class destination.

The PATTERN of LEAVES

WITH WALT'S DEATH IN LATE 1966 and a fruitful decade of activity and growth from 1958 to 1967, the park leaders decided to take a deep breath in 1968. The world was changing outside of the gates, and without Walt, management was trying to figure out the best way to stay relevant and successful.

Still, there were issues to deal with and things to accomplish. Since July 6, 1954, guests had been able to take a helicopter from Burbank to the park. The 20-minute ride was less than one-third the time it took to make the same trip by automobile. The service had even been featured on a number of Disneyland television programs. In January 1968, local residents and motel owners petitioned the City Council to limit the flights. The Council sided with Disney, stating that the value of the heliport outweighed "minor disadvantages" of living nearby. Considering that Disney had invested more than $100 million in the park—including enhancements to the PeopleMover, the park's Main Entrance, and the guest parking lot in 1968—the City Council had very little choice. They understood who was driving the local economy.

One day, Dick Irvine was walking through Disneyland when he realized that very little attention had been paid to lighting the park at night. He asked Rolly Crump and Yale Gracey to assess the lighting and see what they could do. Tomorrowland was so overly lit that a person "could cast a shadow at nine o'clock at night," according to Crump. "On the other hand, when they finished New Orleans Square, they didn't have a single light in place other than a few windows that were lit. When I got down there, all they had were the streetlights."[42]

Crump was responsible for Frontierland and New Orleans Square, while Gracey took on Main Street U.S.A., Tomorrowland, and Fantasyland. Each night over the summer of 1968, they would go out with a crew of electricians and make changes to enhance the magic. Crump had an especially creative solution for New Orleans Square. He projected the pattern of leaves on the buildings to give a sense of depth. He noticed as you got away from the buildings you got a soft flow. He cross-lit the upper parts of the buildings from the different balconies. To emphasize the forced perspective, he used hotter lights lower on the structures. For general area lighting, Crump supplemented the antique lamp posts with lights in the trees as close to the source as he could. The Tomorrowland solution was more straightforward: Gracey immediately removed 50% of the light.

A job at Disneyland was becoming a powerful entry on a resume. Working at the park was so desirable that there were about 30,000 unsolicited inquiries for every 3,000 jobs available. For the first time in 1968, African-Americans were no longer restricted to performer or backstage roles when they were allowed to work at "people contact" positions.

More than 9.4 million guests passed through the turnstiles in 1968, bringing the total attendance to 77 million since opening day.

 # PEOPLE *of* EQUAL CLOUT

SINCE 1962, an immaculate Victorian mansion had sat vacant, high on a hill along the banks of the Rivers of America. On August 9, 1969, the house was opened to the public for the first time, at a cost of $7 million. The Haunted Mansion would become one of the most beloved and durable attractions at Disneyland—a somewhat bittersweet turn of events; although Walt had been heavily involved in its development, it was the first major show to be produced without his final approval.

The Haunted Mansion had been under development for 12 years. The concept had changed many times, but nobody could come up with an idea that would excite Walt. For a couple of years, the project was even put on the back burner. Later on, Marc Davis would be assigned to the project, and he said, "My point of view on all of these attractions is that they are a series of experiences. You aren't telling a story in the Haunted Mansion any more than you are trying to tell a story in the Pirates of the Caribbean." He suggested, "You're showing some pirates in a lot of interesting situations, but you don't really have a beginning or an ending. They're a series of situations, not a story. I think this is why Walt never bought the Haunted Mansion in his time."[43]

When Davis and Claude Coats took over, they threw out much of the prior work and took the project in another direction. This time Davis would take the lead, drafting as many ideas as his fertile mind could conceive with the hope that the best ideas would surface. The process worked.

Coats was in charge of the environments within the attraction. For 20 years, Coats had been painting backgrounds at the Disney studio. The experience taught him how to create a mood, and he had a strong sense of color. He understood how the backgrounds help the audience focus on the story. Over the years he had learned that the same lessons applied to the rides.

The project was restarted in 1967, when Dick Irvine started handing out different parts of the project to the Imagineers. There was no one person responsible for tying all of the elements together. That job was usually reserved for Walt. The talented team tried to collaborate as best they could, but it was hard.

When Walt was alive, the Haunted Mansion was going to be a walk-through attraction with groups of 40 going from scene to scene. To achieve the desired capacity goals, two elevator shafts were built inside the mansion shell. With the success of the Omnimover in Adventure Thru Inner Space, the Imagineers decided that the high-capacity ride system would be the best way to present the Haunted Mansion.

The 131 Omnimover vehicles built for the Haunted Mansion were called Doom Buggies, and two or three guests could be seated in each vehicle from a moving walkway every 3 seconds. Up to 2,618 guests could ride the 786-foot-long track every hour. The Doom Buggies were capable of making 180-degree turns, left and right. Always learning, the Imagineers had made a few improvements over the Adventure Thru Inner Space version, including reversing the angle of the safety bars.

GREAT CAESAR'S GHOST

CONSIDERING ALL OF THE CHANGES in the haunted house concept over the years, the attraction started off much like Ken Anderson had suggested in 1957 and Yale Gracey and Rolly Crump had suggested in 1964. Guests were grouped into parties of 40. They were escorted by a butler and walked into one of two hidden elevators, where they observed a gallery of stretching portraits. After recovering from the surprise of a ghost hanging by the neck above a transparent ceiling, the guests walked down a long, dark hallway with "locked forbidden doors" and into the entry foyer.

From the entry foyer, guests walked into one of two stretching rooms. The stretching room was not just a spectacular effect but also a very practical way to move thousands of guests from the park to the show building just outside the berm. In the stretching room, guests are surrounded by a series of portraits; Marc Davis created the humorous portraits, which slowly reveal the dark side of the mansion's residents. Under one portrait, a door opened for the guests to board one of two elevators. The hydraulic elevators dropped 15 feet, carrying 85 guests; together, the elevators had a capacity of 12,000 pounds.

As guests exited the stretching room elevators, a series of transforming images graced one wall in the gallery. Davis did the concept drawings, and they were rendered by artist Ed Kohn. What guests have experienced over the years is different than originally intended. The original illusion, created by Yale Gracey, was a system that used a canvas framed on the wall and then used rear projection to make the painting slowly change through a number of steps. They decided against using this system because the guests would be moving too fast through the space. Instead, the portraits flashed along with "lightning" outside the windows of the hallway. At one point, Davis suggested that the original effect should be used in a restaurant near the Haunted Mansion.

Continuing down the Gallery was another classic effect, the converse bust, created completely by chance by Gracey and Crump. The two men had been working on a special effect where a human head would morph right in front of the guests' eyes. Crump said, "First you'd see black, then, all of a sudden, the melted section would come on and the face would appear all 'wormy.' Then, slowly, as you got past the melted part, the image would become sharp and the face would appear as a skull. Then the changes would repeat and the face would become normal, then disappear."[44]

To achieve this effect, Crump and Gracey got a "vacu-formed" face of Lincoln made of a clear plastic and fogged the plastic so that it would be opaque. Then they placed it in a frame like a bas-relief bust on a wall. The men aimed a 35-millimeter projector from behind the bust and placed a circular transparent disk in front of the lens and turned the disk with a clock motor. To create the illusion, they melted portions of the disk and sprayed other parts black. As the disk turned in front of the projector, this caused the images on the face to slowly change. They had worked on this effect with Lincoln's face for about a month when it struck Crump that when the effect was turned off and you were standing behind the bust, the eyes seemed to follow him wherever he went. When placed at the end of the corridor, the effect worked properly.

The mansion hallway was loaded with subtle details. The dark wood wainscoting was bordered with faces of skulls. The 31 brass stanchions were made up of bat gargoyles. The doors were carved with lions' heads and outfitted with snake-shaped door handles. The transom grillworks suggested faces of owls. The hallway used forced perspective; the walls narrowed and the ceiling lowered to make it seem even longer and tighter. The room with the loading platform was virtually empty, with only a giant spider and spiderwebs, plus a few urns. Once on board the Doom Buggy, guests ascended a staircase, which was guarded by statues of griffins.

Continuing on their journey, guests entered the Endless Hallway and the Corridor of Doors. Once again, the space was rich in details, such as a red, overstuffed chair with a face embroidered in the fabric and a leftover derby hat sitting next to the umbrella stand. Who could be the owner? The Doom Buggies appeared to disturb an unusual suit of armor that featured a hawk-like beak. The archways surrounding the corpse in the coffin within the Conservatory were carved like growling lions, and there were three sad faces woven into the tapestry below the casket. Even the corner bracings were carved with the faces of animals.

As the Doom Buggies glided through the hallway, guests saw portraits hanging from the walls. Some of the portraits were hung on a downward tilt, and the more observant guests may have noticed that the creatures in those portraits reappeared later in the attraction as spooks popping up all around. Davis designed the memorable wallpaper with eyes, as well as all the knocking doors, the portraits in the hallway, and the bony hands pushing up in the casket (voiced by Xavier Atencio). At the end of the hallway was a clock with a face that was being eaten by a monster with eyes above, gnarled feet below, a barbed tail as the pendulum, and it only struck 13.

Gracey came up with Madame Leota, who appeared inside of a crystal ball gag. Blaine Gibson sculpted the head. She was placed next to a Tiffany lamp with a spiderweb woven into its pattern. Circling above her in the Séance Circle was a wicker table, a drum, a harp, a trumpet, and cymbals. There was also a table with a mysterious box lit by a lamp above, a horn, a bell, and a tambourine.

The Grand Hall was one of the most amazing spaces within any themed environment. There was so much going on it was impossible to take it all in on one journey. That was the point, of course. As the Doom Buggies turned and passed by the scene, guests peered through archways in the shape of screaming faces. The hall had seen better days, but all of the tears in the wallpaper were actually painted on. Even the chairs were menacing, with carved demon faces with long, red-velvet tongues. Guarding the fireplace were cast-andiron cats. Sitting on top of the mantel was the bust of the woman who kept watch on the guests in the Gallery. It was in the Grand Hall that the ghostly occupants of the mansion first appeared in their dimensional form, listening and dancing to a rendition of "Grim Grinning Ghost" played on the organ that originally appeared in the 1954 Disney film *20,000 Leagues Under the Sea* and at the Tomorrowland exhibit. The illusion was created using the Pepper's Ghost effect first employed in Sleeping Beauty Castle. The women appear to be leading the men in the dance. Is this a mistake or did the designers intend to show that things were different in the afterlife?

The Hall was populated with Anthony and Cleopatra, "Great Caesar's Ghost," and a curious fellow named Pickwick hanging from the chandelier, among others.[45] Another resident was inspired by the *Carousel of Progress* show: Granny, knitting a three-armed sweater. Flying high above were banshees that would later reappear in the cemetery riding bicycles.

The Attic acted as a transitional space. The scale of the room greatly differed from the Grand Hall, and it felt claustrophobic in comparison. There were bats flying about, guarding broken musical instruments and the empty musician's cases left by the band playing for Madame Leota. The attic even included a remnant of Ken Anderson's original bride and groom murder-suicide story line: items from ships such as ship's lanterns and hemp ropes across from a ghostly bride.

The bride was not originally in the Attic. Instead, another figure stood there for a very short time. The character was known as the Hatbox Ghost, and it was removed soon after its debut. No one knew what became of the Hatbox Ghost; for many years it was rumored to still exist, but nobody was really quite sure. The illusion was supposed to be a creepy skeleton-headed ghost in an overcoat with one hand on a cane and the other holding a hatbox. When the cane moved slightly, the skeleton head would disappear from the body and reappear in the hatbox. The Hatbox Ghost figure was designed by Davis. Claude Coats sculpted a maquette, which Imagineer Wayne Jackson enlarged into a full-size show element. The special effect was another Gracey creation and used lights to achieve the effect.

There was only one problem. The illusion was not convincing. The head did not vanish completely due its location within the attic. The effect was installed prior to the attraction's public opening and ran during the cast previews. He was located in front of a bunch of props and very close to the Doom Buggies. However, the gag was removed shortly after the grand opening, never to be seen again. The legend of the Hatbox Ghost had grown so large, Disney profited from selling sculptures based on the original design, even though very few guests ever saw the actual figure.

The Doom Buggies exited the Attic through a window. As guests caught a quick glimpse of the decaying cemetery filled with ghostly figures, they became so frightened that they fell backward into the Graveyard. Throughout the environment, the smaller trees seemed scared, while the taller trees seemed angry. Was this a warning?

The Graveyard was a series of comedic gags crafted in the brilliant mind of Davis. Such memorable moments included the graveyard band, the tea party at the hearse, and the conversation at the Egyptian tomb. With a sensitivity to conveying as much information with as little movement possible, Davis proved to be the master of his craft. Creating Audio-Animatronics figures that looked like the Davis drawings and appeared to be transparent was no small feat. The clear plastic bodies were fogged just a little to give a ghost-like effect.

Wathel Rogers, working alongside mechanical genius Ub Iwerks, created the projection system for the memorable singing quartet busts. Disney hired singers Chuck Schroeder, Bobbie Wright, Jay Myers, and Thurl Ravenscroft, also known as the Mellomen, to perform for all eternity. The men recorded a full-length version of the attraction's theme song, "Grim Grinning Ghosts," composed by Buddy Baker with lyrics by Xavier Atencio. A few months later, the singers were brought back to the Studio and made up to look like marble busts, with pock marks and cracks like a piece of marble. It was necessary to restrict the singers' heads during filming. They used five cameras to capture the action and encourage the singers to animate their faces all they wanted. When the Imagineers were done, they were able to project the images on the busts, creating a convincing and memorable illusion. The audience is reminded that a spectacle is not over until the fat lady sings, and that was precisely one of the comedic elements Davis included toward the end of the Graveyard.

As the Doom Buggies entered the Hitchhiking Ghosts scene, the Ghost Host, voiced by Paul Frees, warned us that a ghost "may follow you home." To prove his point, three figures named Gus, Ezra, and Phineas tried to flag down guests; chillingly, they always seemed to catch a ride. This was another effective and inventive use of the Pepper's Ghost effect.

The show was not over, even as the guests disembarked from their Doom Buggies. As they ascended the Speedramp toward the exit, a small figure named Little Leota with a projected face like the singing busts encouraged guests to return. The final gag may have been one of the most subtle, but it epitomized the playful nature of the design team.

unofficial **TIP**

At the Haunted Mansion, Little Leota sings, "Hurry back. Be sure to bring your death certificate, if you decide to join us. Make final arrangements now. We've been 'dying' to have you."

As guests exited, right at the turnstiles, hidden up in the wall was a small speaker. Evil laughter could be heard. The Imagineers had allowed the mansion to have the last laugh.

Over in Tomorrowland, guests began to enjoy the latest in monorail technology. The Mark I and II versions of the monorail had served the park well, carrying 30 million passengers more than 850,000 miles. The Mark III train was different than its predecessors because it ran on a brand-new air-cushioned chassis, was lighter, had more power with four 100-horsepower traction motors, was more easily accessible, and offered a better view. The trains were extended to 137 feet, thereby allowing for five-car trains with room for 127 guests. The two loading platforms had to be extended. The cost of the upgrade was $2.3 million.

Another subtle change had come to Tomorrowland. Once again, fantasy had become reality and Tomorrowland had become Todayland. Men had been going to the moon at Disneyland since 1955. On July 20, 1969, real men achieved the same feat.

The year was a huge success. All of the new attractions encouraged 82,516 guests to visit Disneyland on August 16, setting an all-time, single-day record. The park had attracted more than 85 million guests since its opening in 1955. More than 9.3 million guests passed through the turnstiles in 1969 alone.

The end of the 1960s marked the end of Walt's Disneyland. The park was to become even more dependent on consensus by a group of talented individuals who had worked with the master. Some would be frozen by second-guessing what Walt would have wanted. Others would flourish in the new freedom.

AN ERA PASSED WHEN OLD RED, the last of the Mark III bubble-top monorails, made its final run around the beam on April 12, 1988. Old Red would live another day as the Mousorail, a stretch limousine that traveled the country on promotional visits.

1. "Disneyland in Accord With Zoning Proposal," *Los Angeles Times,* 6 Jan. 1967.
2. Ibid.
3. "Pirates of the Caribbean . . . More Gems from this Disney Treasure," *The "E" Ticket,* Number 32, Fall 1999, 24–37.
4. Alice Davis, "Marc Davis Centennial Celebration" (speech, Club 33 event, Disneyland, Anaheim, CA, 7 March 2013).
5. Ibid.
6. Ibid.
7. Rick West, ed., *Walt Disney's Pirates of the Caribbean* (San Francisco, CA: *Theme Park Adventure Magazine,* 1998).
8. Ibid.
9. Ibid.
10. WED Enterprises, "Pirates of the Caribbean Facts and Figures," internal memorandum, 14 Feb. 1967.
11. Rolly Crump with Jeff Heimbuch, *It's Kind of a Cute Story* (Clearwater, FL: Bamboo Forest, 2012).
12. "Pirates of the Caribbean . . . More Gems from this Disney Treasure," *The "E" Ticket.*
13. West, ed., *Pirates of the Caribbean.*
14. Ibid.
15. Ibid.
16. "Club 33 is a Magic Kingdom Secret," *Anaheim Bulletin,* 14 Sept. 1991.
17. Disneyland, Club 33 membership solicitation brochure, 1967, Anaheim Heritage Center, Anaheim Public Library, Anaheim, CA.
18. Ibid.
19. "Secret of Club 33 Will Cost $9,500 to Crack," *Anaheim Bulletin,* 30 Nov. 1995.
20. Ibid.
21. Disneyland, Club 33 membership solicitation brochure.
22. Bruce Gordon and David Mumford, *Disneyland: The Nickel Tour* (Santa Clarita, CA: Camphor Tree, 2000).
23. Walt Disney, Tomorrowland plaque near entrance to Tomorrowland near the flagpole (Anaheim, CA: Disneyland, 17 July 1955).
24. David Fisher, "Back to the Future," *Disney Magazine,* Fall 1997.
25. Paul F. Anderson, "A Great Big Beautiful Tomorrow," *Persistence of Vision,* Issue 6/7, 1995.
26. Ibid.
27. Sam Gennawey, *Walt and the Promise of Progress City* (Montgomery, AL: Ayefour Publishing, 2011). See this book for the complete EPCOT story.
28. WED Enterprises, "New Concepts in Transportation for High Density Traffic Flow Areas," press release, 1967.
29. Gordon and Mumford, *Nickel Tour.*
30. Disneyland University, *Adventure Thru Inner Space* (Anaheim, CA: Disneyland, 1967).
31. Bob Thomas, *Walt Disney: An American Original* (New York: Disney Editions, Inc., 1994).
32. Disneyland University, *Adventure Thru Inner Space.*
33. Ibid.
34. "Six Minutes of Surrealism," *The "E" Ticket,* Number 40, Fall 2003, 18–31.
35. Dave Smith, "Authors Panel" (discussion, National Disneyana Fan Club Convention, Crowne Plaza Hotel, Garden Grove, CA, 21 July 2012).
36. "Imagineering and the Disney Image," *The "E" Ticket,* Number 30, Fall 1998, 4–16.
37. Ibid.

38. Bob Gurr, *Design: Just for Fun* (Tugging, CA: APP-Gurr Design, 2012).
39. Ibid.
40. WED Enterprises, "New Tomorrowland: Showcase for American Industry," press release, May 1967.
41. "Planners Okay for Park Growth," *Anaheim Bulletin,* 21 Nov. 1967.
42. Crump with Heimbuch, *It's Kind of a Cute Story.*
43. "Marc Davis and the Haunted Mansion," *The "E" Ticket,* Number 16, Summer 1994, 16–27.
44. Crump with Heimbuch, *It's Kind of a Cute Story.*
45. Jason Surrell, *The Haunted Mansion: From the Magic Kingdom to the Movies* (New York: Disney Editions, Inc., 2003).

CHAPTER 7

CARRYING ON:
1970–1984

▌ REPEAT CUSTOMERS

AS THE NEW DECADE BEGAN, most of the focus of the Disney organization and WED was on Walt Disney World, a resort slated to open in Lake Buena Vista, Florida, in fall 1971 that would include a Disneyland East called the Magic Kingdom. Nevertheless, small projects (compared with the upgrades of the 1960s) were also in the works for Disneyland. For example, the park would open a new exhibit focused on Walt's life and contributions. "Walt Disney: A Legacy for the Future," which took the place of the Wurlitzer shop on Main Street, opened January 15, 1970. The exhibit featured 208 awards given to the man during his lifetime; his first-grade school desk with his initials carved into it, from Marceline, Missouri; and a 6-minute film highlighting the California Institute of the Arts (CalArts), which was scheduled to open in the fall. CalArts had been Walt's vision for a new kind of art school that focused on collaboration and the practical application of art in all disciplines. In the film, Walt said, "A completely new approach to training in the arts is needed. . . . That's the principal thing I hope to leave when I move on to greener pastures. If I can help provide a place to develop the talent of the future, I think I will have accomplished something."[1] The exhibit remained open until 1973.

The biggest news: Disneyland broke its annual attendance record. By September 19, 10 million guests had already visited the park in 1970.

In January 1971, Jeron "The Amazing Criswell" King, an American television psychic, had predicted that by 1999, Disneyland would be covered by a plastic bubble, with the weather inside controlled by the flick of a switch. He said the concept would be duplicated in almost every state. He also added that on August 18, 1999, there would be "desolation on earth" and people "will come out of the caves to rebuild and we will dig through the rubble and from the trace of Anaheim and we will wonder, 'What was Anaheim?' "[2] Criswell was wrong on all accounts.

Another quiet adjustment reflected changing public sensibilities: the Indian War Canoes were renamed Davy Crockett's Explorer Canoes on May 19, 1971. Aero Development built six, 35-foot-long fiberglass canoes with flotation tanks. Painted in a birch-bark design, each canoe could carry 18 guests. Guests still had to row, though.[3] One of the first shops to open on Main Street, the Book & Candle Shop, closed in preparation for a remodel of that entire block. The space would be carved into four little shops. Also, Carefree Corner would lose its Insurance Company of North America (INA) sponsorship.

On June 17, the park's 100 millionth guest pushed through the turnstiles. In spite of amazing attendance records overall and high attendance in 1970, the number of guests slipped to 7.8 million in 1971. Local hotel bookings dropped more than 10% compared with those in the previous year, and there was some concern from the Southern California Visitors Council and others that the opening of Walt Disney World would hurt attendance on the West Coast. Buzz Price ran the numbers and concluded that with most of Disneyland's business being local repeat customers, the park wouldn't be hurt. Marketing director Jack Lindquist reminded the public that only 11% of Disneyland visitors came from east of the Mississippi.

Local business leaders hoped that Price and Lindquist were right. In 1955, Anaheim had a population of 30,059 and measured 4 square miles. Just 16 eventful years later, the city had grown to 168,940 residents and 35 square miles. Was Disneyland the sole reason for the explosive growth and prosperity of Anaheim and Orange County? While Lindquist and Anaheim Mayor Jack Dutton felt that the growth was due to the construction of the Santa Ana Freeway, others gave more credit to Disneyland. City manager Keith Murdoch suggested that "south-central Anaheim would very likely be covered with housing units [if Disneyland had not been built in Anaheim]. There would be no Anaheim Convention Center, one of the country's most successful. The city most likely would not have the California Angels."[4] Dutton acknowledged that another benefit Disneyland brought to Anaheim was jobs. Rockwell International, for example, had established its Autonetics plant in Anaheim in 1960 and at one point employed as many as 32,000 people in relatively high-paying jobs. However, as the mayor pointed out, "It's staggering to think what the unemployment problem would be in Anaheim if there weren't amusement parks to offset aerospace."[5]

On December 20, 1971, Roy Disney passed away at the age of 78. He had cofounded the company with his brother in 1923 and was chairman of the board at the time of his death. The leadership of Walt Disney Productions was subsequently reorganized into a four-man council that included Donn Tatum, president; Card Walker, executive vice president and chief operating officer; Walt's son-in-law Ron Miller, executive producer; and Roy E. Disney, Roy O. Disney's son.[6] With both Disney brothers gone, fans worried that Disney parks and films would suffer, but Tatum insisted there was no cause for alarm: "The philosophy will continue to be the same. A constructive approach to amusement, entertainment, and recreation, designed to appeal to the broad family audience throughout the world."[7]

Disneyland's anniversary had traditionally been a time to look forward as well as back, and the park's 17th anniversary, in 1972, would be no different. In a wide-ranging newspaper interview with the *Anaheim Bulletin,* Lindquist revealed a planned expansion in Disneyland's northwest portion that was scheduled to begin in 1974. Frontierland would be extended 9 acres behind the Mine Train, crossing north over the berm. This new part of Frontierland would connect with Fantasyland to the east.[8]

Lindquist also spoke of closing Fantasyland completely for remodeling: "After all, this is show business, and you can't run the same old show forever."[9] One plan would convert the Rivers of America into a transportation link comparable to the railroad encircling the park. Other ideas mentioned in the interview included a return to the Edison Square concept or a Chinatown, or perhaps both.

All of this new development and capacity building would accommodate much-larger crowds. Lindquist predicted that by the late 1970s, average daily attendance would increase to 100,000 to 125,000 people per day, rendering the existing 13,000 parking stalls inadequate. He mentioned that double- or triple-decking the parking could be a solution. Lindquist also quipped, "It would be cheaper to bring in the public by bus and then give each a car in which to leave."[10]

BEARS WHO COULD LAUGH

THE FIRST BIG ADDITION since The Haunted Mansion was Bear Country, which opened on March 24, 1972, as Disneyland's seventh themed land. The $8 million expansion included a new E-ticket attraction, an updated classic ride, an arcade, a new restaurant, a snack bar, and retail stores. Themed to evoke the Great Northwest, the 4 acres were thickly planted with more than 165 imported trees, including coast redwood, locust, white birch, and evergreen elm, plus Monterey, Canary Island, Aleppo, and Italian stone pines. Another 100 trees were moved to Bear Country from other parts of the property. To make room for the new land, once again the Santa Fe & Disneyland Railroad was lengthened and rerouted.

The gateway to Bear Country was a large, simulated-granite wall. As guests passed by, they were greeted by the snores of Rufus, a hibernating bear. A new souvenir shop, Ursula H. Bear's Wilderness Outpost, had an old-time player piano in the back. The Indian Trading Post remained unchanged. Without even moving from Frontierland, Davy Crockett's Explorer Canoes became part of Bear Country. In *The Nickel Tour,* Bruce Gordon and David Mumford declare Bear Country "a major letdown" and "urban renewal at its worst."[11]

As with the Pirates Arcade in New Orleans Square, the park had customized familiar arcade games in Bear Country to extend the theme. Nine machines gave guests the opportunity to shoot at empty honey pots or challenge Big Al in a round of golf. The Mile Long Bar used mirrors to produce the illusion of a bar that goes on forever in both directions.

The biggest attraction was actually an import from Florida: the *Country Bear Jamboree,* a huge hit that had debuted at the Magic Kingdom in 1971. Two identical 307-seat theaters would be built in Anaheim with a capacity of 2,000 guests per hour. This would be the first time a Disney park attraction started out east and came west.

When Walt first got the idea for the bear attraction, he had intended to use it for another Disney project rather than Walt Disney World or Disneyland. In the early 1960s, Walt Disney Productions had actively pursued the development of a ski resort in California's Sierra Nevada Mountains. Walt was working with the State on a site called Mineral King.[12] If it had been built, the resort would have likely changed the development patterns for mountain retreats the same way Disneyland revolutionized the theme park industry. For example, Walt would have included activities for the young people. As Ron Miller said, "Walt knew that his [ski] resort needed something for the kids at night. Other ski resorts ignored them and he didn't think that was right."[13] At the time, Walt had turned to Marc Davis and suggested an attraction that featured a group of bears from the surrounding forest who have been trained to play musical instruments.

Davis started by sketching different kinds of bear bands. His wife, Alice, said, "Marc would do maybe five different bear ideas. He would have a jazz band, a one-man band, a country band, a circus band, and another one. And he would hand these out one at a time to Walt. Marc said it was like handing Christmas presents to a little kid. Walt would be very excited about each sketch. But then he would decide which one he wanted and that's the one Marc would go with."[14] Marc Davis said, "We kept coming back to country music as the logical choice and consequently settled on this as the theme." Davis added, "We wanted to make [the bears] funny looking as well as funny sounding. Many times we'd find a humorous song and draw a bear to match the tune."[15]

Marc Davis recalled a visit from Walt late in 1966. "I had drawings of a 'bear band' that I had done . . . not the 'bear band' that you see down there . . . this was an experimental thing that I had done. I had these things, and Walt laughed when he saw them. He looked awfully bad. He'd been in the hospital, and he'd lost a lung, and so on. He stayed there for about 15, 20 minutes."[16] Davis continued, "Later he came back around . . . and I stopped in my doorway . . . and as he walked down the hall about 40 feet, he stopped and turned . . . he said, 'Good-bye Marc.' And that was it. He died a couple of weeks later. And he never said good-bye, usually. He would say, 'Let's get together,' or 'How about next week?' or something. I'm positive he had a feeling about it."[17]

THE BEARS WOULD PROVE TO BE VERSATILE. In November 1984, the robotic musical bears performed *The Country Bear Christmas Special*. For the first time, an attraction would be redressed for a holiday. The year before, Marty Sklar was inspired by drawings from two animation programmers who sketched each character in different costumes. WED project designer Dave Feiten said, "Thanks to a new computer animation console that was developed by WED for Epcot Center in Florida, it took us seven weeks, or about one-fourth the time, to complete the new program as it took to do the original *Country Bear Jamboree* program in 1972. And when we are finished with this show, it will take 10 minutes to re-load the previous program and an additional two days to change sets and costumes."[18] This was the first time this technology had been used in Disneyland. The process was used once again in February 1986 with the *Country Bear Vacation Hoedown,* a humorous look at the great American pastime.

After Walt died, Davis continued to develop the bear attraction idea for the ski resort. When development was canceled, WED leadership realized it would be a good addition to the Magic Kingdom. *Country Bear Jamboree* represented a departure from earlier attractions. The latest Audio-Animatronics shows, Pirates of the Caribbean and the Haunted Mansion, were ride-through musicals where guests only got a glance at the characters. However, Davis wanted to return to the *Tiki Room* format and have the guests sit in one place and enjoy the show. The show featured 22 animated musical robots. The characters included 18 bears, and the star of the show was Big Al, who was based on Imagineer Al Bertino.

The new show helped to improve attendance slightly to 8.4 million in 1972. All of those guests pouring into Bear Country found a new place to eat in February 1973. The Golden Bear Lodge served the usual hamburgers and hot dogs, and it had an attached dining area with a spectacular view of the Rivers of America. The name would soon be changed to the Hungry Bear Restaurant, sponsored by Wonder Bread.

▨▨▨ BRONZED BABY SHOES

THE BIG PUSH FOR IMAGINEERS IN 1973 was Walt Disney Productions' 50th anniversary. The park paid tribute to its founder with the opening of *The Walt Disney Story* in the Main Street Opera House on April 8, 1973.[19] The new show replaced *Great Moments with Mr. Lincoln*. It also reused many of the items from the Walt Disney Legacy exhibit, which had closed and had been replaced by "Disneyland Presents a Preview of Coming Attractions," an exhibit that featured artist renderings and models of future plans. Over the years, guests could study the models for Splash Mountain, Discovery Bay, *America Sings*, Space Mountain, and the new Fantasyland.[20] The park announced that Mr. Lincoln would return in the future "as part of the Hall of Presidents," a stirring presentation featuring all [36] U. S. presidents, and climaxed by the inspiring words of Abraham Lincoln." No opening date was specified.[21]

According to a press release, *The Walt Disney Story* had begun in 1970 with "the idea of presenting the background and philosophy of Walt Disney to the public." The Imagineers gathered tens of thousands of photos and more than 70 hours of tape recordings, and they edited the materials into a 28-minute film "narrated" by Walt via footage from old interviews. The displays were organized by Disney's accomplishments:

Walt Disney the Film Maker, the TV Pioneer, the Naturalist, the International Ambassador, and the Artist and Impresario.[22]

Walt's formal and working offices from Burbank were moved intact and put on display. In the formal office was a bell given to him by the Coast Guard and used by his secretary to tell him when it was time for lunch, a model of an airplane he was considering buying just prior to his death, Diane Disney's bronzed baby shoes, a collection of miniatures, and a grand piano. Walt had spent most of his time in the working office, which housed a bulletin board with a map of Disneyland circa 1966, a fireman's hat, and a pigeonhole cabinet where he kept his scripts. The exhibit opened on April 8, 1973, with his widow, Lillian Disney Truyens, as special guest.

In September, the *Carousel of Progress* closed after six years and was moved to the Magic Kingdom in Florida. The Pack Mules Through Nature's Wonderland closed in October. Van France said, "The mules served as a good attraction for several years. I don't think they made any money and 'working the mules' was in about the same category as 'working the Shooting Gallery' or even 'the Buckets.'" These were considered very hard jobs. He added, "Those who dream of the 'good old days' never spent eight hours a day lifting, strapping, and unlifting people off of mules."[23]

Attendance rose to 9.5 million in 1973.

On January 3, 1974, Walt Disney Productions entered into an agreement to purchase the Disneyland Hotel from the Wrather Corporation.[24] The price tag was set at $55 million for the 60-acre complex.[25] Card Walker said it gave the Walt Disney Productions the "potential to master-plan and develop" the entire property. (The agreement would later fall through; subsequent merger talks between Disney and Wrather were put on hold until 1988.)

The success of Disneyland was creating massive traffic congestion on local Anaheim streets, and Orange County Transit District officials could no longer ignore the problem. One recommendation was to build a freeway ramp at West Street that went directly to Disneyland. Another proposal was for a two-tier street at major intersections. The lower level would be used for local traffic and the upper level used for through traffic. The cost for the two-tier street was projected to be between $1 million and $1.5 million. The transit district was unable to identify funding sources for either project, so neither project moved forward at the time.

County officials also authorized a study to identify the location for a major transportation activity center that could accommodate any kind of transportation mode, including automobiles, buses, or rail. The $80,000 study was completed in August 1976, and it indicated that a system centered on Disneyland would return a net income of $1,184,200 in the first five years. A system centered at Anaheim Stadium, favored by many members of the transit board, would show a deficit of $565,700 during the same period. In 1986 a site for the multimodal center was selected near Anaheim Stadium; after multiple delays, the facility has been slated to open in late 2014.

JASON CHANDLER

IMAGINE THE *MARK TWAIN* PERMANENTLY DOCKED in front of the Haunted Mansion and used as a restaurant. Imagine an undersea restaurant inside of the *Nautilus* from 20,000 Leagues Under the Sea with the *Columbia* moored nearby. Imagine Tom Sawyer Island cut in half and your being able to walk from Fantasyland all the way to Bear Country. Those were just some of the ideas being considered in 1974 for Discovery Bay, the brainchild of Tony Baxter.[26]

Baxter had been inspired by the stories of Jules Verne, H. G. Wells, and San Francisco in the gold rush days, and he wanted to bring those kinds of experiences to Disneyland guests. The land would appear to be a scientific outpost in the style of San Francisco's Barbary Coast, and it was to be a celebration of "the Victorian Age of Invention." With the 1974 release of the film *The Island at the Top of the World,* Baxter felt the time was right to pitch the mystical new land. Tucked away behind Tom Sawyer Island, the land would include a tunnel going under the railroad tracks to Geyser Falls, the signature thrill ride for Discovery Bay. A path would connect Fantasyland to Bear Country, allowing guests for the first time to walk all the way around the Rivers of America. Big Thunder Mountain Railroad would have been built at the southern entry and the backstories for the two attractions intertwined.

Discovery Bay and Big Thunder Mountain Railroad were originally conceived to complement one another, fashioned around the legend of Jason Chandler, who, some say, lived in a town called International Village in the Big Thunder region around 1849. Chandler invented a drilling machine capable of boring into Big Thunder Mountain, where "the veins of gold ran so deep, it was rumored they could produce a mother lode that would bring a man enough wealth to last a hundred lifetimes and more."[27] However, one day a cave-in buried 26 miners alive. Chandler and his drilling machine were called into action, and he rescued the miners. Just as they emerged from the mine, a massive earthquake shook the ground, opening up a rift in the earth that swallowed Chandler and his drill. The miners tried to rescue him but to no avail. Not only had Jason Chandler disappeared, but all of the gold in the mountain was buried with him. "The mountain had gone bust, and it became just a matter of time before only ghosts resided there."[28]

At the entrance to Discovery Bay, the Imagineers planned an international shopping and dining area called the Crossroads. The E-ticket attraction would have been Geyser Falls, a thrill ride for guests to experience a dormant geyser as it roared back to life and propelled them skyward in a mine-shaft elevator. The Hyperion airship from *The Island at the Top of the World* would house another ride where guests flew to mythical lands in an Arctic fantasy. A boat ride through time was proposed, as was a fireworks shooting gallery and a greenhouse "filled with a botanist's exotic experiments."

However, *Island at the Top of the World* was a box office failure, so Discovery Bay did not get the green light. "Discovery Bay was probably one of the biggest disappointments for me," said Tony Baxter. "I still believe that to visit a Jules Verne place, along a frontier river, where this eclectic collection of inventors, dreamers and schemers of that period are being funded to create their visions of the future . . . that would have been a fabulous place to see. So when Island came and went, so did the Discovery Bay concept. It wasn't that we had a bad idea . . . it was the fact that we tied it to a weak property."[29] The elaborate model was put on display on Main Street.

In 1984, the project was revived. Unfortunately, Jack Lindquist estimated that the cost of the project would exceed the $55.5 million budget set aside for a new Fantasyland and that it would take three or four years to build. Once again, Discovery Bay was shelved.[30]

Marc Davis had been itching to do another Audio-Animatronics musical. In 1972, he had partnered with Imagineer Al Bertino to work on some concepts for the Carousel Theater. With the *Carousel of Progress* leaving for Florida, there was some prime real estate available. Bertino later said, "At first we thought about a show on music around the world. But this looked too complicated. So we kicked it around and decided to concentrate on American musical heritage. The American Bicentennial was coming up and that helped us make up our minds."[31]

The concept was easier said than done. The team needed about 40 songs to represent 200 years of American music. They started with a list of more than 1,000. "We tried to place every tune into a certain time span of American music, grasp a feeling for the melody and picture in our own minds a character to capture the comical aspects of the song," said Bertino. "The mood we wanted to create for the attraction was built around humor, so, in listening to this large volume of music, our goal was to pick out the joke from a song and eventually draw to it." Davis added, "We even had a piano player come into our offices to perform tunes for us. One day we listened to more than 150 songs in just one sitting."[32] He said of the process, "There were times when we were searching for a character to fit a song. Other times it was just the opposite. We had the tune we liked and we needed a character to match." Davis said, "We tried to get the laugh-type songs. We tried them out on many people to get their reaction before the final selection was made."[33]

Not only was it challenging to narrow the song set to fit the show, but the show also had to fit the constraints of the Carousel Theater. This meant there would be an opening, four acts, and a closing. Each segment would last 3 minutes and 15 seconds. Davis and Bertino identified the four acts as the Early South, Old West, Gay Nineties, and Modern Times, and they selected music to match each location and era. "Yankee Doodle" was performed in every scene as the transitional tune. Buddy Baker conducted the orchestra.[34]

America Sings opened on June 29, 1974, at an estimated cost of $6 million. The hosts were Sam the Eagle, voiced by Burl Ives, and Owl, voiced by Sam Edwards. Wathel Rogers programmed 114 Audio-Animatronics characters for the 24-minute show. The team really took a liking to the robotic cast. Bertino said, "They have become our friends. We believe in them. We don't think of them as pieces of machinery. We don't want the [audience] to, either. We want them to think of our characters as real persons. If we don't believe in them, then no one is going to." Davis thought that Walt would have liked the show. He said, "[Walt] loved the creative things and the things that were new. I believe that he would have loved this show."[35]

unofficial **TIP**
Although never named during the show, the Owl in *America Sings* was named Ollie.

In some ways, the show was cursed. On June 23, a few days before the opening, Bertino had fallen into a stage pit, but, fortunately, he was not seriously hurt. At the grand opening, a large American flag was displayed upside down. Those minor incidents paled, though, when, for the first time, a cast member died while on the job. According to press reports, 18-year-old Deborah Stone "somehow fell between the stationary stage and a wall of revolving audience platform."[36] She became the only cast member fatality in the park's history.

America Sings closed on April 10, 1988. In a way, the breakthrough technology of the revolving Carousel Theater made it impossible for the show to succeed. The theater could handle more than 4,000 guests per hour. Compared with something like Dumbo, which could only handle 600 riders per hour, even crowds of 2,000 guests per hour would be perceived as a failure. The Carousel Theatre would sit empty for many years.

Investment in the park topped $150 million in 1974. Although the park set attendance records for Christmas Day (34,500) and Easter (49,750), annual attendance dipped to 9 million.

A RECEPTACLE *of* EXPERIENCE

DISNEYLAND HAD BEEN flying guests to the moon since July 1955, and they continued the flights until 1975, well after the last real astronaut landed on the moon in December 1972. On January 5, 1975, the last rocket left the launchpad in Disneyland, and a new destination was entered into the attraction's navigation computer. Starting on March 22, guests traveled to Mars, the forbidding red planet. The new show was renamed Mission to Mars and was very similar to the moon version. It used Mars footage shot by a NASA satellite. The show was still sponsored by McDonnell Douglas.

Not everyone was so enchanted with the Disneyland attractions. In May, Dr. Michael Brody of Washington, D.C., presented his paper, "The Wonderful World of Disney—Its Psychological Appeal" to delegates at the American Psychiatric Association's 128th annual convention, which was held across the street from Disneyland at the Anaheim Convention Center. According to press reports, Dr. Brody stated that Disneyland was "literally booby-trapped with oral, anal, castration, and obsessive themes." He stated that many of the Disneyland rides were examples of the "mastery of castration," where "a vague fear is followed by immediate relief." In his analysis, he concluded that children were frequently frightened by Disney stories. Dr. Brody also had issues with the level of "control" and "passivity" within the park, where guests "become a receptacle of experience."[37]

Los Angeles Times columnist Jack Smith reacted to the paper with his well-known wry humor. "I've always known that Disneyland was

Sodom of oral, anal, castration and obsession themes; but at least you're out in the fresh air."[38] When asked for a reaction, a Disneyland spokesperson said, "We've heard about it, of course. But we haven't seen or read anything." He also mentioned that 7,000 association members and their families had visited Disneyland for a special private party, "successfully suppressing, at least to all outward appearance, any undue anxieties of whatever variety, castrative, aggressive or obsessive."

Brody was not alone in his analysis, however. Critic Richard Schickel authored *The Disney Version,* one of the earliest critical looks at Disney's influence on American culture. He said, "Disney's machine was designed to shatter the two most valuable things about childhood—its secrets and its silences—thus forcing everyone to share the same formative dreams." He added, "As capitalism, it is a work of genius; as culture, it is mostly a horror." Schickel was especially concerned with Disneyland. There is "no sex or violence, no release of inhibitions, no relief of real stresses and tensions through their symbolic statement, and therefore no therapeutic effect."[39]

Schickel further opined, "I felt that there were severe limits on [Walt Disney's] imagination, despite what everybody says. I thought he was a technological genius. I thought he had a certain genius in the economic realm. I thought that at a certain point artistically he became stunted. I was never, peace on all of you who work there, a big fan of the theme parks. The substitution of ersatz reality at that level seems to me kind of dangerous, but that's a lonely voice in the wilderness now because you can't walk into a restaurant or anything else without encountering some form of Disneyfication. Everybody has a theme and a damned *Tiki Room* or something."[40]

Influential architect Charles Moore disagreed with Schickel. "People often use Disneyland as a synonym for the facile, shallow and fake. It just doesn't wash: This incredibly energetic collection of environmental experiences offers enough lessons for a whole architectural education in all the things that matter—community and reality, private memory and inhabitation, as well as technical lessons in propinquity and choreography."

With Walt gone, Schickel questioned the future direction of the park. He asked, "What goes on in Disneyland now? There are obviously tons of variations. They keep building new rides and improving old rides, all of that stuff. The fundamental thing with Disneyland, Disney World, for all I know, Tokyo Disney, is that they sell nostalgia and cuteness. There are these ersatz adventures that always come out in a happy place and a little fake alligator gets shot in the thingy. I think that stuff is dangerous." He added, "It's pandering to the lowest common denominator of American thought, culture, and life. You can't argue with it, it's hugely successful, but I don't think there's anything in there that is authentically heartfelt. I think it is conventionally heartfelt."

San Francisco Chronicle columnist Herb Caen also had issues with Disneyland and its cultural impact. In 1976 he wrote, "Disneyland lies somewhere between 1984 and 2001,[41] glittering and gleaming in the rain." He noticed, "It is a children's wonderland artfully geared to adult tastes" and "the adults chuckle, the children are frightened." He called it "the generation gasp." He felt "the disturbing thing about Disneyland [was that] the line between the real and the false keeps disappearing." [42]

In "The Dark Side of Disneyland," a two-part essay in *Art Issues* magazine, poet and author Donald Britton was even more downbeat. He said, "In counterpoint to its more obvious 'sweetness and light' aspects, throughout the park one finds evidence of a profoundly morbid preoccupation with death, violence, and human decay." Snow White's Scary Adventures is "the quintessential Disneyland ride [because] its core conflict is the primary energizing drama of Disneyland itself: the threat to youth and beauty by old age and death."[43] *Los Angeles Times* columnist Randy Lewis joked of Britton, "This guy must have done great on essay tests."[44]

One can only speculate how Walt Disney would have responded to this discourse; but we do know that Walt simply believed, "You can't live on things made for children or for critics. I've never made films for either of them. Disneyland is not just for children. I don't play down."[45]

A MILESTONE
in AMERICANA

BECAUSE OF PUBLIC DEMAND, Mr. Lincoln returned to the Opera House on June 12, 1975, and joined the ongoing "Walt Disney Story" exhibit. Along with a newly programmed Audio-Animatronics figure, the park brought in the 1:64 scale model of the United States Capitol building shown at the 1964–1965 New York World's Fair. The 16-minute show used a slide show for the prologue.[46]

For the 20th anniversary in July, Retlaw wanted to do something special. As the custodian of Walt's beloved steam trains, Retlaw president Bill Cottrell wanted to restore the Disneyland Railroad's original observation car and create a gilded, plush Victorian private coach for the park's many visiting heads of state and dignitaries. By this time, more than 45 heads of state, members of royalty, and other high government officials had visited the park. A State Department official said, "Walt sold America and Americana to foreign dignitaries. I have no doubt that Walt Disney and Disneyland, in a very real way, have contributed to better understanding and a friendlier attitude on the part of world leaders to the U.S."[47]

The observation car had been mothballed in 1966 in favor of new rolling stock. In June 1974, it was relocated in a new train barn backstage. Cottrell began the restoration project by researching privately owned railcars. He worked closely with Walt's widow, Lillian, to create something that her husband would have approved. Railroad Car No. 106, as it was also known, was repainted in a burgundy color and trimmed in red and green with red doors. The four corners were embellished with 23-carat gold leaf scrolls.

The interior was refinished in solid mahogany, stained-glass windows near the ceiling, and claret-colored drapes, trimmed with gold fringe. On the floor was a deep red-rose-patterned Victorian carpet. The love seat and two matching chairs were upholstered in claret-colored fabric. Cottrell found some era-appropriate antiques to furnish the car, including five marble tables and a brass jardiniere for a potted palm tree. Photos of the Disney family adorned the walls.[48]

The gold ceiling lights came from the original car, as did the newly reupholstered seats. On display was the yellow ⅛-scale model caboose that Walt personally built for his backyard railroad, the Carolwood Pacific. It was traditional to name such a fine railcar after a woman, so the observation car was christened the *Lilly Belle*. A Disneyland spokesperson said, "We selected a name we thought Walt would have chosen." The first passenger was Mrs. Lillian Disney Truyens and her husband, John, on July 17. Emperor Hirohito of Japan and his empress also were passengers in 1975.

As was the custom, Disney management took advantage of the anniversary celebration to reveal some of the plans for the future. Card Walker, president of Walt Disney Productions, quipped, "It would be fun to have Walt quarterback us today and tell us where we have gone wrong. I'm sure we haven't done it right. I guarantee you that and I am not saying that maliciously."[49] He knew that Walt was never satisfied and always thought anything could be improved. Walker said a Pinocchio dark ride was in the works, as well as an attraction based on the film *Fantasia*. Two new thrill rides were planned, including "a raft journey through an all-new Primeval World, complete with steaming swamps and menacing prehistoric beasts."[50] Another attraction was Thunder Mesa, "a thrilling train adventure set in the very middle of early western history." The addition of new Audio-Animatronics figures to the Jungle Cruise was planned "for our guests who visit us two and three times each year."

The City of Anaheim had benefited greatly from the taxes generated by Disneyland, the economic multiplier effect on local businesses, and the prestige that came with being the host city. From 1955 to 1975, the park had paid $19.2 million in property taxes and had collected $13.7 million in sales tax. Disney said in 1975 that a "reasonable estimate" on the Anaheim economy is no less than $1.5 billion. Anaheim Mayor William J. Thom said the city would have experienced "sizeable natural growth, but by no stretch of the imagination would it have been anything like what we have seen with Disneyland. The park is an institution, a milestone in Americana."

In 1975, Anaheim community leaders wanted to build a new, modern Civic Center and they proposed a 5% admission-amusement tax to pay for it. Disneyland vice president of marketing Jack Lindquist argued, "It's not an admission tax, it's a Disneyland tax." Mayor Thom's justification for the tax was that tourists "demand services at the same time—increased police protection, increased fire protection. They use our streets." Plus, "It's a voluntary type of taxation. You don't have to pay it to live."[51] The tax initiative failed.

When Disneyland opened in 1955, the horses on King Arthur Carrousel were painted in a variety of colors, including black, tan, brownish red, and gray. In 1975 that would all change. John Hench recognized that most children wanted to ride the white steed. They all wanted to be the hero. Imagineer Kim Irvine led an effort to have all of the horses repainted Arctic white. They also changed the canopy and added the Sleeping Beauty paintings to the center pole housing. Their goal was to create a stronger visual link between the carousel and the castle.

Attendance at the park in 1975 was booming, with 5% gains over the previous year. The park set a new record for July 4 with 79,680 guests, which also marked the second busiest day in the park's history. Christmas Day attendance was also a new record, with 41,840 guests. More than 9.7 million guests pushed through the turnstiles in 1975.

By 1976, Disneyland was old enough to have a past, and there was a growing interest in preserving and celebrating it. On January 9,

The Disneyana Shop opened on Main Street inside the Crystal Arcade and next to the watch shop. The store was a joint project between Disneyland and Walt Disney World. Chuck Ousley, Main Street production director, said, "The purpose of the shop was really to expose our guests to something that really ties in with the history of Disney and the characters." He added, "We're really lucky that we don't have to worry about making a profit."[52]

Many of the items for sale came from a buyer in Florida and Disney archivist Dave Smith. Some of the items for sale included bisque figures from the 1930s to the middle 1950s, animation cels, and dolls. Items ranged in prices from $1 for a cutout from an old 1938 Post Toasties cereal box to a $3,000 set of Seven Dwarfs dolls. When a guest purchased an item, he or she was given a specially designed card explaining when the item was originally sold or made. One cast member who worked in the shop commented, "You just don't realize how many people collect these things. One man drove all the way from San Jose to buy a bronze figure of Winnie the Pooh."[53]

The LOVE BUG

WALT AND THE TEAM AT WED had invented the theme park industry back in 1955, but by 1975 the industry was going through a major transition and beginning to leave them behind. New technology was being exploited to create extreme thrill rides, and roller coasters with inversions were becoming the hot new attraction. It started in 1975 when Knott's Berry Farm in nearby Buena Park introduced Arrow Dynamic's Corkscrew as the centerpiece of its new Roaring 20s themed area. The Corkscrew was the world's first steel coaster to successfully turn people upside down. North of Disneyland in Valencia was Six Flags Magic Mountain; in 1976 they opened the American Revolution, the world's first modern coaster with a vertical loop. A few days later, Cedar Point in Ohio opened another Arrow Corkscrew that had three inversions. Suddenly, the Matterhorn seemed very tame in comparison.

Thrill rides were never a priority at Disney. Neither Disneyland nor the Magic Kingdom at Walt Disney World opened with one. In the case of Florida, Marty Sklar said, "Right off the bat, we had misjudged the audience in a lot of ways. We thought that Florida would have a lot older population, and if you look back to the Opening Day menu for Walt Disney World, there were no thrill rides, and a lot of theater shows."

The question for the Imagineers was how to bring thrills to the park while still being Disney. Dick Nunis said, "We don't just want more thrill rides. We want thrill attractions with stories to go with them."[54]

For Disneyland, the Imagineers were also working on other ideas, which never opened. For example, the proposed Herbie the Love Bug Ride slated to fit into Fantasyland was based on the first two films in the popular Disney series, *The Love Bug* (1969) and *Herbie Rides Again* (1974). One could think of the attraction as an updated, technology-driven version of Mr. Toad's Wild Ride. Up to four passengers would climb inside their own Love Bug, and the ride would begin at the starting line for a race. As the race started, Herbie would pop a wheelie and almost run over a bunch of chickens. As they scattered, the car would run along the side of a cliff on only two wheels. What was sure to be one of the most memorable elements was inspired by the first film, when the Herbie vehicle would split down the middle, dividing the members of the party between the two halves, which would then pass a cactus on opposite sides. Trying to make up ground, the vehicle would weave its way through other race cars. From that point, it would be just one gag after another. The ride vehicle would blast through a shack, leap over a San Francisco skyscraper, almost run into a cable car, skip over water, and even climb the Golden Gate Bridge.

Another proposed thrill ride was geared toward children. Dumbo's Circusland would be a five-acre area both inside and outside of the berm adjacent to It's a Small World. Circus-themed spaces went all the way back to some of the earliest ideas for Fantasyland as penned by artist Bruce Bushman. Animator Ward Kimball also contributed to the planning.

The centerpiece would have been Mickey's Madhouse. Like Space Mountain at Walt Disney World, this ride would have been a Wild Mouse roller coaster in the dark. Guests would have entered the world of black-and-white cartoons of the 1930s and traveled through an environment where they would be unable to see what was in front of them. The Casey Jr. train would have been extended and given a second stop within Dumbo's Circusland. A dark ride called Circus Disney, featuring Audio-Animatronics Disney characters and a new Pinocchio ride, would be squeezed in as well. At the center of the land would be a playful fountain with the fireman clowns from the animated film.[55]

When the Jungle Cruise reopened on December 18, it had gained seven new scenes and 31 new Audio-Animatronics animal characters. A number of the scenes were first installed at the Magic Kingdom. The

Cambodian ruins were now guarded by a trio of King Cobras and a nearby Bengal tiger. The African veldt segment was enhanced with new animals, while a group of gorillas was spotted invading a base camp. The two threatening gorillas were replaced with a water buffalo protecting her calf from a python. The landscaping was trimmed back of overgrown vines, and dead plants and trees were removed. [56]

From an operational point of view, a change to the boats was the big news. For more than 20 years, the sharp turns at Schweitzer Falls and the Hippo Pool created a wake that would lift the rear of the boats, and they would derail from their track. To alleviate this problem, a fin was added to the guide wheels. Now the boats could navigate the turns without stopping the attraction.

Park attendance had increased to 9.5 million in 1975. On May 22, 1976, Elsie Mae Houck, of Tulare, California, became the 150 millionth guest to enter Disneyland. For the American Bicentennial, the park hosted 75,640 guests on the Fourth of July and celebrated with the largest fireworks display in the park's history.

SIMPLER PLEASURES

THE LAST MINING TRAIN to pass by Cascade Peak ran on New Year's Day 1977. More than 30 million guests had taken the tour through Nature's Wonderland, but the ridership at the Mine Train had been declining for years. One of things that made the attraction special was the occasional interaction with the Pack Mules. When the Pack Mules closed in 1973, the audience could sense that something was missing. This spiral downward was not aided by the pace of the attraction. Guests expected more, and the attraction had to compete with Pirates of the Caribbean and the Haunted Mansion for one of the precious E tickets. The one highlight remained the Rainbow Caverns finale.

The Imagineers considered updating the animation or adding new scenes, but priorities were changing. Marc Davis was asked to take a look at the attraction and see if there was anything he could do to bring back its popularity. As he had done before for the Jungle Cruise, he worked with Imagineer Al Bertino to dream up a number of new gags. In one scene, a bear searching for honey finds his head stuck in a log. Another scene featured a bear trying to catch a leaping fish. There were even marmots popping up near Cascade Peak.

It was too late. The park was under a lot of pressure to add more thrill rides, and the Mine Train Through Nature's Wonderland took up a lot of land. As the attendance declined, the number crunchers would budget less and less for maintenance and nostalgia would not be enough.

The little mining town of Rainbow Ridge would be recycled as part of Big Thunder Mountain Railroad. The Balancing Rock Canyon remained in Big Thunder Ranch. The Saguaro, the bobcat on the cactus, the peccaries, and the mountain sheep made their way to the Magic Kingdom version of the roller coaster. Some of the animals were just buried out back. Cascade Peak would survive until August 1998, when it was finally dismantled.

RACE *through* SPACE

IT WAS TIME TO ADD A NEW THRILL RIDE, and the two projects that were furthest along in development were Big Thunder Mountain Railroad and Space Mountain. It was decided that children were more interested in space than the Wild West. Plus, Walt and John Hench had talked about Space Mountain as far back as the late fall of 1964, but it was not until the mid-1970s that the technology had caught up with the vision. Hench declared, "We didn't just build this because we needed another thrill attraction. Walt always intended this to be here, and we never abandoned the idea."[57]

The attraction was rushed to completion and opened in the Magic Kingdom at Walt Disney World on January 15, 1975. Six months later, ground was broken for the Disneyland version. Space Mountain opened on May 27, 1977, and lines ran all the way down Main Street U.S.A. to the flagpole. At the opening, Hench conceded, "What you are going to see today is not quite the same as the original, but it is pretty close."[58]

Space Mountain was to be a journey into outer space and experiencing the unknown. This illusion would be realized through the use of controlled lighting, projected images, and the speed of the roller coaster. The technological hurdle was the ability to control multiple vehicles on the same track simultaneously in the dark. The solution was a new computer system that would slow the trains in different brake zones to keep a safe distance between them.

Forty-five concrete pilings grounded the building, while 36 steel support beams formed the conical roof. The enormous show building was 200 feet in diameter and reached 118 feet high to the top spire, with an interior space of more than 1.8 million cubic feet. The structure was placed 15 feet below grade so as not to tower above everything else. The main roof structure of the 48,960-square-foot building was made of precast concrete and steel T-beams. The span between the T-beams was narrow at the top and wide at the bottom, creating the illusion of a much larger cone. The design was timeless and powerful.

With such a large show building, things were getting tight behind Main Street, and Tomorrowland had to build up instead of out. In 1965, John Hench had worked on a plan for a two-level building, with guests entering from the second level. They considered having the roller coaster lifts on the outside of the structure but decided that the lighting could be controlled better in an enclosed structure. Guests entered the Observation Deck just past the entrance, where rockets with glow strips along their sides sped past a large window. The lighting was a subdued blue to enhance the effect.

Inside the dome were 3,450 feet of pressurized tubular steel track. The track configuration allowed the rockets to run alone at the top of the dome and to run side by side at the lower level, giving guests the impression they were racing other rockets that had glow-in-the-dark panels on the side. Instead of single-file seating with seat belts and two tracks like the Florida version, Disneyland's rockets were side-by-side seating with a lap bar that could hold up to 12 passengers on a single track. Nylon wheels and ball bearings were used in a roller coaster for the first time instead of polyurethane and regular automotive bearings. The rockets could reach speeds of 32 mph.

To reach a capacity of 2,160 guests per hour, a computer weighed each rocket and set the intervals between them. The rockets climbed three chain-lifts. The first was just outside the Space Port Launch Portal, the second was as they climbed through a meteor shower, which led to the Solar Energizer tunnel. The third was at the top of the tunnel past a geodesic satellite. Many turns later, "faster than the speed of light" and through "intergalactic superspace," the rockets reentered "through a cosmic vapor curtain."[59] Imagineer George McGinnis worked on many of the special effects. He was able to combine many established technologies in a way that created something entirely new.

After two years of construction, the park held a grand opening ceremony on May 27, 1977, featuring Project Mercury astronauts Captain Scott Carpenter, Colonel Gordon Cooper, Senator John Glenn, Captain Walter Schirra, Admiral Alan Shepard, Donald "Deke" Slayton, and Betty Grissom, widow of Gus Grissom. According to the press release, after their ride they were heard to proclaim it was "just like the real thing!"

The roller coaster was not the only new element of the $20 million project. There was the two-story Starcade electronic arcade with more than 60 electronic games. The 1,100-seat Space Stage became the first permanent amphitheater at Disneyland, with concerts during the day and a special Cosmic Concert show at night incorporating electronically adapted contemporary music with choreographed dancing and special lighting. In a press release, Disneyland described the show as "a complete visual and sensual experience." A 32-channel sound system with an early use of monitor speakers for the performers was also installed.

For those looking for something to eat, they could visit the 670-seat Space Place fast food restaurant where you could find "Solid Fuel, Liquid Fuel, and Booster Fuel."[60] The WEDway PeopleMover was realigned to include a preview of Space Mountain, and it made a trip through a new space called the Superspeed Tunnel, where film images were projected along the side walls, providing the illusion of speed to the slow-moving trains.

Another park icon was getting a makeover. The walk-through attraction inside of Sleeping Beauty Castle opened in 1957, and it was a delightful diversion, but it was beginning to show its age. On November 5, the plywood flats that made up the scenes were replaced with doll-like dioramas with limited animation, reminiscent of the windows in the Emporium on Main Street U.S.A. Because the original displays were built before the film was completed, they did not reflect the final story that most guests would be familiar with. That issue was reconciled during the transformation. It was also felt that the increased sophistication of the newer Audio-Animatronics shows made the walk-through feel dated. This update was meant to resolve both of those issues.

Each of the scenes was described in beautiful hand-decorated books. One of the new scenes was Aurora dancing with the make-believe prince made up of her forest animal friends dressed in a red hat and cloak. The Tchaikovsky score played in the background. The space where the goons used to live was sealed up and unused. Only the wooden doors with metal hinges remained.

The opening of Space Mountain and an updated version of the Main Street Electrical Parade helped to set a new attendance record at 10.5 million guests.

While Space Mountain was thrilling guests in 1977, the park took the opportunity that September to close the Matterhorn Bobsleds for an extensive $4 million rehab. In May 1978, the Matterhorn Bobsleds reopened, resembling something that was closer to Walt's original concept.

According to John Hench, Walt always wanted to include a snowman in the Matterhorn. He said, "We just thought it was time that we gave this elusive character a home."[61] A total of three abominable snowmen were installed within the caverns: one for each ride track, as well as one visible from both sides. To complete the effect, a pair of glowing red eyes and a startling growl greeted the riders at the top of each lift hill. Blaine Gibson sculpted the 8-foot snowman character. Imagineer Harriet Burns worked on the attraction; she recalled, "I was up on a ladder finishing the top of [the Abominable Snowman], and when I came down—let's just say I could tell that he was a real man! Fred [Joerger] had 'adorned' him while I was out to lunch!"[62] The snowman was nicknamed "Harold" by cast members.

The Imagineers also installed new special effects, including an enclosed lift hill with the sound of howling winds and snowstorms raging on either side, an interior filled with glowing ice crystals, and fully realized ice caverns that replaced the visible girders and support beams. There was fog at the top of the lift hill, and the interior was air-conditioned to be at least 30° cooler than outside on a summer day.

To increase capacity by 70%, new tandem bobsleds were installed that could seat up to eight people. The bobsleds were based on the rockets used at the Magic Kingdom's Space Mountain. The entire chain lift had to be replaced to deal with the heavier load, and the entire track was reinforced. Booster motors were placed in strategic places to push the sleds along. New functional systems, such as a new computer system, control podiums in the pit area, and an updated maintenance area, were part of the project. The sleds were designed to move faster, hitting a top speed of 30 mph.

Because of the additions to the Matterhorn Bobsleds, once again Disneyland broke attendance records, with almost 10.4 million guests. Other factors that affected attendance included the devaluation of the dollar, which caused foreign guest attendance to jump 14.8%, and lower airfares that translated into a jump of 10.5% from out-of-state guests. The attendance in 1978 was an achievement, made all the more remarkable given that Orange County also had the heaviest rain in 88 years.

▌ DO IT *with* INTEGRITY

MARC DAVIS WAS PROUD of Pirates of the Caribbean, but he was not satisfied. He wanted to top himself, and he figured the best opportunity would be in Florida. When the Imagineers were developing the Magic Kingdom in Florida, Pirates of the Caribbean was left off the roster because it was felt that a ride based on a nearby environment would not feel exotic or foreign enough. For Frontierland in the Magic Kingdom, Davis imagined a new show called the *Western River Expedition,* presented inside the largest show building ever built at a Disney park. The show would have been a musical comedy romp through the Wild West with plenty of "cowboys and Indians."

To hide the massive show building, it would be dressed as a mesa. To add kinetic energy to what was going to become the backdrop for Frontierland, a train ride was proposed that took guests from the top of the Mesa down along the front. Tony Baxter was in charge of the train component and began to wonder what would happen if they moved the train from on top and placed it in front of the mountain. One benefit would be the option to build the *Western River Expedition* first and then add the train later. As was the custom, he built a model. What he did not know at the time was management would take his advice, but not in the way he intended.

When the Magic Kingdom opened in 1971, the number one complaint from guests was the lack of a Pirates of the Caribbean ride. The attraction had become closely identified with Disney because of the television show, and the public expected to find Pirates in Florida. Disney decided to give the people what they wanted, and a shortened version of Pirates of the Caribbean was installed in Adventureland at the Magic Kingdom in Florida. Western River Expedition was deemed redundant and was shelved. However, Tony Baxter's impressive model pushed the roller coaster project to the front. A ride meant for Florida would be built in Anaheim first. Construction began on July 1, 1977, and the attraction opened on September 2, 1979.

For many guests, a visit to Disneyland meant conquering the three mountains: the Matterhorn Bobsleds, Space Mountain, and Big Thunder Mountain Railroad. The three thrill rides made Disneyland relevant in the changing market they created.

The $15.8 million Big Thunder Mountain was set in the gold rush era of the Old West. According to the press release, the adventure "takes guests on a harrowing journey through danger-filled caverns and deep sandstone gorges, encountering swarming bats, crashing landslides, and rumbling earthquakes along the way." Baxter described the ride as "a collection of individual embellishments orchestrated into a cohesive show."[63]

The 104-foot mountain was modeled after "the charming and fanciful rock formations of Bryce Canyon," according to Baxter, who felt the inspiration was a natural fit.[64] He had heard so many people comment that Bryce's colorful hoodoos looked like something that could be found in Disneyland. In tribute to Walt's 32nd anniversary gift to Lillian, the tip of the mountain reflects the same massing as the tip of the Petrified Tree in Frontierland. Considered the most elaborate rockwork texture and shape formation ever attempted at the time, artists painted the top 30 feet before it was lifted into place. This became the color standard for the rest of the paint job, which covered 9.5 acres of total surface space.

"The challenge for us was to do it with integrity, so the ride tracks didn't look like a plate of spaghetti," Baxter said. "I pride myself that when you look at Big Thunder, nowhere does it look like the rockwork was built around the train. It always looks like the train had to configure to the mountain."[65]

The six mining trains had colorful names: *I.M. Brave, U.B. Bold, I.M. Fearless, U.R. Daring, I.B. Hearty,* and *U.R. Courageous.* Each one had a locomotive with no engineer and five cars. Each train carried 30 guests, and the attraction had a capacity of 2,400 guests. They traveled along a 2,671-foot track at a top speed of 28 mph. The attraction covered a compact 3.8 acres.

Guests encountered 11 animated figures during their 3-minute, 15-second trip. Following in the footsteps of Pirates of the Caribbean, at the speed the trains were going, it would be impossible for the guest to take it all in on just one ride. The design philosophy was to give them more than they could see and they would keep coming back.

The ride had three lift hills. The first lift hill was 30.4 feet long and was inside of a tribute to Rainbow Caverns. The second was 36.5 feet long; it carried guests past a goat chewing on a stick of dynamite. The final lift was 28.3 feet inside a tunnel; guests on the final lift found themselves right in the middle of an earthquake.

Bill Evans was responsible for transforming the Mine Train Through Nature's Wonderland landscape into something that would support a mountain haunted by a runaway train. He started by reusing the piñon trees he planted in 1954. Imagineer Pat Burke was in charge of finding many of the hundreds of authentic mining relics that dress the Big Thunder set.

Imagineers removed the main Fantasyland food stand and built a new pathway, the Big Thunder Trail, to connect Fantasyland with Frontierland. Many of the trees along the trail were planted when the park opened in 1955.

Attendance grew to 10.4 million guests in 1979. The Thanksgiving weekend set a record with 166,059 guests. By this point, Disney had invested more than $206 million into the park.

The SILVER ANNIVERSARY *and* BEYOND

IN 1980 WALT DISNEY PRODUCTIONS was preoccupied with the development of Epcot Center in Florida, and the most notable physical change at Disneyland was limited to the Main Gate, which got a major face-lift. New ticket booths, turnstiles, and a landscaped mall were added. Otherwise, the focus for 1980 was the park's 25th anniversary. Instead of major changes or new additions to the park, most of the new offerings were entertainment related, including a new parade and a 25-hour birthday party. The anniversary activities also featured "Celebrate the Lands," a weekend set aside for each land when guests could ride that land's attractions for free as often as they wanted.[66] The anniversary celebration, in part, drove record attendance, with 11 million guests going through the turnstiles.

The Anaheim City Council amended the height limits for buildings surrounding Disneyland in April 1980. This was the first revision since the limits had been put in place in September 1964. Under the new rules, the allowable building heights north of the park were reduced by as much as 50 feet, but the limits west and southwest were increased by 25 feet. To verify their building designs, developers were asked to fly a balloon at the height of any proposed development to confirm that the building would not be visible inside of the park.[67]

The 200 millionth guest visited Disneyland on January 8, 1981.[68] On March 30, Walt Disney Productions reached an agreement to purchase Retlaw Enterprises. Roy E. Disney was the only member of the board to vote against the negotiation.[69]

The only real action was a proposal by a joint venture between the Wrather Company and Hilton to build a 1,500-room convention center hotel with an expansion of the Disneyland Monorail connection.[70]

ENJOYMENT *of*
QUIETER ATTRACTIONS

AT THE TIME THE TICKET BOOK was introduced in October 1955, it was a way to minimize the perception that a visit to Disneyland meant reaching into your pocket all day. However, the unintended consequence was a system that helped guests to organize their day while maximizing the capacity of the park's assets. By grouping the attractions into value groups, guests had to ration their experiences. They were subtly forced to slow down. The tickets also provided the cast members an opportunity to make contact with every single guest. The system worked so well that other parks, such as Knott's Berry Farm, copied Disneyland's example.

When Six Flags purchased Magic Mountain in 1979, they introduced a new approach to tickets: a single general admission ticket with unlimited use of the rides. Magic Mountain was in the process of becoming the thrill ride leader in Southern California with the additions of the American Revolution looping roller coaster and the humongous Colossus wooden roller coaster—so their approach to ticketing was closely watched by Disney.

Starting on June 20, 1981, Disneyland management began to experiment with an "Unlimited Passport" for the general public. Disneyland had crafted an unlimited use ticket in 1977 but had never sold it to the general public; only members of The Magic Kingdom Club had been able to purchase this type of ticket. The Passport, which cost $10.25, eliminated the need to buy individual attraction tickets. Guests also had the option to purchase a book of eleven tickets for $9.25.[71] The reaction was immediate and positive. An $8 "Summer Night Passport" was also made available for guests arriving after 7 p.m.[72]

The test was a winner for Disneyland financially, but its implementation would have a significant and possibly unfortunate impact on the way guests would experience the park in the upcoming years. Disney historian Jason Schultz suggested that "a new era was unintentionally born." He opined, "Once all rides become included with the cost of admission, people tended to prioritize the bigger, and more thrilling rides—the ones which until recently had cost more."[73] While guests spent more time on the marquee attractions, they tended to ignore the smaller attractions that gave the park so much of its character.

On June 16, 1982, the last ticket book was sold, leaving only the Unlimited Passport available to guests.[74] Columnist Carol Crotta wrote,

"Answer me this, without a ticket book, who's going to go on Mr. Toad's Wild Ride? And how about the Mike Fink Keel Boats? Don't you care about the Mike Fink Keel Boats? It's just a further assassination of what little tradition there remains in our increasing alienating society."

Attendance topped more than 11.3 million guests in 1981 but fell to 10.4 million visitors in 1982. Some parks like the San Diego Wild Animal Park and Six Flags Magic Mountain enjoyed outstanding success in the early 1980s, while Disneyland began to suffer.

WHAT HAVE WE DONE?

WHEN ROLLY CRUMP BECAME the supervising art director of Disneyland in 1967, he began to look around at what needed to be updated. Disneyland was almost 30 years old and was beginning to show its age. One of the areas of the park in most distress was Fantasyland. The years had taken their toll on the dark rides, and they were beyond repair. Crump and Imagineer Raellen Lescault proposed a major rehab of the entire land.[75] The goal was to update the existing attractions to current Disney standards.

When Fantasyland was originally built, the early facades were made out of fiberboard. Although the facades looked fine from a distance, upon close inspection the Imagineers could see that the only thing holding it all together were the layers and layers of paint. Beneath the paint, the fiberboard had begun to buckle. After surveying the site, the project team concluded that the dark rides' facades were falling apart. The flats inside the rides had been repainted so often they did not even resemble the characters they were trying to portray. In Snow White, they even discovered that the signs said TO THE WITCH'S COTTAGE and TO THE DWARFS' CASTLE.

Imagineer Tony Baxter was assigned the role of chief show designer for Fantasyland and was in charge of figuring out what the Imagineers were going to do and to make sure it got done. One of the objectives was to update the special effects to get beyond the use of black light and incorporate new technologies such as fiber-optics. But first he needed to knock everything down so they could start over. Dumbo had been removed in November 1981 and the Fantasyland Theater had closed in December. Snow White, the Mad Tea Party, and the Big Thunder Trail closed at the beginning of 1982, and the entire area was put behind the standard Disney 8-foot construction wall.[76]

"The hardest thing for me was not the designing of a new Fantasyland, but being there the day that they tore down the original," Tony

Baxter said. "We came in after the bulldozers were gone that day, and I remember looking at the Fantasyland Theater and the Snow White building. The mural had been ripped off in shreds, and there were pieces of the 'frightening trees' from inside [lying] on the ground. The Theater's two big Mickey signs were [lying] there, and the strings of twinkle lights were down on the ground . . . they had fallen, too."[77] As the group stood stunned, suddenly and unexpectedly the strand of lights flickered on. Baxter thought to himself, "Oh my God, what have we done?"[78] He realized, "We knew it was too late to stop, we were committed, and if anything at the Park was pure 'Walt,' it was Fantasyland."[79]

Since the Fantasyland station was closed, savvy guests figured out they could ride the Skyway round-trip, get a view of the construction site, and monitor the progress. In April, portions of Fantasyland—including Peter Pan, Mr. Toad, and Alice in Wonderland—reopened to accommodate the seasonal crowds. The Storybook Land Canal Boats remained open on the weekends and holidays throughout construction.

On August 29, 1982, the last tuna sandwich would be served on the Chicken of the Sea Pirate Ship Restaurant. Skull Rock and the restaurant had to be moved to make room for Dumbo. The plan was to reinstall the Pirate Ship and Skull Rock just past the exit from Storybook Land. The project would have created a new layered environment. The Canal Boats path would be extended to come out from behind Skull Rock and pass in front of the Pirate Ship. In the lagoon would be a crocodile that would surface as the boats passed. A new seating area and multilevel viewing platform would face a small stage where guests could watch a pirate show.

Budget problems forced the delay of Alice in Wonderland and killed the Pirate Ship makeover. The removal of the Pirate Ship was especially difficult for the Imagineers. They tried to save the intricate, hand-carved plaster details. The plan was to carefully remove them, but the back panel was shattered when the truck hit a bump. They discovered they were built in place and therefore incredibly delicate. Skull Rock did not fare any better. The rock sculpture was supposed to be moved around the corner along with the Pirate Ship, but, when those plans were scuttled, the rock was simply removed. By the holidays of 1982, demolition was complete.

The project team was assisted by Imagineer Ken Anderson, who had worked on the original Fantasyland with Walt. Anderson was critical to the success of the project. His senior status allowed him to act as a calming factor and to settle any differences between the creative people. He was enthusiastic about the update, and that became reassuring to the others.

To reduce the notorious congestion and allow for more room for the guests, the King Arthur Carrousel was moved northwest 20 feet to the spot where the Mad Tea Party had stood, and Dumbo was moved toward what had been the Skull Rock location. The Fantasyland Theater was removed and replaced with a new dark ride, Pinocchio's Daring Journey. Baxter moved the Mad Tea Party from the central courtyard to a spot just in front of Alice in Wonderland.

The new facades were meant to be "consistent with the original medieval village fairground motif with some renaissance fair in Bavaria added in."[80] Each dark ride's facade was built in a style that reflected the individual theme of that attraction. Disneyland fans recognized the remodel to be a tribute to Walt's original vision for his most personal land. They all had heard the story that Walt wanted it this way but had run out of money, but it turned out that that was also part of the fantasy. "We had kind of made those things up, all about how Walt had wanted the original Fantasyland to be richer," Tony Baxter said many years later. "We assumed that stuff was true. We knew how much Walt really liked Storybook Land . . . we knew he liked the 'old world' look of that ride. And much of the Castle courtyard area, with Merlin's Magic Shop and Tinker Bell Toy Shop and so forth, had a little of that look."[81] Merlin's Magic Shop set the standard for the quality they were trying to achieve. The result was an environment that seemed like it had been there for many, many years.

New Fantasyland opened on May 25, 1983, at an estimated cost of $55.5 million. Walt's original vision for Fantasyland was much different than what he could afford in the 1950s. He had taught his artists, "Fantasy, if it's really convincing, can't become dated for the simple reason that it represents a flight into a dimension that lies beyond the reach of time."[82] This time, the Imagineers would achieve Walt's goal.

As guests walked across the drawbridge and passed through the portal, they saw a new steel canopy for King Arthur Carrousel. In front of that, guests enjoyed the new *A Sword in the Stone* show, where Merlin the Magician would seek one guest who had the power and magic to pull the sword from the stone. The addition of the decorative element was an afterthought. Surprisingly, it was to become one of the details most noticed by guests and taking a photo trying to extract the sword would become a rite of passage.

A third generation of Dumbo the Flying Elephant was installed where the Pirate Ship had once stood. This Dumbo had been destined for Euro Disneyland but was diverted to Disneyland at the last minute when that project faced delays. There were now 16 flying elephants instead of 10, and all of the decorative mechanisms were plated with real gold.

 # FEAR *and* CONQUEST

ALONG WITH MOVING ATTRACTIONS around to create better pedestrian flow, the Imagineers were able to expand the dark rides by 25%. The Snow White, Peter Pan, and Mr. Toad dark rides were updated.

"You remember two things, the things that scare you and the things that make you laugh," designer Brock Thoman said. "Fear is part of growing up. Not milquetoast scary, not cute, but real fear! Overcoming that fear makes a child feel he's accomplished something."[83] Fear and conquest were the emotions the Imagineers were trying to embed in the revamped version of the attraction. The Imagineers wanted to make sure that parents understood how scary the ride was inside. Instead of the lighthearted festival tent facade of the original, guests had to pass through a German Gothic castle made of heavy dark-gray stones. Occasionally peeking out through an upper floor window was the Wicked Queen.

The queue passed through a narrow, claustrophobic corridor and a dungeon laboratory scene with scary sounds and the shadow of a crow. All of this was an effort to discourage adults from letting skittish children ride the attraction. The change was successful. Complaints about how scary Snow White was had diminished due to the scary preshow area.

Another benefit from the new design was that much of the queue was now under shelter, providing much-needed shade. Instead of an entrance with a simple mural outlining the story line of the dark ride, the new version of Snow White had an impressively themed loading area with a three-dimensional exterior of the Seven Dwarfs cottage that cleverly hides a support column behind the chimney.

The remodel would also be the first time that Snow White actually appeared in the attraction. Originally, the attraction put the guest in the role of Snow White, but nobody seemed to get it. Instead, they would go on the ride and wonder where Snow White was. Changing the guest's point of view was another reason to update the dark rides.

Once on board the little mining cars, guests passed through the Dwarfs' cottage, complete with Snow White, and then entered the Dwarfs' diamond mine. From the mine until the approach to the queen's castle was 100 feet of additional track, created by moving the back side of the show building into an area that once was part of Nature's Wonderland. However, it was still not enough room. The Imagineers wanted to add a scene with the prince but ran out of space and put up a sign that read AND THEY LIVED HAPPILY EVER AFTER instead.

Peter Pan's Flight had always been a guest favorite. The classic ride always had a long line. The front facade was pulled forward into the courtyard to allow for longer tracks and new scenes. A hat shop was removed to make extra room. The flying galleons were new and larger, and the track system was upgraded. Inside were new Audio-Animatronics characters, such as Captain Hook and Peter Pan dueling on the mast, Wendy reading to the boys, and the Lost Boys. New stars guided guests toward Never Land Island, and the ending was changed to a view of Smee in a rowboat and Hook standing on the open jaws of the crocodile.

Next door at Mr. Toad's Wild Ride, the external updates were major, but inside was still the classic thrill ride with minor changes. As they had done for Peter Pan, the Imagineers pulled the Mr. Toad facade forward so that it looked just like the model in the Storybook Land Canal Boats. The loading area and ride exterior were enlarged, and more space was created by replacing the hat shop next door.

Inside, the Toad vehicle now crashed through a fireplace with fiber optic sparks hitting the floor. A Town Square scene was added: the cars rushed past a fountain, the Green Dragon Inn, and a statue of Toad and Cyril. After 5 seconds in front of the prosecutor, the guests were off to a short stay in prison, then escape, with a flurry of tunnel, headlight, explosions, and a bigger and better "Jaws of Hell" with a "green dragon" with respiratory challenges.

Just across the courtyard was a new dark ride replacing the Fantasyland Theater. The facade for Pinocchio's Daring Journey was influenced by Tyrolean architecture and the distinctive look of the animated film. "Rides like Pinocchio's Daring Journey play on childhood fears, such as the loss of a parent and the joys that follow a reunion," said Tony Baxter. "A lot of Disney films used that security versus insecurity contrast."[84]

Pinocchio followed the tradition of the other dark rides by starting in incandescent light during the happy puppet show and then moving into blacklight as the cars approach the Stromboli scene. The attraction was technically very advanced, including the first use of holography to transform Lampet into a donkey, the use of the Pepper's Ghost effect to make the Blue Fairy disappear, and fiber optics on the floor of Geppetto's puppet shop.

Although the year started optimistically, attendance levels continued to drop. Disneyland greeted 9.9 million guests in 1983.

KIND *of* CRAZY *and* ECCENTRIC

HISTORY DOES REPEAT ITSELF, even at Disneyland, and Alice in Wonderland would once again be late for her very important date—her opening in Fantasyland. Like the 1955 Fantasyland, the budget ran out of money and the dark ride was deferred for a year. Originally planned for a 1983 opening, the revamped ride welcomed guests on April 13, 1984.

The project was a reflection of the skills, interests, and experiences of the second generation of Imagineers. The original Alice was a series of little vignettes in the dark. The updated version would be more immersive and try to capture the color and mood of the original film. The sets would reach from wall-to-wall, and previously missing characters would be added. There were more animated three-dimensional figures, and special effects and black light would play a different role in this version. Black light was a technological marvel in the 1950s but would become an overused cliche by the 1980s.

The 16 original caterpillar cars were reused and placed on a new chassis, and the Caterpillar's shoes were added to the roof of the former mushroom ticket booth. The facade of the ride was also changed to increase Alice's appeal to men. Over the years, the cast members noticed that men were embarrassed to sit in the caterpillars. With the refurbishment, the track was rerouted, a large tree was planted out front, and by moving the Mad Tea Party nearby, the whole area became a mini-land dedicated to Alice. The operations booth for the Mad Tea Party was the home to the March Hare, and the Mad Hatter Gift shop was the cottage of the White Rabbit.

Inside, the Upside Down Room was replaced with Tweedledum and Tweedledee and a fully sculpted White Rabbit and his cottage. The Oversized Room was removed and replaced with a larger Garden

of Live Flowers. For the first time, a three-dimensional Alice was looking at the Caterpillar sitting on a giant mushroom. It is the Caterpillar
that left the shoes on top of the mushroom outside.

Like Snow White, the first-person perspective had been changed,
and for the first time Alice could be seen in the ride hidden away
across from the Caterpillar. The Alice figure was found in storage in
Florida, where it was part of the 1971 Mickey Mouse Review attraction. The Mad Tea Party was replaced with the Royal Rose Garden
and Queen's Court and the track expanded slightly.

"Alice in Wonderland always intrigued me because half of it was
outside," remembered Baxter. "As a kid, I used to sit up there on Snow
Mountain, which back then was just a mound of dirt [Holiday Hill]
with some benches. You could look down on Alice, and I was always
fascinated with the track." He said, "It was convoluted, and it seemed
to lend itself as part of a wonderland world, kind of crazy and eccentric.
I thought that it was an amazing layout, but as a kid I was always a
little disappointed. You could see from the top of the vine that you'd
just reach the ground and that was the end of the ride."[85] Baxter wanted
to make sure children were not disappointed with the updated version,
and a new finale was added. As the caterpillars burst out of the second-floor door, they wound their way down the vine and entered The
Unbirthday Party with the Mad Hatter and his friends. Baxter made
sure the show "ends with a bang."

Wonders of China, a $1 million Circle-Vision 360 film, premiered
on September 8, 1984. The film was produced by Jeff Blyth and took
guests to many areas that had never before been filmed by Western-
ers. The scenic wonders included remote areas in Tibet, the Gobi
desert, and Xinjiang Province. The Great Wall, the Forbidden City,
and swooping shots over the Yangtze River were also featured. The
film joined a growing library of Circle-Vision 360 films. The park
would begin to rotate *Wonders of China* with *American Journeys.*
America the Beautiful was retired.[86]

Great Moments of Mr. Lincoln returned to the Opera House on
Main Street on December 22, 1984, with a completely new and very
impressive figure. Disney Imagineers collaborated with the University
of Utah's Center for Biomedical Research to improve on the existing
generation of Audio-Animatronics, and once again Mr. Lincoln was
to be used as the showcase. This time, the Imagineers had access to
technology developed by scientists to maneuver artificial limbs. The
outcome was a concept called "compliance." Imagineer Marc Miller

explained, "Generally, robotics will hold a very rigid stationary position, but the technology in Lincoln allows him to give a little, so any roughness is not centered in one joint. It's balanced out over the body so it's more like human movement."[87] Imagineering programmer Dave Feiten said, "It was kind of scary to see how realistic we could make him with the new technology. I couldn't resist pushing the animation movements as far as the new system would let me. I guess I sort of went too far. When I finished the program, we discovered that I had turned him into a hyperactive campaigning politician."[88]

Some of the programmers who had worked on the original Lincoln figure were not impressed with the update. Blaine Gibson said, "I feel that the original Lincoln as programmed by Marc [Davis] and Wathel [Rogers] was much more tastefully done than the one they have in Disneyland now. The current figure is holding some papers, now, and he flails around too much. I think that he was much more dignified when he had his hands behind his back the way they did it originally."[89] Gibson suggested, "You can over animate things, too. I've always thought that the lack of capabilities, back then, forced them into devising animation which was actually more interesting, and it let the audience use their imagination." Rogers agreed. "We made him move slow and dignified, because of our limitations."[90]

Attendance at the park hit a 10-year low in 1984 with only 9.9 million visitors. The summer season was the quietest in 20 years. Things got so bad that Disney launched an unprecedented promotion in partnership with then local fast-food chain Carl's Jr.: guests could receive a free children's ticket with the purchase of the $2.49 bacon cheeseburger. Much of the blame for the reduced attendance was placed on the 1984 Summer Olympics in Los Angeles, which may have lured away many potential guests.

KEEP CHANGING *the* SHOW

FROM 1971 TO 1983, many of the Disney company's creative and financial resources had been dedicated to the development of the $900 million Epcot project in Florida. Jack Lindquist said, "Nobody in this company had time to do or think about anything down the road except for Epcot."[91] By 1984, Disney corporate director Raymond Watson instituted the creation of a long-range master plan for the Anaheim property. Working closely with Disney CEO Ron Miller, Watson looked toward the horizon and started to make plans.

Building a new theme park on the 40-acre strawberry field across West Street north of the Disneyland Hotel seemed an obvious goal. In order not to compete directly with Disneyland—the same way Epcot did not compete directly with the Magic Kingdom—the leaders considered a park based on non-Disney characters such as E.T. or roles from George Lucas films At the same time, it was determined that the Southern California market was already saturated and becoming stagnant, suggesting that there would be no demand for a new park before 1995. Recognizing that Anaheim was not Florida, planners recommended a strategy to improve food, merchandising, and pay greater attention to teens and guests over age 45.[92]

Many of the park's most memorable attractions were based on the films from the Studio, but by 1984, successful Disney film properties had become scarce. There was a period of 15 years after Walt's death where the animation department really struggled and the lack of compelling source material made ride development very difficult. The last Disney-produced movie that truly touched the audience was the 1967 animated version of *The Jungle Book*. The Imagineers tried to come up with ideas for films like *The Black Hole, Tron, Robin Hood,* and *Island at the Top of the World,* but the poor box office showings usually killed the project. Nobody wanted to be reminded of the failures. The park had been surviving on unique thrill rides like Space Mountain and the nostalgia of being a Southern California tradition, but that would not be enough.

The Imagineers needed fresh new stories to exploit if Disneyland were to thrive. The park needed to remain relevant to a new generation of park goers. This point was hammered home to Tony Baxter when he recalled a time at Disneyland when he saw a "5-year-old little girl, with her 25-year-old mother, watching the Alice in Wonderland float going past in the parade. The little girl pointed to the Caterpillar and said, 'Mom, what's that?' and the mother said, 'Oh, I guess it's a worm or something.' And I suddenly realized that the girl's mother wasn't even born when *Alice in Wonderland* was at the theaters."[93]

Tony Baxter started at WED in 1970 and was part of the second-generation of Imagineers. Unlike the original Imagineers, who had to experiment to figure out what the public would like, this group had grown up with the park and understood what was possible. However, Baxter and many of his peers were frustrated. The Disney film division was struggling to create the timeless stories of Walt's generation, and good source material was becoming scarce. They felt that the company had to look outside to find the newest generation of mythmakers.

He had been courting George Lucas for a long time, and knew he was a fan of the park with fond memories. He recalled, "I was at Disneyland the second day it opened," and the mini-freeway was his favorite "until I could drive."[94]

"George Lucas will talk endlessly about the importance of myth and building on things that are born in us, allowing us to feel as people," Baxter said. "I thought, 'Gosh, these guys have learned the lessons so well that right now, they are more Disney than Disney.'" A meeting was set up between George Lucas and Disney President and CEO Ron Miller at Miller's winery, the Silverado Vineyards in Napa Valley.[95]

Baxter got there earlier than Lucas. "Ron drove us around in his Jeep showing us the winery and the process of wine making. He let us sample his first vintages . . . he was really in his element." The Millers' home was in an old Victorian-type ranch house. The team was waiting to have lunch in the backyard when "up drove a BMW and George Lucas climbed out and said, 'Hi guys!'" Baxter's thoughts at that moment were, "Ok, the lady who is serving the potato salad is Diane, Walt's daughter, the guy in the BMW just revolutionized the film industry, and Ron is the President of the Walt Disney Company . . . it doesn't get any better than this!"[96]

The conversation was very productive. There was talk of creating an entirely new land adjacent to Tomorrowland with as many as seven attractions based on Lucas's movies, including an aircraft-simulator ride. Imagineer Randy Bright said, "We are talking about a substantial project. We have explored with him the possibility of introducing the George Lucas mythologies into this Disneyland environment."[97]

The moment would be short-lived. Within six months, Ron Miller was gone, and Michael Eisner and Frank Wells had entered the picture.

1. Vernon Scott, "Disneyland Salutes Walt," *Fresno Bee,* 6 Feb. 1970.
2. George Comboe, "Disneyland Under a Plastic Bubble?," *Anaheim Bulletin,* 29 Jan. 1971.
3. Disneyland Operations Department Group II, *Background Information: Adventureland, Frontierland, New Orleans* (Anaheim, CA: Disneyland, 26 Jan. 1970).
4. John Gregory, "Disneyland: It's Here in All Its Glory—Now What?," *Los Angeles Times,* 5 Dec. 1971.
5. Ibid.
6. "4-Man Council Runs Disneyland," *Anaheim Bulletin,* 22 Dec. 1971.
7. Ibid.
8. Ann Terrill, "Disneyland Won't Ever Stand Still," *Orange County Register,* 23 July 1972.
9. Ibid.
10. Ibid.
11. Bruce Gordon and David Mumford, *Disneyland: The Nickel Tour* (Santa Clarita, CA: Camphor Tree, 2000).
12. Sam Gennawey, *Walt and the Promise of Progress City* (Montgomery, AL: Ayefour Publishing, 2001). This book provides the full story of Mineral King.
13. Ron Miller, interview with author, The Walt Disney Family Museum, 21 Jan. 2012.
14. Neal Gabler, Harriet Burns, Alice Davis, Blaine Gibson, and Richard Schickel, "The Life & Legacy of Walt Disney," panel discussion, Annenberg School for Communication, University of Southern California, 15 Nov. 2006.
15. Disneyland, "Disneyland's Hilarious Country Bear Jamboree Inspired by Walt Disney and WED Imagineers," press release, 1972.
16. Gordon and Mumford, *Nickel Tour.*
17. Ibid.
18. Disneyland, "Disney Animators Perform Bearable Artistry," press release, Nov. 1984.
19. "A Moving Salute to Our History," *Disneyland Line,* 15 Feb. 1991.
20. "A Disney Showcase for Synergy," *Disneyland Line,* 4 Sept. 1992.
21. Disneyland, "Disneyland Begins Construction of The Walt Disney Story," press release, 22 Jan. 1973.
22. Disneyland, "New Disneyland Addition Nearly Three Years in the Making," press release, Feb. 1973.
23. Van Arsdale France, "Backstage Disneyland: A Personal History" (unpublished manuscript, 1980).
24. Walt Disney Productions and Wrather Corporation, press release, 3 Jan. 1974.
25. "100 Acre Expansion Told D'Land Shareholders," *Los Angeles Times,* 8 Feb. 1973.
26. E. Scott Reckard, "Disneyland Doodlers Toy With Old Idea for New Attraction," *Los Angeles Times,* 4 Sept. 1998.
27. Ryan Harmon and David Mumford, "Did You Hear the One About," *Disneyland Line,* 1995.
28. Ibid.
29. "Magic Kingdoms Then and Now," *The "E" Ticket,* Number 22, Winter 1995.
30. Bruce Horovitz, "Executives Study Major Disneyland Expansion," *Anaheim Bulletin,* 7 March 1984.
31. Disneyland, "Disneyland's *America Sings* Will Tell the Story of the Nation Through Humor and Song," press release, June 1974.
32. Jack Boettner, "*America Sings:* Disneyland's New Wonder," *Los Angeles Times,* 13 June 1974.
33. Ibid.
34. Disneyland, "*America Sings* Will Tell the Story of the Nation."
35. Boettner, "*America Sings.*"

36. "*America Sings* Will Re-open After Shutdown," *Anaheim Bulletin,* 10 July 1974.
37. Eleanor Hoover, "Disneyland Analyzed," *Los Angeles Times,* 10 May 1975.
38. Jack Smith, "A Mickey Mouse Rap at Disney," *Los Angeles Times,* 18 May 1975.
39. Richard Schickel, *The Disney Version* (New York: Simon and Schuster, 1968).
40. Ibid.
41. George Orwell, *1984* (London: Secker & Warbug, 1949); *2001: A Space Odyssey,* dir. by Stanley Kubrick (MGM, 11 April 1968).
42. Herb Caen, "The Plastic Fantastic," *San Francisco Chronicle,* 22 Dec. 1976.
43. Donald Britton, "The Dark Side of Disneyland," *Art Issues,* Issue 4/5, 1996.
44. Randy Lewis, "Writer Paints Different Picture of Disneyland," *Los Angeles Times,* 6 Aug. 1989.
45. Dave Smith, *Walt Disney Famous Quotes* (Lake Buena Vista, FL: Walt Disney Theme Parks and Resorts, 1994).
46. "A Moving Salute to Our History," *Disneyland Line,* 15 Feb. 1991.
47. Mary Lou Hopkins, "She's No Run-of-the-Track Car," *Los Angeles Times,* 17 Oct. 1975.
48. Ibid.
49. Jack Boettner, "Disney's 'Magical Little Park' After Two Decades," *Los Angeles Times,* 6 July 1975.
50. Ibid.
51. Susan Pack, "Anaheim Admission Tax Hit By Disneyland, Angels Officials," *Orange County Register,* 23 July 1975.
52. Vicki Liberman, "Shop on Main Street," *Orange County Register,* 23 Feb. 1976.
53. Ibid.
54. Jonathan Volzke, "Lucas's Star Tours blasts into D-land," *Anaheim Bulletin,* 10 Jan. 1987.
55. Jack Boettner, "New Attractions Slated for Disneyland," *Los Angeles Times,* 20 Feb. 1977.
56. "Disneyland Jungle Cruise Again Open," *Orange County News,* 16 Dec. 1976.
57. Disneyland University, *Space Mountain* training manual (Anaheim, CA: Disneyland, undated).
58. Jack Boettner, "Disneyland Unveils Its Space Mountain," *Los Angeles Times,* 29 April 1977.
59. Disneyland University, *Space Mountain* training manual.
60. Ibid.
61. "Disneyland's Snowing Bobsledders With an Abominable Apparition," *Los Angeles News Tribune,* 22 May 1978.
62. "Flair and Versatility," *The "E" Ticket,* Number 44, Summer 2006.
63. Disneyland, "Creation of Big Thunder Mountain Railroad Typifies Disney History of Creative Teamwork," press release, 15 Sept. 1979.
64. Ibid.
65. Ibid.
66. "Free Adventureland Trip Marks Anniversary Fete," *Anaheim Bulletin,* 26 Jan. 1980.
67. "Building Height Limits in Disneyland Area Revised," *Los Angeles Times,* 26 April 1980.
68. "Disneyland Welcomes Our 200 Millionth Guest!," *Disneyland Dispatch,* 8 Jan. 1981.
69. Walt Disney Productions and Disney News, "RETLAW," press release, 30 March 1981.
70. Bette Reinhartsen, "Monorail Expansion Eyed," *Anaheim Bulletin,* 18 Nov. 1980.
71. "The Office of Admissions," *Disneyland Line,* 5 March 1993.
72. "Disneyland Sets New Passport," *Anaheim Bulletin,* 12 June 1981.
73. Jason Schultz and Kevin Yee, *Jason's Disneyland Almanac: 1955–2010* (Orlando, FL: Zauberreich Press, 2011).
74. "The Office of Admissions," *Disneyland Line.*

75. Rolly Crump with Jeff Heimbuch, *It's Kind of a Cute Story* (Clearwater, FL: Bamboo Forest, 2012).

76. Bill Guy, "Fantasyland Renovation Update," Disneyland notice to cast members, 13 Oct. 1981.

77. "Magic Kingdoms Then and Now," *The "E" Ticket.*

78. Gordon and Mumford, *Nickel Tour.*

79. Ibid.

80. Disneyland, "New Fantasyland Announced," memorandum to employees, June 1981.

81. "Magic Kingdoms Then and Now," *The "E" Ticket.*

82. Gordon and Mumford, *Nickel Tour.*

83. Ibid.

84. "Magic Kingdoms Then and Now," *The "E" Ticket.*

85. Ibid.

86. Herman Wong, "Circle-Vision 360 Takes Its Sixth Turn at Disneyland," *Los Angeles Times,* 17 Nov. 1984.

87. "A Moving Salute to Our History," *Disneyland Line.*

88. Ibid.

89. "Wathel Rogers and Audio-Animatronics," *The "E" Ticket,* Number 25, Winter 1996.

90. Ibid.

91. Cathy Taylor, "Disneyland Back on Front Burner with 5- and 10-year Master Plan," *Orange County Register,* 8 March 1984.

92. Harrison Price Company to Walt Disney Productions, "A Second Gated Attraction in Anaheim at the Strawberry Patch," 12 June 1984 to 1 Sept. 1984, Series I: Reports, 1952–2003; Commercial Attractions, 1959–2003, Theme Parks and Attraction Parks, Project Class: A1; report number 212, box 7, folder 141–142; Harrison "Buzz" Price Papers, CFM2003_12, Special Collections & University Archives, University of Central Florida Libraries, Orlando, FL.

93. "Tony Baxter—Disneyland's Idea Guy!," *The "E" Ticket,* Number 46, Summer 2006.

94. Steve Daly, "An Easy Ride for Disney?," *Entertainment Weekly,* 3 Feb. 1995.

95. Ibid.

96. Ibid.

97. Charles Siler, "Disneyland Plan: 'Star Wars' Shine in Designers' Eyes," *Orange County Register,* 6 Dec. 1984.

CHAPTER 8

NEW IDEAS:
1985–1996

The FIRST, the FASTEST, the FINEST

IN SEPTEMBER 1984, Michael Eisner had been named CEO of Walt Disney Productions, and he was joined by Frank Wells as president. Eisner humbly said of the firm's founder, "Walt Disney was a genetic accident. He was a genius, and all geniuses are genetic accidents. His shoes are impossible to fill and never will be filled, and this company must recognize that."[1] He then set out immediately to put his own permanent stamp on the company. With all of the changes in the boardroom, the talks between Disney and George Lucas had initially come to a halt, but Eisner was willing to revisit the relationship. Lucas remembered, "When the new administration took over, they [Eisner and Wells] seemed to have more enthusiasm, and we started more serious talks about working on a ride together."

> **unofficial TIP**
> Michael Eisner worked at Paramount, and Franks Wells came from Warner Bros.

Eisner was also trying to court entertainer Michael Jackson, and in December 1984 he had Frank Wells call Imagineering president Carl Bongirno and Disney World president Dick Nunis to ask if they could develop an attraction with Jackson. In *Work in Progress*, Eisner explained, "Jackson was a huge fan of our parks, sometimes visiting several times a month, in and out of disguise. Our notion was to put him in an extended 3D music video."[2]

Jeffrey Katzenberg of Walt Disney Pictures met with Jackson in January 1985 to make a pitch for a 3-D movie using a new 70-millimeter film system in operation at Walt Disney World and combine that with in-theater special effects. Jackson was interested but wanted to work with somebody like George Lucas or Steven Spielberg. Because Imagineering had already been talking with George Lucas, they felt there might be a real opportunity in moving forward. Lucas recruited Francis Ford Coppola to direct the movie.

The talks were productive, and by February 1985, Eisner announced plans for a new attraction designed in collaboration with director George Lucas. Eisner said the ride would utilize technologies never before seen in a Disney theme park. The Imagineers struggled with the finished concept, and the original opening date of June 1986 was overly optimistic.

On March 29, 1985, the Frontierland Shootin' Arcade replaced the original shooting gallery. Guests could choose from 18 guns and shoot at 97 animated figures in the 1,280-square-foot arcade. They had 1½ minutes to unload 20 shots. Over in Adventureland, the Jungle Cruise was drained once again to inspect and completely rehabilitate the track, The Kilimanjaro rapids segment was rebuilt, and the landscape replanted and enhanced to create a dense, mysterious, live-vegetation rain forest from the moment guests left the dock.

Once again, rumors of Disneyland's being sold were rampant. This time, the rumors came straight from the top—from Disney CEO Eisner. One idea under consideration was to sell individual attractions to other companies; Disney would continue to manage the attraction, but the new owner would take over the operation and profit. Eisner was quoted as saying that he had been in talks with Hyatt Hotels and Marriott Hotels about a joint venture in Florida. He cautioned that "we're not going to sell any assets that we won't continue to manage." However, he added, "I don't want to mislead you. Where there's smoke, there's fire."[3] Walt Disney Productions stock rose on the news.

The new Walt Disney Productions leadership team "wanted to show the world that Disney was waking up, that it was different [than the old guard]," according to Tony Baxter. He figured Eisner and his colleagues were movie guys who believed that it only took one blockbuster hit to turn things around. As it would turn out, it would be a fateful meeting between Baxter and Breck Eisner, Michael's 14-year-old son, who changed the course of Disneyland history.

On September 29, 1984, just after Michael Eisner was hired to run Disney, he visited his Imagineers to see what they were up to. He told his team, "As you know, I'm really new to this business, but my son goes to these parks all the time. So I thought I'd let him guide me on what's good."[4] The Imagineers first pitched Star Tours. Breck was enthusiastic. "Dad, we've just got to do that . . . it's unbelievably cool!" With that, the Imagineers got the green light to proceed. Splash Mountain also got the nod at that meeting. Then Eisner asked, "Now that we have these two ride ideas, we open them when . . . next year or what?" It was Baxter who got to break the bad news. "Star Tours will take three years and Splash, which is a lot more elaborate, will take five." Eisner was used to having things done on his schedule, and Baxter could see that "he about died."[5]

Although Eisner knew that he could probably make more money concentrating on Florida, he felt Disneyland had an important role to play. "Disneyland remains the flagship, the experimental place to do things that could translate to our other parks," he said. "To keep Disneyland on the leading edge, we'll be constantly looking at new ways to combine art and technology, just as Disney has always done. But the main emphasis will remain—that we're there to entertain and be creative and fanciful, while we look to the brighter side of things."[6]

Disney marketing people were looking at the demographics and knew that they needed to attract a different age group. "Obviously, we have never had trouble attracting families to Disneyland, but we have never been satisfied with our percentage of the teen market," according to park spokesman Al Flores.[7] Disneyland wanted to ride on the music television wave and bringing an edgier type of entertainment to attract a different audience: young adults and older teens. They looked around and saw that Studio K at nearby Knott's Berry Farm had been highly successful, attracting up to 2,000 dancing teenagers a night.[8]

With that inspiration, Videopolis was born. Videopolis opened on June 22, 1985, at a cost of $3 million. It only took a mere 105 days from design to installation—a development schedule that even Eisner could appreciate. The park purchased some of the staging elements used at one of the 1984 Los Angeles Olympics facilities. Bongirno described the project as "the first, the fastest, and the finest—it is the first attraction completed under the new Eisner–Wells team; the fastest construction project we've ever completed; and the finest dance facility of its kind anywhere."[9]

Videopolis was strategically placed near It's a Small World. The location was out of the way, and the sound could be directed away from Fantasyland and toward the backstage area. Dancers enjoyed a 5,000-square-foot dance floor with a sophisticated light show mounted on a giant grid structure that slowly lowered from the ceiling. Three camera crews captured the dancers and projected the images on two 16-foot screens and 70 video monitors. The venue was packed with all sorts of state-of-the-art effects, like a large computerized display wall and a system of "light sticks" that played tricks on the dancers' eyes. The venue was not without its critics. One mother wrote to the *Anaheim Bulletin* about "Punkers in Fantasyland." She charged that since the dance club opened, "It's Halloween every day."[10]

On August 4, 1985, 3-year-old Brooks Burr became the 250 millionth guest to pass through the turnstiles.[11] He would not be the only one celebrating Disneyland's 30th anniversary. Much of the interest was sparked by the park's 30th anniversary and an advertising and promotional blitz commemorated with the gift of a car to every 30,000th guest. Another factor contributing to the high attendance was that starting on February 6, the park was open seven days a week year-round. Since 1955, the park had been closed on Monday and Tuesday from September through May. Although the closed days had given crews an opportunity to perform maintenance out of guests' view, the "dark" days disappointed many guests with less-flexible travel plans.[12]

WE'LL BUILD YOU *a* THEATER

IN FEBRUARY 1986, a vote at the annual shareholders meeting in Kansas City, Missouri, changed the company's name from Walt Disney Productions to the Walt Disney Company (WDC). A company executive said, "It will be a lot more comfortable to operate being known as the Walt Disney Company because Disney is no longer only involved in motion picture and entertainment productions, but has real estate and consumer merchandise ventures as well."

With Epcot's success bringing older, more-affluent guests to Florida—guests less prone to seasonal travel—WDC began to look for opportunities next to Disneyland. A 1986 report identified up to 30 acres within the Disneyland berm for expansion. Edison Square, a very early concept, was revived for consideration as a second Main Street. The new land would be located east of Tomorrowland in the space used for backstage functions. To make additional room, Disney purchased the 5-acre Global Van Line building and planned on moving its administrative staff into a new structure on that site.[13]

Once again, the 40-acre strawberry field across West Street was a site of interest. WDC was beginning to recognize that themed shopping and entertainment districts were becoming the next big real estate trend. Simply stated, the fashion was to raise merchandising "to the art form of entertainment," and Epcot was pointing the way. A second gate in Anaheim would focus on food, shopping, and entertainment instead of rides. Liquor would be served, and any rides in the vicinity would target teenagers, a group Disney had trouble attracting.

The leadership team also considered a nighttime entertainment center based along the lines of the historic Church Street Station development in Orlando, with a dynamic mix of nightclubs, restaurants, and shopping. During the day, the facility would take on a festival marketplace atmosphere, like Faneuil Hall Marketplace in Boston and South Street Seaport in New York.[14]

The company also hinted that the future of Disneyland would be attractions based on "illusions created with sophisticated computer software" so that "when the public becomes bored with an attraction, instead of knocking down a multimillion-dollar attraction, Disneyland can simply replace the software." Dick Nunis suggested that the park would try to open a new major attraction every two or three years and that all of them would have to have a corporate sponsor to defray the development costs.[15]

On May 2, 1986, the outdoor Space Stage was reopened as the indoor Magic Eye Theater sponsored by Kodak. Because the Michael Jackson 3-D epic was not yet ready, *Magic Journeys,* a 3-D film from the Imagination pavilion at Epcot Center, was used as a placeholder. *Magic Journeys* used Eastman Kodak's polarized, double 70-millimeter process that employs special glasses to allow guests "to see with two camera 'eyes' instead of just one," according to a press release. This process created a sense of depth. *Magic Journeys* had been shown the summer before at the outdoor Space Stage. The movie was closed on September 8, so Jackson's film, *Captain EO,* could be installed with its special effects.

Captain EO made its debut September 18. The 3-D film also opened at Epcot Center in Florida. From the very beginning, the Jackson attraction was a high priority for Michael Eisner. He wanted to get something going that would proclaim to the world that the Disney parks were still relevant. Imagineer Tony Baxter said, "We put in *Captain EO,* because Michael Jackson had been riding on the forefront of pop culture at that time."[16] For the $10 million production, Jeffrey Katzenberg, Disney motion picture and television division chairman, coordinated an all-star team that included Jackson, George Lucas as executive producer, and Francis Ford Coppola as director. The choreography was done by Jeffery Hornaday, who also worked on the musicals *Flashdance* and *A Chorus Line*. Writer Rick Rothschild drafted three screen scenarios, and Jackson and George Lucas independently chose the same story.

When work first began on *Captain EO*, it was not going to have in-theater effects. It was assumed that the film people would make an entertaining musical film and the Imagineers would design an appropriate theater. This changed at one critical meeting when somebody stood behind the model of the theater and blew cigarette smoke to show when the smoke was going to billow out. Everybody loved it.

The 12-minute, Kodak-sponsored film was considered the most expensive film ever, considering its running time. The theater was loaded down with more than 240 special effects. There were lasers firing from the screen over the heads of the audience. The screen had tiny shutters that would open to let the lasers fire. The screen was embedded with fiber optic "stars," and liquid nitrogen fog bellowed out from under the stage. Getting everything to coordinate precisely with the effects on the film was a very difficult challenge.

The press was not kind. Charles Solomon of *The Los Angeles Times* said, "For all its wondrous imagery, *Captain EO* is nothing more than the most elaborate rock video in history. Like a hollow chocolate Easter Bunny, its glorious surface over a void." *The Chicago Tribune* said, "The movie thrusts its characters into danger immediately. They are flying into your face, lasers blasting, just as you learn their names. Within such a short time you can't empathize with their plight. But the novelty of the 3-D effect is enough to occupy you through the start, though the plot is overcomplicated for the time available."

There was a lot of vacant land where Nature's Wonderland had once stood, so it was converted into the 2-acre Big Thunder Ranch. The attraction opened on June 27, 1986, and was "a combination petting zoo, exhibit area, and restaurant," according to Al Flores, a park spokesperson. He added, "It will feature an 1880s-style ranch house that will serve as a museum, an area where children can pet farm animals, and exhibitions of such ranch chores as harness making and horse grooming."[17] The ranch house was built from an 1894 barn Disney moved from Santa Ana. The burros came from the Bureau of Land Management; for only $75, qualified guests could adopt one to take home.[18]

LITTLE GALLERY

ALSO IN 1986, Imagineer Tony Baxter was trying to figure out how to deal with the congestion in front of Pirates of the Caribbean. He proposed connecting Adventureland to New Orleans Square with an elevated walkway that crossed over the Pirates queue. The bridge would be built in almost the exact same spot as the footbridge that was in place when the park opened. As he was working on this project, Baxter realized that if he added a pair of sweeping staircases, they would lead to what was meant to be Walt and Roy Disney's private second-floor apartment, the Royal Suite. The 3,000-square-foot apartment idea had been abandoned after Walt's death in 1966, but Walt's and Roy's initials could still be found woven into the wrought iron railing.[19] It sure seemed like the perfect place for something.

At the same time, John Hench was looking around for a space for a small art gallery. He remembered that Walt always wanted to have an art gallery to showcase the work done by the Imagineers and other Disney artists. Walt had told Hench, "We ought to have ourselves a little gallery next to the Commissary. Some of these guys around here are very good artists."[20] Hench thought the idea could work for Disneyland. He said, "Now we have several decades of marvelous art to share with the public, art which was instrumental in turning Walt's dreams for the Parks into reality."[21] The question was where to put the gallery. A celebration of art inside of Walt's personal residence seemed like a perfect fit, and the team began to prepare the space.

At the top of the staircase, the Imagineers added French doors that led into the space meant for the living room. Original artwork adorned the walls, and most exhibits featured models or other artifacts. The master bedroom and guest bedroom were used as galleries, the dining room was turned into a retail space, and the small kitchen became a sales counter. The climate-controlled courtyard remained, even though the heating and air-conditioning system was not used. Guests were allowed to sit on the balcony to enjoy an incredible view of the Rivers of America.

The Disney Gallery opened on July 11, 1987. The Art of Disneyland was the first exhibit and featured rarely seen original concept drawings and scale models of park attractions.[22] Many other shows followed. The Disney Gallery closed August 7, 2007, so the space could be converted into the Disneyland Dream Suite as part of a promotion. It reopened on October 2009 inside of the old Bank Building on Town Square.

ONE CONTINUOUS TAKE

MICHAEL EISNER HAD ENDORSED his son Breck's enthusiasm for Star Tours because he recognized that it was in the Disney tradition of creatively blending cutting-edge technology with good, old-fashioned storytelling. During the research phase, the Imagineers tried every sort of training simulator, including helicopters, passenger planes, and jet fighters. The simulator technology was basically a large tabletop supported by hydraulic pistons for legs. As the pistons moved up and down, the platform would tilt and twist and faithfully re-create almost any motion encountered in a flight situation. While in London, the team visited the Rediffusion Company to test one of their motion-based simulators used for training fighter pilots. It took them 20 minutes to climb into the machine and get strapped in. Obviously, this would not do in a theme park environment. The Disney team successfully solved the problem and were awarded several patents for the loading and unloading process.

unofficial **TIP**
The Disney marketing team called the show Star Rides until WDI reminded them that there are no rides at Disneyland, only attractions. Tom Fitzgerald coined the name Star Tours.

Star Tours opened on January 9, 1987. The $17 million project came together in only 18 months from research to grand opening—half the time that Baxter originally estimated in the seminal meeting with Breck Eisner. The story for the attraction was set just after the film *Return of the Jedi*. The villain, Darth Vader, is dead and the Star Wars have ended. The Rebel Alliance was trying to rebuild, and it created a pleasure tour service to showcase former Rebel and Empire bases. They decided to place a depot at Disneyland to entice Earthlings to visit the other planets. This particular trip is to Endor.

The queue was a big part of the experience. The guests wound their way down the same curving walkway that had been installed for Adventure Thru Inner Space. In the tradition of showing off the ride vehicle before guests arrive, a StarSpeeder 3000 was seen undergoing repair after an unpleasant meeting with an Imperial starship. Guests would notice the familiar shape when boarding, helping to suspend their disbelief. Along one wall was a huge display showing commercials for a trek to Tatooine and cocktails at the Mos Eisley Cantina.

In the next room was the Droidnostics Center, a factory with Go-Bot G2 robots repairing droids. The two Audio-Animatronics workers had once been singing geese in *America Sings*; in their new incarnation, the characters talked to guests as they passed by. Overhead conveyor belts were in constant motion carrying parts to an unseen destination; and as a tribute to Adventure Thru Inner Space, a miniaturized Atomobile was mixed in with the baskets of robot space junk.

George Lucas liked the technology, but he wanted to put a new spin on the story. Disneyland was famous for nothing going wrong. Lucas suggested the ride should start out like any other attraction, with the ride vehicle simulating it was on a track. Just ahead, out the front window, guests would see another vehicle just like theirs blasting off into space successfully. When it was their turn, something would go horribly wrong. They would take a wrong turn, blast through the maintenance doors, and begin their "misadventure."

The hapless pilot was RX-24, Rex, voiced by actor Paul Ruebens, and he took guests on a wild 4½-minute ride. Even the Mighty Microscope from Adventure Thru Inner Space made an early cameo appearance as the Star Speeder was first leaving the space station.

The film was a challenge. In the *Star Wars* movies, the cuts were anywhere from 2 to 3 seconds to 40 seconds. Star Tours is almost 3 minutes of one continuous take. The 70-millimeter film was synchronized with the motion simulator and was believed to have the longest special effects sequence anywhere.

unofficial **TIP**
In Star Tours, C3PO is voiced by actor Anthony Daniels, reprising his role from the films.

Star Tours was an instant hit. The Imagineers took an existing technology, repurposed it as a ride conveyance, and married that to one of the strongest mythologies of the 20th Century powered by the instantly familiar musical score from composer John Williams to create something entirely new.

The attraction was a huge success, and it triggered a whole new industry. Soon, virtually every shopping mall had a simulator. The novelty quickly wore off, but the popularity of Star Tours remained. The difference between Star Tours and its many imitators was how the preshow immersed the guests in the world of *Star Wars* and introduced the ride vehicle so that it was more than just a movie inside of a moving box.

It was suggested that another benefit to the technology is that a new film could be shot and the ride could be reprogrammed. However, at the grand opening, George Lucas suggested that people should not expect a 3-D Star Tours anytime soon. Lucas was right in his prediction about that. The 1986 version of the attraction lasted until July 27, 2010; on June 3, 2011, it was replaced by Star Tours: The Adventure Continues.

IT'S NOT JUST DISNEYLAND

IN DECEMBER 1986, the American Society of Mechanical Engineers recognized the Disneyland Monorail system as a Historic Mechanical Engineering Landmark.[23] At the beginning of 1987, guests began to see sleek, Learjet-like Mark V trains gliding on the beam. Produced to replace the Mark III trains that had been serving guests since 1969, the Mark V trains officially opened on April 17. Designed by Imagineer George McGinnis, the six-car trains were made of fiberglass instead of steel and featured on-board computers, wheelchair access, and an advanced suspension system. New bodies were placed on the original chassis, and the doors slid shut instead of swinging shut. To the disappointment of many children, the bubble dome for the pilot was eliminated. The monorails were built by MBB Co.[24]

Also in 1987, Disney officials began to talk again about expansion plans. They hinted to the public that a second gate was under consideration and it might be a 52-acre World's Fair–type theme park incorporating the more popular elements of Epcot. The cost of the project was estimated to be $1.2 billion. Construction on the project would begin in 1992, with an opening date in 1998. Jack Lindquist said, "We've lived off what was started in 1955. Now we have to take a big bold step up to take it to its full potential."[25] The hope was to extend guest stays to multiple nights like they did at Walt Disney World. Disney wanted to build a resort right in the heart of a highly urbanized area. The goal was to attract as many as 20 million visitors to Disneyland every year.

Lindquist outlined some of the areas available for expansion. He suggested that the 43.3-acre back lot area north of the park could accommodate as many as four new themed lands. Office functions would be moved to a new building on 5 acres along the freeway purchased from Global Van Lines. He mentioned the 40-acre strawberry farm across West Street. This was not a new idea; plans going back to the 1960s had looked at that parcel as a potential expansion area. Lindquist also clarified that the 102-acre parking lot was no longer an area under consideration.[26]

The key to success, according Lindquist, was the proposed 4,387-acre Katella Redevelopment Project connecting Disneyland to the Anaheim Stadium and a proposed multimodal transit station—a station similar to the one that had been proposed in 1976. The plan called for a $15 million PeopleMover-type system that connected the transit station and Disneyland to parking structures at the edge of the redevelopment area. The Anaheim Convention Center was going through a $50 million expansion, and organizations such as the Anaheim Committee for Traffic Solutions—made up of Anaheim officials, motel and hotel owners, and local businesses—thought it was time to clean up the area and reduce traffic congestion. Lindquist said, "It's critical that it's not just Disneyland, but Disneyland and the city, the Visitor and Convention Bureau, the Angels and Rams. It's going to take a major effort both in planning and financing a system." Disney supported the transit initiatives, even after the Katella Redevelopment Project was rejected by the Anaheim City Council. Their hope was that some sort of public action meant that the project could be paid for with public financing.[27]

Another element of the expansion plans included running the Edison transmission lines underneath the parking lot. At the beginning of 1987, Edison and Anaheim officials authorized a $146,000 study to replace two existing 66,000-watt power lines with one new 220,000-watt line underground. The old power lines had been in place since 1935. The cost of such a project was estimated at $40 million.[28] Disney and Edison both felt the other party should pay, and discussions continued.

On January 21, 1988, the Walt Disney Company entered into a 50–50 joint venture agreement with Industrial Equity Ltd. of Hong Kong to purchase the assets of the Wrather Corporation for $152.3 million. Included in the agreement was the 1,174-room Disneyland Hotel in Anaheim and the right to build hotels on the West Coast with the Disney brand. Jack Wrather had gained the rights when he made the deal with Walt before the park opened. Other assets included the Vacationland Campground north of the hotel and control of the *Queen Mary* ocean liner and Spruce Goose World War II aircraft in Long Beach. The RMS *Queen Mary* was a retired ocean liner that sailed primarily in the North Atlantic Ocean 1936–1967. The Spruce Goose was the derogatory nickname given to Howard Hughes's H-4 Hercules airplane, the largest flying boat ever, with the largest wingspan of any aircraft in history. Disney also acquired 47 acres of parking lot and retail space in Long Beach adjacent to the tourist attractions, as well as the Biltmore in downtown Los Angeles. Most important, Disney believed they gained the right to create 236 acres out of tidal water in the Port of Long Beach. Typically, coastal waters in California could not be filled in for recreational purposes, but Disney felt it could overcome such a limitation.[29] In March, Disney bought out its partner for $85.2 million and gained full control of all of the properties.[30]

Critter Country opened on November 23 in the northwest corner of the park. Because Splash Mountain would be the featured attraction, calling the area Bear Country made no sense. The solution was found right in the movie *Song of the South*. At one point, Uncle Remus begins his story of Br'er Rabbit and Br'er Fox and tells the children, "It wasn't yesterday nor the day before, but it was a long time ago . . . back when the critters were closer to the folks and the folks were closer to the critters . . . and things were better all around." The Indian Trading Post had become the Briar Patch, the Wilderness Outpost became the Crocodile Mercantile, and the Mile Long Bar became the Br'er Bar. The restrooms behind the facade of the George E. Russell Co. Mine Brokers and the Miners Union were removed to make room for Splash Mountain, and new restrooms were built on the lower level of an expanded Hungry Bear Restaurant. Even the train tracks were moved west to make more room. Fowler's Harbor was redesigned with the Seafood Shanty eatery and a dock to view the *Columbia*.

The LONGEST, STEEPEST, HIGHEST

IDEAS FOR NEW ATTRACTIONS can come from anywhere. In the summer of 1983, Tony Baxter had been working on a request from Dick Nunis, who wanted a flume ride like Knott's Berry Farm's Timber Mountain Log Ride. Baxter said, "He wanted something like Pirates of the Caribbean but more exciting. I wanted to help him but I didn't really know what to do."[31]

Because Baxter did not live close to Disneyland, he began to ponder Nunis's request while stuck in traffic on the Southern California freeways. Nothing was coming to him until 1984, when discussions started with George Lucas about ideas for Tomorrowland. One of the ideas was to close *America Sings* and tear down the Carousel Theater. Baxter felt like it would be a terrible waste of valuable Audio-Animatronics characters when the lightbulb lit up. Why not recycle them for the log flume ride?

When thinking about potential story lines for the ride, Baxter relied on his intimate knowledge of Disney animation and thought that the rarely seen *Song of the South* would make for a perfect fit. Bruce Gordon remembered, "Tony came up with the idea and suggested it that morning, and by the end of the first day, we knew what the show was going to be. That's the fabulous part of the attraction. We heard the idea and it just clicked. It was just a natural."[32] Stone added, "The three of us—Tony, Bruce Gordon and myself—literally spent the next three days in Tony's office preparing about 30 storyboards and outlining the entire project."[33]

At the same 1984 meeting when the Imagineers pitched the Star Tours concept to Michael Eisner and his son, Breck, they also presented the model for Splash Mountain. Baxter felt this would be a harder sell because the attraction was based on an obscure Disney animated film. Once he started to describe the drop as "the longest, steepest, and highest," Michael Eisner got very interested. He asked, "Can you guarantee it will be the longest, steepest, highest . . . make sure it's all those things?" Breck was even more excited and said, "That's even better!"[34]

The ride was originally known as the Zip-a-Dee River Run, but Michael Eisner told his team, "We've got this movie coming out [in 1984] with Daryl Hannah called *Splash*. That's a better title. Let's get some synergy with that movie. Maybe you could put one of those audio figures you have . . . of Daryl Hannah at the end of the ride waving to the people." Baxter's first thought was "A mermaid? You already admitted you don't know anything about this business. Why don't you let it go?" However, Baxter said, "[Eisner] was insistent about the name Splash, so we expanded it and came up with Splash Mountain. At the time we were all troubled by that because the movie was in the theaters and it didn't seem like a good fit at all. Now, as the movie has gone into history, the name Splash Mountain has no connotation with the Daryl Hannah movie. In hindsight, that first day, I think Eisner made a good call insisting on the name Splash. If we had called it the Zip-a-Dee River Run, how boring would that have been?"[35]

Although the concept for the flume ride came together very quickly, its placement in the park was a much more difficult decision. The ride required a 100-foot run-out for the drop. Bruce Gordon said, "We needed something to draw people back to Bear Country. It was very underutilized as an area."[36] Imagineer John Stone remembered, "We had done a concept that sort of looped the dead end of Bear Country back with the Haunted Mansion over the chiller plant between Pirates and the Mansion." The chiller had been built in 1971 and provided cold water to cool many of the attractions. The problem, according to Stone, was "it required changing a lot of things and a number of unnecessary expenses. We ended up taking the berm that was in Bear

Country between the Mansion and the Hungry Bear Restaurant and situated the ride right there. Though it appeared to be quite small, we found out that there was an incredible amount of space and fit just perfectly."[37] The ride was contained in two show buildings. One faced West Street and the other was under the eight-story mountain. The connection was known as the Burrows.

As was the Disney tradition, guests got a peek at the ride vehicles before boarding. While in line, the logs rounded Chickapin Hill and the guests could see other logs hurtling down the final drop. Stone said, "We did this on purpose. For a lot of people, seeing a boat come down a drop is almost as exciting as going down it themselves."[38]

Splash Mountain is based on one of the original stories written by Joel Chandler Harris. It is the story of Br'er Rabbit, who wants to go on a journey and learns that paradise could be found at home. Throughout the attraction he is chased by a hungry Br'er Fox and Br'er Bear. When Br'er Rabbit is finally caught, he escapes by tricking his foes and jumping into the Briar Patch. Guests learn that the Briar Patch is where he was born and bred. The moral of the story is if you are looking for adventure, the best place to find it is in your own backyard. The show was made up of 15 scenes, with 9 scenes featuring Audio-Animatronics characters. Along the journey, the logs floated past the Old Mill, the Bog, the Swimming Hole, and the Hollows. A visit to the Laughing Place was almost a psychedelic experience before the logs were taken up the lift hill.

The park had hoped to open Splash Mountain in November 1988. However, the attraction was plagued with technical issues. Disneyland was late in adding a flume ride to its roster, and Eisner wanted to do something different. Flume rides typically move slow and get guests wet. Eisner wanted the logs to move fast, and he wanted the guests to stay dry. Disney hired the premier builder of such rides, New Hampshire–based O. D. Hopkins, but everything was new and it was not working. Bob Stevens of O. D. Hopkins said, "We did what was needed as far as we're concerned. I don't think anybody could give [Disney] what they wanted."[39]

The financial cost of the delays was mounting. The $20 million original budget had skyrocketed to over $70 million.[40] One estimate suggested if the delays took another six months, it would also cost the park $13 million in lost revenues. With a market made up primarily of local visitors, new attractions were the one sure way to boost business. An additional pressure to open came from a prescheduled cross-promotion with McDonald's starting on February 10, 1989.[41] Even so, the attraction ultimately did not open until July 17, 1989.

The seven-passenger logs took 10 minutes to travel along a half-mile concrete flume and encounter five drops along the way. The first drop provided a transition similar to the one experienced in Pirates of the Caribbean. The guests go from a gentle outdoor ride with real grass and rough rocks and fall into a show building bursting with bright cartoon colors.

Splash Mountain featured the most intricate, dimensionally detailed rockwork at any Disney park at the time. Inside, there were no walls that divided the show scenes. Guests could look way to the other end of the bayou without giving away the story. It was different than Pirates of the Caribbean. In that classic ride, most of the action takes place far away from the boats. At Splash Mountain, the logs take you right into the middle of what is happening. Baxter suggested, "There's a theatrical magic in that, when it's done, it looks as though you just pulled down the landscape and revealed what's been there all along. Even when it's purposely treated as bad architecture . . . in fact, it's good theater."[42] The top of Chickapin Hill was 87 feet, or 10 feet taller than Sleeping Beauty Castle.

Of course, the biggest thrill element was the final drop of 52.5 feet at a 47-degree angle with a top speed of 40 mph. The logs plummet through the Briar Patch and the guests are sprayed with 12 water cannons before skirting the Rivers of America. The rails at the end of the large drop are adjustable to control the amount of splash that occurs when the boat enters the water. The angle of entry into the water can also be controlled, which determines how fast the boat slows down.

Because one of the goals had been to recycle the Audio-Animatronics from *America Sings,* the group inventoried the 100 figures and then tried to match them to characters in *Song of the South*. The 21 figures that could not be matched up were put on the showboat at the end, which was 50 feet wide by 30 feet high. That scene was placed in a 35-foot-tall room, which was the largest space of any single scene in any attraction ever created by the Disney team.

Another innovation was that the entire set was made of cement. The trough for most conventional log rides was made of fiberglass. By making the trough out of cement, the Imagineers could paint it any color and camouflage it to look like a river. They were also able to take advantage of the bypass troughs and design lakes and wider areas that appear to be rivers and bayous. Another benefit was that

SPLASH MOUNTAIN WAS CLOSED in 2005 for new logs with better rider protection. In addition to single seats instead of a bench, which allowed people to slide forward during the drop, an extra seat for an adult and child was added in the back row.

Disneyland maintenance could drain the [475,000-gallon reservoir] every night, for both maintenance and inspection.

As was the tradition, Disneyland used its 34th anniversary to provide a preview of upcoming attractions and shows. Michael Eisner announced that an Indiana Jones attraction was in the works, along with an update to Tomorrowland and the possibility of a second gate. He mentioned the proposed theme park opportunity in Long Beach that had been made possible by the purchase of the Wrather Corporation. He added, "With the Pacific Rim and the appeal that California has throughout the country, there's no question that [both the Long Beach park and the second gate at Anaheim] could be made to work. But it's years away."[43]

One change that was more immediate was the marquee out front. Since 1958, the blue-and-white Disneyland marquee on Harbor Boulevard had been a landmark. In October 1989, Disneyland decided to freshen things up with a brand-new, high-tech marquee that was one-third larger and featured a fiber-optic message display capable of showing photographs. The trademark slogan, "The Happiest Place on Earth," was retained. The new marquee was placed 60 feet south of the original to give visitors a better idea of where the actual entrance was located. The old marquee was dismantled and placed into storage.[44] This 1989 marquee would last until 1999, and then be sold in pieces on eBay.

For 15 years, guests could get a peek into Disneyland's future at the Preview Center. That display was closed in 1989 and replaced with the Disney Showcase, a merchandise store that featured items related to Disney films. Another change to Main Street was the closure of the Town Square locker facility to make room for an expanded Emporium. In Frontierland, Fowler's Harbor was remodeled with new buildings and landscaping. Guests could now walk around the *Columbia* and get a close look.

On September 1, 1989, Claudine Masson of Chateaux, France, became the 300 millionth guest. Attendance in 1989 was a respectable 14.4 million guests.

The **DISNEY DECADE**

IT WAS A VERY OPTIMISTIC TIME at the Walt Disney Company, and Disney CEO Michael Eisner was about to kick it up a notch with the announcement that the 1990s would be known as "The Disney Decade."[45] This ambitious program of expansion in the theme park and resorts division was unprecedented in scope.

Disneyland was certainly slated to get its fair share of goodies. To start, the park would feature shows developed in collaboration with some of the new creative partnerships that Eisner was forging. He started with Warren Beatty. In June 1990, the *Dick Tracy Musical Revue: Diamond Double Cross,* opened, and the hope was to establish *Dick Tracy* as the new Disneyland comic book franchise. Eisner suggested more entertainment offerings for 1991, including a project by director George Lucas. The *Young Indiana Jones Adventure Spectacular* was proposed as an "action-packed live extravaganza" that would give Disneyland a stunt show to compete with the *Miami Vice* show at Universal Studios. The Muppets would star in their own live show called *Here Comes the Muppets,* as well as a new daytime parade called the Magnificent Muppet All-Star Motorcade.

To celebrate Mickey Mouse's 65th birthday in 1993, the 4.5-acre Mickey's Starland would open adjacent to It's a Small World. The Muppets would finally get a permanent attraction in Mickey's Starland with *Kermit the Frog Presents Muppet-Vision 3-D.*

A new Tomorrowland would debut in 1994. The concept was known as Tomorrowland 2055, set 100 years after Disneyland opened. "The planet Earth, it turns out, had finally been discovered by alien civilizations from planets throughout the universe. And once they found out we existed, what earthly beacon did they head for? Why, Disneyland, of course!" read one publicity release. The area would have been an environment of other-worldly plants and animals. The multistory theme that began with the Space Mountain complex would be extended throughout the area with a skywalk connecting all the attractions. Strobing fiber-optic "approach lights" would have been

MICKEY'S STARLAND WAS RENAMED MICKEY'S TOONTOWN in 1993, and *Muppet-Vision 3-D* would open up first at the Disney-MGM Studios theme park in Florida in 1990. Eventually *Muppet-Vision 3-D* made its way back west with the opening of Disney's California Adventure in 2001.

embedded into the concrete. There was even the suggestion that the men's restrooms would be equipped with "mood sensing" urinals.

Star Tours and Space Mountain would be joined with four new attractions. Alien Encounter would be a departure from the traditional Disney attraction, with the horror film monster terrorizing the guests using binaural sound and olfactory effects. The Carousel Theater would get a brand-new show called *Plectu's Fantastic Galactic Revue,* in which aliens from another galaxy have been stranded at Disneyland and have decided to put on a show for the guests. Similar to *America Sings,* the show would feature an all–Audio-Animatronics cast. The hope was that Michael Jackson would provide the voice of the host character. The Circle-Vision 360 theater would also get a new film exploring "the scenic wonders and culture of Western civilization." The attraction would combine the film with Audio-Animatronics and in-theater effects. Finally, a new 3-D film produced by Lucas would debut in the theater where *Captain EO* was located.

In 1995, the focus would be on Disneyland's 40th anniversary and a Little Mermaid attraction in Mickey's Toontown. Then in 1996, Dick Tracy would find a permanent presence with Dick Tracy's Crimestoppers. This big-budget Audio-Animatronics ride would "recruit guests to shoot it out with gangster bad guys."[46] This would be the first attraction to open in a whole new part of the park called Hollywoodland.

The rest of Hollywoodland would premiere in 1999. This all-new land would be "an idealized re-creation of Hollywood Boulevard in the '30s and '40s, complete with shops and restaurants amid an atmosphere that marked the 'Golden Age of Movies.' " Four new attractions would nestle up against a giant backdrop of the Hollywood Hills with the famous sign. Toontown Trolly was going to take the simulator technology of Star Tours to a whole new level. Based on the film *Who Framed Roger Rabbit?* guests would go "on a wild ride through the cartoon world of Toontown." Close by would be another attraction inspired by the *Roger Rabbit* film, Baby Herman's Runaway Baby Buggy Ride. The roller coaster would "zoom through the sets of Toontown Hospital, fly down stairs, crash through doors and bound over beds."

From the Disney-MGM Studios, which had opened in Florida in 1989, would come The Great Movie Ride, a ride that "travels through some of the most memorable scenes from classic films of yesteryear" and features "the most complex and realistic Disney Audio-Animatronics technology ever developed." Another Florida attraction, *Superstar Television,* was also on the roster of attractions.

An expansion of Disneyland Hotel was also part of the plan, as was the development of a second theme park in Anaheim or Long Beach. The Disney Decade promised to transform the world of the theme parks and provide Eisner the chance to create a legacy that he hoped could be equal to Walt's. Only time would tell.

Although the future held much promise, the actual changes in the park were minor. The Blue Ribbon Bakery opened on the northwest corner of Main Street and Center Street in April 1990, replacing the Sunkist Citrus House; later that month, the Pendleton Woolen Mills closed in Frontierland after 35 years.[47] The shop had been one of the original tenants and a personal favorite of the Disney family.

In June 1990, the Emporium on Main Street U.S.A. reopened after an extensive remodeling. The store was the largest in the park, and it got even bigger. The interior was expanded west, taking over the guest locker facility, while new lockers were moved to the end of the east branch of Center Street. The new floors, ceilings, and fixtures were meant to be "more elegant," according to Paul Goldman, a Disneyland spokesman.

Guests may have not been able to buy gum or a newspaper within Disneyland, but they could buy cigarettes—until June 1, 1990, that is, when the Tobacconist shop was converted into Patented Pastimes with crafts, needlepoint, and models. The cigar store wooden Indian remained out front as a silent reminder of times past.

IN 1999 THE CIGAR SHOP AGAIN CHANGED, becoming the 20th Century Music Shop, featuring an innovative use of technology, where guests could create custom CDs from dozens of attraction soundtracks. The machines were removed in 2009. Smoking was banned on January 30, 2000, except in designated areas.

PORT DISNEY

DISNEY'S MANAGEMENT was becoming increasingly concerned with the public realm surrounding the park. The area had been deteriorating for years due to the laissez-faire attitude toward planning within the City of Anaheim. However, there was little the City of Anaheim could do. One planning official described the surrounding properties as "a lot of scrawny little lots with funny configurations. You have developers trying to do something with them, but you don't get a decent restaurant or a hotel on a 200-foot-wide lot." The City lacked the authority and the political will to control development around the park.

City planners wanted to create a Specific Plan for the commercial–recreation district to guide development standards and enhance the area. They proposed a one-year moratorium on the construction of new hotels and motels to study the possibilities, but they allowed developments already in the pipeline to proceed. The development community was concerned about how long the study would take, with all of their projects put on hold. Disney supported the moratorium. Allan Epstein of the Disney Development Company said, "We're strong supporters of the study process and we hope that out of the study will come a vision for the community on where the commercial-recreation area should be heading."[48] He added, "We'd like to see a well-thought-out master plan as opposed to spot development." After completing the study, Anaheim zoning administrator Annika Santalahti felt "it doesn't look like there's a good solution" and it would be unlikely that the city could reach consensus on a plan. When the moratorium was lifted a year later, of the 13 exemptions granted, only one project ever broke ground.[49]

Although the Walt Disney Company was concerned about Anaheim, they did have other options in Southern California. They turned their attention to the assets they now controlled in Long Beach, including the long-term leases for the *Queen Mary* and Spruce Goose, development rights for 47 acres adjacent to those two attractions, and rights to create another 236 acres by filling in a nearby harbor wetland.

In July 1990, Disney announced plans for the new $2.8 billion Port Disney resort. The resort would front both sides of the mouth of the Los Angeles River in Long Beach Harbor. On the port side, the *Queen Mary* would be moved 700 feet north and remain a tourist attraction and a hotel; it would also serve as the resort's marquee. The centerpiece would be DisneySea, a new ocean-oriented theme park where guests would gain "a better understanding of the sea" and explore "the myths, romance, challenges, and mysteries of the ocean—the world's last great frontier."[50] At the center would be Oceana, a gigantic oceanarium that would appear to be a series of futuristic bubbles filled with a variety of marine habitats. People would be able to see the display from walkways above or through underwater portholes below. The attraction would also house the Future Research Center, a state-of-the-art laboratory.

Surrounding Oceana would be immersive lands such as Mysterious Island with Captain Nemo's Lava Cruiser thrill ride, Heroes'

Harbor with it's Aqua-labyrinth water maze, and a re-creation of Long Beach's oceanfront when it was a popular amusement park. Project manager David Malmuth said, "Our goal is to sensitize millions of visitors each year to the enormous challenges and opportunities of our seas—our most precious resource—in a setting that encourages play and fantasy." [51]

There would be a new waterfront shopping and entertainment district with ferry service connecting the resort to Queensway Bay adjacent to downtown Long Beach. A total of 3,900 hotel rooms were proposed, including two new hotels built adjacent to the park. The 500-room Port Hotel would provide luxury accommodations and a waterfront setting. The 1,400-room Canal Hotel would include a 150-slip guest marina and waterfront promenade. The Port of Long Beach would be responsible for a new cruise ship terminal with five cruise ship berths, a 15-acre park, and a 250-slip marina.

On the city side would be three more hotels, including the 900-room Tidelands Hotel along the waterfront with a 6-acre park, the 400-room all-suite Shoreline Hotel with its own shopping center, and the 700-room Marina Hotel adjacent to the Long Beach Convention Center. A new 17-acre park was part of the plan, as were enhancements to Shoreline Drive.

The assumption was that the project would open in two phases, with the first coming online in 2000 and the second by 2010. Disney hoped to attract 10 million guests in the first year and more than 13 million by the time the second phase was completed.[52]

The SEVEN WONDERS of the WORLD

IN A MOMENT of unfortunate corporate synergy, the Motor Boat Cruise was renamed the Motor Boat Cruise to Gummy Glen on March 15, 1991. Part of a promotional program called the Disney Afternoon Avenue, plywood characters from Disney's animated *Gummy Bears* television series made Gummy Berry juice along the waterway. The new theme lasted until November 10 and was then removed.

unofficial **TIP**
The Motor Boat Cruise closed in 1993, and the dock became a rest area renamed Fantasia Gardens.

On May 8, 1991, the Walt Disney Company announced preliminary plans for a $3 billion expansion in

Anaheim. The Disneyland Resort was to become a multiday destination just like Walt Disney World. To encourage guests to remain
on the property during their stay, Disney planned to create a 550-
acre, pedestrian-friendly Garden District with a new theme park, an
updated Disneyland Hotel, three new hotels, and much more.

The new theme park would be WESTCOT Center and was referred
to in the press as a World's Fair–type park similar to EPCOT Center. It
would have been divided into two areas: Future World and the World
Showcase. The Future World section would include the Wonders of
Living, the Wonders of Space, and the Wonders of Earth pavilions.
The World Showcase section would include pavilions representing
Asia, African, Europe, and the Americas. Pavilions combined, guests
would be able to visit "the seven wonders of the world."

Some of the proposed attractions included a revamped version of
Adventure Thru Inner Space using simulator technology, a "raft ride
down the mythical Congobezi River in Africa," and a "roller coaster
on the Great Wall of China."[53] There would be a Tivoli Gardens playground for little children.[54] What was sure to be the highlight of any
trip would have been the 45-minute World Cruise. The boat ride
would play a similar role to the Disneyland Railroad, with stops every
9 minutes at each of the pavilions. In between, guests would see scenes
reflecting the theme of the next stop.

The hotel expansion would be unprecedented. The Disneyland
Hotel would be upgraded and expanded. The New Disneyland Hotel,
a 800-room resort based on the Hotel del Coronado, would be added.
The Mission in Santa Barbara would inspire the low-rise, 960-room
Magic Kingdom Hotel, and the 1,800-room WESTCOT Lake Resort
would take on the flavor of the Beverly Hills Hotel. The added occu-
pancy was estimated to total more than 5,100 rooms. The hotels
would be built along West Street, and the theme park would be built in
Disneyland's 102-acre parking lot.

An attraction for locals and visitors alike would be the Disney
Center, a new waterfront shopping and entertainment district set on
a 6-acre lake. The lake would be surrounded by buildings inspired
by the Catalina Casino, the Venice Boardwalk, and the Palisades.
A 5,000-seat amphitheater called the Disneyland Bowl would be
located near Harbor Boulevard. Guests would park their cars in
huge structures at the edges and take PeopleMovers to the front
gates. An elevated PeopleMover system would connect all of these
activity nodes.

It was estimated that the new resort would bring as many as 12,500 new jobs and that the resort total employment could top 15,400. Disney anticipated generating $45 million in taxes per year to Anaheim, $9 million to Orange County, and $70 million to the state of California. The project was supposed to break ground in 1993 and be operational in 1999.

With the Port Disney in Long Beach project already announced, Anaheim found itself in competition for Disney's development dollars. Peter Rummell, who was Michael Eisner's go-to guy for real estate matters, cautioned the community, "As a business judgment it's too risky to build both at the same time in the same markets."[55] This was meant as a warning to some Anaheim community leaders who had suggested that Disney should help pay for some of the negative effects that had come with its growth. The local school districts were looking for as much as $91 million in assistance. Housing advocates were also concerned about the need for more affordable housing for the projected increase in the workforce. In spite of Rummell's caution, Anaheim officials were confident that a deal could be struck.

After the Walt Disney Company made its announcement, Long Beach city officials were excited and optimistic about hosting a Disney resort. However, Disney began to run into opposition from the powerful California Coastal Commission and environmental groups such as the Sierra Club. The 1976 California Coastal Act did not allow for landfill to be used for recreational purposes. Disney needed the Commission's approval for the required 236 acres of landfill. Without the additional land, the Disney project could not move forward. To get around this limitation, Disney sponsored Senate Bill 1062, which would exempt Disney from the Coastal Act.[56] State Senator Henry J. Mello (D-Watsonville) said, "They're trying to fill ocean waters. That's the biggest sin man can commit on this planet as far as I'm concerned, whether it's Disney or anybody else." By June, the bill died in the Legislature. In hindsight, Robert Sulnick, executive director of the American Oceans Campaign, said, "Disney went about this in an ivory-tower approach, which was either naive or arrogant on their part."[57]

Author Mike Davis felt that both cities were getting a raw deal and that they were their own worst enemies. He laid the blame on the lack of a progressive property tax due to California's Proposition 13 (People's Initiative to Limit Property Taxation, a 1978 amendment to the state constitution that reduced tax rates on homes, businesses, and farms by nearly 60%) and the lack of federal aid from President

George H. W. Bush's administrations as cities "pauperize each other in Darwinian struggles over scarce tax resources." Davis said, "Disney officials have long been critical of their founder's improvidence in failing to control the periphery of his original park," so they wanted "to build a better mousetrap in Southern California." He noted that the difference between Anaheim and Orlando was that in the latter, Disney was the government and could reap tax advantages in maintaining the infrastructure. In Anaheim, the company was "as fixated with externalization of costs as with internalization of sales and profits."[58]

For both projects, Disney put together extensive community outreach efforts to minimize opposition. In Anaheim, on June 5, 1991, Disney consultants facilitated a Scoping Meeting, which was required by the California Environmental Quality Act (CEQA) for the Environmental Impact Review (EIR) process. The meeting gave project opponents an opportunity to voice concerns about traffic, noise, housing, and water. Kerry Hunnewell, vice president for the Disney Development Company, said that Disney representatives were "gratified by the positive response" and were "committed to studying the issues that have been raised."[59] He added that "major urban development requires that the public and private sectors work together, and we are fortunate to be working with people who clearly understand that."

One of the opponents was a recently formed neighborhood group called Anaheim H.O.M.E. More than 200 residents gathered at their first meeting, and many were angry. "Why is the city thinking about using eminent domain to condemn private property?" asked resident John Gordon. Steve White, secretary of the group said, "They're going to park 16,000 cars right next to our homes. The whole Disney parking lot is only 14,000 cars right now. Can you imagine 16,000?" White suggested if the project had to move forward "we should see what we can get out of the project that can benefit us."[60] One idea was for the city to retain ownership of the proposed parking structures and keep the fees rather than the city's buying the land, building the structures, and then leasing them back to Disney.

The parking structures and the circulation enhancements were critical to the success of the entire expansion project. Disney lobbied for federal funding for a $395 million highway project that would include freeway off-ramps leading directly into the resort's parking garages. The company suggested it could be considered a "demonstration project" in order to bypass the state government planning process. Part of the program was to design a citywide PeopleMover system but only build the first leg on Disney property, with no commitment to build the rest of the network. Existing parking capacity was only 14,000 vehicles. The new west parking structure would be six levels and hold 16,700 vehicles. The east structure would be even larger, with seven levels capable of holding 17,600 vehicles. Both would be accessed by dedicated freeway off-ramps.[61]

The *Anaheim Bulletin* had always been bullish on Disneyland, but even they felt that this request was an injustice. In an editorial published in July, they stated, "We find the whole thing offensive, especially that a giant corporation like Disney, who will later charge us admission to their park, wants us to help pay for its construction."[62] *The Los Angeles Times* came out against Disney. They said, "Part of the problem is timing," and "the result is that Disney's request looks outsized; and its strategy of proposing a Disney-originated plan allowed critics to argue that little direct public benefit would result."[63] A U.S. Senate subcommittee rejected Disney's bid for federal money to pay for the parking lot. The *Anaheim Bulletin* concluded, "The Disney Company has finally gotten its comeuppance."[64]

40-FOOT PINK ELEPHANTS

THE RIVERS OF AMERICA were drained once again starting on September 9, 1991, but this time the park installed a new $30 million show called the *Imagination River Spectacular* at the southern end of Tom Sawyer Island. The show was born during a charrette (an intensive planning and design session) two years before, when Michael Eisner gave his creative team 48 hours to come up with 20 major ideas. Entertainment vice president Bob McTyre said, "We gave him a whole laundry list of what we could do."[65] Ideas ranged from a patriotic extravaganza to a spotlight on Disney's early years. Eisner chose the high-tech water show based on familiar Disney themes.

The project was inspired by new technology that the Imagineers discovered in a small town in France. During a community festival, the town had projected films onto water screens. Disney improved upon the water screen technology and combined it with advanced projection systems, lasers, pyrotechnics, and controlled fire effects. According to McTyre, the show would have "weird distorted images" popping in and out of thin air like magic, fire-breathing dragons, and "40-foot pink elephants marching across the water in the darkness out of nowhere." He added, "We're all interested in these things, and we put it through the Disney sieve, the Disney point of view. Of course, what we do is going to take on a '90s sensibility."[66]

To maintain the illusion of a rural river during the day, the show's infrastructure had to be hidden. To that end, the Old Grist Mill was removed and a new one built where the bait shack had been. The show equipment room was camouflaged as a Cider Mill. Just in front was a new stage with a 20-foot sliding door. A basement was built 15 feet below the river bottom to house a 43-foot inflatable dragon. Also hidden on the island were a number of hydraulically elevated lifts, including two light towers, a Mickey Mouse lift, and one for Maleficent, the villainess from *Sleeping Beauty*, whose lift reached 32 feet in the air. Along the New Orleans Square waterfront were three retractable show light towers. The magnolia trees that Bill Evans had saved so many years before finally met their end in order to improve site lines.[67]

The show, eventually renamed *Fantasmic!*, debuted on May 13, 1992. Upon hearing the news, local neighbors were not as excited as the planners had been. Margaret Douglass, who lived in a mobile home park nearby, said, "Once a night is bad enough; now we're gonna have fireworks three times a day? That'll go over like a time bomb in this area." Disney historian Jason Schultz has suggested the show "was a game changer for the crowd patterns at Disneyland."[68] The west side of the park was particularly quiet in the evenings until the debut of *Fantasmic!* Now that side of the park became very congested virtually every evening.

A CHRISTMAS PRESENT

ON DECEMBER 12, 1991, the waiting was over. Anaheim had won. The letter to the City of Long Beach read, "Our efforts to develop the proposed DisneySea project in Long Beach have been discontinued."[69] After a year-long assessment, Disney felt they had a better chance of actually getting something built within the target time frame in Anaheim than in Long Beach. Even with the all-powerful California Coastal Commission stating they would not get in the way, Port Disney was being held up in the environmental review process and by the requirement that Disney coordinate with 26 regulatory agencies. The pro-Disney Anaheim City Council was deemed to be an easier partner to deal with.

Disney felt the WESTCOT project could be "a catalyst for the revitalization of the entire Anaheim Commercial Recreation Area" and become "a world-class tourist destination."[70] Construction was slated to begin in 1993, and the project completed in 1999. Disney was expecting up to $1 billion in additional public money to improve the area infrastructure, street improvements, increased sewer capacity, and increased public safety needs. Anaheim Councilman Bob Simpson said, "I don't know how the city could have gotten a better Christmas present."[71]

Peter Rummell once again was the voice of caution. He told Anaheim community leaders that even though Disney was not going to build in Long Beach, "We have not made a final decision to build in Anaheim. The economic feasibility still has to be proven. We've never before undertaken a project like this in an urban environment."[72] Kerry Hunnewell reminded the community, "There has to be some way for us to work out some form of public–private financing mechanism in order to fund the infrastructure projects we need right now."[73]

The next day, the Walt Disney Company announced it would acquire the Melodyland Church property across the street from Disneyland. They also announced that they would not renew the leases for the *Queen Mary* and Spruce Goose when they expired in July 1993.[74] Many of the proposed elements for the Long Beach park would make their way to Tokyo when the Oriental Land Company opened DisneySea in 2001.

The announcement of the expansion overshadowed what had been another down year for attendance. The economic recession had taken its toll. The park was able to reach 11.6 million visitors in 1991, but this was a far cry from the 12.9 million in 1990, much less the 14.4 million in 1989.

The initial euphoria about Disney's expansion plans was starting to wear off for some Anaheim leaders by 1992. Residents adjacent to the commercial–recreation district were becoming increasingly concerned with the scale of the project. For example, in the planning process Disney needed to acquire 15 properties to build a large parking structure. They were able to purchase seven of the properties but had suggested to the holdouts that they would force the City to use their power of eminent domain if necessary. Some longtime property owners did not take this threat lightly.

One of the holdouts was Odetics, a high-tech recording-equipment manufacturer. The company had been on its 14-acre site since 1969. Chairman of Odetics Joel Slotzky was not pleased when he heard the news that Disney planned to take his land. He said, "The only notice we got was a phone call from someone at Disney a few hours before the announcement. Nobody at the city informed us about this. We looked at the newspaper this morning and said, 'Hey, that's us.'" He added,

"We're not happy campers."[75] Odetics fought against the project and succeeded in being excluded from the property consolidation.

Another holdout was Hiroshi Fujishige. His family had purchased 58 acres near Katella Avenue and Harbor Boulevard in 1953.[76] Anaheim had wanted to buy his strawberry farm since the development of the Convention Center back in the 1960s. Some say that Fujishige was holding out for more money. He said, "It's too big for me to comprehend. If I had more schooling and knew what all these deals were, I might have been out of here a long time ago. At this time and age, you've got to keep doing what you know best." One close friend said, "He has an Oriental Omniscience about him. Some say he's crazy watching his strawberries grow. I think he knows something we don't know." The pressure to sell over the years was a contributing factor to the suicide of Fujishige's brother in 1986. Fujishige said, "This land means quite a bit to me. My brother died for it."[77]

In 1991, a planning document showed the Fujishige farm as a potential site for a third Disney theme park.[78] The family sued. At the time, Carolyn Fujishige wrote the city, "We will never sell our property to the Disney Company or to anyone affiliated in any way with the Disney Company." It would not be until August 1998 that the company would be able to take control of the property. Newspaper reports suggested the purchase price was somewhere between $65 million and $78 million for 52.5 acres. The family intended to farm the remaining 3.5 acres.[79] On March, 29, 2010, the property became the Toy Story Parking Lot.

Project opponents decided to get the attention of the City Council by questioning the practice of city officials receiving free tickets to the park. In 1991, City Council members distributed 276 tickets with a face value of $7,590. In April 1991, the practice was put on hold, awaiting a decision from state officials if this was a violation of any gift laws. If so, it could prevent a number of the council members from voting on any project affecting Disneyland's expansion plans. Although no wrongdoing was ever acknowledged, the practice was never reinstated.[80]

NORMAL SEASONAL ADJUSTMENTS

THE INDIANA JONES FRANCHISE was loaded with abundant material for ride concepts—too many, it seemed. Like John Hench and Bill Martin before him, Tony Baxter had suggested creating a layered environment with multiple attractions intertwined. Guests would travel through the jungle (the queue) and arrive at the "Indiana Jones Expeditions" base camp. Once there, they could choose to board a transporter and tour the ruins, step into an ore car and ride through a mine, or walk through a labyrinth. The Jungle Cruise and the Disneyland Railroad would pass by, giving guests on those rides a peek of the camp. However, the Imagineers had to start narrowing down the list, and by the end of March 1992 it was decided to focus on developing the Enhanced Motion Vehicle (EMV) transport vehicles. The labyrinth was reconfigured to become the queue for Indiana Jones and the Temple of the Forbidden Eye, and the ore car roller coaster was put on the shelf.

In September 1992, the park announced the closing of three of its oldest attractions. Soon to be extinct were Mission to Mars, the Motor Boat Cruise, and the Fantasyland Autopia. Although the park claimed the closures were part of "normal seasonal adjustments," a park spokesperson admitted it was "possible but not probable" that they would reopen.

To give guests a preview of what to expect in Mickey's Toontown, the Toontown Railroad Depot opened on November 25, 1992. It was a remarkable cartoon version of the original Frontierland Depot and representative of the architecture for Toontown. To further enhance the area, It's a Small World's all-white facade was painted in pastel colors that duplicated Disneyland Paris.

At the end of 1992, more details about the Disneyland expansion project were revealed. The proposed iconic centerpiece would be Spacestation Earth, a giant gold globe surrounded by a translucent web. At 300 feet, the height of a 23-story building, it would be the tallest structure in Orange County. The globe would rest over a large lake and enclose a new thrill ride. Neighborhood reaction was negative. Steve White, vice president of Anaheim H.O.M.E., said, "It's really hard to conceptualize a giant golf ball sitting at Harbor Boulevard. It might be appropriate in the middle of swamps in Florida. But in our residential area, it seems a tad inappropriate."[81] The plans called for buildings ranging in height from 50 feet to 250 feet in WESTCOT, but height limits for buildings outside of the park would again be reduced so external structures could not be seen inside the new park. Former Mayor Bill Thom joked, "I guess they can visually intrude on themselves."[82]

Another change was the consideration of an admission price for Disneyland Center, the shopping and dining district. Once thought to be an amenity for local residents, the Disneyland Center concept was evolving. Kerry Hunnewell said, "What we showed a year and a half ago was a first cut."[83] Mayor Tom Daly's reaction was, "That would be a huge change. One of the most striking aspects of this project has been its major commitment to public space."[84]

Just about the same time, the suggestion of an admission tax was floated before the City Council once again. The City was looking at ways to fund the $500 million in infrastructure improvements expected of them, including the two giant parking garages. Disney reminded the City that it "has historically been opposed to any admissions tax" and suggested that such a tax could derail the expansion. In spite of a city deficit of $20 million and the possibility of layoffs for city employees as well as severe budget cuts, the City Council backed down again.

Tourism was down for the third year. Local officials blamed the decline on the recession, an earthquake, and civil unrest related to the Rodney King police brutality case verdict. Disneyland attendance dropped to 11.6 million in 1992.[85]

While the Walt Disney Company continued to talk with the community, what the public did not know was that the company was starting to have second thoughts about their expansion plans. The lack of confidence in California tourism, the delays in the entitlement process, and the slow start for EuroDisneyland were making Michael Eisner concerned.

A COMPLETE CHARACTER COMMUNITY

WHAT IS MICKEY'S TOONTOWN? As the story goes, according to Disney show writers, Mickey Mouse was feeling trapped due to his fame. Between 1928 and 1931, he had made 30 cartoon shorts and he practically lived at the Studio. He decided to buy a suburban house in one of the exclusive "Toon Only" cities said to exist outside of Hollywood. Mickey's Disney friends moved out to the suburbs with him, and he decided to make a film studio out of his barn so he wouldn't have to drive into Hollywood quite so much. One day in the early 1950s, Walt came to Mickey's Toontown for a visit. Walt was one of the very few non-Toons allowed. Walt talked about his idea for a park, and Mickey suggested he should build it right next door to Toontown. In 1990, the residents of Toontown decided they wanted to open the place up to non-Toon guests.

The reality, according to Imagineer Joe Lanzisero, was a "mandate … to create a one-on-one experience with Mickey Mouse."[86] The area was designed for guests who were 3–9 years old, and the town was vaguely based on Mickey's Starland, which opened in the Magic Kingdom in 1988. The new area in Disneyland was also inspired by the success of Camp Snoopy at Knott's Berry Farm. One Knott's spokesperson said, "They took a page from our playbook."[87]

On January 26, 1993, the 3.2-acre Mickey's Toontown opened at the north end of the park, just beyond the railroad tracks. Disney promoted the addition as "a complete character community" with a "downtown, a suburban neighborhood, and rural areas that feature Disney characters at home, work, and play."[88] Show producer Dave Burkhart said, "You aren't just going to see a set; you're going to experience a living, breathing, three-dimensional cartoon environment. Everything is exaggerated. There are no straight lines or conventional architecture. Nothing is 'real' in Mickey's Toontown. It's composed completely of cartoon elements."[89]

Joe Lanzisero explained, "We spent weeks in the Disney Archives and art libraries, researching sixty years of cartoon history. But there was no definitive Mickey's house or Goofy's house. It was up to the Imagineers to invent them."[90] He suggested, "No one has ever built buildings that look fat and inflated with air with no right angles. In many cases, our drawings and character elevations and the structures holding them up had very little to do with each other."[91]

Lanzisero felt that "there is a flow and rhythm to this land you won't find anywhere else. All the architectural elements follow certain lines, none of which are straight. Everything has a strong internal logic that makes sense, but it can only make sense in Toontown."[92] Mickey's Toontown was divided into three areas: Downtown Toontown, Toontown Square, and Mickey's Neighborhood.

Downtown Toontown became home to many interactive exhibits and photo opportunities, including the dog pound, where children snuck between the rubber bars; the fireworks factory, where they detonated cartoon explosives; and the post office, where cartoon characters had talking letter boxes. Children could try to lift the dumbbell at the nearby Horace Horsecollar's Gymnasium. Also nearby was the Toontown Fire Department and the Camera Shop, where ringing the doorbells could get an unexpected response. Even the manhole covers and post office box talked back to the guests. The two stores, the Gag Factory and the Toontown Five & Dime, became very popular.

Toontown Square was a cleverly disguised food court with three restaurants: Daisy's Diner, Pluto's Dog House, and Clarabelle's Frozen Yogurt. Throughout the area were other embedded gags, such as the facades for the 3rd Little Piggy Bank, the Planning Commission with a poorly planned sign, the Department of Street Repair with its sign in disrepair, the Department of Ink & Paint, the Toontown Sckool, the Library, and the Toontown City Hall with an animated Glockenspiel tower. Cartoon characters performed on a bandstand in the center of the square. The Goofy Water talking drinking fountains guaranteed a laugh. Beth Dunlop said, "[Toontown] is also very funny, layering joke upon joke, and offering up a good solid parody of real towns."[93]

The backdrop to Mickey's Neighborhood was the 40-foot-tall Toon Hills. Perched on the side of the hill was a sign that looked vaguely reminiscent of the HOLLYWOOD sign, a famous Los Angeles landmark. In Mickey's Neighborhood, guests could explore the classic yellow and red California bungalow where Mickey lived. As guests toured the living room and den, they enjoyed an incredible collection of Mickey's mementos. A doorway led to his garden and Pluto's doghouse. The garden path led to Mickey's barn, where guests could pose for pictures with Mickey on the set of *Steamboat Willie, The Band Concert, Thru the Mirror,* or *The Sorcerer's Apprentice.*

Right next door was Minnie's purple painted house. As guests wandered through her house, they could eavesdrop on Minnie's answering machine, sample the perfume on her dressing table, and experiment with her fashion options via a dressing room computer. Minnie had a lot of photos of Mickey, and she collected magazines like *Cosmousepolitan* and *Mademouselle.* In her kitchen, guests could turn a switch on her stove and bake a cake, or turn on the dishwasher to see the dishes transform into a balancing circus of tableware. Inside of the Cheesemore refrigerator was every type of cheese imaginable. Linking Mickey and Minnie's houses together was a wishing well out back.

Goofy's Gas had more food and, of course, the restrooms. Interactive public pay phones allowed guests to make calls and insert cartoon sounds. In Goofy's Bounce House, children could literally bounce off the walls, floor, furniture, and even the fireplace. In the yard were spinning flowers, popcorn stalks, watery watermelons, and squashed squashes.

One of the associates of a high-level Disney executive visited Walt Disney World and returned with complaints that there was not very much for her toddler to do. Suddenly, it became a companywide initiative to place as many toddler playgrounds in the parks as possible. Disney corporate lawyers were not pleased because the Bounce House was the site of frequent accidents caused by overzealous children flying into each other.

Next to Goofy was the *Miss Daisy,* Donald Duck's boat filled with interactive elements. Children could climb on a net; play with the periscope, whistle, bell, and foghorn; and ride a spiral slide from the upper deck to the boiler room. Upon close inspection, it becomes obvious that the boat is actually Donald. The top of the wheelhouse is Donald's hat, the bow is painted like his shirt, and the whole shape looks like a duck bill.

The only ride that was ready when Mickey's Toontown opened was Gadget's Go-Coaster from *Chip 'n Dale's Rescue Rangers.* It was a miniature roller coaster, made from oversize combs, toothbrushes, matches, scissors, and wooden block toys. Animated frogs squirted water over passing riders as they rode in cars that looked like they were made from hollowed-out acorns. Just beyond was the Chip 'n Dale Tree Slide and Acorn Crawl. There were two slides inside of the tree house and a pit filled with thousands of plastic acorns for younger children to dive into, roll in, and crawl through. Unfortunately, the maintenance crew had to close the pit frequently to clean up "accidents," so the acorns were soon removed.

Connecting all three areas together were the two Jolly Trolleys. The cartoon-shaped trolley had a giant wind-up key on top, and it would pitch and weave as it made its way around the two fountains at each end of the land. One of those fountains was known as Mickey's Fountain and featured pads in the pavement that triggered various audio and animation effects. The Jolly Trolley would not last long, and one was sold on eBay.

On March 17, 1993, the Tahitian Terrace closed; it reopened on July 1 as Aladdin's Oasis. One thing that was consistent during the Eisner era: If somebody was making money, Disney was keen to copy

GOOFY'S BOUNCE HOUSE became Goofy's Playhouse in March 2006. The yard was ripped up and replaced with rubberized ground covering, toys, and features aimed at 18- to 30-month-old toddlers. One immediate problem was the use of reflective clear-coat paint on items the children might touch. While the paint looked good, the items got so hot that they had to be closed down during the middle of the day.

that idea. In nearby Buena Park, two dinner shows, *Medieval Times* and *Wild Bill's Western Extravaganza,* were packing in the customers. During a Facility Development Team meeting, Executive Show Producer Eddie Sotto remembered, "Someone mentioned the plans to rehab the waterfall for the Tahitian Terrace. I wondered if there were anything we could do to the facility, and I asked what if we did an *Aladdin* show. It just took off from there."[94] David Mumford was assigned the design responsibilities for the $1 million showcase, and he came up with a venue that would allow for up to eight shows a day.

PARTNERS

BY 1993, Anaheim businesses and residents were starting to take up positions on opposite sides with regards to the Disneyland expansion. Local business leaders and major corporations organized as Westcot 2000 in support of the project.[95] They were bolstered by an optimistic economic benefit report drafted by Chapman University.[96] Jack Lindquist insisted, "The Disney project and the Disneyland Resort is the right project in the right place at the right time. It's what Anaheim needs, it's what Disney needs, it's what California needs."[97] The *Orange County Register* weighed in on the issue of responsibility and suggested Disney "is an environmentally responsible company and is always eager to be a good neighbor" and that they "could handle the building and operation of some public facilities, such as roads, that benefit it most directly." In exchange, government officials would lessen the environmental regulatory restrictions and even "consider the notion of eventually turning over the freeways to private businesses like Disney."[98] Most of the opposition came from residents raising questions about noise, traffic, and other effects on local services, such as schools and water.

On April 28, 1993, the Anaheim Planning Commission took up the expansion proposal for the first time. The Planning Commission expected large crowds, so the meeting was moved from City Hall to a ballroom at the Inn at the Park hotel. More than 750 people attended the meeting. By May, the Planning Commission had approved Disney's plans with 63 conditions, including the development of at least 500 affordable housing units and child-care services for park employees.[99]

City of Garden Grove officials were starting to complain that their needs were not being addressed by Disneyland. Consultants for Disney suggested that traffic concerns in Garden Grove were not their problem. Federal law stated that mitigation was only necessary if traffic counts on the freeway exceeded a 10% increase. The project was unlikely to cause that level of traffic in Garden Grove, so the company felt no obligation to fund local transit efforts.

However, Disney was listening to the Anaheim community and started to make concessions. A condominium adjacent to the property hired an attorney, and the homeowners got Disney to change elements of the proposed 16,700-car parking structure at the corner of Walnut Street and Ball Road. The massing of the structure was redesigned with setbacks to lessen the visual blight, and a 42-inch sound wall was proposed to lessen noise impacts. A frustrated Kerry Hunnewell complained, "That's, what, our fourth redesign of that garage?"[100]

The giant, 300-foot-tall Spacestation Earth, which was to be the centerpiece of WESTCOT, was changed to a slender 300-foot-tall spire. At the base would be a 35-foot-wide revolving blue and green globe. Underneath the spire would be a learning and entertainment center, with the nation's largest saltwater aquarium. The change in the massing of the icon was less motivated by neighborhood complaints than by the visual intrusion into Disneyland that the globe would have made. "By going to a slender shape, it's almost totally invisible from Disneyland," according to Tony Baxter. He added, "The castle symbolizes fantasy and happiness. The spire symbolizes hope and inspiration for the future." [101] Mayor Tom Daly of Anaheim said, "I like the distinctiveness."[102]

To reduce noise impacts, the 5,000-seat Disneyland Bowl amphitheater would be moved "as far away from anybody as geographically it could be," said Marty Sklar.[103] The Disneyland Center shopping and dining complex would no longer charge a $30 admission fee like Pleasure Island at Walt Disney World. In fact, the entire shopping mall was being scrapped. "We've brought the shops within the park," said Kenneth Wong, president of Imagineering. Instead, the lake would be surrounded by landscaping.[104] Local residents were disappointed by the removal of this public amenity. "That would have been a nice feather to give the people something back," said longtime resident Sally White.[105]

They also announced an innovation in Disney resorts, something Michael Eisner wanted to do at the proposed Disney's America theme park in Virginia. The "Live the Dream" project called for three mini-hotels totaling 1,000 rooms inside the theme park. The facilities would be themed to Europe, Asia, and the Middle East. Guests would be allowed to use some of the attractions after-hours.[106]

Keith Murdoch, who was city manager when Walt first proposed to build in Anaheim, said, "If we had to go through all these hoops to establish Disneyland in the beginning, it probably wouldn't have been done."[107] Disney officials did warn Anaheim officials that if the EIR was challenged in court, it would kill the deal. Kerry Hunnewell said, "The project economics are very marginal now."[108]

With all the negative noise and implied threats, speculation became rampant as to what would happen if Disney decided not to proceed with the WESTCOT project. Although Disney had committed to pay the $502,000 engineering fee to design the freeway off-ramps that would lead directly into their parking structures, officials at the California Department of Transportation (Caltrans) were concerned. "You can't come in and ask us to incorporate these elements and then just say, 'Okay, we changed our minds,'" said Raouf Moussa. "If Disney called off the deal, the city of Anaheim would pay the bill."[109] To make up for the shortfall, some predicted the city would finally impose an entertainment tax on Disneyland admissions.[110] Adding to the concern was Eisner's statement in November that he was "not willing to invest in projects that promise no return" and suggested that they could stop reinvesting in the park and then let it run its course.[111]

On June 22, the Anaheim City Council certified the Disney Resort EIR. Mayor Tom Daly said, "It would be an understatement to say this is a milestone in the history of the city." Opposition leaders were not happy. "It was more of a ceremony than a meeting," said Jeff Kirsch of Anaheim H.O.M.E. The *Orange County Register* wanted the project to succeed and was concerned that "school officials might play selfish, greedy games that could scuttle the entire project."[112] However, an agreement between Disney and the Anaheim City School District to invest $2 million in the schools up front resolved that issue.[113]

Not satisfied with the City Council action, neighborhood organizations sponsored a petition drive to place the approval of the project on the ballot. They did not succeed. The Disney public relations effort was aggressive and based on a sophisticated marketing campaign to garner public support. There were constant hints that if the objections continued, something much smaller or nothing at all might get build. By October, most of the obstacles were slipping away, including the settlement of a lawsuit brought by five key properties: four motels along Katella Avenue and the Schlund family, who owned 14 acres that Disney wanted to control.

Back in 1962, sculptor Blaine Gibson had tried to capture the likeness of his boss in bronze. However, he was not satisfied with the result and he wanted to destroy the bust. The management at Retlaw had already taken possession, though, and they asked him to try again. Gibson noted, "Some people are kind of ticklish about busts and statues of themselves while they're still alive. They get a sense that we're trying to rush them."[114]

A few years later, after Walt had died, Gibson was working on a medal for CalArts. Walt's wife, Lillian, had refused to give permission to create a bust, portrait, or a statue. So it came as a surprise when Marty Sklar contacted Gibson and asked if he wanted to give the bust another try for Disneyland. Gibson figured that Eisner was behind the effort this time, and that he had finally convinced Lillian Disney to give her permission, which she did.

Sklar had suggested a life-size statue of Walt holding Mickey's hand while Mickey was holding an ice cream cone. Gibson started with some crude sketches, but he preferred to work in three dimensions and was known for doing what he felt was right, even if it did not match the drawings exactly. Sklar, Jack Lindquist, John Hench, and Gibson began to have concerns about the ice-cream cone. They felt it made Mickey appear a little too immature and it favored one lessee, like the Nestlé Company or Carnation. The group agreed that Mickey should just have his arm to his side. Due to the change, Gibson felt that the statue put more emphasis on Walt.

unofficial **TIP**
At some point over the years, Walt had told sculptor Blaine Gibson that he wished he was 1 inch taller. Gibson remembered that and decided to satisfy Walt's wish by making the statue 1 inch taller than life-size.

The statue was unveiled at the center of the Plaza Hub on November 18, 1993.

The economy was in the doldrums, and Disneyland was trying its best to attract guests. The opening of Mickey's Toontown bolstered the summer a bit but not enough. Disneyland's attendance was still down slightly in 1993, to 11.4 million visitors.

HIGHLIGHTING ITS ESSENCE

ON JANUARY 17, 1994, a 6.7-magnitude earthquake struck Northridge, about 50 miles northwest of Disneyland. The tremor was felt as far away as Las Vegas, almost 300 miles northeast of the epicenter. Chapman University economists predicted a 10% drop in Southern California tourism, and they were right. The earthquake, a weak economy, and the disappointing dearth of visitors coming to Los Angeles for the World Cup soccer championship all added up to a significant drop in attendance at Disneyland. Only 10.3 million guests passed through the turnstiles. The tough times at Disneyland resulted in layoffs and a management restructuring to "streamline the operations."

Much better news was the January 26 opening of Roger Rabbit's Car Toon Spin. It was the largest and longest dark ride ever designed for any Disney theme park, and it was the first time that guests could control their point of view. The innovative dark ride tried to capture "the crazy, zany cartoons of the '40s and '50s," according to show designer Joe Lanzisero. He had worked on the feature film *Who Framed Roger Rabbit?* and said, "The concept for the attraction grew out of a suggestion from Michael Eisner. In the early planning stages of Mickey's Toontown, he had suggested we utilize Roger Rabbit in one of the attractions."[115] The movie came out in 1988 and from a design perspective, Lanzisero said the "concept worked out well, since Roger is closer in temperament to what Toontown is all about, which is the cartoon shorts." He noted, "We aren't trying to tell the entire story of *Who Framed Roger Rabbit?* but rather highlighting its essence. I think our dark rides work best when we can take you someplace where you can't go in reality."[116]

unofficial **TIP**
Roger Rabbit's Car Toon Spin was based on a mid-1970s concept by Tony Baxter for an Ichabod Crane attraction where guests would ride in a spinning pumpkin.

The queue was one of the most remarkable features. Guests walked past gags lifted straight out of the cartoon world. Norman Doerges of Disneyland explained, "We know we are going to have a wait. So how can we make that wait time as enjoyable as possible?"[117] The solution was the creation of a preshow that became the first act. The lengthy queue was designed so that a guest could only see about a dozen people in front of and behind them, thereby hiding the size of the crowd. Some of the gags included a door where Bongo, the gorilla doorman, told guests to scram; Baby Herman's apartment, with the star in his crib smoking a stogie; and a trip through the room where the infamous Dip that erases 'toons was being brewed. Many of the building facades appeared to have faces.[118]

unofficial **TIP**
After a major accident at Roger Rabbit's Car Toon Spin in 2000, where a 4-year-old child fell under a vehicle and was severely injured, the attraction was shut down for 10 months to install new safety measures, including a door, taller sides, updated training procedures, and a sensor skirt around the bottom of the vehicle to stop it immediately if it bumps something 8 pounds or heavier. The child never fully recovered from the incident and died in 2009.

Once guests arrived at the loading area, which was dressed as the Toontown Cab Company, they were loaded into Lenny the Cab, Benny's cousin, and sent on a mission "to save Jessica Rabbit from the paws of the evil weasels, while avoiding a Toon's ultimate weakness—the Dip." Just as they turn the first corner, the cab hits a puddle of slimy Dip, and that causes the cab to spin around. Guests could control their modified Omnimover vehicle by turning a wheel similar to the Mad Tea Party. There were 16 Audio-Animatronics figures inside the ride, along with 59 animated props. Guests witnessed Jessica's kidnapping, crashed through the Bullina China Shoppe, were blown skyward in a power plant explosion, and fell into the Gag Warehouse. They narrowly escaped from the weasel's clutches with a portable hole, a gag taken from the Warner Brothers 1955 cartoon short "The Whole Idea."

MAKING US THINK TWICE

BOOSTERS OF THE DISNEYLAND EXPANSION were beginning to feel confident. The negotiations between Disney and Anaheim were almost done. Many of those who had objected to the expansion started to settle, including Garden Grove and the school districts.[119] Even the last lawsuit against the project by Tiffy's Restaurant was settled.[120] However, the Walt Disney Company was starting to have buyer's remorse.

Kerry Hunnewell, the Disney executive in charge of the project, had resigned just before the holidays in 1993, and the financial pressures from the failing EuroDisneyland were making Michael Eisner uneasy about really big projects. Eisner said, "I don't even know if there's going to be WESTCOT. We're at a real crossroads. We had a very big investment in Europe and it's difficult to deal with. This is an equally big investment. I don't know whether a private company can ever spend this kind of money."[121]

Hunnewell's boss, Kenneth Wong, said the process "has taken longer to get this far than we expected." He added, "We still don't have a project that pencils out. We have been pretty honest about that." The city was becoming increasingly frustrated as well. City Manager James Ruth said, "If this is an exercise in futility then we want to know about it."[122] Anaheim Mayor Tom Daly noted, "It's clear that there are internal business decisions and a variety of competitive factors which are influencing Disney's decision to move forward with WESTCOT." Eisner tried to reassure the community, "We are committed to Anaheim. Remember, Walt mortgaged his house to build Disneyland."[123]

It seemed that everybody was now waiting for Disney to commit, including Caltrans. Dealing with traffic congestion was one of the biggest concerns within the community and region. Caltrans was preparing for the long-awaited $1.6-billion widening of the Santa Ana

Freeway through Anaheim. In February, the agency agreed to commit $50 million in freeway ramps and a connection to a parking garage that would serve Disney. Lisa Mills, chief deputy at the Orange County Transportation Authority said, "We decided we couldn't afford to wait for their decision any longer, because of the widening project reaching that point and having to make construction and design decisions now, not later."[124]

The recent earthquake, fires, floods, and riots had put a damper on the Southern California tourism industry. The public relations battle surrounding the now-defunct proposal to build Disney's America, a history-based theme park in Virginia, had caught Eisner by surprise.[125] The staggering financial losses at Disneyland Paris took their toll. Disney lost $514.7 million from the European project. Roy E. Disney said, "Clearly, EuroDisney is making us think twice about a lot of things. WESTCOT is down the list a little bit."[126]

Eisner was looking for a new strategy. Disney told city officials that it might be another year before they announced what they were going to do, if anything, in the expansion areas. Disney officials said one condition for moving forward was a promise of up to $1 billion in public funding for infrastructure improvements, placing the burden back on public officials.[127]

When Disney had suggested that they only wanted to build 1,800 hotel rooms in the first phase instead of 4,600, Anaheim officials became very concerned. The Walt Disney Company had overbuilt the number of hotel rooms at EuroDisneyland, and that was a significant factor in the financial losses. From the City's point of view, this change undermined the tax revenue assumptions that would pay for the public improvements. The City was looking at spending up to $300 million to expand the sewers, redesign the streetscapes, create pedestrian walkways, and move the utility lines underground.[128] Mayor Daly said, "Anaheim residents tell me they want the area around Disneyland cleaned up, improved, beautified, and modernized."[129] He could only do this if Disney built the massive project they were proposing.

The JUNGLE CRUISE TRADING CO.

IN JULY 1994, THE JUNGLE CRUISE reopened after a six-month-long refurbishment. At the same time, ground was broken for the construction of Indiana Jones and the Temple of the Forbidden Eye.

Adventureland was the smallest land within the park and was notorious for its bottlenecks. The solution was to move the Jungle Cruise loading dock back to its original location, 15 feet into the jungle, and build a new two-story Boathouse. The course of the river was changed to accommodate the queue for the Indiana Jones ride.

To fit in better with the future E-ticket attraction, the Jungle Cruise became rooted in a different reality for the third time. When the attraction opened in 1955, it was a serious look at the jungle in keeping with the True-Life Adventure film series. Twenty years later, it took on a comic tone with the influence of Marc Davis. In keeping with the theme of the upcoming Indiana Jones attraction, the 1994 ride was transformed into a jungle outpost set in 1935. An extensive backstory was developed for the cast members, and the first new script in 10 years was introduced. Fully one-fifth of the script was revised. All of the jokes were set in the 1930s time frame, so any jokes about freeways were banned.[130]

The two-story Boathouse was an abandoned 1911 Victorian house at the edge of the jungle, built around the Dominguez palm tree that had been on the site since 1896. The structure had gone through several owners, including a river merchant, boat repair service, and now the Jungle Cruise Trading Co., a group of enterprising down-and-out skippers who had turned to tourism. The Boathouse was divided up into themed areas. The ground floor was a ticket booth, boat maintenance, and shipping. On the upper floor, guests wandered through three areas, including an infirmary, dispatch office, and the lounge. An Audio-Animatronics hornbill and cobra were moved into the boathouse. The upstairs provided plenty of room for an overflow queue and kept people out of the crowded pathway.

Fitting in the Indiana Jones queue was a major challenge. There was only 50 feet of frontage between the Jungle Cruise and the Swiss Family Treehouse. Bill Evans was brought in to survey every tree in the jungle. The landscape reflected 35 years of growth, and many of the plants were original. Five hundred trees were tagged and either relocated or saved. Some of the enormous bamboo had to be removed. Starting in October 1994, the queue was opened to the public as an attraction in its own right. This was a first for Disney, and it remained this way for six months until the actual ride opened.

Trying to stay relevant to younger audiences, Imagineer Kim Irvine was assigned to rename a couple of the Storybook Land Canal Boats after current characters. The two new boats would be the *Ariel* and the *Belle*. While she was selecting the names, she thought, "We really ought to start updating the Show by putting in scenes from our newest animated classics."[131] The intention was to install a Little Mermaid set, but Michael Eisner was so impressed with the concept he wanted an Aladdin model built as well. Toad Manor was removed and was replaced by the city of Agrabah. The little model had gold-leafed turrets, a reflecting pool, and miniature "palm" trees. Each tiny tree was in its own planter and attached to a drip irrigation system. The buildings incorporated fiber-optic lighting effects that simulated flickering candles. Past the canopy of Cecile Brunner roses was the Caves of Wonder, which had once been the site where guests could find the Wicked Witch from *Snow White*. Toward the end of the ride were scenes from *The Little Mermaid,* including Prince Eric's ship at anchor in the harbor and a glimpse into King Triton's kingdom. Other elements within the ride were rehabbed, and the landscaping was updated.

An ACCIDENT WAITING *to* HAPPEN

WALT WAS PROUD OF THE SKYWAY. It was another example of reconfiguring an existing technology in a way that nobody ever really thought of before and creating something new. In this case, the something new was a ski lift–type gondola transformed into a transportation system that gave his guests a chance to fly above the park and get a sense of their surroundings. The Skyway provided that kind of experience—it was as though they had been sprinkled by Tinker Bell's pixie dust. After carrying 150 million guests, the Skyway's last day of operation was November 9, 1994. The two support towers were removed within a week, and the pass through the Matterhorn was sealed up.[132]

The park blamed recent laws for making improvements financially infeasible. The Skyway was not accessible to those using wheelchairs, and it no longer met the safety codes for aerial tramways. After all, it was the first one in the United States, and the regulations had come later. To bring the Skyway up to code would have required elevators and other major modifications. The Imagineers considered a new, larger system with six-person gondolas that would be enclosed, air-conditioned, and heated. The trip would be faster, and, due to the size of the new buckets, and the new cable would go around the Matterhorn.

A third station to Critter Country was also considered.[133]

Park officials suggested that the Skyway was also a victim of declining popularity. Tony Baxter suggested the closure was all about saving money. He said, "Part of the dilemma with the Skyway was the cost of operating the park overall. Every time you add a new attraction like Indiana Jones, the cost of operating the park becomes more expensive. The result is a prevailing attitude that when something new opens up, something old should come down to offset the cost."[134] Park president Jack Lindquist was blunter. He said, "I am glad [the Skyway] closed. It was an accident waiting to happen."[135]

An initiative to repaint all of Main Street U.S.A. began in the fall of 1994. Disney claimed the project to be the most extensive rehabilitation of that part of the park since the grand opening. The project was partially motivated by the need to remove lead paint, which had become increasingly regulated since 1977. On many surfaces there were as many as 30–40 coats of paint. Special teams wearing hoods, masks, and gloves had to go in and strip the walls.

Main Street was primarily made up of four large buildings made pedestrian friendly by facades that emulated much smaller shops. The frequent doors and windows created a lively rhythm as guests walked down the street. "As we converted certain buildings on Main Street, such as the Emporium 'annex,' we put a new color scheme on the facade," said Imagineer Kim Irvine. "We just couldn't change the interior color scheme and leave the outside; we had to do the whole building from start to finish."[136] The new color scheme was much brighter, just like Main Street U.S.A. in Florida. Disneyland's original Main Street was painted in more realistic colors, with lots of grays and tans.

Irvine said, "The individual facades were not as evident because the more mundane colors prevailed in the overall color scheme." The new exterior paint schemes reflected the products that could be purchased inside. The Candy Shop was painted in seafoam green, peach, and cream. "For Disney Clothiers we selected shades of grays, blues, and wine, similar to the colors you'd find in a man's necktie," according to Irvine. "Originally that was supposed to be a man's clothing store, so they wanted it to look masculine." The bank building was refaced in marble, the train station got a new roof, and all of the original wood ornaments along the street were removed and recast in either fiberglass or a resin-type material. The original wood structures were reinforced structurally. The project would continue into 1995.[137]

INVISIBLE TECHNOLOGY

FOR THE DISNEYLAND RESORT EXPANSION plan to work, the Walt Disney Company had to lobby public officials for assistance during a recession. Even with federal, state, and city money tight, the politicians did what they were asked. Congress allocated transportation funds, California Governor Pete Wilson arranged for $60 million in state funding, and the city of Anaheim rezoned the area and increased the hotel tax to pay for infrastructure improvements. But things were changing at Disney.

At the beginning of 1995, David Malmuth took over from Kenneth Wong as the head of the expansion project.[138] Wong was put in charge once Kerry Hunnewell left at the end of 1993. Malmuth had worked on the Port Disney project and said, "We have to figure out a project that works financially and that is also a creative home run."[139] It did not take long for the team to realize that it was a bigger task than they could accomplish; by January 30, the development team had failed to come up with the right answer, and it was over. The Disneyland expansion was not going to happen the way it had been first sold to the public four years earlier.

The Walt Disney Company walked away from options to purchase six parcels of land, including 10 acres at Harbor Boulevard and Freedman Way where Melodyland stood. This was the site where they had planned to build a 12,000-space parking structure and transportation center. Disney officials met with the City to explain why they were not renewing those options; Malmuth recounted, "We concluded that, at today's land prices these options just were not economic. It did not make sense given the price." According to Disneyland President Paul Pressler, "What we had originally envisioned was a very large resort. What we are looking at today is the ability to break it into component parts and build on it." He added, "We are going to build a second gate, absolutely." One senior Disney executive who was instrumental in the design of EPCOT, Marty Sklar, was not so sad to see the WESTCOT center project die. "I prefer not to spend six to seven years of my life on something that's already been done."

The introduction of new technologies during the period of 1985 and 1990 made things possible that were unimaginable just a few years before. When Star Tours debuted in 1987, there was nothing quite like it. The Indiana Jones attraction was in response to the changing habits of a new generation of children. Born into a world of video games, they were used to nonlinear stories, delivered in rapid fashion with a certain level of control. They are used to electronics and less impressed with mechanical effects. Their preference is entertainment that was unpredictable, non-repetitive, and energetic. "What I really like about this Indiana Jones ride is that it takes the technology of Star Tours and then throws it back in time in a way where it's not just a gimmick," said Tony Baxter. "This ride goes somewhere. You really go into the environment, and everything that happens, happens because of your being in there."[140] Indiana Jones Adventure and the Temple of the Forbidden Eye opened on March 3, 1995.

According to Baxter, Indiana Jones was his baby.[141] He came up with the concept and the basic story line. Although Baxter was not a mechanical engineer, he developed the principles of the ride system. The engineers created a mock-up as a way to develop the technology.

The critical piece of technology was the troop transport. The solution was the creation of the patented Enhanced Motion System (EMS), engineered by Bill Wolf and Ed Fritz. Basically, the vehicle was a motion simulator similar to Star Tours, but on a moving platform. The chassis supported the hydraulic motion passenger carriage on top. They wanted to create a vehicle that would feel like a four-wheel truck that was capable of going anywhere. When management felt the EMS could work, then they would commit to building the attraction.

A test track was set up in a facility in Valencia, California, near Magic Mountain and about 60 miles northwest of Disneyland. They worked on the vehicle development for more than two years. Not only did they have to prove the vehicles could operate, but they also had to demonstrate that they could be reliable from 8 in the morning to midnight every day. It was also the highest-capacity thrill ride in the park.

During the testing, Michael Eisner went to see the progress on the EMS. The engineers built about half the ride and had the ability to change the programming and the lighting in real time. Baxter said, "Michael was impressed and joked that if we spread flyers around the Magic Mountain parking lot we could get a bunch of people up to our test facility to have the ride of their lives."[142] Then they gave George Lucas a ride. According to Baxter, he "showed up eating two chocolate donuts with a cup of orange juice. I thought, 'Uh-Oh!' When he got off he had beads of sweat on his forehead, and said that it was fine . . . he didn't want to go on it a second time, though. I figure it passed its test if it scared the bejesus out of George."[143]

With the EMS concept proven, production on the rest of the attraction started in earnest. The 15 vehicles each weighed 12,800 pounds and could carry 12 guests. They wanted to call them Jeeps, but that was a Chrysler trademark. Each vehicle was operated by a dedicated programmable logic control (PLC) system, and that was linked to another computer in the control room. The PLC ran the ride systems, kept it safe, told the transports when they could go or when they had to wait. The transports were connected to a 2,500-linear-foot bus bar that provided AC power and the communications line to the master control system. The result was that each vehicle could be programmed differently, with up to 160,000 possible combinations. Guests endured or enjoyed (depending on their point of view!) a random experience while moving through a physical space. To achieve this level of sophistication, each of the vehicles had more computing power than the entire control system for Space Mountain.

Each of the vehicles had three different soundtracks on board. One was music, one was effects and dialogue, and one was motor sounds; and they were all programmable and variable. John Williams's film score was adapted, arranged, and then rerecorded by a 90-piece orchestra at Todd AO studio in Hollywood under the direction of Richard Bellis.[144]

Indiana Jones Adventure and the Temple of the Forbidden Eye was set in 1935. Indiana's good friend Sallah had found a piece of a treasure map that showed the way to the idol Mara, according to the elaborate story conceived by the Imagineers. Set in The Lost Delta of India, Mara promised that those who visited the temple "pure of heart" would receive one of three gifts: eternal youth, dazzling wealth, or the ability to see into the future. Another friend, archaeologist Marcus Brody, funded an expedition, and one month later Indy figured out the trick. "The eyes of the idol! That's the trap! Don't look into the eyes of Mara." Once the word got out about the discovery, tourists flocked from everywhere. Indy tried to warn them, but many did not take his advice. In fact, he said, "Records indicate that many have come . . . but few have returned." As any fan of the film series knows, Indy was not fond of crowds and preferred to work alone. So Sallah put together the transports to keep the tourists busy while Indy continued with his work.

If the guests did not look at the eyes of Mara, all was well. However, somebody always looked. "It's not an adventure about characters you're watching and not one controlled by a pilot or someone else," said Baxter. "It's not. It's determined by you going through it and participating in it."[145] He said of Pirates of the Caribbean, "Everything happens whether you are in there or not . . . as if you were eavesdropping on something already underway." For Indiana Jones, "Had you made the right choices at the beginning, you would have gone on to your reward, but because you didn't . . . you're caught in a mess and you're trying to find your way out. All the explosions and catastrophes happen because of you being there."[146]

One of the most spectacular elements to Indiana Jones was the queue. Like the Haunted Mansion and Pirates of the Caribbean, designers had to place the huge show building outside the berm in the Eeyore section of the Disneyland parking lot. At three stories and as long and wide as a football field, it was so large that the designers had to move some of the monorail pylons.[147]

The eighth-of-a-mile queue became an attraction in itself. Guests started at the archeological base camp and staging area in the Temple courtyard. The Troop Transport out front with the Lost Delta Expeditions logo was the famous truck under which Indiana crawls in *Raiders of the Lost Ark*. It was found in England, and the golf balls used for the filming were still on the vehicle. The placement of the truck was to suggest that this would be the type of vehicle the guests could expect to ride in. The generator ran the lights throughout the queue, with the result that the lights would flicker in time with the generator. Imagineer Pat Burke found many of the machinery artifacts, just like he did for Big Thunder Mountain Railroad. In the background was a vintage radio broadcast, with frequent reports of guests who have gone missing after a visit to the temple. Imagineers left a treat for sharp-eyed guests: a figure of Walt hidden among the artifacts. A ramp that looked like it was set up to move artifacts out of the temple served two functions. It avoided the stairs in front of the temple and it made wheelchair access easier. However, in time, wheelchair access would be through the exit tunnel.

It is no coincidence that there were snakes carved in the newel posts on the stairs leading up to the temple. Just past the entrance, guests encountered a mural of the deity Mara with subtle hints on what needs to be done in order to receive a reward. However, the obelisk in the next room was not so kind; it suggested the types of punishment for those not worthy. Ways to perish included snakes, rats, fire, and spikes. The queue became a walk-through of labyrinthine rooms and narrow passages. The tunnel was designed to force people to walk in pairs, which made the line appear to be moving faster.[148] This concept of forcing guests through tight spaces and into a large entrance room had been a longtime Disney tradition, as seen in the Attic segment of the Haunted Mansion and the tunnel before the *Wicked Wench* in Pirates of the Caribbean.

Throughout the queue were warnings written in Maraglyphics. When the attraction first opened, guests were handed a decoder card so they could translate the various warnings and suggestions while they waited in the queue. Those who did learned that "Only one spring can restore youth and vigor, choose wisely." There was also a subtle reminder in Maraglyphics that the ride was sponsored by AT&T.[149]

Continuing down the path, guests came to the Bamboo Canyon, which were actually large doors that allowed the Jungle Cruise elephants to be moved backstage for maintenance. Just beyond were the Bat Caves. The Spike Room was inspired by a scene in *Indiana Jones and the Temple of Doom* and had an inscription near the round stone door at the gateway, "The Gates of Doom are Ever Open." There was an interactive element where the falling ceiling was held up by one bamboo pole. If a guest in the know ignored the DO NOT TOUCH sign, the animated ceiling would fall a couple of inches. The Block Room next door, inspired by *Raiders of the Lost Ark,* was originally meant to have the same type of interaction; had it been fully developed, guests would have been warned to avoid stepping on diamond tiles on the floor.

The Rotunda, also known as the Calendar Room, was a large space with pictographs representing the natives offering gifts to Mara while wisely shielding their eyes. Their mantra was "Plow the field, plant the seed, reap the harvest, tribute to Mara." Another interactive element was the archaeologist, voiced by Imagineer Eddie Soto. As guests waited in the Rotunda, there was a rope with a warning sign: DO NOT PULL THE ROPE! HANDLING DELICATE ARTIFACTS. Of course, given human nature, there was always a guest who would pull the rope, and the consequences were quite humorous, involving an annoyed and ultimately unlucky excavator.

In the Film Room, guests watched the safety film, cleverly disguised as a 1935-era "Eye On The Globe" newsreel. A vintage 16-millimeter film projector, a slide projector, and an old Eeyore parking sign were set above the audience on scaffolding. The next room was Dr. Jones's Office. It was built out of crates labeled with the addresses of his friends, including one for Star Wars' Obi Wan Kenobi. The bulletin board was rich in details, including a themed map of the entire attraction with its many variations.

By the time the guests reached the loading dock, they had been fully immersed in the world of Indiana Jones and the Lost Delta. The queue set the stage the same way Frontierland did for the *Mark Twain* and New Orleans Square did for Pirates of the Caribbean and the Haunted Mansion.

Another signature Disney design detail included in Indiana Jones was that guests were able to preview the loading and unloading process in operation before they boarded. To access the loading area, guests walked upstairs and crossed over to the platform, passing by artifacts ready for shipment. For Indiana Jones, the preview was a necessary feature, as Disney tried to maintain two loading platforms, with each transport launching every 18–36 seconds.

The ride began in the Chamber of Destiny. If guests cleared their minds and allowed Mara to peer into their souls, they could determine which door to open. Sallah had set up antique mirrors so guests could see ahead of them, and typically their vehicle would go through a different door than the preceding vehicle. The illusion was achieved by one entry point and five doors that could swing from side to side in 18 seconds. The design objective was to create a slightly different experience every time the guest rode the attraction. Creating sets with interchangeable components made this possible.

As the transports entered the Hall of Promise—a narrow corridor with a steep grade—the room's decor changed to reflect the reward. If the prize was the "Treasure of Mara," then the walls would be lined with glittering gold. If the prize was "timeless youth and beauty," then blue-tinted walls would be covered with murals of old pilgrims turning young again. Finally, if the prize was Mara lifting "the curtain of time" with future knowledge, then the guests would be engulfed by a sky filled with 5,000 fiber-optic stars. The room was also one of the rare times guests could see the track.

A sharp turn to the left and the transports entered the Tunnel of Torment. This segment had been programmed by Imagineer Dave Durham to give the illusion that the vehicles were silently floating toward the Gates of Doom. It was inspired by the motion of the ghosts that emerged at the end of *Raiders of the Lost Ark*.

In front of the Gates of Doom, the guests met Indiana Jones for the first time. He was trying to hold the door closed while a mysterious vortex swirled behind him. The spell then broke, and the transport fell to the ground. Unfortunately, Harrison Ford's voice could not be used in the attraction due to cost and creative control. He was also negotiating for a fourth film at the time.[150]

Another narrow passage led to the huge Cavern of Bubbling Death. From the top of the passage, guests looked into the inner chamber; this outlook was described as the "Christmas Morning" view due to all the action below. The cavern was 100 feet by 140 feet and 50 feet tall. There is a 45-foot skull of Mara. The inspiration for having the ride wind in and out of this large room was the Glory Hole at Knott's Berry Farm's Calico Mine Train.

The first side room was the Mummy Chamber, a segment inspired by the scene in *Raiders of the Lost Ark* when Marion and Indy break through a wall in the Well of Souls and find themselves covered with mummies. A fan produced a 60-mph wind to enhance the sensation of speed. Maintenance did not clean the room, and the cobwebs were allowed to accumulate. One mummy was wearing a pair of Mickey Mouse ears. While driving through the Insect Room, guests heard the shells of the insects popping underneath them. Back into the Cavern, the transports must cross the Rope Bridge. Each vehicle reacted differently as they crossed. Some would stall or cross over quickly, while others would tip to look over the edge or would shudder as though the rear wheel had fallen off.

On the other side was the Snake Room. Guests were confronted with 2,129 sculpted, carved, painted, or living representations of snakes.[151] There was one that was 50 feet long; Imagineers had chosen that scale to emulate a close-up. Unique to Indiana Jones, the vehicles would become the storytellers in the show. For example, as the transporters approached the large snake, it would seem to recoil from the attack.

Quickly escaping from the snakes, guests headed straight for the Mara Skull, where there were more than 2,000 replicated human skulls. Down through the lower level of the Cavern was the Rat Room, with the vermin projected on a mist screen. The sound of the little rat feet could be heard through the transport. In the Dart Room, a segment inspired by the opening sequence in *Raiders of the Lost Ark,* compressed air jets blasted the guests from both sides.

The climax of the attraction was the Rolling Ball segment. Here, Indy was hanging from a rope, calling out to those in the transport to help him down. Unexpectedly, a 16-foot boulder started to roll toward the guests. The transport reacted by suddenly backing up. The remarkable illusion was inspired by a drive-through car wash. One day Tony Baxter was sitting in an automobile going through a car wash and he noticed that although he was sitting still, the moving machinery around him created the illusion that he was moving backwards. He took this idea and applied to the ride. In this segment of the ride, only the walls in the room were actually moving; then the transport rushed forward and guests saw the giant ball smashed and a weary Indy waving goodbye.

Baxter was proud of the attraction. He said, "So to be able to replace the Avatar and actually be the person in that world is the whole joy of it . . . to be able to actually go to places in an imaginary world." He noted, "We've taken the effects and dramatics of a simulator and put it into a real environment. No one's going to know that on the ride, because there's no opportunity to see the motion simulator in action. It absolutely feels as if the vehicle is doing everything it appears to be doing."[152]

Over the years, enhancements were made to the attraction, while some of the special effects disappeared. The Indiana Jones and Gates of Doom effect was upgraded in 2010, and in 2012 the ride went down for months as part of a major refurbishment and reopened at the end of the year.

The ANAHEIM PROBLEM

MUCH OF NEW ORLEANS SQUARE had remained pretty much the same since it opened in 1966. In 1995, the park merchandising department wanted to transform the quiet corner into a place where it is Mardi Gras every day. In the spring, the "new" New Orleans Square opened. The stodgy One-of-a-Kind shop, a store Walt had personally put in place, was transformed into a store where guests could design their own hats. T-shirts joined the pirate gear at the Piece of Eight store, while Le Gourmet added a scent dispenser pumping out the smell of pralines. Mlle. Antoinette's Parfumerie went unisex, and the new Le Bat en Rouge was designed by Imagineer Eddie Soto in a Gothic style to "celebrates the spirit of Halloween all year long."[153]

Over in Fantasyland, the Matterhorn Bobsleds reopened in the spring after a lengthy rehabilitation. A new exterior feature was the addition of a rockwork "teacup handle" visible only from the Mad Tea Party. More obvious was the removal of the holes where the Skyway had once passed through. The open sides were sealed up and a new Glacier Grotto was installed inside, with eerie clouds, spooky sounds, and massive stalactites. Inside one of the ice caverns was a tribute to Walt Disney Company President and CEO Frank G. Wells, an avid mountain climber who had climbed six of the highest mountains on each of the seven continents before he died in a helicopter accident in 1994. Ride control systems were updated, including new computers and software, as well as the lift hill mechanism.[154]

For the park's 40th anniversary, a Time Castle with more than 60 items was sealed and lowered into a vault in front of Sleeping Beauty Castle. The vault, which was not to be opened until Disneyland's 80th anniversary on July 17, 2035, was filled with a "Mickey" cast member name tag, a 1995 pay stub, a laser disc player, and lots of 40th anniversary memorabilia.[155]

On August 2, 1995, a group of about 40 high-ranking Walt Disney Company executives assembled in Aspen, Colorado, for a three-day brainstorming session to deal with "The Anaheim Problem."[156] The group was broken up into five teams, and it was the job of each team to develop its own concept. Kenneth Wong said, "We had all kinds of crazy ideas. If you could look at them all, it would be hilarious. You wouldn't be able to trace any linear logic—the creative process doesn't work that way."[157] Ideas ranged from a trip along Route 66, sports-related themes, and a celebration of the natural world.

At the end of the retreat, the different design teams pitched their concepts to Michael Eisner. The Disney CEO sat quietly and listened to each of the presentations. After Eisner heard the pitch from Disneyland President Paul Pressler and Imagineer Barry Braverman he said, "You know what? California is the big idea. We can do everything we want to do under that umbrella. People are seeking that perfect, idealized California, and we will be able to deliver it to them."[158] With that, Disney's California Adventure theme park was born. Anaheim was finally going to get a second gate.

One more piece in the Disneyland Resort concept was put into place in December 1995: For the first time in 40 years, Disney owned two hotels adjacent to the park. They purchased the 502-room Pan Pacific Hotel from the Tokyu Corporation for an estimated $36 million. Built in 1984, the hotel was on 4.6 acres, south of the Disneyland Hotel on West Street and adjacent to the monorail station. Disney had tried to buy the hotel in 1991, but the two sides could not agree on a deal. In 1995, the hotel was remodeled and renamed the Disneyland Pacific Hotel.[159]

Attendance skyrocketed in 1995 to more than 14.1 million guests, making Disneyland the most visited theme park in the world. The 40th anniversary and the new Indiana Jones attraction were credited for the big crowds.

1. Dick Kleiner, "New Chief of Disney Studio Makes Plans," *Los Angeles Daily News Tribune,* 13 Dec. 1984.
2. Michael Eisner with Tony Schwartz, *Work In Progress* (New York: Hyperion Books, 2001).
3. "Walt Disney's Promise," *Anaheim Bulletin,* 31 May 1985.
4. Eisner with Schwartz, *Work In Progress.*
5. Ibid.
6. Ibid.
7. Barry Koltnow, "Disney Hopes Videopolis is Teen Magic," *Orange County Register,* 21 June 1985.
8. Bruce Horovitz, "Disneyland Will Open Teen Nightclub," *Los Angeles Times,* 23 April 1985.
9. Randy Bright, *Disneyland: Inside Story* (New York: Abrams, 1987).
10. Katherine Bird, "Punkers in Fantasyland," *Anaheim Bulletin,* 21 July 1985.
11. Julie Anne Dart, "Lucky Little Visitor to Disneyland Wins Big," *Los Angeles Times,* 25 August 1985.
12. Cheryl Downey Laskowitz, "Disneyland to be Open Every Day of the Year," *Orange County Register,* 6 Sept. 1985.
13. Gary Harmon, "Disneyland Plans Expansion, Major New Attractions," *Anaheim Bulletin,* 23 June 1986.
14. Harrison Price Company to Disney Development Company, "Specialty Center Business, Opportunities at Disney–Anaheim," Oct. 1986, Series I: Reports, 1952–2003; Real Estate and Other Development, 1960–2000; Festival Markets and Shopping Centers, Project Class: B18, 1967–2000; report number 205, box 32, folder 675; Harrison "Buzz" Price Papers, CFM2003_12, Special Collections & University Archives, University of Central Florida Libraries, Orlando, FL.
15. Bruce Horovitz, "Disneyland Sets Sights on Huge Park Expansion," *Los Angeles Times,* 22 June 1986.
16. "Tony Baxter—Disneyland's Idea Guy!," *The "E" Ticket,* Number 46, Summer 2009.
17. Amalia Duarte, "Disneyland Buys Wood From Demolished Bar," *Los Angeles Times,* 30 Oct. 1985.
18. Gary Harmon, "Disneyland to Offer Burros for Adoption," *Anaheim Bulletin,* 20 May 1986.
19. Angela Rocco DeCarlo, "The Disney Gallery: Disneyland's Second Floor Surprise," *Disney Magazine,* Summer 1994.
20. Disneyland, "Welcome to the Disney Gallery," press release, 1987.
21. Ibid.
22. Ibid.
23. "Our Own Super Highway in the Sky," *Disneyland Line,* 9 Sept. 1994.
24. Joe Ascenzi, "Disneyland Monorail Gets Facelift with a New Train," *Anaheim Bulletin,* 29 Jan. 1987.
25. Barbara A. Serrano, "Expanding the Magic Kingdom," *Orange County Register,* 26 July 1987.
26. Ibid.
27. Chris Richard, "Disney Official Says Company Might Support Redevelopment," *Anaheim Bulletin,* 6 June 1988.
28. Joe Ascenzi, "New Power Lines May Go Up in Disneyland Parking Lot," *Anaheim Bulletin,* 13 Feb. 1987.
29. Juanita Darling, "Disney May Get Long Beach Land," *Orange County Register,* 13 Jan. 1988.
30. Juanita Darling, "Disney Buys Rest of Wrather," *Los Angeles Times,* 30 March 1988.
31. James B. Stewart, *DisneyWar* (New York: Simon and Schuster, 2005).

32. "Splash Mountain: A Zip-a-Dee River Run," *Disneyland Line,* Winter 1988.
33. Ibid.
34. Eisner with Schwartz, *Work In Progress.*
35. "Magic Kingdoms Then and Now," *The "E" Ticket,* Number 22, Winter 1995, 12–23.
36. "Splash Mountain: A Zip-a-Dee River Run," *Disneyland Line.*
37. Ibid.
38. Ibid.
39. Kathleen Murray, "Pushing Back Splash Mountain," *Orange County Register,* 31 Jan. 1989.
40. Vicki Vaughan, "Planning Ensures Ride Isn't All Wet," *Orlando Sentinel,* 16 Sept. 1991.
41. Ibid.
42. Blair Howell, "Make Way For Splash Mountain," *Disneyland Line,* Dec. 1988.
43. Mary Ann Galante, "Disneyland Hopes to Duplicate 1985 with 35th Birthday Party," *Los Angeles Times,* 19 July 1989.
44. Allison Samuels, "Disneyland Erects New 'Happiest' Sign," *Los Angeles Times,* 23 Sept. 1989.
45. Disneyland, "Disneyland Celebration Announces Start of 'Disney Decade,'" press release, 12 Jan. 1990.
46. Ibid.
47. "Renovated Disney Emporium Set to Open Soon," *Orange County Register,* 23 May 1990.
48. Debra Cano, "Disney Backs Tourist Area Effort, Asks City to Delay Developments," *Anaheim Bulletin,* 16 March 1990.
49. Brett Sporich, "Building Moratorium in Tourist Area Lifted," *Anaheim Bulletin,* 18 Sept. 1991.
50. *Port Disney, Long Beach, California: preliminary master plan executive report* (Anaheim, CA: Walt Disney Company, July 1990).
51. Jeff Rowe, "Long Beach Considers a Seaside Theme Park," *Orange County Register,* 27 Nov. 1991.
52. Kotin, Regan & Mouchly, Inc., "Economic and Fiscal Impacts Port Disney" (Long Beach, CA: Walt Disney Company, Oct. 1990).
53. Ricky Young, "Freedom to Create," *Orange County Register,* 22 Dec. 1992.
54. Ibid.
55. Gina Shaffer, "Schools Lay Claim to Disney's Future," *Orange County Register,* 30 March 1993.
56. David Malmuth, "A Note to the Long Beach Community From David Malmuth," *Port Disney News,* 1991.
57. Mark Gladstone, "Disney's Coastal Theme Park Plan in Rough Waters," *Los Angeles Times,* 29 May 1991.
58. Mike Davis, "Will Cities Enter Mickey Mouse Deals to Survive?," *Los Angeles Times,* 11 Aug. 1991.
59. "Disneyland Resort Update," *Disneyland Neighborhood News,* Oct. 1991.
60. Brett Sporich, "Group Plans to Fight Parking Structure," *Orange County Register,* 16 May 1991.
61. "Mickey Mouse Deal," editorial, *Orange County Register,* 18 July 1991.
62. "Unequal Burdens," editorial, *Anaheim Bulletin,* 16 July 1991.
63. "Disney Should Pay," editorial, *Anaheim Bulletin,* 20 July 1991.
64. Ibid.
65. Ricky Young, "Disney Attractions to be Technological Treats," *Orange County Register,* 9 Aug. 1991.
66. Ibid.
67. "Building on Our Imagination," *Disneyland Line,* 27 Sept. 1991.

68. Jason Schultz and Kevin Yee, *Jason's Disneyland Almanac: 1955–2010* (Orlando, FL: Zauberreich Press, 2011).
69. Jack Lindquist, Ron Dominguez, and Kerry Hunnewell, Disneyland letter to William Griffith (Anaheim, CA, 12 Dec. 1991).
70. "Disneyland: Extending the Magic," *Disney News*, Spring 1992.
71. Terri Vermeulen, "City Leaders Thrilled Over Disney Pick," *Anaheim Bulletin*, 13 Dec. 1991.
72. Ricky Young, "Disney Will Build Resort in Anaheim," *Orange County Register*, 13 Dec. 1991.
73. Ibid.
74. E. Scott Reckard, "Disney Dumps *Queen Mary*, Spruce Goose," *Anaheim Bulletin*, 7 March 1992.
75. LoriAnn Basheda, "City to Cooperate on Disney Plans," *Anaheim Bulletin*, 10 May 1991.
76. William F. Powers, "Anaheim Strawberry Farmer is Dean of Disney Holdouts," *Washington Post*, 14 March 1994.
77. Kevin Johnson, "Strawberry Field Forever? Disney Can't Buy the Farm," *Los Angeles Times*, 31 March 1991.
78. *The Disneyland Resort: Preliminary Master Plan* (Anaheim, CA: Walt Disney Company, March 1991).
79. Lisa Richardson, "Anaheim Farm Now Disney's Land to Expand," *Los Angeles Times*, 16 Aug. 1998.
80. "Notes: Districting Discussion," *Anaheim Bulletin*, 11 April 1992.
81. Ricky Young, "Disney's Big, Big World," *Orange County Register*, 16 Dec. 1992.
82. Ibid.
83. Ricky Young, "Disney May Charge Admission to Six-Acre Shopping Zone," *Orange County Register*, 19 Dec. 1992.
84. Ibid.
85. Jeff Rowe, "OC Tourism Down Again for 1992," *Orange County Register*, 12 Jan. 1993.
86. Chris Woodyard, "Next Stop: Toontown, U.S.A.," *Los Angeles Times*, 21 Jan. 1993.
87. Ibid.
88. Ibid.
89. Ibid.
90. Ibid.
91. Ibid.
92. Ryan A. Harmon, "Toontown 92803," *Disneyland Line*, 7 Jan. 1994.
93. Beth Dunlop, *Building a Dream: The Art of Disney Architecture* (New York: Disney Editions, Inc., 2011).
94. Randy Lewis, "Rolling Out the Magic Carpet," *Los Angeles Times*, 3 July 1993.
95. Jeffrey Miller, "Westcot Backers Shun Small Protest," *Orange County Register*, 23 April 1993.
96. Chris Woodyard, "Executives Speak Up for Disney Expansion Plan," *Los Angeles Times*, 26 March 1993.
97. David Heitz, "Hoteliers Bemoan Dead-end," *Anaheim Bulletin*, 6 May 1993.
98. "Disney's Path," editorial, *Orange County Register*, 28 March 1993.
99. Matt Lait, "Disneyland Resort Clears Major City Hurdle," *Orange County Register*, 20 May 1993.
100. Ricky Young, "Parking Structure Revamped," *Orange County Register*, 17 April 1993.
101. Chris Woodyard, "Needle Replaces Sphere in Disney Resort Plan," *Orange County Register*, 23 April 1993.

102. Ibid.
103. Ricky Young, "Disneyland Shelves Plan for Park to have Lakefront Retail Area," *Orange County Register,* 23 April 1993.
104. Ibid.
105. Ibid.
106. Ricky Young, "Disney's Sweet Dreams," *Orange County Register,* 23 April 1993.
107. Hetz, "Hoteliers Bemoan Dead-end."
108. Jeff Rowe, "Disneyland Expansion Losing Momentum?," *Orange County Register,* 7 Nov. 1992.
109. Ricky Young, "If Disney Drops Expansion, who funds off-ramp redesign?," *Orange County Register,* 23 Dec. 1992.
110. Matt Lait, "Anaheim Mayor Backs Admissions Tax at Disneyland," *Los Angeles Times,* 17 Oct. 1992.
111. Jeff Rowe, "No More Magic Kingdom," *Orange County Register,* 22 June 1993.
112. "The Disney Dilemma," editorial, *Orange County Register,* 25 April 1993.
113. Matt Lait, "Schools Will Get $2 Million in Disney Resort Accord," *Los Angeles Times,* 15 Sept. 1993.
114. "Walt Disney's Sculptor: Blaine Gibson," *The "E" Ticket,* Number 21, Spring 1995.
115. "Taking Our Guests Out for a Spin," *Disneyland Line,* 7 Jan. 1994.
116. Ibid.
117. Chris Woodyard, "Wait Until You See Disney's New Attraction: a Fun Line," *Los Angeles Times,* 26 Jan. 1994.
118. "Taking Our Guests Out for a Spin," *Disneyland Line.*
119. Sarah Catz, "Transit Center is a Win-Win Project for the Public and Disney," *Orange County Register,* 31 July 1994.
120. Matt Lait, "Last Foe of Disney Resort Settles With City," *Los Angeles Times,* 9 March 1994.
121. Chris Woodyard and Matt Lait, "Disneyland Plans Dim as Project Chief Resigns," *Los Angeles Times,* 21 Dec. 1993.
122. Matt Lait and Chris Woodyard, "Is Anaheim Next in Line for a Rejection by Disney?," *Los Angeles Times,* 24 Dec. 1993.
123. Matt Lait and Chris Woodyard, "Anaheim Shaken by *Disney News,*" *Los Angeles Times,* 22 Dec. 1993.
124. Jeffrey Perlman, "Officials Pledge $50 Million for Disney Ramps," *Los Angeles Times,* 26 Feb. 1994.
125. William F. Powers, "Eisner Blasts Critics of Disney Virginia Park," The *Washington Post,* 14 June 1994.
126. Jeff Rowe, "Disney: a small, small time?," *Orange County Register,* 12 Dec. 1993.
127. Lait, "Mayor Backs Admissions Tax."
128. Gina Shaffer and Jeff Rowe, "Anaheim Spending Plan Boosts Disneyland Area," *Orange County Register,* 3 July 1994.
129. Gina Shaffer, "Massive Anaheim Face Lift?," *Orange County Register,* 10 June 1994.
130. "To a Thirties Theme," *Disneyland Line,* 22 July 1994.
131. Anne K. Okey, "Oh No! We've Been Swallowed by Monstro," *Disney News,* Fall 1994.
132. Jerry Hirsch, "Disney due to decide on park," *Orange County Register,* 5 Nov. 1994.
133. "Saying Goodbye to the Disneyland Skyway," *The Brake Zone,* Nov./Dec. 1994.
134. "Magic Kingdoms Then and Now," *The "E" Ticket.*

135. Jack Lindquist, interview with author, 22 Sep. 2012.
136. Kris Bromberger, "A Turn-of-the-Century Look for the 21st Century," *Disneyland Line,* 23 Sept. 1994.
137. Ibid.
138. Chris Woodyard, "Malmuth Appointed to Head New Disney Project," *Los Angeles Times,* 18 Jan. 1995.
139. Jeff Rowe, "Quiet man at helm of expansion project," *Orange County Register,* 5 Sept. 1994.
140. "If Adventure Has a Place," *The "E" Ticket,* Number 46, Summer 2009.
141. Ibid.
142. Steve Daly, "An Easy Ride for Disney?," *Entertainment Weekly,* 3 Feb. 1995.
143. Ibid.
144. Disneyland, "Indiana Jones Adventure Fact Sheet" (Anaheim, CA, undated).
145. Patrick Alo, "Uncovering the Indiana Jones Adventure," *Disney Magazine,* Spring 1995.
146. Ibid.
147. Steve Daly, "An Easy Ride for Disney?"
148. Jeff Rowe, "Wait is Half the Fun," *Orange County Register,* 31 May 1996.
149. Disneyland, "Indiana Jones Adventure Temple Queue and Pre-show," press release, Jan. 1995.
150. Steve Daly, "An Easy Ride for Disney?"
151. "Themed Adventures," *Disney Magazine,* Spring 1996, 38–61.
152. "If Adventure Has a Place," *The "E" Ticket,* Number 46, Summer 2009.
153. "Nouvelle Orleans," *Disneyland Line,* 28 April 1995.
154. "Makeover for a Mountain," *Disneyland Line,* 21 April 1995.
155. Matthew Walker, "Disneyland's 40th Anniversary 'Time Castle,'" startedbyamouse.com, 30 March 2005.
156. "Disney Moves Forward," *Orange County Register,* 15 Oct. 1998.
157. Matt Lait and Greg Miller, "The Anaheim Problem Has a Happy Ending," *Los Angeles Times,* 18 July 1996.
158. Eisner with Schwartz, *Work In Progress.*
159. Debora Vrana, "Disney Acquires Pan Pacific Hotel in Anaheim," *Los Angeles Times,* 12 Dec. 1995.

CHAPTER 9

THE RESORT:
1996 *and* ONWARD

▌ PLAY *at the* EDGE

EVERY TIME MANAGEMENT asked Walt for a new administration building, he would reply with, "I don't want you guys sitting behind desks. I want you out in the Park, watching what people are doing and finding out how you can make the place more enjoyable for them." That was then. Michael Eisner had a different philosophy. He fancied himself as a patron of fine architecture, and he would give his managers what they wanted in 1996.

Eisner hired Pritzker Architecture Prize–winning architect Frank O. Gehry to design an office building on the property they purchased from Global Van Lines. "We wanted something functional that would meet operational and administrative requirements, and the budget was very modest. Also, the building was right on the freeway," said Gehry.[1] The Team Disney Anaheim building opened on February 15, 1996, at a cost of $35.6 million, according to city records. The project took seven years.

The whimsical building had two very different sides. Facing inward, the building's wavelike facade was painted a bright yellow. "The yellow is a color you don't use in a building; it's a color you use in making a cartoon," said Gehry. "I wanted to show you can play at the edge and stay within abstracts. You don't have to literally make the Disney images." He said of this side of the building, "I wanted it to be joyful. I wanted to play with the forms and create a sense of movement."[2] Architectural historian Beth Dunlop described it as "highly animated, conjuring images of some of Gehry's liveliest structures, including his 'Fred and Ginger' houses in Vienna and his Walt Disney Concert Hall in downtown Los Angeles."[3]

The facade facing the Santa Ana Freeway was a profoundly different statement. The forbidding 800-foot flat surface with deep-set windows appeared to peek out over a castle turret or a cow catcher from an old steam locomotive. It was sheathed in quilted stainless steel panels, which had been dipped in chemicals that deoxidize the surface. This created a dynamic patina that changes from yellow to purple to green as you look at it from different directions.

Dunlop noted, "Team Disney is four stories tall; like its counterpart in Lake Buena Vista in Florida, it is a skyscraper turned on its side, with almost 300,000 square feet of space. Though the lobby is bright magenta, work spaces are more subdued and feature pastel hues. Interior materials are classic Gehry—chain-link fence, plywood, undulating stairways."[4] The building could accommodate up to 1,250 cast members, and there was a seven-level parking structure capable of holding 1,600 vehicles. Inside were a 200-seat auditorium and a 400-seat cafeteria. One unintended consequence was that the new building blocked the view of the Matterhorn from the freeway—the first signal for many children that Disneyland was nearby.

ERASING LEO FREEDMAN

WITH MORE THAN 50,000 GUESTS on many days, Walt felt that Disneyland was more like a city than a theme park. At one point he wanted an official post office, which the United States government wouldn't do, and he wanted Caltrans to list Disneyland on one of their big green signs along the freeway.

Walt was to get neither while he was alive, but a $1.6 billion Santa Ana Freeway widening project in the late 1990s was an opportunity to implement at least one of Walt's wishes. To make it easier for guests to find their way to the resort parking lots, the Anaheim City Council decided to rename two streets. In 1998, Freedman Way would be renamed Disney Way.[5] This would be the primary access route for guests arriving from the south. Freedman Way was named after philanthropist Leo Freedman, who at one point owned the Grand Hotel, Melodyland, and the Celebrity Theatre. Freedman's family was opposed to the name change, especially after having given the city nearly $500,000 over the past few years through their foundation. In 1999, West Street would be renamed Disneyland Drive. That street was originally named West Street in 1857 when it formed the western boundary of the original German Colony of Anaheim.

The 10-story, 240-room Grand Hotel was originally named the Crest and was built in 1965 by Wilbur Clark, who was best known for the Desert Inn, El Rancho Vegas, and Stardust Hotels in Las Vegas. Freedman had wanted to also build a 22-story office tower between the hotel and the freeway but was thwarted by the height limitations imposed by Disney and Anaheim in 1964.

When the Walt Disney Company unveiled their plans for the expanded Disneyland Resort in 1991, the Grand Hotel site was shown to be part of the seven-story parking structure, even though the company did not own the property. Attorney Daren Brinkman, who represented the hotel, said, "That killed our advance bookings from tour groups and conventions. They didn't think the hotel was a going concern."[6] The hotel suffered and eventually went bankrupt. The Walt Disney Company acquired the $8 million mortgage in 1993 and began foreclosure proceedings in early 1995. Just before finalizing the foreclosure, the judge gave the existing owners a reprieve, and the hotel went up for bid. Disney won with a bid of $13.3 million. Disney took possession on April 26, 1996.

unofficial **TIP**
On March 22, 1998, at 6:55 a.m., the Grand Hotel building was imploded and the debris removed. The site would be used for temporary parking and held in reserve for later development.

There were rumors that Disney would operate the hotel until they needed the land, but that did not happen. The company immediately gutted the hotel and let it sit vacant for two years.

The park did make some minor changes in 1996. On May 14, Tom Sawyer Island was renamed Tom and Huck Island to promote a new video release. The name change did not last long.[7] One of the shops that Walt Disney had personally conceived of, the One-of-a-Kind Shop in New Orleans Square, was closed. Inspired by Space Mountain in Disneyland Paris, an audio system synchronized to a soundtrack was installed in the Disneyland Space Mountain trains. Each train had its own self-contained audio system and incorporated a sophisticated series of timing checks and balances both in the ride operating system and within the audio itself. Legendary surf guitarist Dick Dale provided the soundtrack with a recording of Camille Saint-Saens's "Le Carnaval des Animaux."

In the past, these types of changes happened quietly, and Disney management could pretty much do as they liked. Walt always insisted that the show be kept fresh and that change was necessary. Sometimes City Hall might get flooded with letters or complaints, but usually the Public Relations team could overcome the residents' frustrations.

> IN AN INTERVIEW WITH THE *Orange County Register* in April 1998, Disney-
> land president Paul Pressler said that when he started, "I didn't quite understand
> in its entirety the public trust we have as caretaker for the Disneyland brand." He
> learned, "People want to hold onto their memories and their past, and we
> appreciate that," but "we cannot turn Disneyland into a museum." He noted,
> "We must be constantly moving forward." While in charge, he would be respon-
> sible for the development of the expansion of the Disneyland Resort and the
> acquisition of the Disneyland Pacific Hotel. In December 1998, Pressler would be
> elevated to run the entire theme park division for the Walt Disney Company.

What Disney management was not prepared for was a new phe-
nomenon: the rise of Internet critics. A growing number of guests were
watching the company's every move, and they did not like what they
saw. Many felt that greed was encroaching on Walt Disney's legacy.
American studies professor Karal Ann Marling studied the critics and
said, "It's as if their childhoods are preserved in amber there. Disneyland has had such a profound emotional impact on its visitors that
they feel they have a stake in what happens."[8]

Popular websites such as the independent Disneyland Information
Guide run by Al Lutz gave voice to the park's most loyal fans. Lutz and
others placed the blame on Disneyland president Paul Pressler for the
deterioration of Walt's high standards of cleanliness and service. Lutz
said, "It's the difference between a park run by a showman and one run
by shopkeepers." Pressler was the public advocate for the expansion
project, and his success at getting things done at a lower-than-expected
cost had put him on the fast track up the corporate ladder.

WELCOME CENTER
for CALIFORNIA

ON JULY 12, 1996, DISNEYLAND OFFICIALS met with local
leaders in the Opera House to unveil plans for the expansion project.[9]
The general public and the press would learn of their plans on the
park's 41st anniversary a few days later. As announced, the new Disneyland Resort would include Disney's California Adventure—a
55-acre theme park—the 750-room Disney's Grand Californian Hotel
that would face into the park, and a 200,000-square-foot Disneyland
Center shopping and entertainment district. The goal was to turn the

area into a multiday tourist resort like Walt Disney World. Disney was growing increasingly concerned that the constant regional discounting and annual passes had started to turn the park into a regional theme park rather than a world-class destination.

The new park was meant to be a departure from the traditional Disney theme park. The Eureka Adventure area would represent the wild areas of the state with a whitewater-rafting ride, a hang glider ride, and underground caverns that guests could explore. The Golden Beaches section would feature a recreation of a coastal amusement park where guests could watch surfers, extreme sports demonstrations, and street artists and musicians. The Waterfront Village would show how California works. Miniature sourdough bread and chocolate factories would be on display, as well as the Silicon Valley garage where the first personal computer was assembled. Agricultural displays would round out the offerings. The Hollywood section of the park would feature an animation display and a real, functioning ABC television studio.

Disney hoped to attract 7 million guests a year and estimated that the new venues would generate up to $700 million in new economic activity to the city every year. Local business leaders were pleased with the announcement. Anaheim Chamber of Commerce President Floyd Farano said, "We hope this whole project gets on the way as soon as possible and it doesn't get pushed back any further than the target date of 2001." John Poimiroo, director of California's Division of Tourism, said the park "will be like a welcome center for California. People will be inspired to explore the state." The history-based theme park that Michael Eisner wanted to build in Virginia had found a home in California.

On October 8, the Anaheim City Council voted to approve the expansion plans. In the development agreement, Anaheim agreed to allow the Walt Disney Company to expand on their 490 acres around Disneyland, to pay for $200 million in infrastructure improvements, and to borrow $560 million to pay for the improvements, as well as to expand the convention center. In exchange, Disney would be exempt from any new parking or admission taxes for 15 years, and Anaheim would not be able to compel the entertainment giant to finish the project if Disney again decided the project was not economically feasible. The Walt Disney Company agreed to open a new park by June 30, 2001, that would be of "Disney quality comparable to other resorts."[10]

The next hurdle was a vote on Measure B, which would retroactively increase the hotel tax by 2% for the city to fund the infrastructure improvements demanded by Disney. On November 5, the measure passed, and the city was authorized to sell $560 million in bonds to pay for the cost of rebuilding the infrastructure serving the resort and expanding the convention center.

The good news continued when Disneyland attendance rose to 15 million guests in 1996, setting a new record. Hotel bookings in the area were up more than 10% over the previous year.

The LIVELY LASS

QUIET CHANGES WERE HAPPENING everywhere at Disneyland in 1997. On January 5, the Rocket Jets attraction on top of the People-Mover station was dismantled and removed as part of the next Tomorrowland update. New trams greeted guests in the parking lot.[11] The Gibson Girl Ice Cream Parlor—named after the Charles Dana Gibson illustrations popular in the late 19th and early 20th centuries—was expanded from a tiny little restaurant into "a true Victorian ice cream parlor," according to Disneyland executive Mike Berry. The shop was repainted white and cool shades of pink and green, and the counter from the Carnation Ice Cream Parlor was moved to the Gibson Girl parlor.

In March, driven by demands for a sit-down restaurant on Main Street, Imagineers moved the Carnation Cafe to West Center Street to make room for the Blue Ribbon Bakery.[12] The bakery was decorated in dark wood, polished brass, and had large bakers' display cases. Carnation Cafe reopened on Center Street as a European bistro-style cafe with outdoor seating.

When the Pirates of the Caribbean reopened in March, some of the rougher edges had been removed and the attraction was "politically correct." Imagineer Bob Baranick was the project manager, and he said the biggest change came to the sequence of lusty pirates chasing women. Originally, there was one pirate that sat along the shore and promised to "share" if guests can spot "the lively lass."

unofficial **TIP**
Many of the new figures for Pirates of the Caribbean came from Epcot's World of Motion attraction.

She was hiding inside of a barrel right next to him. In the new version, the pirates' sin had changed from lust for women to gluttony, and the pirates who had been chasing women were now carrying food and wine. One woman was chasing a pirate who stole her baked goods with a rolling pin. Other pirates were drinking straight from the barrel in a gag first drawn by Marc Davis many years before. Tony Baxter said, "We don't want to put anyone in a jeopardy role."[13]

Disney spokeswoman Susan Roth admitted, "This is one way to bring the ride into tune with the '90s."[14] Clarence Page, a columnist for the *Chicago Tribune,* said, "Chalk up another victory for Disney revisionism. Lust in Disney's Fantasyland is OK, as long as it is for food."[15] The ending was all about redemption and retribution, with pirates trying to escape up the final ramp with stolen treasure, only to be foiled by the women.

For the second time, Disneyland temporarily closed one of its attractions to change it into a holiday show. The It's a Small World holiday attraction reopened on November 27, and a new holiday tradition was born. On the outside, the distinctive facade was decorated with more than 50,000 multicolored lights. Inside, guests boarded the familiar boats to find a glistening winter wonderland. The holiday decorations reflected the style and traditions of each country, and many of the robotic children were wearing new costumes. Park president Paul Pressler said, "We've very carefully gone through and depicted the holidays as they're celebrating around the world."[16]

Minnie Pepito from Las Vegas became the 400 millionth visitor on July 5.[17] Park attendance dipped to 14.25 million guests in 1997.

■ IMAGINATION *and* BEYOND

ON JANUARY 22, 1998, after almost a decade of planning and detours, construction started on Disney's California Adventure. The first step toward a multiday resort was set in motion. At the same time, Anaheim was getting ready by committing $8.7 million to install new street lights and sidewalks in the surrounding neighborhoods. The street improvements were to be completed in time for the grand opening.

At Disneyland, the primary question at the time was what to do with the submarines. The low-capacity attraction was expensive to maintain and to operate, but it was one of Walt's originals. Marty Sklar was a big fan of the attraction and called it "unique in all the world." WDI figured a dose of Imagineering magic and a new show using the latest technologies would inject new life into the aging attraction. Some of the new technologies included a new sound system, projection effects, and dynamic seats to create a thrill ride. Sklar said, "Just putting audio in could make it so exciting with what we can do with audio today. The submarines right now have just one speaker in them and that's just one example."[18] Sklar also felt the Imagineers could overcome the capacity issue. Taking matters into their own hands, on May 15, the Imagineers set up a tent over one of the submarines, embellished with a sign that read, ATLANTIS EXPEDITION IMAGINEERING PREPARATION BASE.

Unfortunately, Imagineers had failed to inform Disneyland management about the sign, and Disney quickly denied to the press that a change was coming to the submarines. Park president Paul Pressler said, "We know the show today isn't as relevant as it was. We know that in the future we need to do something in that location, but we have not made a decision on the subs, and we won't make a decision until we know what we want to do in the future there."[19]

The management was not impressed with the box office success of *Atlantis* and announced on July 29 that they planned to mothball their fleet of submarines after 39 years of operation. They said that a replacement would debut in 2003 but provided no details. A spokesperson said that the reason for the closure was that "the vast majority" of guests wanted "something more exciting." For 2 hours after the park closed on September 8, cast members were granted one last chance to ride the subs. At the end of the evening, Manny Mendoza, who had worked on the attraction in 1959, lowered the ceremonial banner for the last time and gave it to Donald Duck in his sailor suit.[20]

From the beginning, the biggest problem with Tomorrowland had always been staying ahead of the future. The first-generation Tomorrowland was an Atomic Age "Science-Factual" vision of life in 1986. The second-generation Tomorrowland had opened in 1967, and it was Walt's optimistic vision of A World on the Move. How do you top that and create something that would remain relevant for more than just a few years?

Imagineer Tony Baxter was put in charge of creating a third-generation Tomorrowland. "Keeping Tomorrowland fresh and forward-looking represented a great challenge for Disneyland," said Baxter. "We have met that challenge with a balanced design which takes advantage of classic Tomorrowland experiences, while introducing some new and innovative attractions and theming to the entire area. The result will be a themed land filled with excitement and kinetic energy."[21] The theme for the newest version of Tomorrowland would be Imagination and Beyond. Baxter suggested this would be "the future of our dreams."

The budget for the project was set at an estimated $100 million, including the creation of a new E-ticket attraction to replace the WEDway PeopleMover. This was not much money for such an ambitious project. To maximize the limited funds, the WDI team decided to reuse the existing structures to the greatest extent possible. Instead of designing new buildings, they focused on content and storytelling, according to Baxter. "If you can do anything you want, often everybody sits around saying, 'What are we going to do?'" Baxter recalls. "But we had existing buildings, and we had a mission to make them more beautiful." He did concede, "Economics are a consideration in everything we do. That's part of the challenge."[22]

So what does tomorrow look like? Baxter felt the 1982 film *Bladerunner* made it difficult to repeat the optimistic tone of Walt's all-white version without being corny. The public's expectations had changed. He said the movie "was a dark, apocalyptic future of crime, overpopulation, grime and acid rain. This was a more paranoid future. It's fine for a 2-hour movie, but not something you want to re-create at Disneyland. America changed in the 1970s. People developed a cynical view of the future."[23]

Looking back, Baxter said of the original Tomorrowland, "It was a very naive and innocent view of the future, where everybody would be flying around on saucers wearing gold lamé suits."[24] Of the 1967 version, "The naivety of Buck Rogers and flying saucers gave way to corporate salvation, where big business and all the resources of industry were going to build the future. It reflected the nature of the country of the time and was paralleled by the space program."[25]

Baxter and his team decided that instead of predicting what the future would be, they would change the question to What would we like the future to be? According to Imagineer Bruce Gordon, Michael Eisner suggested, "The future is Montana. Everybody wants to live in the forest, away from the urban city, but still have the benefits of technology."[26] Eisner felt that this was a "calmer, reassuring future based in hopes, dreams, and romance rather than a portrayal of future reality." "Our vision was almost the antithesis of the current version of the future," Baxter said. "Instead of living in densely packed glass-and-chrome highrises, you'd like to escape to the woods, get a cabin by a lake, telecommunicate, and go out and fish! We even laughed at one point and said, 'Well, then let's just hang a new shingle over Frontierland that says, "Tomorrowland!"'" He added, "Our goal is to get people dreaming about the world of the future again—where you welcome the future, rather than being afraid of it. We want the future to be reassuring—a delightful place to live in, a place for people."[27]

So instead of looking forward, the design team looked backward to the visionaries of the past: Jules Verne, H. G. Wells, and Leonardo da Vinci. No longer was the future an optimistic bright white; the color palette reflected Discoveryland in Disneyland Paris with browns, golds, and greens. Baxter said, "We wanted to capture that moment of inspiration, that imaginative vision of futurists from Leonardo Da Vinci to George Lucas . . . rather than create a specific time period in the future."[28] Another benefit of the paint scheme was the ability to defer maintenance. The white Tomorrowland required repainting every two years.

"We wanted to create a comfortable Tomorrowland, somewhere where you might want to live, as opposed to a sterile or apocalyptic vision of the future," Bruce Gordon said of the challenge.[29] "Our future is optimistic, comfortable and warm." For example, "We came up with the idea to create an edible food product for the new Tomorrowland: cabbages, citrus, spices, fruit, broccoli. This landscape does two things. First, it sends a subtle optimistic ecological message: we're going to be OK . . . the world will be fine . . . there will be enough food for everyone. Second, it's very interesting to look at; it has an unusual, unexpected shape." The plan was to plant seasonal crops like pumpkins or corn. In addition, there would be kiwi vines, strawberries, grapes, persimmon trees, purple cabbage, and citrus trees. Gordon commented, "This has been one of the most interesting things about this project—to watch people stop and look at the landscaping trying to figure out what it is. 'It's cabbage.' 'No, it's not, cabbage doesn't look like that.' These people are spending their Disneyland day trying to figure out the landscaping. The Land really looks beautiful."[30]

The Astro Orbiter spinner ride was removed from on top of the PeopleMover station and placed at the entrance of Tomorrowland, at the same distance from the hub as the Sleeping Beauty Castle drawbridge. The 64-foot-tall brass and gold moving astronomical model of planets and constellations was meant to be a "striking new landmark," with a design inspired by Leonardo da Vinci's art and mobiles. It was an exact duplicate of the Orbitron at Disneyland Paris and surrounded by rockwork, which Tony Baxter described as a mini-berm. The replacement for the Astro Orbiter on the "theme" tower was a "performing sculpture" called the Observatron, which would come alive every 15 minutes, spin, and play uplifting music. The Imagineers claimed it was "sending messages into deep space, looking for intelligent life."

The new Tomorrowland opened on May 22, 1998. Every part of the land had been touched in some way. Mary Blair's playful mural was covered up by a new one celebrating Disneyland's past interpretations of the future. The Premiere Shop was redesigned to look like a vehicle warehouse. Another nod to the past was a scaled-down, 60-foot replica of the *Moonliner Rocket* built from the 1955 blueprints. The rocket marked the entrance to Redd Rockett's Pizza Port, which replaced the Flight to Mars attraction. The restaurant was decorated with vintage attraction posters from the collection of Imagineer Tony Baxter. The 2,500-square-foot "American Space Experience" exhibit commemorated 40 years of the National Aeronautics and Space Administration (NASA) with interactive displays, models of the Mars Pathfinder and the Mars Sojourner rovers, and an actual moon rock. It closed October 26, 2003.

Cosmic Waves was described as a "colorful, highly kinetic sculpture representing the imaginative world of tomorrow." At the center was a 12,000-pound granite ball that moved easily on a thin film of water. To get to the ball, guests had to negotiate a maze created by waterspouts that formed walls and doors. (After a few years, the fountains were shut down, and the area was redecorated with planters surrounding the ball.)

The showiest and most expensive new attraction was the $25 million Rocket Rods. Walt Disney Imagineering replaced the slow-moving WEDway PeopleMover with a high-speed thrill ride. While under development, the attraction was known by many different names—including the Speed Cycles and Rocket Sleds—before Imagineers settled on Rocket Rods XPR (for Experimental Prototype Rocket).[31] The vehicles were designed to look incomplete, suggesting that guests were trying out an experimental high-speed transportation system. Guests were really riding in a prototype. The attraction borrowed technology under development from the problem-plagued Test Track at Epcot. The odd vehicles had an unusual one-one-one-two seating arrangement (three single-seat "rows" with a two-seat row at the back) and were placed on the existing PeopleMover beam. They accelerated rapidly on the straight stretches and had to slow down as they entered the unbanked curves. Rocket Rods was the fastest and longest-distance ride ever at Disneyland, hitting speeds of up to 35 mph. The PeopleMover took 16 minutes to get around the circuit. The Rocket Rods did the trip in 3 minutes. Eisner took great pride in the Rocket Rods. He said, "As a 'type A' impatient person, I was happy to participate in speeding up the PeopleMover."[32]

The Rocket Rods queue was themed as the 50th anniversary celebration of the fictional Tomorrowland Transit System. The walls were adorned with giant blueprints of the Flying Saucers and the Submarines. Also on display was a Mark III monorail, a pair of WEDway PeopleMover cars, and two original Rocket Jets. The queue wound its way inside the CircleVision theater, and excerpts from *Magic Highways U.S.A.*—first shown in 1958 on the Disneyland television program—were projected onto the nine screens. The queue continued down a tunnel and up to the former PeopleMover platform.

There was only one problem with the Rocket Rods: they were prone to frequent breakdowns. Issues included axle problems, overheated motors, and software glitches. Disney Imagineers underestimated the operational and technical complexities of the original concept and ended up committing to a product way too early in the development process. The team working on the repairs began to refer to the various vehicles as Pintos, Mercedes, Rolls-Royces, and Humvees, depending on their reliability.[33] The ride was shut down in July for repairs and reopened in October. Even then, it did not work, and it was shut down for another month as they tried to repair the attraction.

On September 28, 2000, the Rocket Rods finally closed officially. There was a sign out front stating it would reopen in the spring of 2001, but that never happened. Park president Cynthia Harriss said, "The high-speed attraction was never able to perform to its designed show standards." She candidly added, "The problem was a budget-conscious decision to run the high-speed Rods on the PeopleMover's unbanked track."

Imported from Florida was the 3-D film, *Honey, I Shrunk the Audience*. Based on the 1989 film *Honey I Shrunk the Kids,* guests arrived to watch Professor Wayne Szalinski and his family receive an award—setting off 18 minutes of mayhem inside the 575-seat theater. The floor was mounted on a gimbal and was able to move in synchronization with the film.

Another Florida import was Innoventions, which opened in October. Imagineer Barry Braverman had put together a corporate showcase for the Carousel Theatre. Although the platform of the theater still rotated, there was no show inside. Instead, guests had the opportunity to view and interact with "products and concepts from the world's leading industries," according to a press release. Tony Baxter said he wanted visitors to feel the rush he got in "seeing the latest cutting-edge gizmos at the annual Consumer Electronics Show in Las Vegas." The focus was on technology that might be available within the next six months.[34]

Marking the entrance was a triangular sculpture. "We were sitting at a drafting table with a 30–60 triangle and a rough sketch of Innoventions," Baxter recalled. "We slid the triangle on top of the elevation, and it just happened to be the right scale. It seemed to be made for it."[35] Guests entered the showcase via the slow-moving platform and were greeted by an Audio-Animatronics character named Tom Morrow, voiced by actor Nathan Lane. The futuristic robot was stripped of the skin that hid his mechanics, and he was programmed to stay active and remain "onstage" while the theater rotated and the next group walked in. Then a live host would greet the audience and make a quick presentation on one of the five featured realms: Home, Entertainment, Workplace, Sports/Recreation, and Transportation. At the center of the showcase was an artificial tree with branches incorporating computer chips and other bits of technology. Guests exited on the second floor and took a curved ramp down through the logo and back into Tomorrowland.

Throughout June, Disneyland management presented to cast members some of the potential expansion plans. "We just wanted to show what additional opportunities are available to us," said Disney spokesman Ray Gomez. The Disneyland Center shopping and entertainment would double in size from 200,000 square feet to 400,000 and would include four nightclubs, a 14-screen multiplex, a 40,000-square-foot World of Disney store, an ESPN sports bar, and a DisneyQuest virtual reality amusement center.[36]

Much of the growth would also come from the expansion of the hotels. The Disneyland Hotel would gain an additional tower, and two new hotels would be built. A 2,000-room hotel would be built on the Simba parking lot, which was south of the Disneyland Pacific Hotel, while an all-suite hotel would rise out of the Pinocchio parking lot, north of the Disneyland Hotel. The Grand Californian, then under construction inside of the new theme park, would add an additional 250 rooms to its already proposed 750. There were even rumors of a third theme park that summer.[37]

On October 6, Disneyland announced that it would limit the hours of more than 20 of its attractions in an effort to save money on labor. The plan was to stagger the opening and closing times of more than 20 attractions.[38] This was not an insignificant change. Historically, all of the Disneyland attractions were open whenever the park was open, unless there was an extraordinary circumstance, such as the energy crisis of 1979. Management believed that the plan would not only reduce labor costs, but that it would also encourage shopping and dining.

Public reaction was immediate and unfavorable. Cast members received training on how to deal with guest complaints by offering suggestions for other activities. Compounding guest frustrations was the maze of construction walls on the east side of the park while Tomorrowland was under construction. Fans began an e-mail campaign, something unprecedented at Disneyland. According to Al Lutz, founder of the independent Disneyland Information Guide website, "The tone has been annoyed, but polite and respectful." The e-mail campaign generated negative press, and the park began to walk back from the policy the next day. Paul Pressler admitted, "We definitely stubbed our toe on the operating hours."[39]

HIP, IRREVERENT, and CONTEMPORARY

EXCITEMENT WAS BUILDING for Disney's California Adventure. With the public eager to monitor the construction, the park opened a preview center on October 14, 1998. Inside the specially constructed tent were conceptual drawings and scale models. An observation deck allowed guests a look at the construction. At the opening of the display, Imagineer Barry Braverman spoke with the press and said, "This will be a very pop-culture park in contrast to Disneyland. It is about the here and now. It will be hip, irreverent, and contemporary, where Disneyland is rooted in fantasy."[40] The design team wanted to create a sampler of the best of California.

Braverman described the park, which was scheduled to open in early 2001. On opening day, the 55-acre park would have 22 shows and attractions, at least 15 restaurants, a 2,000-seat theater, and a dozen shops. The project was slated to cost $1.4 billion for the theme park, a new hotel, and a shopping complex. Expected attendance was pegged at 7 million visitors the first year. At the entrance, guests would pass by California spelled out in large concrete block letters, walk under the monorail track disguised as the Golden Gate Bridge, and head toward a large metallic sculpture in the Sun Court. This area would act as the hub. "We want people to feel like they are walking into a postcard for California," said Braverman.[41]

One section of the park would be Condor Flats, described as "a high-desert Air Force test facility of the 1940s." The marquee attraction would a hang-glider simulation called Soarin' Over California. While standing in the queue, guests would be entertained by computer-generated graphics of famous aircraft flying overhead. Ten acres were set aside for the Grizzly Peak Recreation Area, an area intended to represent the California mountain wilderness and to include opportunities for extreme sports, such as a whitewater-rafting ride, as well as a children's playground themed like a Scout camp with zip lines, rock climbing, and rope bridges.

The Bountiful Valley Farm would be a demonstration farm where guests could see what basic food crops look like. Michael Eisner was a big fan of "edutainment" and said this is something that people will find compelling. Two children's play areas were planned as well, and there was talk about bringing the 4-D film *It's Tough to Be a Bug* from the recently opened Disney's Animal Kingdom in Florida. Appealing to adult guests would be the Robert Mondavi winery restaurant and tasting area adjacent to the farm. A food court themed as Cannery Row of Monterey would be nearby.

San Francisco would be represented by the rotunda from the Palace of Fine Arts and Victorian facades housing artisans' workshops. Braverman called it "a little bit of the Sawdust Festival at Laguna Beach." The main attraction would be *Circle of Hands,* a film that highlighted all the different peoples who came to California and contributed to its success. "This is an emotional show, the one where we want to pull on people's heartstrings," according to Braverman.[42]

*un*official **TIP**
The Sawdust Festival is an annual arts and crafts festival featuring local artists who build the festival village each year. Since it started in the mid-1960s, the event has been popular with guests from all over the world.

With the real Hollywood only a short freeway ride north, the theme park version would be an illusion. "As you enter, the area looks very opulent and over-the-top," Braverman said. "But as you walk through, you discover that it is all a Hollywood set—false fronts, etc."[43] The *Muppet-Vision 3-D* film from Disney-MGM Studios park in Florida would be the marquee attraction. Braverman noted, "The Muppets give this park a strong character franchise that differentiates it from Disneyland." There would be Superstar Limo, a dark ride where "the limo visits a drive-through tattoo parlor and riders find tattoos projected onto their bodies." A 2,000-seat Broadway-style theater would present two different shows daily, and there would be a 40,000-square-foot Art of Animation display; the highlight of that display would be a room with projected images of Disney villains who battle other characters. Suddenly, the floor would drop away, suspending the guests in mid-air, right in the middle of the conflict.[44]

The largest section of the park would be Paradise Pier, an homage to California's tradition of ocean-side amusement parks. Ironically, much of the new park would be dedicated to exactly the thing Walt was try-ing to get away from: carnival games. The big ticket item would be California Screamin', a steel roller coaster built to look like a wooden one. There would also be a swing ride, a spinning carnival ride, an ocean-themed carousel, an off-the-shelf wild mouse roller coaster, and possibly a small version of Knott's Berry Farm's parachute ride.

"We are impressed with the scale of the Walt Disney Company's investment in Anaheim and by the concept that undergirds this $1.4 billion project," said a *Los Angeles Times* editorial. However, they were disturbed by the level of public dollars committed to the project and unsure if the park's theme would work. Two-thirds of Disneyland visi-tors were California residents. Would a park designed to celebrate the state have broad enough appeal? The newspaper suggested that the new park was merely an amalgam of theme parks: The Hollywood section was a mini Universal Studios, Paradise Pier had thrill rides like Six Flags Magic Mountain, and the historic California theme mirrored Knott's Berry Farm. Braverman justified the creative decisions. "I think what we are doing here is so unique in the way these themes are reflected in the design, attention to detail and storytelling. We have a very unique expression of the essence of California."[45]

In the meantime, attendance at Disneyland had struggled and was down 4%, to 13.5 million guests in 1998.

MORE PRODUCTIVE TIME

AT THE BEGINNING OF 1999, Anaheim lost another landmark. The Golf N' Stuff miniature golf course, which had opened in 1970 just across the street from the Disneyland parking entrance on Harbor Bou-levard, closed in January. The 2.42-acre site was cleared to become part of the road widening of Freedman Way.[46]

The Jungle Cruise was updated again with new boats that were 4 feet longer. Bill Evans convinced them to take the awning covers off the Jungle Cruise boats so that guests could really experience this voy-age through the jungle. He was rightly proud of the way the jungle had matured. When the park opened, the primary objective was to restrict the guest's view. Over time, some of the trees grew to more than 70 feet and the ground covering was lush and dense like a real jungle. The Disneyland jungle included giant fig trees from China, Australia, and India, as well as African coral trees and bottle trees.

Also in Adventureland, rumors were afoot about changes to the Swiss Family Treehouse. The artificial tree was beginning to show the wear and tear of millions of guests and decades of weather and was ready for a major overhaul. Looking for inspiration, Tony Baxter turned to early drawings from the Disney animated film *Tarzan*, which was scheduled to be released on June 18. Baxter was impressed with the scenes of the lead character surfing in the branches of the trees. "The mythology of Disneyland needs to be in touch with where kids are today," he said. "We think *Tarzan* might do as well as *The Lion King*. It is a beautiful film."[47] *Tarzan* did, indeed, seem like a natural fit.

On March 4, 1999, park spokesperson Tom Brochette tried to quell the rumors and said the park had decided against making any changes because they felt the project could not be done in time for the film's premiere. Then, suddenly, the attraction was closed the next day.

That was not the end of the tree house, however. "The creative people figured out how to make the pieces fit together," said Brochette. "They made another attempt and were successful."[48] The attraction reopened as Tarzan's Treehouse on June 19, 1999. The Imagineers were able to design and install the changeover in just six months. The most noticeable change was the addition of a second "rotted" tree stump and an 18-foot-high suspension bridge connected to the original tree. The new element added a bit of fun and a great view of Adventureland, and it served as a visual block between Adventureland and New Orleans Square.

Guests walked up 72 steps and down 67 steps to view three-dimensional scenes from the film. The tree house was filled with special effects such as a "magic mirror" that showed scenes from the film and Jane's "sketch pad" with animation by *Tarzan*'s principal animator, Glen Keane. At the base of the massive tree was a camp with interactive elements, including a gramophone that played "Swissapolka" from the original attraction. In 2007, the attraction had to be closed down and reengineered. The addition of the suspension bridge had added stress to the original tree.[49]

Although Disneyland had several queues that were attractions in their own right—most notably Indiana Jones—waiting in line was never the most loved part of a visit to Disneyland. The earliest queues were simple switchbacks. Then Walt started to adapt the hidden queue concept that he had seen at Knott's Berry Farm. Later, Imagineers realized that the queue could become the first act in the show and that it gave them an opportunity to enhance the attraction and add entertainment value. Still, one of the biggest negatives cited by guests in surveys was waiting in line.

The British loved their amusement parks, but it turned out that they didn't like to wait in line, either. Alton Towers Resort, a popular theme park in England, had developed a successful virtual queue system that allowed guests to make a reservation and come back to a much shorter line. The Walt Disney Company followed their example and created Fastpass. First put into operation at Walt Disney World, a Fastpass system was installed at Disneyland on July 28, 1999. The system was first tested at Space Mountain for four days.[50] Guests used their admission tickets to receive an appointment to return to the ride at a later time, and at the appointed time could then board the ride with little to no wait. Guests could also choose to wait in a standby line without a ticket. A Disney spokesperson said, "The intent is to provide guests with more productive time in our parks. People go on to what you might consider the secondary attractions in that area of the ride they have the FASTpass for."[51] The ticket books had provided the same advantage, but with the adoption of the unlimited passport, guests began to skip the smaller attractions. The test was deemed successful and plans were being made to install the system permanently at Space Mountain, Indiana Jones Adventure, Splash Mountain, and other popular attractions.

In 1999, on the eve of the turn of the century, 13.5 million guests visited Disneyland.

SPEED PARKING

ONE ATTRACTION IN TOMORROWLAND that had not been updated in 1998 was the popular Autopia rides in Fantasyland and Tomorrowland. However, modification plans had been put in place in October 1998 when Disney signed a sponsorship agreement with Chevron. The Fantasyland and Tomorrowland Autopia had already closed on September 6, 1998; the new version opened on June 29, 2000.

Autopia's miniature freeway had been a hit from the beginning, and the ride had been remodeled in 1959, 1964, and 1968. With a new sponsorship deal, the Imagineers were able to update both the cars and the track. Jason Holts designed the new car bodies, which were available in three different styles: cute, sports, and off-road. The fiberglass bodies were "humorously themed" and finished with a paint that changed color depending on the light. They slightly resembled the Claymation talking cars used in the Chevron commercials. Each vehicle weighed 474 pounds. The brake system was integrated with the throttle; when the driver lifted his or her foot, the vehicle stopped. There was an accelerator pedal along one side for the cast members, and the car would shut down automatically after 2 minutes of inactivity. Top speed was limited to 7 mph, and a trip around the track took approximately 4 minutes and 15 seconds. Each car had a license plate with the initials of one of the design team members.[52]

The Fantasyland and Tomorrowland tracks were combined to create four travel lanes. Each track was approximately a half-mile long, a few hundred feet longer than the tracks they had replaced. Guests passed through a "car park" with an original 1955 Mr. Toad car and a 1956 Midget Autopia car on display. There was a small portion of the track that simulated driving off-road. The queue had been redesigned to look like grandstands, and guests passed by little dioramas featuring the cartoon cars of Chevron fame.

Another change at Disneyland in 2000 was parking. Starting on July 24, guests arriving in their own cars were now directed to park in the seven-story, 10,250-car Mickey and Friends Parking structure at the northeast corner of Disney's property. The structure cost $90 million; it was financed by Anaheim hotel taxes and had been built by the city. Disney leased back the garage and pocketed any revenues. Parking in the structure was handled differently than in the typical parking structure; the new approach was based on the concept of speed parking. Michael Eisner was quite excited about speed parking; and in a *Los Angeles Times* interview, he even claimed credit for it. Guests paid a fee and then drove to the top of the ramp, where cast members guided them to specific parking spaces. All spaces faced the same direction, so exiting simply meant driving forward and going back down one ramp. The driver did not need to change ramps and did not need to back up into traffic to exit. It did not work. In practice, the park found that guests had to walk toward incoming traffic. The facility was closed down and re-striped for traditional parking.

Another change was the renaming of the Disneyland Pacific Hotel, which become Disney's Paradise Pier Hotel on November 1. The 15-story, 502-room hotel offered guests early admission into Disneyland, as well as an exclusive entrance into Disney's California Adventure theme park after it opened in 2001.

With Disney's California Adventure under construction and the Disney organization feeling optimistic, talk had already begun on the potential for a third theme park in Anaheim. Disneyland president Cynthia Harriss said, "Creating the magic of a new Disney park requires us to take a long-term view. We are starting that process now, working with Anaheim residents, businesses, and civic leaders to identify opportunities that will ensure that the Anaheim Resort Area remains a world-class destination for the decades ahead."[53] The new park would be located on 78 acres east of Harbor Boulevard and south of Katella Avenue. Rumor had it that the third park might include a water park modeled after Typhoon Lagoon at Walt Disney World or that it might be a theme park that combined "brand-new attractions along with the best of Disney rides, shows and entertainment experiences from around the world." The goal was to have the third park open in 2010.

In the meantime, Disneyland hosted 13.9 million guests in 2000.

The SECOND GATE

AS 2001 STARTED, *Great Moments with Mr. Lincoln* was closed once again for another update. Nobody seemed to notice, as all eyes were focused on the opening of the long-awaited expanded Disneyland Resort. After more than a decade of planning, the project was becoming a reality. Imagineering General Manager Timur Galen said, "If Disneyland had started as the only development in a sea of green, it was now the only green in a sea of asphalt."[54] That was the same line used word for word by Disney executive Kerry Hunnewell a decade before to describe the WESTCOT project.

The first component to open was the Grand Californian Hotel and Spa on January 2. The 750-room hotel had been designed by architect Peter Dominick. Architectural critic Beth Dunlop described the hotel as an "homage to the creative forces at work along California's coastline at the dawn of the last century—with inspiration drawn from groups ranging from the Arroyo Craftsmen to the Plein Air Painters."[55] Never before had such a large structure been inspired by the Arts and Crafts movement. Dunlop noted, "The spaces are carefully manipulated—small and tight and then huge and soaring—to perfect effect. The bracketed, vaulted wood ceilings seem to embrace the spaces." She felt that Dominick "mastered the great romantic gesture, using authentic materials to create a full travel experience."[56]

The check-in area was a tribute to San Francisco's exquisite Sweden-borgian Church, which was considered to be the first Arts and Crafts structure in California. Throughout the public spaces, artisans had been commissioned to add custom furniture and decorative pieces. The two vice presidential suites and two presidential suites were inspired by architects Frank Lloyd Wright and the Greene brothers, Charles and Henry. The hotel also had 20,000 square feet of meeting space, the award-winning Napa Rose restaurant, and the Storytellers Cafe.

The next opening was Downtown Disney, on January 12. Galen said that the 300,000-square-foot non-gated shopping, dining, and enter-tainment center possessed "its own unique 'sense of place,' evoking the feeling of stepping into a garden paradise. Its lush environment con-nects the expanded Disneyland Resort and embodies our vision for the guest experience which the entire complex will offer." To create "a lush, garden-like complex by day that transformed to a bright glittery zone at night, the mall was lined with Cuban laurel trees that Disney had rescued from Culver City where they were about to be destroyed."[57]

Originally known as the Disneyland Center, the mall connected Disneyland and the California Adventure to the Disneyland Hotel. Major tenants included a 12-screen, AMC stadium-style movie the-ater, the House of Blues, a Rainforest Cafe, Ralph Brennan's Jazz Kitchen, an ESPN Zone, and many more venues. The 40,000-square-foot World of Disney store was the second-largest Disney store in the world. Along Harbor Boulevard, a new transportation center designed by renowned landscape architect Martha Swartz had been installed. Dubbed the "Christmas Tree Lot" by online fans, the East Esplanade was, according to Disney press releases, "inspired by gardens of the classical Baroque Period, where episodic events or spaces are joined through a linear progression of the pedestrian through the spaces."

Imagineer Barry Braverman was the creative leader for the project. "First thing, we threw out the rulebook."[58] He wanted to turn away from all of the lessons learned over the years during the development and operation of Disneyland and Walt Disney World. "When we started working on [Downtown Disney] there was a tremendous amount of suspicion in the air because it was so different," he said. "This wasn't to be a theme park in the traditional Disney sense." Braverman knew he was trotting on sacred ground. He admitted, "Frankly, if we had tried to compete with Disneyland on its own terms, we would have failed."[59]

Instead of immersing guests within a single theme, "This is a park that is very open in its views," said Braverman. "You can stand at the park's entry plaza and see the gateway to Golden State; you can see the California Grizzly Bear icon high atop Grizzly Peak; you can see the gates to Hollywood; and you can see Paradise Pier's massive roller coaster, along with so much more. Here we have a park that embraces 'visual intrusion' and turns it into an attribute that draws guests into the environment and the excitement happening throughout."[60] Braverman felt, "You can navigate easily in this park and, in that way, it feels intimate and understandable. Then as you wander into an area, Hollywood Pictures Backlot for example, you become immersed in that experience. There's a combination of comfortable large view and overpowering short view that happens."[61]

In an opening-day press release, Braverman stated, "There's a kind of brash California attitude that we wanted to capture. Much more pop culture and MTV with a little tongue-in-cheek thrown in. It's shorthand, impressionistic and cinematic." It was Disney's Postmodern theme park. Even the company admitted it was the "most unusual theme park in the Disney family." The new park opened to great fanfare on February 8 with a crowd estimated to be less than 8,000 guests.

Guests entered Disney's California Adventure through the Sun Plaza and were greeted by the world's largest ceramic mural of California landmarks. The Monorail track was disguised as the Golden Gate Bridge, and just beyond was a large north-facing sun sculpture with computerized heliostats to constantly reflect the sun toward the icon. From there, guests could choose from three different paths. To the east was the Hollywood Studios Backlot with Superstar Limo dark ride, *Muppet-Vision 3-D* film, and the 50,000-square-foot Disney Animation exhibit with three interactive displays. To the west was Condor Flats with the park's one hit attraction, Soarin' Over California. Continuing toward the west was the Grizzly River Run raft ride and the Redwood Creek Challenge Trail. To the south, guests could walk past the Golden Vine Winery sponsored by Mondavi, the Mission Tortilla Factory, and The Bakery Tour, and then to a large lagoon with a wave machine. The park's signature attraction was *Golden Dreams,* a sometimes painfully accurate film look at California history.

On the other side of the lagoon was Paradise Pier. It had the Sun Wheel Ferris wheel, the California Screamin' roller coaster, the Orange Stinger swing ride, and the Maliboomer space shot ride. There was also a temporary mad mouse coaster called Mulholland Madness, plus the Golden Zephyr and the King Triton Carousel. Other attractions included a couple of children's play areas and the 3-D film *It's Tough to be a Bug!* from Florida.

Critics were not very kind to the new park. John Cora, a former Disney executive, said, "Disney's highest priority in developing the park was to keep costs down." The park was estimated to have cost $650 million. It opened with a large number of high-end restaurants and heavily themed shops but few attractions. Cora said, "Part of the problem is Paul [Pressler] came from retail. He thought retail and still thinks retail. We spent enough money overbuilding retail and food to add three or four major attractions to the park."

Beth Dunlop stated, "As originally planned, California Adventure was a generalist's theme park, telling a larger, and in many ways more abstract, tale of the history of the Golden State. It did not ultimately tug at enough heartstrings or conjure up strong subliminal (or overt) responses."[62] Sculptor Blaine Gibson said, "I'm not saying this to defame Mike Eisner, but he came up with California Adventure right adjacent to Disneyland. People went in there and they'd say, no, I want to go back to Disneyland. My feeling is that Disneyland had heart. Walt and the people he chose to work on it, everybody, put their heart into what they did. And a lot of the other kinds of parks are done by people who do it professionally but they don't have that same intense feeling about it."[63] Possibly the most damning comment came from John Hench; when asked his opinion of California Adventure, he said he preferred the parking lot.

The science-fiction novelist Cory Doctorow said, "There's lots you can say about Eisner that isn't very flattering, but the one thing you can say is that under Eisner's leadership, there has been a definite focus on innovation, at least in Florida. At Disneyland, unfortunately, they brought in these idiot McKinsey consultants, they stopped spending any money on R&D and they bought all these off-the-shelf midway rides, with Ferris wheels, for the California Adventure. They built this incredibly dreary, boring, banal theme park that is like an extremely clean but less-fun version of the Santa Monica pier, and, unsurprisingly, it's a ghost town. You could fire a cannon down the main drag without hitting a tourist."[64]

HIT *and* MISS *in* *the* NEW MILLENNIUM

MARK RAMIREZ OF LYLE, TEXAS, became the 450 millionth visitor to Disneyland on March 15, 2001.[65] While most of the action focused on the grand opening preparations for Disney's California

Adventure, there were some changes taking place inside Disneyland. The Tomorrowland Terrace was converted from a nighttime entertainment venue to a kid-friendly activity space called Club Buzz on June 30. Guests were disappointed to learn that Jungle Cruise skippers were no longer able to shoot at the charging hippos. Although many groups attributed political motives to the decision, Disney management said they made the change because their now more-sophisticated guests no longer found the sequence believable. (The decision was quietly reversed in October 2004, and guns with blanks returned to the Jungle Cruise.[66])

On July 17, *Great Moments with Mr. Lincoln* reopened in the opera house with a new show, *Journey to Gettysburg*. The show's gimmick was binaural sound, and the Audio-Animatronics technology had also been upgraded. Guests were handed headphones on entry to the theater, and the 3-D sound technology provided the sensation that the action was taking place all around them. A gag with a soldier getting a haircut was especially effective. The story line followed a young soldier from photographer Mathew Brady's studio to the battle of Gettysburg and led to the show's climax with Abraham Lincoln reciting the Gettysburg Address. (The poorly received show was shuttered on February 21, 2005.)[67]

unofficial **TIP**
The Nightmare Before Christmas holiday overlay was so popular that it has become an annual holiday attraction. For the 2002 season, the soundtrack was adapted by John Debney to use elements composed by Danny Elfman. A different gingerbread element is added to the ballroom scene every year.

With the success of the holiday overlay at It's a Small World, it was only a matter of time before other attractions were included on the holiday overlay roster. The holiday overlay for 2001 was inspired by the 1993 Disney animated hit, *Tim Burton's Nightmare Before Christmas*. Based on a poem Burton had written when he was a Disney animator, the film depicted a collision of two holidays, Christmas and Halloween. Steve Davidson from the Disney Entertainment Department designed the holiday overlay for the Haunted Mansion. The exterior featured a coffin sleigh, hundreds of flickering candles along the roofline, and a field of pumpkin heads. Inside, the graveyard was covered in snow.[68] An original soundtrack composed by Gordon Goodwin did not include any music from the film because the rights had not been secured in time for the 2001 holiday season. The attraction reopened on October 5 and was an incredible success.

The September 11, 2001, terrorist attacks virtually put a stop to international travel and resulted in a worldwide recession. WDC put in place 800 expense-saving measures—including layoffs and a freeze in hiring and salaries—with the hope of saving up to $250 million. Security was visibly increased; for the first time, uniformed police were seen onstage, in the public areas. Still, 13.3 million guests visited Disneyland in 2001, in part due to California Adventure's grand opening and the resort expansion earlier in the year.

With all of the action happening over at the struggling Disney's California Adventure, Disneyland was put pretty much on the back burner. On September 28, 2002, the Matterhorn Bobsleds closed for routine refurbishment and reopened in early December. Attendance fell to 12.7 million guests in 2002.

King Arthur Carrousel reopened on March 5, 2003, after 14 months of extensive renovations that included improved access for disabled riders. A loading ramp was installed, as was a four-seat bench that could be lifted for wheelchairs. Four horses were removed to accommodate the new bench. In addition, most of the original wooden parts were replaced by metal, and a new computer control system was installed.[69]

A CHANCE *to* BE *with* POOH

A.A. MILNE'S WINNIE-THE-POOH franchise was a merchandise cash cow for the Walt Disney Company, and the theme parks wanted in on the action. On June 4, 1999, the bear and his friends had replaced Mr. Toad's Wild Ride at the Magic Kingdom. On September 4, 2000, Tokyo Disneyland opened the remarkable, state-of-the-art Pooh's Honey Hut at a reported cost of $150 million. Disneyland would get a much simpler ride; the Many Adventures of Winnie the Pooh, estimated to have cost $35 million, opened on April 7, 2003. The opening date had been selected to coincide with the release of the animated film *Piglet's Big Movie*.[70]

The attraction was a simple dark ride, with honey pot vehicles that would bounce along the track for no apparent reason. Bruce Gordon described the ride, "It's not a story about Pooh. We wanted to give guests a chance to be with Pooh. The idea is they've just joined Pooh and his friends, who are off on one of their many adventures. I think we pulled that off."[71] The original Country Bear theater became a room filled with Heffalumps and Woozles.

It was suggested that Critter Country would be remodeled to look like the 100-Acre Wood from the Milne books, but the only real change was that all references to bears were removed—well, except for Pooh, of course. The Mile Long Bar was transformed into Pooh Corner, a

British country cottage that included a display candy kitchen. A character meet-and-greet area was also installed.

On September 5, 2003, tragedy struck when train #2, the *I.M. Brave,* derailed on Big Thunder Mountain Railroad. Guest Marcelo Torres died in the accident, which was determined to have been caused by a mechanic who did not tighten bolts and attach a safety wire to a wheel assembly. The assembly fell off, leading to a partial derailment in which the lead passenger car slammed into the locomotive's undercarriage as the train entered the last turn of the tunnel immediately preceding "B-Lift." Torres died of extensive internal bleeding resulting from severe blunt force trauma to his chest causing, among other injuries, rib fractures and lacerations to his lung. Within weeks after Big Thunder Mountain Railroad was reopened in 2004, two more nonfatal accidents happened.[72]

Attendance stayed flat in 2003 with 12.7 million visitors. The relatively good news was that attendance at Disney's California Adventure had jumped 13% to 5.3 million, which was still well below Disney's forecasted 7 million.

50 YEARS

WALT HAD SAID, "Disneyland is the star. Everything else is in the supporting role."[73] For many years, the park was fussed over like a diva, and guests arrived with high expectations. As Disneyland approached its golden anniversary, the years of cost cutting, deferred maintenance, and lack of attention and resources were finally beginning to be noticed by even the most casual visitor. In the past, this piecemeal approach to maintenance would have been frowned upon.

Rolly Crump described the park as "a gorgeous salad because of the ingredients. There is a little bit of something in there for everyone. The attention to detail is one of the most important pieces of it, because there is so much in there." As an example, he also pointed to "the little figures making popcorn in the popcorn wagons. Those little things are the croutons, or the little bits of oregano, that are in the salad that make it so delicious. I really feel like that was why Disneyland was always so successful. I hate to say it, but the rest of the

unofficial **TIP**
As far back as opening day, trash containers were placed every few yards and were "specially designed to blend with the set." An early press release from the 1950s proudly proclaimed, "Although there are no 'Anti-litterbug' signs, guests are amazed to see other visitors walk several yards to insert an empty popcorn box in a container rather than clutter the constantly clean pavement."

theme parks were nothing more than just lettuce and tomatoes."[74]

By 2004 WDC management was more concerned about defending itself against a takeover effort by cable giant Comcast than it was in investing in major changes in Disneyland. Still, there were some improvement initiatives. New park president Matt Quiment and his team set about implementing Project Sparkle, a campaign to repaint and repair almost every building after years of neglect.[75] Virtually every trash can was painted at a considerable cost. Throughout the park, welcome enhancements were added to some of the most popular attractions. The facade for It's a Small World was restored to the original gold and white with nighttime lighting of blue and white. Inside the attraction, the entire sound system was replaced, and a new digital version of the original 1964–1965 New York World's Fair soundtrack was installed. In the Haunted Mansion, Madame Leota now levitated over the séance table. Tomorrowland was repainted in white, silver, blue, and violet.

The park reached a major milestone when Bill Trow from Australia became the 500 millionth guest on January 8, 2004. By March, new permanent security gates were installed in the Esplanade to reduce congestion and improve security.[76] Changes also came to the Fastpass system when it was removed from a number of attractions, including Pirates of the Caribbean, Winnie the Pooh, Star Tours, and others.[77] In November, guests were stunned to see Tinker Bell flying around the castle during the fireworks show. For many years, she had just simply slid down a zip line from the top of the Matterhorn to a landing pad just behind Fantasyland. In 2004, through the use of a sophisticated system of cables, winches, and pulleys, she could go up, down, forward, and backward.

Another quality improvement was *The Enchanted Tiki Room*. Due to pressure from sponsor Dole, the attraction had been closed for a lengthy refurbishment. When it reopened on March 12, 2005, all of the Audio-Animatronics had been repaired, the dust that had caked up on the birds was removed, the soundtrack digitized, plus the sound system and lighting had been upgraded. The faded preshow film had also been replaced, and it was shown on a new projection system. The original lacquered bamboo-look chairs, purchased in early 1963 when the attraction was going to be a Stouffer's restaurant, were reused. Tony Baxter said, "[The improvements at *The Enchanted Tiki Room*] revolutionized the industry. It's the first time sound and movement have been sequenced to a three-dimensional performance. To me it's important. It should belong, if only as an institution."[78]

Buzz Lightyear Astro Blasters opened on March 17, 2005, as an attempt to fuse the world of theme park rides with the virtual world of the Internet: Guests could experience the ride at the theme park while others could participate online. Disney executive Roger Holzberg said, "It's a paradigm that hasn't been tried before."[79] The backstory for the attraction was that the evil Emperor Zurg had cornered the world's supply of batteries, and Buzz Lightyear and 722 little green men needed the help of the guests to defeat the villain. The attraction borrowed many elements from the Tokyo Disneyland version. The attraction was fitted into the northern show building in Tomorrowland. As guests entered the queue, they were greeted by an Audio-Animatronics Buzz Lightyear. The face used projection technology similar to the Madame Leota effect in the Haunted Mansion.

In the park, guests rode in specially fitted Omnimover vehicles armed with two guns and a joystick that spun the vehicle 360 degrees. To execute the mission, guests used an infrared pistol to hit targets and to accumulate the highest number of points. The gun lit up to confirm the shot, and the vehicle was capable of displaying each player's score on a dashboard. The sets were made up primarily of simple three-dimensional figures and two-dimensional flats. The targets ranged in value, and frequent guests could ring up some very high scores. The top 10 scores of the day were displayed on a monitor at the end of the ride. The average score for a 6-year-old during the testing phase was 317,000 points.

The online component of Buzz Lightyear Astro Blasters consisted of a website that randomly assigned players to ride along with the in-park guests. The online players could activate targets, enabling higher scores for those actually riding. Nine webcams were installed in the attraction. The online component opened on June 6. Another popular feature of the online feature was that in-park riders could send themselves e-mail with their pictures and scores.

In preparation of the park's 50th anniversary celebration, Locomotive #5, the *Ward Kimball,* joined the Disneyland Railroad fleet on June 25, 2005. In honor of Kimball, one of his creations, Jiminy Cricket, was painted on the Lantern. The train had originally operated at Cedar Park in Sandusky, Ohio, since 1961.[80]

Even the Jungle Cruise received some updates. The overgrown jungle was tamed, and piranhas were added to the water in the rapids area. Turnabout being fair play, one of the chimps at the base camp was handed a gun and started shooting at the boats, with the baboons—originally from the African veldt—contemplating the ensuing mayhem.

PART OF THE REFURBISHMENT of Space Mountain was to install lighting effects that could be used for future overlays. For example, on January 2, 2006, the attraction was renamed Rockin' Space Mountain. The lights within the dome were turned on, projections of dancers filled the room, and a new soundtrack by the rock band Red Hot Chili Peppers was installed. The overlay lasted only three months, never to return.

In September 2009, the ride was redressed as Ghost Galaxy, a Halloween overlay. It featured new projections, creepy onboard music, screeching ghosts and ghouls, and frightening visual effects. Ghost Galaxy was definitely a more amped-up version of the regular Space Mountain, and park management was now trying to decide how to make it clear this could be a very scary experience for school-age children.

Another classic attraction that received a major update was Space Mountain. After being closed more than two years, it reopened on July 15, 2005. Guests found a new track had been built using the original layout—which resulted in a much smoother ride—a reconfigured entryway, and a much darker interior. The iconic conic dome had been resurfaced with a building material infused with "Space Mountain white" that required no painting. New linear magnets were installed to replace the chain lifts, and a new soundtrack by Michael Giacchino replaced Dick Dale. The show building was much darker, and glowing side panels on the rockets were removed. The re-entry tunnel was also extended.

On July 17, 2005, Disneyland celebrated its 50th anniversary. In honor of the occasion, the park donated an original Dumbo elephant and Tea Cup to the Smithsonian's permanent collection.[81] The United States House of Representatives also approved a resolution congratulating the park on this milestone. Disneyland had truly become an American institution. The celebration was a huge hit, and attendance reached 14.26 million by the end of the year. The year ended with Michael Eisner's stepping down earlier than announced. Bob Iger became Disney CEO on October 1, 2005.

MENTAL REAL ESTATE

IN 2006 THE PAMPERING CONTINUED. Pirates of the Caribbean received a modest remodel with major implications. The attraction was closed for three months; when it reopened on June 26, the most notable change was the introduction of three Captain Jack Sparrow figures throughout the attraction. Sculptor Chris Turner modeled the figure after Johnny Depp, who played Sparrow in the hugely successful Pirates films. The Curse of the Black Pearl was placed in an all-new Treasure Room. Other changes included a water screen "waterfall" in the transition tunnel with Davy Jones, played by Bill Nighy, warning the guests of impending doom; a Captain Barbosa figure, voiced by Geoffrey Rush, taking over from Blackbeard and commanding the Wicked Wench to fire on the fort; and music from the film's Battle Scene. Also new were a pair of skeletons in the Crew's Quarters, playing a game of chess that neither could win, and compressed air cannon jets in the fort battle that simulated the blasts of cannon balls flying nearby. The sound and lighting systems had been completely updated, with more than 250 new speakers and new lighting fixtures.[82]

Another way that the Imagineers thought to exploit the popularity of the Pirates of the Caribbean movies was to redress Tom Sawyer Island. At one point, they considered cannons that guests could fire that would cause parts of New Orleans Square to collapse, as well as a larger tree house with slides and climbing nets. There was even talk of Fort Wilderness becoming a high-tech play area like Fortress Explorations at Tokyo DisneySea.

Although those changes were never made, Imagineers did modify Tom Sawyer Island by creating the Pirates Lair, which opened on May 25, 2006, at an estimated cost of $28 million. The most noticeable addition was a new two-level centerpiece play area with the rock-work reshaped to discourage climbing and the sharp edges softened. Near the barrel bridge were new interactive play elements, including a winch that lifted the remains of a pirate skeleton out of the water and pumps that drained a boat. Special effects were installed in Injun' Joe's Cave, but Fort Wilderness was closed to public access. Many of the landscape design elements were influenced by the need to comply with the Americans with Disabilities Act (ADA). A big draw was a pirate stunt show performed on the island during the first season. As part of the refurbishment, the rafts were replaced and named the *Anne Bonney* (a famous Irish pirate who plundered ships in the Caribbean in the 18th century) and the *Blackbeard*. The new rafts were a foot wider, rode about 8 inches higher in the water, and were several feet longer.

The *Los Angeles Times* attacked the changes in an editorial that said that, while many children may not know who Tom Sawyer was, "there will always be kids whose curiosity is sparked by all these unknown references. They might even be interested enough to put down the remote and crack open a book." Disney claimed the overlay was loosely linked to stories Mark Twain had written in which Tom and Huck Finn dreamed of being pirates.

The Haunted Mansion also added some new elements. The Attic was updated with a story line based on one of Marc Davis's portraits in the Stretching Room of a widow bride sitting on top of her dead husband's tombstone, which is adorned with an ax. The Attic was filled with portraits of Constance, the killer bride, and the increasingly wealthy men she married, whose heads would mysteriously disappear and reappear in the portraits. Just before the Doom Buggies fell out of the attic window, guests could see the figure of Constance animated with a projected face.

The big new attraction for 2007 was another update to a classic attraction: The Finding Nemo Submarine Voyage opened on June 11 to long lines. Tony Baxter said, "There's a term, 'mental real estate' that I think is very interesting. If you think of the word mermaid, Disney kind of owns that now because the first thing that comes to mind is Ariel from *The Little Mermaid*. If you go to any aquarium in the world, you can bet they're going to have Clown fish on display because the kids love them, and when they see them they say, 'Oh, it's Nemo, it's Nemo!' You've taken a thing that is generically owned by the public and transformed it into something where the mental real estate of it is owned by the Disney Company."[83]

The new show started out much like the original: The submarines cruise through the lagoon before entering an extended show building. At that point, guests could hear the hydrophones picking up sounds that suggested the fish were talking. That is when guests first met Mr. Ray and his class from the film *Finding Nemo*.

Instead of three-dimensional figures, the characters were digitally projected onto screens built inside of boxes. The water remained between the little portholes and the screens, creating a convincing illusion. The illusion was very impressive and very expensive to maintain. Due to air-quality regulations, the submarines were rebuilt with electric motors instead of diesel engines. To accommodate all of the new effects, the show grew from its original 9 minutes to 14 minutes.

TINKERING

ON OCTOBER 17, 2007, the Walt Disney Company announced that it would spend $1.1 billion over the next five years to fix Disney's

unofficial **TIP**
To help signal that a major change was at hand, the park was renamed Disney California Adventure on June 11, 2010. When California Adventure formally reopened on June 12, 2012, Disney CEO Bob Iger said of the Disney California Adventure makeover, "The park can stand on its own. Along with Disneyland, it will finally enable them to become the destination resort we envisioned."

California Adventure. Once again, Disneyland would take a back seat to one of its sister parks. California Adventure was estimated to have originally cost $600 million, but it was a critical and fan failure from its opening day. Over the next few years, much of the management's attention had been focused on fixing that troubled park. The 2007–2012 project would include a new entry called Buena Vista Street, a reworked Paradise Pier with a Little Mermaid dark ride, and a new nighttime water fountain and special effects show called the *World of Color*. The project would also include Cars Land, a new 12-acre immersive environment, based on the Disney-Pixar film *Cars*, with three attractions: Radiator Springs Racers, Luigi's Flying Tires, and Mater's Junkyard Jamboree. California Adventure would go from being a "hip" take on California culture to one that celebrated a romanticized version of the state.

With much of the attention going to California Adventure, Disneyland continued to tinker around the edges, including changes in the 200-odd block on Main Street in 2008. The Carnation Café took over the bakery and added seating under a brass awning on Center Street. Guests looking for baked goods on Main Street could now go to the Jolly Holiday Bakery, which repurposed the long-closed Plaza Pavilion. For the first time, Mary Poppins had a permanent presence in the park: The inlaid mosaic at the entrance looked like a sidewalk drawing by Bert from the Tea Party Scene. The interior reflected 1901–1910 Edwardian era decor.

Pixie Hollow was added October 28, 2008, on the spot where the House of the Future once rested. This became a meet-and-greet area for Tinker Bell and her expanded roster of fairy friends. A musical fountain out front entertained guests while they waited to be shrunk to the size of a pixie.

Another early attraction was also updated: The long-shuttered Sleeping Beauty Castle walk-through reopened on November 21, 2008. The new version was a return to the original Eyvind Earle vision, with updated special effects using the latest technologies. Gone were the echo room and the goons staring back at the guests.

Even the Disneyland Monorail was updated. The first of three five-car Mark VII monorail trains opened to the public on July 4, 2008.

Designed by Imagineer Scot Drake, they were a tribute to Bob Gurr's original Buck Rogers design but with a few new touches. The design was a blend of old and new with the signature 1950s bubble-dome noses, while the lower sweep of vestigial tail fin looked more modern and was reportedly inspired by ground effects on modern sports cars.[84] Disney watchdog Al Lutz said, "Seeing how the original trains were directly inspired by the General Motors car offerings of 1959, it seems appropriate."

The Mark VII trains were built in British Columbia and came with a special paint that changed color in the sunlight. The interior had a central bench seat that faced out toward the windows, and recessed LED lighting in the cabin matched the color of the train. For the operators, a computer-controlled, six-speed drive system was installed, as well as more cameras, a new public address system, and a more-comfortable seat for the pilot. The capacity remained at 120 guests, and the top speed remained the same at 30 mph.[85]

The new trains were originally scheduled to begin operation in February 2009, but they were plagued with mechanical and clearance problems. To save weight, the trains were not air-conditioned. Due to recommendations from the WDC legal team, ventilation was limited to fixed windows that only popped out a couple of inches at the bottom. This resulted in trains that could not run if it was hotter than 80°F. One solution was to add a vent made from the escape hatch. Ultimately, new windows were installed that were similar to those on the earlier versions of the monorail.

Another problem was that the chassis and suspension system had been incorrectly designed in such a way that it was not making the clearance between the chassis itself and the concrete beam. The trains could not make the turns. It was determined that there was a discrepancy between the original blueprints and the drawings that had been generated from the reversed engineering done on a cannibalized Mark V train. Monorail Red finally debuted on July 4, and Monorail Blue would go online in September.

unofficial **TIP**

Problems continued to plague the Mark VII monorails. At one point in 2011, all three monorails were parked and brought up to date.

On February 6, 2009, It's a Small World reopened after an extensive rehabilitation. The public relations department said the reason for the 10-month closure was to remove "layers and layers" of fiberglass that had built up in the water flume over the years. They also said that many of the flats were original to the 1964–1965 New York World's Fair.

However, website publisher Al Lutz claimed there was another reason. He pointed out that in 1960, the average American male weighed 166 pounds and the average woman was 140 pounds. By 2009, the men's average grew to 195.3 pounds, while women grew to 170.2 pounds. Lutz said there were two spots, one at the Canadian Mounties and the other near the Scandinavian geese, where the boats frequently bottomed out and got stuck. He discovered, "They've even built a platform next to that curve because they've had so many problems." One or more guests would exit, and the boats could then continue on their way.[86] When It's a Small World reopened, the new flume was 1 inch deeper, and the new boats were made of a colored plastic resin shaped from a mold that was more buoyant than the original wood.[87]

The concept for the updated attraction was borrowed from the version of the attraction under construction at Hong Kong Disneyland and featured 29 new characters from Disney and Pixar animated films, designed in the signature style of the ride. Characters included Alice on a chess board in the England area, Abu from Aladdin near India, and Simba in the Africa section. Musical counterpoints incorporating each character's theme music were integrated into the soundtrack. To replace the rain forest segment, Imagineers designed a new scene, the Spirit of America, which depicted American Indians dancing and farm children singing. For many guests, the ride became a treasure hunt to find the new characters.[88]

On December 17, 2009, *Great Moments with Mr. Lincoln* returned to the Main Street Opera House once again. The new show revisited featured elements from the 1965 Disneyland version and presented an experimental Audio-Animatronics human figure. Of the new Mr. Lincoln, Imagineer Tony Baxter said, "We felt that rather than have the frozen face with the mouth moving, we'd challenge ourselves to bring the entire head to life."[89] He explained, "We never use technology for technology's sake. When you do that, it's a gimmick." Looking back, "The first motion picture was of people dancing around on a screen, and when people first saw a train coming at them on film, they ran in fear from the theater. But once people understood what movies were, then you had to tell them a story," he said. "That happened with Audio-Animatronics. You could put dolls, Lincoln, and birds in front of people and they'd say, 'This is a miracle . . . these things are moving!' And then, all of a sudden people needed to have more than that."[90]

Imagineers wanted a figure so precise that a guest could watch the show without sound and read his lips. Baxter, who expected guests to zoom in with their video cameras, was satisfied with the results. "Mr. Lincoln is good enough to get in real close."[91] He said, "You'll be able to hear him smack his lips and hear him get another breath." In the past, Mr. Lincoln's actions had been controlled with a combination of hydraulic and electronic components. This new figure had a completely electronic head. The soundtrack was remastered from the original recordings of Royal Dano as Lincoln and Paul Frees as the narrator. The theater was also outfitted with a new state-of-the-art audio system.

Even not-so-long-ago attractions made a comeback. On January 3, 2010, the last rat was released from *Honey, I Shrunk the Audience,* and the *Captain EO* tribute moved in on February 23, 2010. Many of the original special effects—including the lasers—were missing, but the movable floor from the previous show was used during the finale.

When the Rivers of America attraction was drained for periodic maintenance in 2010, a mountain of debris was removed, including hundreds of cellphones, liquor bottles, a computer tower, and half a canoe. That in itself was not unusual; what was different this time was how Disney handled the water. In the past, the waterways had been drained directly into the Anaheim sewer system. This time, the 6 million gallons of water were sent to holding ponds, where it seeped into the groundwater supply. The recycled water was then used to refill the waterway.[92]

The Rivers of America reopened in May. The show was divided into four segments, allowing guests to pass through the Mississippi, Columbia, Potomac, and Rio Grande Rivers. The park planted more than 4,000 new shrubs and 130 new trees to enhance the illusion. For example, in the Columbia region, deer drank from a creek while American Indian braves guarded Tom Sawyer Island. In the Rio Grande region, mountain lions hid in tall grass while an osprey on top of a winch watched the boats passing by. The friendly American Indian camp was refreshed with a corral for two live ponies; and the burning cabin, which had been vacant and nonfunctioning for years, became the home of river boatman Mike Fink and his keelboat, the *Gullywhumper,* which was placed out front. Sixteen of the figures were repainted, and 10 new figures were added, including a tribute to an early Marc Davis drawing of a skunk and two raccoons on a log. On the infrastructure side, the 2,500-foot track for the *Mark Twain* and *Columbia* was replaced, as were 9 of the 11 docks.

Since Star Tours opened, one of the promises of its technology was the ability to install a new film and reprogram the simulator. On June

3, 2011, that promise was finally realized with the opening of Star Tours: The Adventure Continues. The new show was based on all six of the *Star Wars* movies. The biggest difference was the upgraded 3-D technology and the ability to provide a random experience. The show was divided into three acts, with two different versions of the first act, three different second acts, and two different endings—a total of 54 variations. A new loading and unloading system was installed to increase capacity.

Attendance remained steady, with 14.8 million guests in 2007 and 14.7 million in 2008. However, attendance exploded to 15.9 million in 2009, due in part to heavily discounted tickets and resort packages, as well as a promotion that offered guests free admission on their birthdays. The good times would continue with nearly 16 million guests in 2010 and more than 16 million in 2011.

Things continued pretty much the same in 2012, with the Matterhorn Bobsleds reopening on June 15 after a six-month, $1.3 million extensive makeover. Gone were the classic bobsleds where riders could share a seat with another member of their party. Jim Crouch, project field director suggested, "People didn't like to snuggle up so much. They wanted their space." Instead, the new high-tech bobsleds had three individual seats and safety systems alerting the cast members if anyone was not wearing his or her seat belt. The retro paint scheme reminded guests of the two-toned look of the Matterhorn decal on the front of the 1959 sleds. Along with the new seating arrangement, a new single-rider line was installed.[93]

Over the years, more and more snow had been added to the mountain because it was a lot easier to paint than to match the surrounding rock. During the 2012 rehabilitation, a 20-level scaffolding system was deployed, and the mountain was carefully painted from top to bottom. The Imagineers had studied and tried to copy the snow patterns of the real Matterhorn. Glass beads were mixed in with the white paint to provide the illusion of wet snow. Twenty-three pine trees that had been missing for years were replanted. Crouch said, "It really makes the mountain come to life."

As 2012 was coming to a close, there were no major announcements for any grand initiatives. Disneyland had become a middle-aged icon, loved and adored by the public for what it had been and what it had meant to them. But it was at the crossroads of where it wanted to go. What path would it choose as it approached its 60th birthday?

1. Marla Dickerson, "They're Getting a Bit Goofy at Disneyland," *Los Angeles Times,* 16 Feb. 1996.
2. Jeff Rowe, "Disney Building a Stunner," *Orange County Register,* 13 Aug. 1994.
3. Beth Dunlop, *Building a Dream: The Art of Disney Architecture* (New York: Disney Editions, Inc., 2011).
4. Ibid.
5. Marla Jo Fisher, "Driving Mr. Disney," *Orange County Register,* 2 March 1996.
6. Penny Love, "Grand Moves Hint at Disney Expansion," *Orange County Register,* 13 Dec. 1995.
7. "The Huck Stops Here," *Orange County Register,* 7 May 1996.
8. Karal Ann Marling, *Designing Disney's Theme Parks: The Architecture of Reassurance* (New York: Flammarion, 1997).
9. Marla Jo Fisher, "Officials Glimpse Disney Plans," *Orange County Register,* 13 July 1996.
10. "Disneyland Expansion," *Anaheim Bulletin,* 10 Oct. 1996.
11. Marla Jo Fisher, "New Disney Ride: Whiz-Bang Trams," *Orange County Register,* 21 Nov. 1997.
12. "The New Taste of Main Street U.S.A.," *Disneyland Line,* 14 March 1997.
13. Jeff Kramer, "Subtly Gentler Pirates Debuts at Disneyland," *Orange County Register,* 8 March 1997.
14. Ibid.
15. Clarence Page, "The PC Brigands are Scuttling Disneyland," *Chicago Tribune,* 9 Jan. 1997.
16. Laura Bleiberg, "Small World's Seasonal Makeover," *Orange County Register,* 26 Nov. 1997.
17. "Disneyland Welcomes its 400 Millionth Guest," *Anaheim Bulletin,* 10 July 1997.
18. Jerry Hirsch, "Rift Surfaces Over Disney's Sub Ride," *Orange County Register,* 17 May 1998.
19. Jerry Hirsch, "Keeper of the Kingdom," *Orange County Register,* 5 April 1998.
20. Nancy Wride, "A Bon Voyage," *Los Angeles Times,* 9 Sept.1998.
21. Disneyland, "Disneyland Announces Plans to Launch Tomorrowland into the World of Imagination and Beyond," press release, 5 Jan. 1998.
22. Ibid.
23. Jerry Hirsch, "Almost Time to Go Back to the Future," *Orange County Register,* 10 Feb. 1998.
24. Ibid.
25. Ibid.
26. Ibid.
27. Ibid.
28. Marla Dickerson, "Disneyland Steps Back to Get Ahead," *Los Angeles Times,* 22 March 1996.
29. Disneyland, "Disneyland Announces Plans to Launch Tomorrowland into the World of Imagination and Beyond," press release, 5 Jan. 1998.
30. Ibid.
31. "Rocket Rods," *Orange County Register,* 28 Feb. 1998.
32. Jerry Hirsch, "Front and Center with Disney CEO Eisner," *Orange County Register,* 22 May 1998.
33. Jerry Hirsch, "Rocket Rods Grounded as Disneyland Fixes Ride," *Orange County Register,* 11 July 1998.
34. Daryl Strickland, "Tomorrowland Aims to Dig Up the Past," *Los Angeles Times,* 26 March 1998.
35. Disneyland, "The New Tomorrowland," brochure (Anaheim, CA: Disneyland, 1998).
36. E. Scott Reckard, "Disney Hints at Even Bigger Plans," *Los Angeles Times,* 27 June 1998.
37. "2001 and Beyond," *Disneyland Resort Planning News,* July 2000.
38. Jerry Hirsch, "Some Disneyland Attractions to Limit Hours," *Orange County Register,* 3 Oct. 1998.
39. Jerry Hirsch, "The Price of Magic," *Orange County Register,* 27 Oct. 1998.

40. Marla Jo Fisher, "You Can Imagine, Too, at Disney Preview," *Orange County Register,* 19 Oct. 1998.
41. Jerry Hirsch, "Creating the Premier Theme Park," *Orange County Register,* 14 Oct. 1998.
42. Ibid.
43. Ibid.
44. Ibid.
45. Ibid.
46. Marla Jo Fisher, "Anaheim's Golf N' Stuff Leveled After 29 Years," *Orange County Register,* 6 Jan. 1999.
47. Jerry Hirsch, "Swiss Family Tree House to be Replaced by Tarzan Attraction," *Orange County Register,* 17 March 1999.
48. Jerry Hirsch, "Disney Changes Plan: Tarzan Gets Tree House," *Orange County Register,* 10 March 1999.
49. Jerry Hirsch, "Swiss Family to be Evicted from Treehouse?," *Orange County Register,* 25 Feb. 1999.
50. Jerry Hirsch, "Disney Plan: Ride While You Wait," *Orange County Register,* 23 July 1999.
51. Heather MacDonald, "System Intended to Cut Disneyland Waiting Sputters," *Orange County Register,* 29 July 1999.
52. Danielle Herubin, "Start Your Engines," *Orange County Register,* 20 June 2000.
53. Jerry Hirsch, "A Third Disney Park Seems Likely, But It's Not a Sure Bet at This Point," *Los Angeles Times,* 18 Aug. 1998.
54. Disneyland, "Presenting Downtown Disney," press release, 2 Jan. 2001.
55. Dunlop, *Building a Dream.*
56. Ibid.
57. Bernard Wolfson, "Disney opts to pack up trunks," *Orange County Register,* 3 Jan. 2000.
58. Fisher, "You Can Imagine, Too."
59. Ibid.
60. Ibid.
61. Ibid.
62. Dunlop, *Building a Dream.*
63. "Wathel Rogers and Audio-Animatronics," *The "E" Ticket,* Number 25, Winter 1996.
64. Cory Doctorow, *Down and Out in the Magic Kingdom* (New York: Tor Books, 2003).
65. "Disneyland Honors its 450 Millionth Guest," *Orange County Register,* 16 March 2001.
66. Michelle Himmelberg, "Jungle Cruise Visitors Get Another Shot at Fun," *Orange County Register,* 8 Oct. 2004.
67. "Disneyland Unveils New and Improved Lincoln Attraction," *Orange County Register,* 17 July 2001.
68. "Disney's Haunted Mansion to Get a Holiday Makeover," *Orange County Register,* 24 July 2001.
69. Michelle Gabriel, "Making the Disney Rounds," *Orange County Register,* 19 Feb. 2003.
70. Michelle Himmelberg, "Fun Pooh-sonified," *Orange County Register,* 10 April 2003.
71. Ibid.
72. "Disney Ride Draws Criticism," *Orange County Register,* 10 July 2004.
73. Van Arsdale France, "Backstage Disneyland: A Personal History" (unpublished manuscript, 1980).
74. Rolly Crump with Jeff Heimbuch, *It's Kind of a Cute Story* (Clearwater, FL: Bamboo Forest, 2012).

75. Wendy Lefkin, ed., *Disney Insider Yearbook: 2005 Year in Review* (New York: Disney Editions, Inc., 2006).

76. Michele Himmelberg, "Reality vs. Fantasy," *Orange County Register*, 10 March 2004.

77. "Disneyland aims to improve FastPass," *Orange County Register*, 20 July 2004.

78. Mary Susan Herczog and Steve Hockman, "What Would Walt Say?," *Los Angeles Times*, 24 Dec. 1995.

79. Michele Himmelberg, "Buzz to Cross Cyberspace," *Orange County Register*, 17 March 2005.

80. Steve DeGaetano, *From Plantation to Theme Park: The Story of Disneyland Railroad Locomotive No. 5.*, The Ward Kimball. (Wake Forest, NC: Steam Passage Publications, 2006).

81. "Disney's Dumbo Gets a New Home in D.C.," *Orange County Register*, 9 June 2005.

82. Sarah Tully and Chantal Lamers, "Yo Ho, Yo Ho!," *Orange County Register*, 26 June 2006.

83. Jim Fanning, *Finding Nemo In the Disney Theme Parks* (New York: Disney Editions, Inc., 2009).

84. Sonya Smith, "Disney Rolls Out New Mark VII Monorail," *Orange County Register*, 10 July 2008.

85. Sonya Smith, "Walt's New Ride," *Orange County Register*, 24 April 2008.

86. Kimi Yoshino, "Disneyland's Weighty Affair," *Philadelphia Inquirer*, 18 Nov. 2007.

87. "Small World Cast Grows," *Los Angeles Times*, 5 Feb. 2009.

88. Adam Townsend, "It's a New Small World," *Orange County Register*, 5 Feb. 2009.

89. Sarah Tully, "High-Tech Mr. Lincoln Set to Return to Stage," *Orange County Register*, 17 Dec. 2009.

90. Ibid.

91. Ibid.

92. Eleanor Hoover, "Disneyland Analyzed: It's a Freudian Wonderland," *Los Angeles Times*, 5 May 2010.

93. Hugo Martin, "Peak Performance is Aim of Matterhorn Renovation," *Los Angeles Times*, 8 Feb. 2012.

EPILOGUE

WALT DECLARED, "Disneyland is the star. Everything else is in the supporting role."[1] Like many movie stars before and since, the park's story is familiar. At the start, her popularity took off like a rocket. Then, as she matured, she explored more challenging roles. Over time, she had moments of brilliance, but those became fewer and farther between, and she began to coast on a well-deserved reputation. Walt knew that his star needed to constantly reinvent herself while staying true to her inner forces based on timeless principles. This is how he had lived his own life.

Perhaps the greatest illusion on display at Disney is what Jeff Kurtti suggested when he said that frequent visits to the park are "revelatory in the drastic change you will see —and the almost complete lack of change you will see."[2] The park has always been "in a state of becoming," as Walt would later say about a different project.[3]

When Tony Baxter studied the evolution of Disneyland, he realized that the earliest attractions relied on the technique of placing the guest onstage in popular movie genres based on "the Disney mythologies for their storylines" or characters from American history.[4] Baxter said, "What is interesting from a designer's point of view is how Walt built a park from the images that made him comfortable as a child."[5]

Baxter suggested, "Disneyland defined the term 'virtual reality.' Today, the term is associated with a video game or a cyber environment, but for me, the Jungle Cruise is virtual reality! It's as authentic a jungle as you can possibly have in the desert in Southern California— that's the virtual reality of it."[6] *Los Angeles Times* columnist Jack Smith joked in 1969, "[Disneyland] is better than the real thing. It is the jungle without tsetse flies; New Orleans without humidity; a pirate ship without scurvy; a Matterhorn without cold; a Main Street, U.S.A., without litter."[7] He noted that the park's formula of success was "respect for the past, real illusions, Prohibition, clean streets, and every day is a parade."[8]

The park also attracted early critics. Orrin Klapp, a sociologist from San Diego State, suggested, "America is changing right from under us and so many of us have no real traditions. You have this hankering for a past, even if it's not yours and it's a phonied-up one." Walt was attacked in *The Nation* in 1958 when critic Julian Halevy suggested Disneyland is where "the whole world, the universe, and all man's dominion over self and nature has been reduced to a sickening blend of cheap formulas packaged to sell."[9]

However, the park also had its defenders. Ray Bradbury wrote a letter to the editor of *The Nation* and confessed, "I admit I approached Disneyland with many intellectual reservations, myself, but these have been banished in my seven visits. Disney makes many mistakes; what artist doesn't? But when he flies, he really flies. I have a sneaking suspicion, after all is said and done, that Mr. Halevy truly loved Disneyland but is not man enough, or child enough, to admit it."[10]

Gladwin Hill of the *New York Times* felt the same way as Bradbury when he tried to define Disneyland's success. "Many factors have entered into it. But to pinpoint a single element, it would be imagination—not just imagination on the part of its impresarios, but their evocation of the imagination of the cash customers." He noted, "Walt Disney and his associates have managed to generate in the traditionally raucous and off-times shoddy amusement park field, the same 'suspension of disbelief' which has been the secret of theatrical success down the corridors of time. In the theatre the vital ingredient is not realism, but a blending of the real with the imaginary. The entertainer invites the audience to meet him half way. This is what has been successfully achieved at Disneyland."[11]

By the 1960s, Baxter said, the emphasis was on musical attractions such as *The Enchanted Tiki Room,* It's a Small World, Pirates of the Caribbean, and the Haunted Mansion. John Bright of *The Nation* was much kinder than Halevy had been; Bright wrote that Disneyland "is the only major amusement park in America which does not stimulate and capitalize upon hostile aggression and competitiveness. Nor upon fright. Its thrills are derived from and targeted to the child in us. I'm sure Dr. Spock would concur." He added, "Through the most intelligently managed system of controls—from parking to adventuring and dining—an entirely new kind of crowd behavior is stimulated. The same people who grow raucously assertive at ball games and prize fights and in other amusement parks, here comport themselves with a conspicuous good nature and freedom from irritation that has been remarked by observers less than by biased press agents. Squalling infants, even at fatigue peak in the evening hours, are rare."[12] Dick Nunis proudly said, "The thing that has made Disneyland successful from the very beginning is that Walt Disney believed in giving the guests a good value and a good show all the time. We established standard operating procedures for our attractions . . . which are always there to give our guests a good show."[13]

This competency helped Disneyland compete during the thrill-ride era of the 1970s and 1980s. The park stuck to the fundamentals. "All in all, a concern for the needs and comfort of people has become much more evident today in many ways," Disney Legend John Hench said. "Perhaps the astonishing success of Disney theme entertainment and its inherent concern for people have served to accelerate this new awareness of 'the human factor.' Even so, in the wake of these changes and others which could at least indirectly trace their lineage to a Disney influence, both Disneyland and Walt Disney World remain unique while their popularity continues to grow."[14]

A trip to Disneyland would become a rite of passage for many Americans. Social ethics and Jewish Philosophy professor Laurie Zoloth-Dorfman proclaimed, "Disneyland is the secular American version of Lourdes."[15] Gerald Peary of the *Boston Globe* opined, "Going to Disneyland became the quintessential way to experience America, like seeing the Eiffel Tower when in France or checking out Egypt's pyramids. Surely, no 20th-century construction has been so analyzed, and by scholars in so many fields: architects, anthropologists, psychologists, sociologists, semioticians, cultural historians."[16]

Bradbury wrote, "Disneyland is a perfect city all to itself. Yes, it's designed for fun, but you can learn from the totality of the experience of Disneyland . . . how to treat people, how to protect them from the heat and how to move them in lines where they are entertained and not bored out of their skulls." Bradbury felt that Disneyland was "the total of things that didn't have to be done but are done anyway."[17]

As for the future? Disney is betting billions of dollars that the next trends are interactive queues and rides with a heavy dose of technology to personalize and ration guest experiences. The interactive ride was inspired by guests who were no longer content to sit passively but wanted to control their point of view—like Roger Rabbit's Car Toon Spin and Buzz Lightyear Astro Blasters—or who demanded a random experience, such as Indiana Jones and Star Tours. However the technologies evolve, we can be sure they will continue to take guests places they have never been.

One thing is constant, however. Architect Charles Moore said, "In an uncharitable sea of suburbia, Disney has created a place, indeed, a whole public world, full of sequential occurrences, of big and little drama, of hierarchies of importance and excitement, with opportunities to respond at the speed of rocketing bobsleds or of horse-drawn street cars. No raw edges spoil the picture at Disneyland; everything is as immaculate as in the musical-comedy villages that Hollywood has provided for our viewing pleasure for the last three generations."[18]

Walt certainly did not create this unspoiled place on his own. Don D. Jackson, M.D., wrote, "Disney was a master executive capable of harnessing vast numbers of talented people to work out the details of his childlike vision. Like an innocent, Disney did not recognize the ordinary limitations implied by knowledge. All his creative productions realize the visions of childhood—they reach beyond the stars."[19] He added, "As do many creative people, Disney enacted the hope and idealism of modern-day innocence—the persistent belief, in the face of overwhelming technological reasons for why 'it can't be done,' that men can achieve whatever they can conceive."[20]

Disneyland may have very well come out of Walt's frustration with the business of filmmaking. He may have been looking for something new to spark his intellectual interest. He wanted to find a project that was never complete, "in the can" as they say in Hollywood. Walt understood creativity was the gathering and understanding of information and rearranging it into something new. Van France observed Walt "knew about all things practical. His life was a total educational process and he always retained the best possible instructors."[21] So Walt gathered the best and brightest, and they created a revolution in spacial design and storytelling within the public realm. The result, as Walt said himself, is that "Disneyland will never be completed as long as there is imagination left in the world."

1. Dave Smith, *Walt Disney Famous Quotes* (Lake Buena Vista, FL: Walt Disney Theme Parks and Resorts, 1994).
2. Jeff Kurtti, *Disneyland: From Once Upon a Time to Happily Ever After* (New York: Disney Editions, Inc., 2010).
3. *The Epcot Film*, written by Martin Sklar (1966; Orlando, FL: Walt Disney Productions).
4. Remon G. McLeod, "A Marriage of Convenience," *Orange County Register*, 2 June 1985.
5. Ibid.
6. "Tony Baxter—Disneyland's Idea Guy!," *The "E" Ticket*, Number 46, Summer 2009, 4–21.
7. Jack Smith, "A Day in the City: To Disneyland," *Westways*, Sept. 1969.
8. Jack Smith, "How Can Disneyland Sustain Such Success? Let Him Count the Ways," *Los Angeles Times*, 21 July 1983.
9. Julian Halevy, "Disneyland and Las Vegas," *The Nation*, 7 June 1958.
10. Ray Bradbury, letter to the editor, *The Nation*, 28 June 1958.
11. Gladwin Hill, "Disneyland Reports On Its First Ten Million," *New York Times*, 3 Feb. 1957.
12. John Bright, "Disney's Fantasy Empire," *The Nation*, 6 March 1967.
13. Disneyland University, "The Dream Is a Reality" (Anaheim, CA: Disneyland, July 1975).
14. Ibid.
15. John Dart, "Of God and Mickey," *Los Angeles Times*, 28 Nov. 1998.
16. Gerald Peary, "Walt's World," *The Boston Globe*, 19 April 1992.
17. Ray Bradbury, "Disneyland, or Disney's Demon for Happiness," *Modern Maturity*, March/April 2002.
18. Paul Goldberger, "Mickey Mouse Teaches the Architects," *New York Times*, 22 Oct. 1972.
19. Don D. Jackson, M.D., "Awe in Disneyland," *Medical Opinion & Review*, Oct. 1957.
20. Ibid.
21. Van Arsdale France, "Backstage Disneyland: A Personal History" (unpublished manuscript, 1980).

SELECTED BIBLIOGRAPHY

Anderson, Paul F. "A Great Big Beautiful Tomorrow," *Persistence of Vision,* Issue 6/7, 1995.

Baham, Jeff. The *Secrets of Disney's Haunted Mansion*. San Jose, CA: doombuggies.com, 2006.

Ballard, Donald W. *Disneyland Hotel: 1954–1959, The Little Motel in the Middle of the Orange Grove*. Fremont, CA: Magical Hotel, 2011.

Barrier, Michael. *The Animated Man: A Life of Walt Disney*. Berkeley, CA: University of California Press, 2007.

Boag, Wally and Gene Sands. *Wally Boag: Clown Prince of Disneyland*. New York: Disney Editions, 2009.

Bradbury, Ray. "Disneyland, or Disney's Demon for Happiness," *Modern Maturity,* March/April 2002.

Bradbury, Ray. *The Machine-Tooled Happyland*. New York: *Holiday,* October 1965.

Bright, Randy. *Disneyland: Inside Story*. New York: Abrams, 1987.

Broggie, Michael. *Walt Disney's Railroad Story*. Pasadena, CA: Pentrex, 1998.

Burnes, Brian, Robert W. Butler and Dan Viets. *Walt Disney's Missouri*. Kansas City, MO: Kansas City Star Books, 2002.

Burns-Clair, Pam, and Don Peri. *Walt Disney's First Lady of Imagineering Harriet Burns*. Virginia Beach, VA: Donning, 2010.

Crump, Rolly, with Jeff Heimbuch. *It's Kind of a Cute Story*. Clearwater, FL: Bamboo Forest, 2012.

DeGaetano, Steve. *From Plantation to Theme Park: The Story of Disneyland Railroad Locomotive No. 5, The Ward Kimball*. Wake Forest, NC: Steam Passage Publications, 2006.

DeGaetano, Steve. *Welcome Aboard the Disneyland Railroad!* Winter, CA: Steam Passages Publications, 2004.

Disneyland: The First Quarter Century. Burbank, CA: Walt Disney Productions, 1979.

Doctorow, Cory. *Down and Out in the Magic Kingdom*. New York: Tor Books, 2003.

Donaldson, John Stanley. *Warp and Weft: Life Canvas of Herbert Ryman*. Las Vegas: Incanio Press, 2010.

Dunlop, Beth. *Building a Dream: The Art of Disney Architecture*. New York: Abrams, 1996.

Dunlop, Beth. *Building a Dream: The Art of Disney Architecture*. New York: Disney Editions, Inc., 2011.

Eisner, Michael with Tony Schwartz. *Work In Progress*. New York: Hyperion Books, 2001.

The E-Ticket Magazine. San Francisco: The Walt Disney Family Foundation.

Fanning, Jim. *Finding Nemo In The Disney Theme Parks*. New York: Disney Editions, Inc., 2009.

Findlay, John. *Magic Lands*. Berkeley, CA: University of California Press, 1992.

Flores, Russell D. *Seen, Un-Seen Disneyland: What You See at Disneyland, but Never Really See*. St. George, UT: Synergy Books, 2012.

France, Van Arsdale. "Backstage Disneyland: A Personal History." Unpublished manuscript, 1980.

France, Van Arsdale. *Window on Main Street*. Livonia, MI: Starbur Press, 1991.

Gabler, Neal. *Walt Disney: The Triumph of the American Imagination*. New York: Knopf, 2006.

Gabler, Neal, Harriet Burns, Alice Davis, Blaine Gibson, and Richard Schickel. *The Life & Legacy of Walt Disney*. Annenberg School for Communication, University of Southern California, Nov. 15, 2006.

Gennawey, Sam. *Walt and the Promise of Progress City*. Montgomery, AL: Ayefour, 2011.

Gordon, Bruce, and David Mumford. *Disneyland: The Nickel Tour*. Santa Clarita, CA: Camphor Tree, 2000.

Gordon, Bruce, and Tim O'Day. *Disneyland: Then, Now, and Forever*. New York: Disney Editions, Inc., 2005.

Greene, Katherine, and Richard Greene. *Inside the Dream*. New York: Disney Editions, Inc. 2001.

Gurr, Bob. *Design: Just for Fun*. Tugging, CA: APP-Gurr Design, 2012.

Haas, Charlie. "Disneyland Is Good for You," *The New West Magazine*, 4 Dec. 1978.

Harris, Cyril. *Illustrated Dictionary of Historic Architecture*. New York: Dover, 1977.

Hench, John, with Peggy Van Pelt. *Designing Disney: Imagineering and the Art of the Show*. New York: Disney Editions, Inc. 2008.

Kaufman, J. B. *The Walt Disney Family Museum: The Man, The Magic, The Memories*. New York: Disney Editions, Inc. 2009.

Kinney, Jack. *Walt Disney and Other Assorted Characters*. New York: Harmony Press, 1988.

Korkis, Jim. *The Revised Vault of Walt: Unofficial, Unauthorized, Uncensored Disney Stories Never Told*. Orlando, FL: Theme Park Press, 2012.

Kotin, Regan & Mouchly, Inc. *Summary Economic and Fiscal Impacts "Port Disney."* Long Beach, CA, October 1990.

Kurtti, Jeff. *Disneyland: From Once Upon a Time to Happily Ever After*. New York: Disney Editions, Inc. 2010.

Kurtti, Jeff. *Disneyland: Through the Decades: A Photographic Celebration*. New York: Disney Editions, Inc. 2010.

Kurtti, Jeff. *Walt Disney's Imagineering Legends and the Genesis of the Disney Theme Park*. New York: Disney Editions, Inc. 2008.

Kurtti, Jeff, and Bruce Gordon. *The Art of Disneyland.* New York: Disney Editions, Inc., 2005.

Leebron, Elizabeth and Lynn Gartley. *Walt Disney: A Guide to References and Resources.* Boston: G. K. Hall & Co. 1979.

Lefkin, Wendy, ed. *Disney Insider Yearbook: 2005 Year in Review.* New York: Disney Editions 2006.

Lefkin, Wendy, ed. *The Imagineering Field Guide to Disneyland: An Imagineer's Eye Tour.* New York: Disney Editions, Inc. 2008.

Lefkin, Wendy, ed. *The Magic Begins with Me.* New York: Disney Enterprises, Inc. 2005.

Lefkin, Wendy, ed. *Walt Disney Imagineering: A Behind the Dreams Look at Making the Magic Real.* New York: Hyperion, 1996.

Lindquist, Jack, with Melinda J. Combs. *In Service to the Mouse.* Orange, CA: Chapman University Press, 2010.

Malmberg, Melody, ed. *Walt Disney Imagineering: A Behind the Dreams Look at Making More Magic Real.* New York: Disney Editions, 2010.

Marling, Karal Ann. *Behind The Magic: 50 Years of Disneyland.* Dearborn, MI: Henry Ford Museum, 2004.

Marling, Karal Ann. *Designing Disney's Theme Parks: The Architecture of Reassurance.* New York: Flammarion, 1997.

Masters, Kim. *The Keys to the Kingdom.* New York: William Morrow, 2000.

Merritt, Christopher and J. Eric Lynxwiler. *Knott's Preserved.* Santa Monica, CA: Angel City Press, 2010.

Moore, Charles W. *You Have to Pay for the Public Life.* Cambridge, MA: MIT Press, 2001.

O'Boyle, J. G. "Mindsetter: A Cultural Analysis of Disney's Main Street USA," *Persistence of Vision.* Issue 10, 1998.

O'Brien, Tim. *Ripley's Legends: Pioneers of the Amusement Park Industry, Volume One.* Nashville, TN: Ripley's Entertainment, 2006.

O'Day, Tim, and Lorraine Santoli. *Disneyland Resort: A Pictorial Souvenir.* Wendy Lufkin, ed., New York: Disney Enterprises, Inc., 2002.

O'Day, Tim, Jody Revenon, Lorraine Santoli, Leonard Shannon, and The Imagineers. *Disneyland Resort: Remember the Moments, A Magical Souvenir.* Wendy Lufkin, ed., New York: Disney Enterprises, Inc., 2005.

O'Neal, David. *Anaheim Vacation Land.* U.S.A.: Extinct Attractions, 2009.

Price, Harrison "Buzz." *Walt's Revolution! By the Numbers.* Orlando, FL: Ripley Entertainment, 2004.

Schickel, Richard. *The Disney Version.* New York: Simon and Schuster, 1968.

Schultz, Jason, and Kevin Yee. *Jason's Disneyland Almanac: 1955–2010.* Orlando, FL: Zauberreich Press, 2011.

Sklar, Martin A. *Walt Disney's Disneyland.* Anaheim, CA: Walt Disney Productions, 1969.

Smith, Dave. *Walt Disney Famous Quotes.* Lake Buena Vista, FL: Walt Disney Theme Parks and Resorts, 1994.

Snyder, Chuck. *Windows on Main Street: Discover the Real Stories of the Talented People Featured on the Windows of Main Street.* New York: Disney Editions, Inc., 2009.

Stewart, James B. *DisneyWar.* New York: Simon and Schuster, 2005.

Surrell, Jason. *The Disney Mountains: Imagineering at Its Peak.* New York: Disney Editions, Inc., 2007.

Surrell, Jason. *The Haunted Mansion: From the Magic Kingdom to the Movies.* New York: Disney Editions, Inc., 2003.

Surrell, Jason. *Pirates of the Caribbean: From the Magic Kingdom to the Movies.* New York: Disney Editions, Inc., 2005.

Taylor, John. *Storming the Kingdom.* New York: Ballantine Books, 1988.

Telotte, J. P. *The Mouse Machine: Disney and Technology*. Chicago: University of Illinois Press, 2008.

Thie, Carlene. *Disney's Early Years: Though the Eye of a Photographer*. Riverside, CA: Ape Pen Publishing Company, 2002.

Thie, Carlene. *A Photographer's Life with Disneyland Under Construction*. Riverside, CA: Ape Pen Publishing Company, 2002.

Thomas, Bob. *Building a Company: Roy O. Disney and the Creation of an Entertainment Empire*. New York: Hyperion, 1998.

Thomas, Bob. *Walt Disney: An American Original*. New York: Disney Editions, 1994.

West, Rick, ed. *Walt Disney's Pirates of the Caribbean*. San Francisco: Theme Park Adventure Magazine, 1998.

INDEX

ABOUT
the AUTHOR

SAM GENNAWEY IS THE AUTHOR of *Walt and the Promise of Progress City*, a contributor to *Planning Los Angeles* and other books, as well as a columnist for the popular MiceChat website. His unique point of view—built on his passion for history, his professional training as an urban planner, and his obsession with theme parks—has brought speaking invitations from Walt Disney Imagineering, the Walt Disney Family Museum, Disney Creative, the American Planning Association, the California Preservation Foundation, the California League of Cities, and many Disneyana clubs, libraries, and podcasts. He is currently a senior associate at the planning firm of Katherine Padilla and Associates.

Printed in the USA
CPSIA information can be obtained
at www.ICGtesting.com
HW012018140824
4JS00033B/2758